The Argumentative Turn Revisited

The Argumentative Turn Revisited

PUBLIC POLICY AS COMMUNICATIVE PRACTICE

Frank Fischer and Herbert Gottweis, editors

DUKE UNIVERSITY PRESS *Durham & London* 2012

© 2012 Duke University Press
All rights reserved
Designed by C. H. Westmoreland
Typeset in Arno Pro by Keystone Typesetting, Inc.
Library of Congress Cataloging-in-Publication Data
appear on the last printed page of this book.

Contents

INTRODUCTION: The Argumentative Turn Revisited
Frank Fischer and Herbert Gottweis 1

PART I. Deliberative Policy Argumentation and Public Participation

1. Fostering Deliberation in the Forum and Beyond
John S. Dryzek and Carolyn M. Hendriks 31

2. Performing Place Governance Collaboratively: Planning as a Communicative Process
Patsy Healey 58

PART II. Discursive Politics and Argumentative Practices: Institutions and Frames

3. Discursive Institutionalism: Scope, Dynamics, and Philosophical Underpinnings
Vivien A. Schmidt 85

4. From Policy Frames to Discursive Politics: Feminist Approaches to Development Policy and Planning in an Era of Globalization
Mary Hawkesworth 114

PART III. Policy Argumentation on the Internet and in Film

5. The Internet as a Space for Policy Deliberation
Stephen Coleman 149

6. Multimedia and Urban Narratives in the Planning Process: Film as Policy Inquiry and Dialogue Catalyst
Leonie Sandercock and Giovanni Attili 180

PART IV. Policy Rhetoric, Argumentation, and Semiotics

7. Political Rhetoric and Stem Cell Policy in the United States: Embodiments, Scenographies, and Emotions
Herbert Gottweis 211

8. The Deep Semiotic Structure of Deservingness:
Discourse and Identity in Welfare Policy
Sanford F. Schram 236

PART V. Policy Argumentation in Critical Theory and Practice:
Communicative Logics and Policy Learning

9. The Argumentative Turn toward Deliberative Democracy:
Habermas's Contribution and the Foucauldian Critique
Hubertus Buchstein and Dirk Jörke 271

10. Poststructuralist Policy Analysis:
Discourse, Hegemony, and Critical Explanation
David Howarth and Steven Griggs 305

11. Transformative Learning in Planning and Policy Deliberation:
Probing Social Meaning and Tacit Assumptions
Frank Fischer and Alan Mandell 343

CONTRIBUTORS 371
INDEX 375

FRANK FISCHER AND HERBERT GOTTWEIS

Introduction

The Argumentative Turn Revisited

The Argumentative Turn in Policy Analysis and Planning, edited by Frank Fischer and John Forester in 1993, set out a new orientation in policy analysis and planning: a shift away from the dominant empirical, analytic approach to problem solving to one including the study of language and argumentation as essential dimensions of theory and analysis in policy making and planning. The book was instrumental in stimulating a large body of work in policy research and planning in both the United States and Europe over subsequent years. Since its publication, the emphasis on argumentation has converged with other developments in the social sciences focused on discourse, deliberation, social constructivism, and interpretative methods. This new book takes stock of these developments in an effort to further advance the argumentative direction in policy studies.[1]

Drawing heavily at the outset on Jürgen Habermas's critical theory, in particular his critique of technocracy and scientism and his work on communicative action, the "argumentative turn" offered an alternative approach to policy inquiry. Fundamentally, it has linked postpositivist epistemology with social and political theory and the search for a relevant methodology. At the outset, the approach emphasized practical argumentation, policy judgment, frame analysis, narrative storytelling, and rhetorical analysis, among others (Gottweis 2006). From the early 1990s onward, argumentative policy analysis matured into a major strand in the contemporary study of policy making and policy theory development. As one leading policy theorist put it, this postpositivist perspective became one of the competing theoretical perspectives (Peters 2004).

Over these years the argumentative turn expanded to include work on discourse analysis, deliberation, deliberative democracy, citizen juries, governance, expertise, participatory inquiry, local and tacit knowledge, collaborative planning, the uses and role of media, and interpretive methods, among others.[2] Although these research foci are hardly synonymous, they share the special attention they give to communication and argumentation, in particular the processes of utilizing, mobilizing, and assessing communicative practices in the interpretation and praxis of policy making and analysis (Fischer 2003; Gottweis 2006).

First and foremost, argumentative policy inquiry challenges the belief that policy analysis can be a value-free, technical project. Whereas neopositivist approaches embrace a technically oriented rational model of policy making—an attempt to provide unequivocal, value-free answers to the major questions of policy making—the argumentative approach rejects the idea that policy analysis can be a straightforward application of scientific techniques. Instead of a narrow focus on empirical measurement of inputs and outputs, it takes the policy argument as the starting point of analysis. Without denying the importance of empirical analysis, the argumentative turn seeks to understand the relationship between the empirical and the normative as they are configured in the processes of policy argumentation. It thus concerns itself with the validity of empirical and normative statements, but moves beyond this traditional empirical emphasis to examine the ways in which they are combined and employed in the political process.

This orientation is especially important for an applied discipline such as policy analysis. Insofar as the field exists to serve real-world decision makers, policy analysis needs to be relevant to those whom it attempts to assist. The argumentative turn, in this regard, seeks to analyze policy to inform the ordinary-language processes of policy argumentation, in particular as reflected in the thought and deliberation of politicians, administrators, and citizens (Linblom and Cohen 1979). Rather than imposing scientific frameworks on the processes of argumentation and decision making—theoretical perspectives generally designed to inform specific academic disciplines—policy analysis thus takes the practical argument as the unit of analysis. It rejects the "rational" assumptions underlying many approaches in policy inquiry and embraces an understanding of human action as intermediated and embedded in symbolically rich social and cultural contexts.

Recognizing that the policy process is constituted by and mediated through communicative practices, the argumentative turn therefore attempts to understand both the process of policy making and the analytical activities of policy inquiry on their own terms. Instead of prescribing procedures based on abstract models, the approach labors to understand and reconstruct what policy analysts do when they do it, to understand how their findings and advice are communicated, and how such advice is understood and employed by those who receive it. This requires close attention to the social construction of the normative—often conflicting—policy frames of those who struggle over power and policy.

These concerns take on special significance in today's increasingly turbulent world. Contemporary policy problems facing governments are more uncertain, complex, and often riskier than they were when many of the theories and methods of policy analysis were first advanced. Often poorly defined, such problems have been described as far "messier" that their earlier counterparts—for example, climate change, health, and transportation (Ney 2009). These are problems for which clear-cut solutions are missing—especially technical solutions, despite concerted attempts to identify them. In all of these areas, traditional approaches—often technocratic—have proven inadequate or have failed. Indeed, for such messy policy problems, science and scientific knowledge have often compounded problem solving, becoming themselves sources of uncertainty and ambiguity. They thus generate political conflict rather than help to resolve it. In a disorderly world that is in "generative flux," research methods that assume a stable reality "out there" waiting to be discovered are of little help and prone to error and misinterpretation (Law 2004:6–7).

Nothing has contributed more to this uncertain, unpredictable flux than the contemporary transformation of the political and economic world into the one we now confront. One of the most important policy issues to signal these new characteristics has been the environmental crisis. Spanning local and global scales, it has made clear not only the interconnectedness of policy issues, but also the increasing levels of uncertainty and risk associated with them. In addition, the unpredicted collapse of the Soviet Union and the end of the Cold War dramatically altered the international political landscape. With it came the spread of neoliberal capitalism and the promise of steady worldwide economic growth, coupled with the heralded spread of democracy. But this too brought a very different and unpredictable reality.

The failure of this new order to materialize has underscored the nonlinear and often contradictory nature of contemporary politics and policy making. Instead of the envisioned, all-encompassing new order of global and liberal capitalism, the result is new and worrisome varieties of capitalism (often statist in nature), the revival of nationalism, ethnic conflicts, destabilizing waves of migration, unanticipated forms of terrorism, new worries about both nuclear weapons and nuclear energy, rapidly accelerating threats of climate change, and the near collapse in 2008 of the worldwide financial system (Bremmer 2010). In short, such uncertainties, ambiguities, unpredictabilities, and unexpected consequences have become the defining features of our increasingly turbulent times.

Nowhere was this more evident and disturbing than in the nuclear disaster in Fukushima. Almost disbelieving the reports, the world watched the unfolding of a catastrophe resulting from an unforeseen interaction of earthquakes, a tsunami, and sociotechnical mismanagement. The resulting nuclear meltdown and release of radiation were all products of technocratic strategies based on outdated modes of guidance and control. Leading to devastating destruction and the death of thousands, these failures left the nation of Japan in a state of economic disarray, even disaster, for many.

In the economic sphere, the equally disastrous consequences of rationality failures could be observed in the near collapse of the world economy in 2008. Unforeseen by all but a very few economists, the real-world behavior of bankers defied the logics of the economists' models of rational behavior. From this perspective, the problem was as theoretical as it was practical. In what can be described as the Waterloo of the "rational model" of economic policy making, the economics profession largely failed to anticipate the possibility of—let alone predict—the breakdown of the Western banking system in 2008 and the near collapse of the world economic system, a crisis that only could be prevented by a bailout, unimaginable until then, from the governments of the United States and Europe. As leading economists have explained, economic understanding and prediction have rested on the assumption of rational expectations, anticipating individual behavior to conform to the structures of the economist's theoretical models rather than real-world activities (Colander et al. 2009; Friedman 2009). Based on a false belief that "individuals and the economist have a complete understanding of the economic mechanisms governing the world," these models lead economists to "disregard key factors—including heterogeneity of decision rules, revisions of forecasting strategies, and changes in the social context—that drive outcomes in asset and other markets." Such models, as even the causal observer can see, fail to understand the real workings of the economy, both domestic and international.³ As these writers conclude, "In our hour of greatest need, societies around the world are left to grope in the dark without a theory." It represents "a *systemic failure of the economics profession*" (Colander et al. 2009:2).

These concerns have spread beyond the economics profession to the other social sciences. Many political scientists busy themselves adapting this economic model to the explanation of noneconomic behavior. In the United States, the rational choice model borrowed from economics has in fact become the dominant theoretical orientation in political science, with many adherents in sociology as well. Bringing with it a neo-positivist effort to supply empirical and deductive, value-neutral modes of political explanation, as best evidenced by the influential advocacy coalition model of policy change, it has largely failed on its own terms to provide significant, usable findings relevant to policy. And, in the process, it drives out an understanding of the essential role of the subjective and ideational components basic to social and political explanation.

But one doesn't have to rely on a critique of the rational model to identify the failures of a technically oriented form of policy analysis. This is also clear from a more general neglect of the role of culture, values, and ideas. Easily at hand is the case of the Iraq War and its tragic consequences for both the Iraqi people and the foreign policy of the United States. Here one has to point to the failure of Bush administration policy makers to consider the cultural realities of that country, not to mention the Middle East as a whole; they simply looked at Iraq through American eyes and saw what they wished to see.

The tragedy that resulted from Hurricane Katrina in 2005 is yet another example. The destruction the hurricane wrought on the City of New Orleans was only in part a function of inadequately reinforced containment walls; in the aftermath, it also became clear that the failure to address the problem before and after the disaster was also rooted in widely held tacit beliefs about poverty and race.

Yet another tragic example is the catastrophic BP oil gusher in the Gulf of Mexico in the spring and summer of 2010. This was in significant part a failure to appreciate the risks and uncertainties of deep-sea drilling; policy makers either followed the inefficacious regulatory advice of an outmoded administrative culture, relied on unreliable ecological estimates, or accepted BP assurances based on self-serving motives. Each of these instances illustrates especially complex and uncertain problems that do not lend themselves to traditional models of policy making and the kinds of technical analysis that have sought to inform it. In all of these cases, the problem itself was in need of a new definition, one including first and foremost a process of normative interpretation rather then empirical analysis per se. Interpretive analysis, in this regard, needs to coexist and interact with empirical analysis. In recent years, there has been some progress in this direction; many now recognize of the need for interpretive-oriented qualitative research. But interpretive modes of inquiry have to be accepted on their own terms, not just as an adjunct to empirical hypothesis testing and explanation (King, Keohane, and Verba 1994).

For these reasons, policy analysis can no longer afford to limit itself to the simplified academic models of explanation. Such methods fail to address the nonlinear nature of today's messy policy problems. They fail to capture the typically heterogeneous, interconnected, often contradictory, and increasingly globalized character of these issues. Many of these problems are, as such, appropriately described as "wicked problems." In these situations, not only is the problem wanting for a solution, the very nature and conceptualization of the problem is not well understood. Effective solutions to such problems require ongoing, informed deliberation involving competing perspectives on the part of both government official and public citizens.

The argumentative turn literature has made a strong contribution toward bringing back the critical role of discursive reflection and argumentation to both the practices of policy analysis and an understanding of the dynamics of policy making today. On the methodological level, it contrasts the limits of hypothesis-driven neopositivist research with a grounded approach toward policy inquiry that is less characterized by the search for general laws and regularities of society and politics than by contextually situated, ethnographically rich analysis of policy constellations (Clarke 2005). This type of inquiry emphasizes the multifaceted nature of human action that cannot be reduced to empirical variables but views humans as culturally shaped, communicatively based, socially motivated, and emotionally grounded.

In sum, it seems today to be more obvious than ever that the still dominant empiricist orientation in the social and policy sciences cannot adequately grasp this much more complex, uncertain world defined by interconnected networks that blur the traditional boundaries that organize our social political spaces and political arenas. By focusing on argumentation, processes of dialogic exchange, and interpretive analysis, we need to discover how competing policy actors construct contending narratives in order to make sense of and deal with such uncertain, messy challenges. Only through a dialectical process of critical reflection and collective learning can we develop new and innovative policy solutions that speak to contemporary realities. Toward this end, the process must also be supported by a constructivist understanding of the ways in which interpretation and argumentation function in science and scientific expertise. Such understandings, both empirically valid and normatively legitimate, are required to build consensuses capable of moving us forward in the deliberative process of public problem solving.

The contributions in this book build on and supplement the themes developed in 1993 in *The Argumentative Turn*, with contributions based on discourse analysis, deliberative democracy, collaborative planning, interpretive frame analysis, discursive institutionalism, new media, performativity in rhetorical argumentation, narration, images and pictures, semiotics, transformative policy learning, and more. These chapters further develop the perspective against the background of a more complex, ever more connected and networked, heterogeneous, turbulent, and increasingly globalized world. Before presenting the contributions of this book, however, it is useful to clarify some of the key notions used in the following pages.

Communicative Practices: From Argumentation to Discourse—and Back Again

The argumentative turn begins with the realization that public policy, constructed through language, is the product of argumentation. In both oral and written form, as Majone (1989) has reminded us, "argument is central in all stages of the policy process." Policy making is fundamentally an ongoing discursive struggle over the definition and conceptual framing of problems, the public understanding of the issues, the shared meanings that motivate policy responses, and criteria for evaluation (Stone 2002). Whereas this view was relatively new in 1993, there has since been an outpouring of activities—books, articles, conferences, and workshops—related to the argumentative turn, as originally understood.

After its publication, *The Argumentative Turn* became a much discussed and cited book, establishing itself in a relatively short period of time as important orientation in policy studies. Today, it is a contending theoretical and methodological direction with a well-articulated policy research agenda. Much of what emerged took its initial cues from the issues set out in 1993, especially in the interlinking of epistemology, methodology, policy theory, politics, and policy practices. Offering an epistemologically grounded pluralistic agenda for an argumentative and discursive approach to policy analysis and planning that is more sophisticated, the range of contributions now stretches from Frankfurt-style critical theory and Foucauldian poststructuralism to a Bourdieu-influenced emphasis on institutional practices and a neo-Gramscian study of hegemonic discourse. In more specific terms, it includes work on social constructivism, practical reason, deliberation, discourse analysis, interpretive frame analysis, rhetorical analysis, semiotics, performativity, narrative storytelling, local and tacit knowledge, the role of expertise, and participatory policy analysis. Examples of these new tendencies can be found in the chapters of this book.

Fundamentally, the argumentative turn is founded on the recognition that language does more than reflect what we take to be reality. Indeed, it is constituent of reality, shaping—and at times literally determining—what we understand to be reality. A view grounded in the epistemological contributions of philosophers such as Ludwig Wittgenstein, J. L. Austin, and Jacques Derrida, it is reflected in the theories of phenomenology, symbolic interaction, and ethnomethodology, among others. It largely entered policy analysis and planning through an interest in the writing of Jürgen Habermas, giving rise to an argumentative policy turn. This was followed by later developments that often took their cue from the poststructuralism of Foucault and postmodernism, coupled with influences in social constructivism emerging from sociology of science and science studies more generally. Theory and research along these lines have thus focused on the role of interpretation in analyzing policy agenda setting, policy development and implementation, the use of narratives in policy discourse, the social construction of policy findings, citizen participation and local knowledge, participatory policy analysis and collaborative planning, gender and feminist epistemology, identity politics in policy discourse, the analysis of deliberative processes, a return to the role of rhetoric, performativity and dramaturgy, and discourse analysis more broadly conceived. And, not least important, many of those who started with Habermas have continued their project by exploring more closely issues of policy deliberation and discursive democracy (Dryzek 2000). Other Habermasians turned to a focus on the more micro aspects of language and deliberation in policy and policy-oriented work in planning (Forester 1999, 2009). A large number of research projects were inspired by this turn to argumentation and discourse, demonstrating the usefulness of the approach for policy research.

Given the diversity and spread of orientations, however, there is now some variation in terminology. There is, in short, a need for clarification, in particular as it pertains to argumentation. Today, terms like "discourse," "deliberation," "rhetoric," and "argumentation" are frequently used somewhat indiscriminately. These concepts are interrelated yet different. They are all forms of communication but have different characteristics and functions. Insofar as the concept of argumentation has tended to take a backseat to the emergence of discourse, we seek to clarify and revitalize its essential importance. That is, it is not now an outmoded concept that can be replaced with the more fashionable concept of discourse. The focus here is thus primarily on argumentation and its relationship to discourse, deliberation, and rhetoric.

"Argumentation" traditionally refers to the process through which people seek to reach conclusions through reason. Although influenced and shaped by formal logic, the study of argumentation has also turned to informal logic and practical reason. As such, it explores the way people communicate in civil debate and engage in persuasive dialogue and negotiation as well in ordinary conversation. It focuses on the way that people—including opponents—reach and justify mutually acceptable decisions. It thus includes the ways policy analysts and planners seek to advise their clients, politicians, and the public of their conclusions and recommendations.

There is no firm distinction between deliberation and argumentation. This is because deliberation is itself a form of argumentation. We set it off as a procedurally governed form of collective argumentation, as it is mainly employed in the literature of policy and planning. It is used to denote formally structured processes, such as citizen juries and consensus conferences, in which people are brought together to discuss and decide a particular issue by carefully considering the available evidence and competing perspectives. Although it need not be the case, deliberation usually connotes a more moderate, less impassioned approach to reaching conclusions. It is not that there is no passionate engagement, but that the overall process is seen to be governed by pre-agreed-upon understandings about what constitutes appropriate lines of communications. For example, manipulative persuasion and distortion, common to everyday argumentation, especially in politics, is ruled out.

"Rhetoric" and "rhetorical argument" refer to both a field of study focused on the methods of argumentation and particular features of the argumentative process. Although it unfortunately came to have negative connotations in everyday language, rhetoric is an essential and unavoidable aspect of argumentation. Beyond its identification with distortion and manipulation, it deals with the way arguers focus on the relation of the argument and the audience. As such, it hones in on the dialogic of an "argumentative situation." In this type of argumentation, the arguer pays special attention to those he or she is speaking to, their beliefs, backgrounds, intellectual styles, and communicative strategies. Rhetorical argumentation thus seeks to combine logical, propositional argumentation with an appreciation of the speaker and the audience, as well as the role of emotion in the persuasive process. Unlike standard forms of logical argument, which focus on a "given" reality, a rhetorical argument seeks to construct particular representations of reality. The arguer attempts to persuade the audience to see and understand something—an event, relationship, process, and the like—one way as opposed to another.

"Discourse" is employed here more formally to mean a body of concepts and ideas that circumscribe, influence, and shape argumentation. Often the word "discourse" is used casually to refer to argumentation. One of the reasons for this has to do with a negative connotation associated with argumentation, in just the same way that rhetoric is often seen pejoratively. In ordinary communication, arguing is often seen to be impolite. But argumentation, like rhetoric, has also a long formal history related to the advance and appraisal of knowledge. This is the understanding employed here.

"Discourse," by contrast, is seen here to be the broadest and most encompassing of these terms and also serves a different function related in particular to social meaning. For Hajer (1995), discourse is "a specific ensemble of ideas, concepts, and categorizations that are produced and reproduced and transformed to give meaning to physical and social relations." Similarly, Howarth (2000:9) writes that discourses refer "to historically specific systems of meaning which form the identities of subjects and objects." A discourse, in this view, circumscribes the range of subjects and objects through which people experience the world, specifies the views that can be legitimately accepted as knowledge, and constitutes the actors taken to be the agents of knowledge. Discourse analysis thus starts from the assumption that all actions, objects, and practices are socially meaningful and that these meanings are shaped by the social and political struggles in specific historical periods.

Discourse, in this sense, operates at the sociocultural macro level, transmitting basic values and giving cohesion to shared beliefs. Among other things, it supplies society with basic stories and narratives that serve as modes of behavior, both positive and negative. Discourses are thus different in different cultures. The broad discursive framework of Western Christian culture, for example, differs from that of the Islamic world. Both offer different stories and illustrative principles that illustrate how one should behave. There are points of commonality, but there are also essential differences.

Discourses, as such, provide the materials from which argumentation, including deliberative argumentation, can be constructed. Within a discourse there will be conflicting, unresolved elements that emerge from the historical struggles that have shaped the discourse. Discourses will also identify who has the right to speak authoritatively on specific matters. For example, workers and managers will typically subscribe to different goal values; managers and owners will see and understand things differently than labor unions and workers. To take another illustration, the church no longer has the authority to pronounce on matters related to medicine. And laypeople are usually not accepted to be knowledgeable about legal matters requiring judicial judgments. But these understandings change over time. Even though certain lines of argument will be considered out of bounds, there is thus a great deal of room for argumentation within a cultural discourse. Because of unresolved conflicts and even contradictions in a discourse, coupled with the need to always interpret the meaning of new circumstances in light of given social meanings and values, a society will always contain an argumentative struggle that typically becomes the stuff of politics.

While such discourses structure the struggles that ensue among conflicting groups, it is important to understand that social agents are not altogether determined by the social positions afforded by the dominant discourses. Over time, there is a dialectical interaction between social actors—as arguers—and discourse structures that is inherent in the processes of social and political change. In the process, social agents can themselves influence the content of the dominant discourses. Indeed, social struggles are generally related closely to the meanings established and perpetuated by such discourses and their communicative practices. In relatively stable societies, agents—often in the form of discourse coalitions—can manage to bring about change in discursive practices, albeit gradually. But revolutionary situations can give rise to rapid and dramatic changes. Social actors need to be understood both as the products of these preexisting discursive relationships and as the agents of their change. The degree to which agents can cause such discursive change is an empirical question that needs to be examined in the context of the specific circumstances.

Within this overarching conceptualization of discourse and discursive struggle, there are also subordinate discourses that structure specific realms. Because society is differentiated and complex, specific discourses govern the various sectors and subsystems of society. There are political, economic, and environmental discourses, among others. A political discourse, for instance, covers all of the topics that would come up in matters political—concepts, terms, theories, relevant policy issues, and the like. The discipline of political science, an academic discourse, seeks to refine these concepts for the purpose of more precise explanation and understanding. These discourses, as such, are anchored to specific institutional realms, such as the ministries of foreign and economic affairs and a national political science association. In these domains, discussions will be circumscribed and constrained by the terms and concepts of the discourse embedded in institutional processes.

Narration and discourse are often used together, especially by postmodern theorists. Discourses contain narratives, which are essentially stories, either in oral or written form. Fundamentally, narrative storytelling reveals or conveys an experience structured as a sequence of events or occurrences (e.g., a beginning, middle, and ending) through which individuals relate their experiences to one another. In policy inquiry, narrative story lines in the everyday world draw on the vocabularies of the macro epistemic discourses to which the inquiry belongs. The specific role of the story is to furnish communication with particular details that provide the material out of which social meaning is created. They are not arguments as such, but arguments are often included as part of the story. Arguments can also be based on a story or drawn from them. They often are the source of the propositions of arguments and frequently provide evidence for claims.

Finally, the concept of practices requires attention. The term "communicative practices" is used rather loosely to cover various acts of discourse, deliberation, and argumentation. In most formal definitions, in particular those related to language and linguistics, communicative practices involve reaching conclusions through reason rather than intuition. Argumentation, as such, is a communicative practice.

In social theory, the emphasis on practice usually refers to activities that have become routine, regularized, and habitual. Much of this work is based on the contributions of Michel Foucault and Pierre Bourdieu. In their contributions, "practice" refers to modes of communication that appear as unified, with rules about who can use these ways of speaking and boundaries specifying which kinds of issues and topics are a part of them and which are not. "Practice" here typically refers to the construction and reflection of social realities through actions that invoke beliefs, ideologies, identity, ideology, and power. Studying communicative practices not only involves paying attention to the production of meanings by participants as they employ the verbal, nonverbal, and interactional resources that they command, but also requires paying attention to how the employment of such resources reflects and creates the processes and meanings of the community in which local actions occur. Although a practice is goal-oriented, people who participate in a communicative practice may not be consciously goal-oriented, since their goal is built into institutional activities in ways that are no longer immediately available for their conscious examination.

Finally, the power of pictures, images, film, and, in general, visual representation in political discourse, often referred to as indicating a "pictorial turn," is obvious and much-debated (Mitchell 1994). However, the conceptual and theoretical challenges of studying aspects of visual representation in social and political context have only slowly been taken up in empirical social science. Integrating strategies for the study of practices of visual representation into argumentative policy analysis is an important challenge for future analysis and has been taken up also by a number of authors in this book. Especially when controversial and emotional questions are at stake, actors choose innovative ways of communicating their interests, and images function as a powerful rhetorical tool.

All of these communicative practices have a role to play in the focus presented in this book. In the view here, however, it is argumentation that constitutes the primary consideration in the world of policy making. It is through argumentation, identified by the actors, that actors in the political process advance their goals and objectives. Argumentation, from this perspective, draws on discourses, but it also encompasses other essential aspects of communicative practices that are basic to policy politics, such as political rhetoric, structured policy deliberation, performativity, images, and emotional expression. The focus is thus how actors in the public sphere argue, rhetorically and deliberatively, within and across discourses, especially those embedded in the discursive practices of institutions.

The emphasis is important, especially given the traditional—and still prevalent—attempt on the part of many social scientists to eliminate or reduce argumentation and discourse in social and political explanation. They are rejected as being anchored to nonscientific, subjective processes. Explanation, according to conventional social science methodology, particularly in the United States, should be based on objective (particularly material) interests that can be identified, carefully observed, and deductively analyzed. Indeed, it is an approach still today advocated by rigorous rational choice theorists in the social sciences.

But in more contemporary times, it has become clear that ideas, discourse, and argumentation matter. It is not that the point is new. Indeed, a classic statement of this understanding is by Max Weber, who recognized the importance of ideas and argumentation long before modern-day postmodern theorists, among others, turned to discourse and argumentation. Weber formulated the relationship between ideas and material interests this way: "Not ideas, but material and ideal interests, directly govern men's conduct. Yet very frequently the 'world images' that have been created by 'ideas' have, like switchmen, determined the tracks along which action has been pushed by the dynamic of interest" (Weber 1948:280).

There is no better example of this in modern politics than Thatcherism in Britain and its counterpart in the United States, Reaganism. Both political leaders introduced new ideas about governance and economy that switched the political tracks to neoliberalism. Indeed, President Reagan's lasting influence, despite his many policy failures, was his impact on political discourse in the United States. Whereas for more than forty years the Democratic Party forged the dominant political paradigm around economic regulation and social assistance in the name of the "public interest" or "common good," Reagan reshaped the contours of public discourse by replacing government regulation and public assistance with deregulation, free markets, and the interests of the individual, especially the individual as entrepreneur. In the process, the normative terminology of public interest was replaced with an emphasis on self-interest and personal gain. Today, it is scarcely possible to discuss new policy proposals in the United States without first explaining and legitimizing them in terms of the economic language of costs and benefits, a formulation that does not easily admit the traditional concept of the public interest. The public interest, based on values and ideas related to the larger common concerns of society, cannot be easily discussed in terms of cost and benefits; indeed, it is generally understood as morally transcending such narrow economic criteria. When a public interest claim attempts to satisfy a cost-benefit test, it is usually difficult —or impossible—to measure the outcome in terms of monetary value.

Looking closely at the enactment of historically significant legislation, we nearly always discover that shared values are the forces behind the interest groups and social movements that struggled to achieve them— the end of slavery, women's right to vote, anticommunism, civil rights, environmental protection, and antismoking campaigns, to name some of the more obvious examples. More specifically, consider the passage in the United States of the Voting Rights Act of 1964. Only two years before this landmark legislative achievement for the civil rights movement, the prospects for the passage of such legislation looked very doubtful. In just a couple of years, views about equality of opportunity changed so dramatically that they cleared away the long-standing entrenched political opposition that had blocked the path of such legislation for more than a century.

Beyond the broad sweeps of historical change, moreover, there is plenty of evidence to show the importance of ideas in the ordinary course of public affairs. Research shows, as Orren writes, "that people don't act simply on the basis of their perceived self-interest, without regard to aggregative consequences of their action" (1988:13). They are motivated as well "by values, purposes, ideas, and goals, and commitments that transcend self-interest or group interests." Indeed, over the past thirty or forty years a good deal of research has steadily accumulated to support the contention that ideas and values can be relatively autonomous of interests and institutions. Although it is never easy to sort out these influences, such research makes clear that the values of individuals can arise quite independently of their life experiences and can exert an independent influence on their political behavior (Verba and Orren 1985).

There are two levels of analysis that such research brings into play. One has to do with the broad, overarching discourses that structure our ways of thinking and thus communicating. Following theorists such as Foucault and Antonio Gramsci, this turns our attention to concerns about hegemonic discourses such as capitalism and contemporary neoliberalism. By shaping basic social meanings that come to be taken as given—that is, as natural to the social world—they typically operate under the radar. Generally, most people do not even recognize that they themselves are shaped socially and politically by these discourses.

The second level, the level of institutions and action, has to do with argumentation within these accepted discourses. Vivien Schmidt (2001; chapter 3 in this volume), in her theory of "discursive institutionalism," has usefully illustrated the ways in which policy discourses can shape the communicative interactions among political actors who translate problems into policy issues. Analysis of communication within these interactions, as she writes, "can provide insight into the political dynamics of change by going behind the interplay of interests, institutions, and cultures" to explain how change is brought about by "an interactive consensus for change through communication among the key political actors" (2001:3).

This is not to suggest that discursive argumentation can be understood without the variables of interests, institutions, and culture. Indeed, discourse and argumentation are not easily separated from the interests that are expressed through them, the institutional interactions that shape their expression, or the cultural norms that frame them. Communicative interaction can (and often does) exert a causal influence on political change, although the influence tends to be that of an intervening rather than an independent variable. For this reason, discourse and argumentation based on it cannot be *the* cause, but it is often *a* cause of political change (Schmidt 2002). Argumentative communication is only one of a number of multiple causes or influences, although it can at times be the very variable or added influence that makes the difference, especially in the explanation of change (Fischer 2003). It can do this in a variety of ways, including through the conceptual reframing of interests to facilitate consensual agreement or through the reframing of institutional rules and cultural norms governing the play of power.

The reconsideration of ideas and beliefs in political and policy research at this second level owes much to the "new institutionalists" or "neoinstitutionalists," especially those in comparative politics and policy. Long concerned that the existing theoretical approaches to inquiry are insufficient for dealing with the variety and complexity of social and political change in modern societies, these scholars have argued that the analysis of variations in public policy outcomes should more broadly examine the interplay of political elites, interest groups' demands, institutional processes, and ideas in political and policy analysis.

It is not that institutions cause political action; rather, their communicative practices shape the behaviors of actors, causing political action. Supplying them with regularized behavioral rules, standards of assessment, and emotive commitments, institutions influence political actors by structuring or shaping the political and social interpretations of the problems they have to deal with and by limiting the choice of policy solutions that might be implemented. The interests of actors are still there, but they are influenced by the institutional structures, norms, and rules through which they are pursued. Such structural relationships give shape to both social and political expectations and the possibility of realizing them. Indeed, as Weick (1969) and others have shown, it is often the institutional opportunities and barriers that determine people's preferences, rather than the other way around, as is more commonly assumed (Fischer 1990:282–83).

Such research requires a qualitative orientation, but it means moving beyond the standard approaches to include a stronger form of interpretive analysis, or "interpretive policy analysis" as it has emerged in the literature (Yanow 2000; Wagenaar 2011). Interpretive policy analysis goes behind the existing beliefs and their communication to examine how they came to be adopted. This requires an examination of the power relations behind particular argumentative struggles. A critical interpretive analysis emphasizes the political role of communicative activity in both constituting and maintaining power relations. As Keenoy, Oswick, and Grant put it, critical analysts examine "dialogical struggle (or struggles) as reflected in privileging of a particular discourse and the marginalization of others" (1997:147). In the process, such analysis recognizes that discourses "are never completely cohesive, without internal tensions, and therefore able to determine reality" (Phillips 2003:226). As such, they are often partial and inconclusive with crosscutting contradictions and inconsistent arguments. For this reason, they are seldom wholly uncontested.

Part I of this book, "Deliberative Policy Argumentation and Public Participation," begins with the chapter by John Dryzek and Carolyn Hendriks on deliberation. Basic to policy argumentation is deliberation. The emergence and focus on deliberation has in fact been one of the most significant developments in the argumentative turn since the concept was first proposed and includes work in political theory on deliberative democracy. Deliberation and deliberative democracy are topics to which both of these writers have made important contributions. After introducing the conceptualization of society as a deliberative system, Dryzek and Hendriks explore the concept of deliberation and its relationship to other forms of political communication. Drawing on emerging empirical studies, they consider how the quality of deliberative argumentation can be affected by different features of forum design. Rather than compare different types of deliberative forums, they look more broadly at how the authenticity, inclusivity, and effectiveness of deliberation can be shaped by various design attributes such as the structure of the forum, its participants, and the authority and legitimacy of the forum. While design is important for facilitating deliberation, Dryzek and Hendriks also acknowledge the limits of "the forum" and recognize that deliberation occurs in a diversity of spaces including legislatures, courts, social movements, the media, and particular practices such as activism or justification. They conclude that political systems need to facilitate multiple deliberative spaces such that policy making can be informed by a diverse range of argumentation and communication. At the same time, they also argue that variety is not enough; consideration also needs to be given to how different spaces connect to constitute an effective deliberative system.

Moving from the forum to local governance and planning, Patsy Healey takes up the communicative practices involved in collaborative planning processes. Although the role of participation was not new in 1993, its importance in policy and planning has steadily evolved since then. With the development of new techniques and practices, it has come to be widely considered part of good governance practices. Building on her earlier focus on communicative action in planning in *The Argumentative Turn*, she explores here the ways that communicative participatory interaction supports and facilitates the processes of collaborative planning. Based on a relational, constructivist, and pragmatic understanding of social and communicative dynamics, collaborative interactions between planners and citizens emphasize the situated, context-dependent nature of social life. Focusing in particular on problems involved in governing urban places, she illustrates the ways that ideas and practices associated with collaborative planning should be understood as participatory communicative processes rather than technical procedures designed to achieve specific goals. The qualities of these situated communicative interactions and techniques are seen to play an important role in raising awareness among those involved with issues of place, as well as in the need to feed the results of such exercises into the wider deliberative processes through which policy decisions are made. The situated use of these discursive practices, as "art and craft," is essential for the future governance of sustainable urban places.

Part II, "Discursive Politics and Argumentative Practices: Institutions and Frames," begins with Vivien A. Schmidt's chapter on her theory of "discursive institutionalism." Discursive institutionalism is an umbrella concept for approaches that concern themselves with the substantive content of ideas and the interactive processes of discourse and discursive argumentation in institutional contexts. This chapter considers not only the wide range of ideas in discourse, which come in many different forms and types at different levels of generality with different rates of change, but also the ways in which "sentient" (thinking and speaking) agents articulate such ideas by way of a "coordinative discourse." Through these processes, policy actors construct their ideas and a "communicative discourse" through which they make their ideas accessible to the public for discussion and deliberative argumentation, as well as contestation. The chapter also elaborates on the dual nature of the institutional context. This refers not only to the ways external formalized institutions constrain action, but also to the ways constructs of meaning internal to agents enable them to communicate for the purposes of collective action.

Chapter 4 turns to the role of policy frames. In this light of various approaches to frames that have been advanced—from positivist and value-neutral to hermeneutic and interpretive—Mary Hawkesworth sees the need for a critical poststructural analysis of frames. Toward this end, she undertakes a discursive analysis of development policies and planning to show that contrary to explicit claims, the central project of development has not been poverty reduction, but the production, circulation, and naturalization of hierarchical power relations that configure the political economy of the North as the telos of economic development for the global South. In particular, the chapter contrasts standard accounts of development policy and planning with several policy frames drawn from feminist political economy to reveal the hidden power dynamics omitted from dominant development discourses. By contesting the presumption that development benefits everyone, these feminist frames demonstrate the dynamics of class, gender, race, culture, and region that differentially distribute the benefits and burdens of development within and across global sites. In conclusion, Hawkesworth demonstrates the importance of feminist discursive politics in addressing structures of inequality integral to development processes, in both policy research and real-world practical argumentation.

In part III, "Policy Argumentation on the Internet and in Film," Stephen Coleman's chapter on the Internet turns to a new development in policy argumentation. He analyzes the Internet as a relatively new space for policy deliberation. In the process, he considers how the emergence of the deliberation on the Internet reconfigures ways of defining policy problems; how the Internet changes the ways of gathering, organizing, and making sense of knowledge that underpins policy; and ways it facilitates particular modes of policy argumentation. The argument rests on the potential of the Internet to facilitate multivocal policy narratives that surpass the univocal ascriptions of public opinion produced by opinion polling or a national census. Coleman also examines the way it generates collaboration among dispersed policy thinkers, often brought together through uncoordinated policy networks emanating from casual hyperspatial relationships. He then analyzes the Internet's ability to enable forms of public debate and, moreover, knowledge sharing that transcends the talk-based rationalism of traditional argumentation. The chapter concludes by arguing that all of this potential depends on the capacity of the Internet to reshape political efficacy, which, in turn, raises critical questions about how policy scholars understand political sense making.

In chapter 6, Leonie Sandercock and Giovanni Attili bring images and pictorial analysis into argumentative research by exploring important applications of multimedia for urban policy and planning. Raising both epistemological and pragmatic considerations related to the capacities of multimedia as a mode of inquiry, they begin with an account of their postpositivist epistemological orientation, particularly an emphasis on polyphonic narrative analysis through the medium of film as an antidote to the typically bidimensional, cartographic, and quantitative biases of urban policy and planning research. In particular, they examine film as a mode of meaning making, as a tool of community engagement, and as a catalyst for public policy deliberation and argumentation. Exploring what they call a new "digital ethnography," they seek to create a new polyphonic narrative as it relates to Canada's national multicultural philosophy and its translation from the national policy-making level to the streets and neighborhoods where diverse cultures face the daily challenges of coexistence. What kinds of sociological and political imagination at the local level, they ask, could make for peaceful coexistence? Toward this end, they offer a thick description of the role of one local institution in a culturally diverse neighborhood in Vancouver, asking "how do strangers become neighbors?" Interwoven with this inquiry is the account of the making of their documentary *Where Strangers Become Neighbours* and an evaluation of its effectiveness as a catalyst for policy dialogue.

In part IV, "Policy Rhetoric, Argumentation, and Semiotics," Herbert Gottweis takes up the role of rhetoric in policy studies. Though often evoked in political discussion, the concept of rhetoric is still only finding its way into policy making as a conceptual framework. Toward this end, Gottweis introduces the concept of rhetoric as developed in the French "New Rhetoric" tradition of Chaïm Perelman, Ruth Amossy, and Dominique Maingueneau. The concept of rhetoric directs our attention to the centrality of persuasion in policy making and the interplay of what Aristotle called logos, pathos, and ethos as core moments of the process of persuasion. Using stem cell policy making in the United States as a case, he offers a framework for the rhetorical analysis of policy making and argues that processes of persuasion in policy making involve not only arguments but also arguers, images, and the presentation of a self in a process of interaction in which arguing takes place through words and emotions. With persuasion, people try to influence and change one another's mind by appealing not only to reason but also to passions or even prejudice. The politics of persuasion is a politics of disagreement and controversy that goes beyond the exchange of arguments, a politics that counts on the free play of persuasion rather than on the taming of judgment though the imposition of rules of deliberation.

In his chapter on the deservingness in welfare policy, Sanford Schram provides a semiotic analysis on how the unsaid of an underlying discourse allows the said metaphors of policy narratives and the arguments in which they are embedded to indicate points of reference, especially privileged identities that are deeply established in the culture of the broader society. He shows how the metaphors used in contemporary policy narratives about welfare frame their objects of concern in ways that point to implied understandings and arguments found elsewhere. Being on welfare today is assumed to be a sign of not being a "good mother" who is practicing "personal responsibility," demonstrating that the "dependency" associated with taking welfare is analogous to other bad dependencies, for instance, a chemical dependency. These framing metaphors of welfare policy narratives are simultaneously moralizing and medicalizing the problem of welfare dependency as well as immediately suggesting that its treatment be undertaken in ways similar to the treatment of drug addictions. A semiotic analysis enables us to see the deeply embedded cultural biases for political argumentation and social change, for better or for worse. He concludes by arguing that the transformation of social welfare policy for dispossessed single mothers begins with the discursive transformation of how we talk about the problem.

In part V, "Policy Argumentation in Critical Theory and Practice: Communicative Logics and Policy Learning," Hubertus Buchstein and Dirk Jörke return to one of the basic contributions that motivated the argumentative turn, namely, the critical theory of Jürgen Habermas and his theory of communicative action. Since then, the work of Michel Foucault emerged to challenge basic propositions advanced by Habermas, particularly those related to ideal speech and public deliberation. In the chapter, they seek to sort out the debates to which these disagreements have given rise and suggest ways in which these two diverging perspectives might be seen to constructively complement one another. First, they look back to the developments in Habermasian critical theory and their impact on the social sciences, in particular the communicative approach to policy analysis. Habermas's early criticisms of positivism as well as his theory of communicative action have been a crucial steppingstone to bridge the gap between language philosophy and public policy analysis. In the second part, the authors examine the impact of the rise of Foucauldian poststructuralism on critical theory. After reviewing the controversies between Habermasians and Foucauldians, the authors reconstruct and discuss the implications of Foucault's later writings about governmentality for a critical analysis of deliberative policy and politics. Finally, Buchstein and Jörke offer a suggestion about how these perspectives on politics and policy making might be seen as complementing each other.

In their chapter on poststructural policy analysis, David Howarth and Steven Griggs explain how a poststructuralist approach, when combined with elements of critical discourse analysis and rhetorical political analysis, can contribute important tools and concepts to policy studies. Going beyond a minimal and cognitive conception of discourse, in which discourses are simply empirical variables whose impacts can be measured by observation and testing, they offer a constitutive conception of discourse that actively forms practices and social relations. In this approach, discourses do not merely describe, reflect, or make known a preexisting or underlying reality; instead, they are articulatory practices that bring social reality into being for social actors and subjects by conferring meaning and identity on objects and processes. Toward this end, they first set out the ontological assumptions of poststructuralist discourse theory and then show how these assumptions inform their analysis of policy change as an ongoing political and hegemonic struggle. Specifically, they offer a poststructuralist reading of the Gramscian concepts of hegemony and power while employing the Lacanian logic of fantasy to focus attention on the enjoyment subjects procure from their identifications with certain signifiers and figures. Finally, with respect to the methodology, they outline a logic of critical explanation that is composed of five interconnected elements: problematization, retroduction, logics, articulation, and critique.

Finally, Frank Fischer (with Alan Mandell) takes up the topic of transformative learning in planning and policy deliberation. After a presentation of the primary theories of policy learning, focused primarily on technical learning, they turn to the implications of more fundamental policy paradigm learning, as introduced by Peter A. Hall. They thus seek to show the ways that these underlying paradigm beliefs and values have to be part of the work of the planners and policy analysts. Toward this end, the chapter turns to the theory of transformative learning as it has emerged in progressive adult educational theory, in particular as it has developed around the work of Paulo Freire. By focusing on the underlying social assumptions that inform policy formulations, this work offers assistance in bringing these often hidden dimensions of deliberation out into the open and submitting them to a critical assessment. In the process, it helps us to better understand the processes of attitudinal and cognitive change and the ways that they can be facilitated. Two brief examples of facilitation are offered: one concerning participatory planning and the other urban policy development. The chapter closes with a discussion of the implementation of the transformative learning for professional education and practice.

We believe that this book's chapters demonstrate the evolution of argumentative policy analysis from basic concepts built on a range of selected theoretical approaches such as those of Habermas and Foucault toward a more elaborated conceptual framework for systematic analysis. While argumentative policy analysis has gone a long way since it originated in the late 1980s, it continues to grow and further develop today through a process of theoretical refinement and by continuously engaging with the current developments in social theory and responding to the real-life challenges of the ever complex, unpredictable, and messy world of policy making.

Notes

1. This book focuses on public policy rather than policy and planning per se, as was the case with the edition in 1993, in part because policy analysis, as an interdisciplinary mode of inquiry, has been fully taken over by planners as well. Although years ago there were discussions about what distinguishes planning from policy analysis, planners today focus on policy as well. Policy analysis is widely seen as one of the analytical tools of the planner.

2. The orientation has also drawn in some cases on work on discourse and social constructivism in international relations theory. There, too, discourse and argumentation have been important challengers to mainstream orthodoxies.

3. The implicit view behind standard models is that markets and economies are inherently stable and that they only temporarily get off track. The majority of economists thus failed to warn policy makers about the threatening system crisis and ignored the work of those who did. Ironically, as the crisis has unfolded, numerous economists have begun to rethink the need to abandon their standard models and to think about approaches that include more sophisticated behavioral assumptions, including the role of beliefs, argumentation, and emotion (Loewenstein 2007). Some have turned, in the process, to more commonsense advice (Roubini and Mihm 2010). This, in the view of some, is an improvement, but it remains a poor substitute for an underlying model that can provide much-needed guidance for developing policy and regulation. It is not enough to put the existing model to one side, observing that one needs "exceptional measures for exceptional times." What we need are models capable of envisaging such "exceptional times."

References

Bremmer, I. 2010. *The End of the Free Market: Who Wins the War between States and Corporations?* New York: Portfolio.

Clarke, A. C. 2005. *Situational Analysis: Grounded Theory after the Postmodern Turn.* Thousand Oaks, Calif.: Sage.

Colander, D., H. Föllmer, M. Goldberg, A. Haas, A. Kirman, K. Juselius, T. Lux, and B. Sloth. 2009. *The Financial Crisis and the Systemic Failure of Academic Economics.* Kiel Working Paper 1489. Kiel Institute for the World Economy.

Dryzek, J. 2000. *Deliberative Democracy and Beyond: Liberals, Critics, and Contestations.* Oxford: Oxford University Press.

Fischer, F. 1990. *Technocracy and the Politics of Expertise.* Newbury Park, Calif.: Sage.
——. 2003. *Reframing Public Policy: Discursive Politics and Deliberative Practices.* Oxford: Oxford University Press.
Fischer, F., and John Forester, eds. 1993. *The Argumentative Turn in Policy Analysis.* Durham: Duke University Press.
Forester, J. 1999. *The Deliberative Practitioner: Encouraging Participatory Planning Processes.* Cambridge: Cambridge University Press.
——. 2009. *Dealing with Differences: Dramas of Mediating Public Disputes.* Oxford: Oxford University Press.
Friedman, B. M. 2009. "The Failure of the Economy and the Economists." *New York Review of Books,* May 28:30–34.
Gottweis, H. 2006. "Argumentative Policy Analysis." In *Handbook of Public Policy,* edited by J. Pierre and B. G. Peters, 461–80. Thousand Oaks, Calif.: Sage.
Hajer, M. 1995. *The Politics of Environmental Discourse: Ecological Modernization and the Policy Process.* Oxford: Oxford University Press.
Howarth, D. 2000. *Discourse.* Buckingham: Open University Press.
Keenoy, T., C. Oswick, and D. Grant. 1997. "Organizational Discourses: Text and Context." *Organization* 2:147–58.
King, G., R. O. Keohane, and S. Verba. 1994. *Designing Social Inquiry: Scientific Interference in Qualitative Research.* Princeton: Princeton University Press.
Law, J. 2004. *After Method: Mess in Social Science Research.* New York: Routledge.
Linblom, C., and D. Cohen. 1979. *Usable Knowledge: Social Science and Social Problem Solving.* New Haven: Yale University Press.
Loewenstein, G. 2007. *Exotic Preferences: Behavioral Economics and Human Motivation.* Oxford: Oxford University Press.
Majone, G. 1989. *Evidence, Argument and Persuasion in the Policy Process.* New Haven: Yale University Press.
Mitchell, W. J. T. 1994. *Picture Theory.* Chicago: University of Chicago Press.
Ney, S. 2009. *Resolving Messy Problems: Handling Conflict in Environment, Transport, Health and Ageing Policy.* London: Earthscan.
Orren, G. 1988. "Beyond Self-Interest." In *The Power of Ideas,* edited by R. B. Reich. Cambridge: Harvard University Press.
Peters, B. G. 2004. Review of "Reframing Public Policy: Discursive Politics and Deliberative Practices." *Political Science Quarterly* 119(3):566–67.
Phillips, Nelson. 2003. "Discourse or Institution? Institutional Theory and the Challenge of Discourse Analysis." In *Debating Organizations: Point-Counterpoint in Organization Studies,* edited by Robert Westwood and Stewart Clegg, 220–31. Malden, Mass.: Blackwell.

Roubini, N., and S. Mihm. 2010. *Crisis Economics: A Crash Course in the Future of Finance.* London: Penguin.
Schmidt, V. A. 2001. "The Impact of Europeanization on National Governance Practices, Ideas, and Discourse." Paper presented at European Consortium for Political Research Workshop on Policy, Discourse and Institutional Reform, Grenoble, France, April 6–11.
———. 2002. *The Futures of European Capitalism.* Oxford: Oxford University Press.
Stone, D. 2002. *Policy Paradox: The Art of Political Decision-Making.* 2nd ed. New York: W. W. Norton.
Verba, S., and Orren, G. 1985. *Equality in America.* Cambridge: Harvard University Press.
Wagenaar, H. 2011. *Meaning in Action: Interpretation and Dialogue in Policy Analysis.* New York: M. E. Sharpe.
Weber, Max. 1948. *The Social Psychology of the World Religions.* Reprinted in *From Max Weber,* edited by H. N. Gerth and C. W. Mills. London: Routledge.
Weick, K. 1969. *The Social Psychology of Organizing.* Reading, Mass.: Addison-Wesley.
Yanow, D. 2000. *Conducting Interpretive Policy Analysis.* Thousand Oaks, Calif.: Sage.

PART I

*Deliberative Policy Argumentation
and Public Participation*

JOHN S. DRYZEK AND CAROLYN M. HENDRIKS

1. Fostering Deliberation in the Forum and Beyond

The argumentative turn led to appreciation of the variety of forms of communication that could play their parts in public policy processes—and thus also in public policy analysis. These forms include not just argument narrowly conceived, but also rhetoric, testimony, and the telling of stories, narratives, performances, humor, and ceremonial speech. We take it as given that policy analysis now needs to pay strong attention to these communicative forms and the frames or discourses in which they are embedded, and focus here upon the settings in which such communications can occur. These settings range from legislatures to administrative agencies to courts to public hearings to the broader public sphere and also include, crucially, the systems that join all these particular sites. The setting has major consequences for the kinds of communications that can be made and heard. So, for example, courts typically impose fairly strict rules upon who can speak, when, and in what terms; and judges stand ready to rule particular communications out of order.

Sometimes settings are designed to facilitate particular sorts of communications. So, for example, parliaments in Westminster-style political systems are designed to promote adversarial debate. The very design of the chamber distinguishes between government and opposition, with each side facing the other. And all the rules and informal practices are designed to facilitate questioning, challenge, the scoring of points, and the competition of proposals, but not mutual understanding, creativity in the crafting of proposals, or conflict resolution that would be in the interests of all sides.

In recent years, the argumentative turn in policy analysis and planning has converged with the political theory of deliberative democracy and with a movement to institutionalize deliberative forums in political processes. The forums in question include stakeholder dialogues, alternative dispute resolution exercises, collaborative mechanisms, and various designs that rely on lay citizens, such as consensus conferences, citizens' juries, planning cells, citizens' assemblies, and deliberative polls. Most of these developed originally without much input from the theory of deliberative democracy (except for deliberative polls), but theorists are now very interested in these forums for their potential embodiment of deliberative ideals (Smith and Wales 2002; Warren and Pearse 2008). Public policy scholars for their part have recognized affinities between their own work and that of deliberative theorists and are interested in the institutional implications of particular sorts of communication. So, for example, Hajer and Wagenaar (2003) speak of "deliberative policy analysis" that proves especially appropriate for contemporary networked forms of governance that downplay the role of sovereign authority in policy making. These sorts of convergent developments lead to questions about what sorts of communications count as deliberative, how existing practices and institutions might be evaluated in these terms, and how forums might be designed to promote these forms of communication. Important associated issues concern who exactly should participate in these forums and on what terms, and the role that particular forums might play in larger systems of governance.

In this chapter, we emphasize in particular the role of design in promoting authentic, inclusive, and effective deliberation. Our aim is not so much to compare and contrast different types of deliberative forums but to look more broadly at how deliberation might be shaped by various design attributes such as the structure of the forum, its participants, and the authority and legitimacy of the forum.

We recognize at the outset that deliberation does not always need to be designed. Everyday political discussion can contribute to public deliberation (Conover, Searing, and Crewe 2001; Mansbridge 1999). In some instances, strategic or coercive forms of communication can "drift" into more deliberative modes, especially when actors learn to trust each other and have the freedom to shape their own procedures (McLaverty and Halpin 2008). Deliberation might also spontaneously emerge, be it within interest groups (Mansbridge 1992), in the larger public sphere (Habermas 1989), or even international negotiations (Risse 2000). It is worth emphasizing international negotiations on security affairs because on the face of it that is exactly the kind of place where deliberation should not emerge, as actors strive above all to maximize their relative advantage. Risse (2000) shows that communicative action in the Habermasian sense can be found in such negotiations, for example, when Soviet negotiators were persuaded that a united Germany within NATO posed less of a threat than if it were outside NATO.

We also acknowledge that designed forums are not the only settings in which deliberation can occur, and we have already pointed out that it is unwise to focus on any particular forum as the sole and proper location for deliberation. We must always keep an eye on how different forum types connect with each other, with other institutions, with the larger public sphere, and with the content of collective decisions. Here it is most helpful to think of how particular forums function within and help constitute a larger deliberative system (Hendriks 2006a; Mansbridge 1999). A deliberative system links different sites that may contribute to the theoretical requirements of a deliberative democracy. Components of a system might include particular institutions (such as a legislature or courts), particular sites (such as social movements or the media), and particular practices (such as activism or justification).

We begin by clarifying what we mean by "deliberation" and how it differs from other forms of communication. Next we survey emerging empirical research on how deliberation is influenced by various design issues, including structure and rules, participants and their roles, and finally the authority and legitimacy of deliberative forums. We show how design can be used to promote (and inhibit) particular kinds of communication in deliberative forums. At first sight, this conclusion highlights the need for political systems to facilitate multiple deliberative spaces such that policy making can be informed by a diverse range of argumentation and communication. However, more important than simple variety is how the different spaces connect to constitute an effective deliberative system.

What Is Deliberative?

We turn now to clarify what we mean by "deliberation" in the context of public policy. We take a relatively expansive view of what deliberative communication in public policy processes can entail. We thus admit any kinds of communications as long as they can induce reflection on the part of those who attend to the communication, are noncoercive, can connect particular interests to some more general principles, and involve an effort to communicate in terms that others can accept (what

Gutmann and Thompson [1996] call reciprocity, though they emphasize the particular form of argument). Our own expansive view of deliberation is consistent with what we actually observe in more or less deliberative settings concerning controversial public issues, but that does not mean abandoning critical standards for what should count.

Some early theorists of deliberative democracy placed more demanding requirements on the content of deliberation, with an exclusive emphasis on reason giving (e.g., Bessette 1994; Cohen 1989). More recent contributors, such as Fung (2006), argue that quality deliberation should be rational, reasonable, equal, and inclusive. Fung uses rationality here in an instrumental sense: "individuals advance their own individual and collective ends through discussion, brainstorming, information pooling, planning and problem solving" (167). While theorists influenced by Habermas and Rawls would stress public reasons and public interests, Mansbridge et al. (2010:72–80) believe there is a place for self-interest in deliberation, as long as the self-interest in question can be justified to others as reasonable. They refer to "deliberatively constituted self-interest" (77). An example they give is a person who invokes his or her own job security as a reason not to support a potentially costly political action. In Habermasian language, this kind of self-interest might still be interpreted as generalizable interest (because everyone with a job has an interest in their own job security). For Mansbridge et al., this recognition of self-interest entails accepting "deliberative negotiation" that involves a search for mutually acceptable solutions responsive to the particular interests of each party (2010:90–93).

Reason can work against inclusion if it is specified too narrowly. If reasonableness is taken to mean that persuasion should only be on grounds that people can accept by virtue of their own reasonableness, then we are on contentious Rawlsian ground where (for example) rhetoric has no role in deliberation. If political deliberation is conceptualized in the image of a philosophy seminar it provides a big soft target for critics. Most deliberative democrats who have contemplated rhetoric (which can be defined as persuasion in all its forms) actually believe it has important roles to play (e.g., Chambers 2009; Remer 1999).

While taking a relatively expansive view of what kinds of communication can be allowed under the deliberative heading, we should stress that there are some forms of communication that should be ruled out. These include, most notably, command, heresthetic (defined by Riker

[1996] as the manipulation of the choice set of another participant), strategizing, deception, therapy, and coercive bargaining (which works on the basis of threats and inducements).

It is important not to stretch the concept of deliberation too far (Steiner 2008). The most indefensible stretches have actually not been made by deliberative democrats themselves, but by mainstream empirical social scientists and rational choice theorists who have (mis)used the concept of deliberation—presumably because it is so popular—to describe *any* form of political communication, including lies (e.g., Austen-Smith and Feddersen 2006). Against these excessively stretched usages, we need to be careful about what counts as deliberative and what does not (Bächtiger et al. 2010; Steiner 2008). Opinion remains divided on the extent to which deliberation (as a regulatory ideal) should include alternative forms of communication such as storytelling, narrative, and conversation. When it comes to rhetoric, Chambers (2009) is careful to distinguish "deliberative" (designed to make people think and reflect) from "plebiscitary" rhetoric. The latter suffers from the sins of pandering (to existing preferences in the audience), priming (of prejudice), and crafting (i.e., selecting issues to maximize support for the speaker). Dryzek (2010) argues for a presumption in favor of bridging over bonding rhetoric. Bridging attempts to reach differently situated others, bonding to reinforce group solidarity. However, there are circumstances when this test misleads, such that a better test involves asking whether the rhetoric in question contributes to the establishment or maintenance of an effective deliberative system linking competent and reflective actors. If we follow the advice of Young (2000) and include, in addition to rhetoric, storytelling (or testimony), and greeting as admissible and valuable forms of communication, then we also need tests to distinguish defensible from indefensible uses of these forms.

We note in passing that what counts as deliberation can be connected to, and learn from, other literatures relevant to policy that have addressed communicative questions. Most notable among these is the literature on conflict resolution, mediation, and what is called consensus building (Susskind, McKearnan, and Thomas-Larmer 1999). The term "consensus building" is actually somewhat unfortunate from the point of view of deliberative democracy, which in recent years has been busy trying to escape unrealistic notions of consensus as an ideal, which is associated with Habermas in particular. In the conflict resolution literature, consensus building really means agreement building; protagonists can accept the agreement for very different reasons (including fear of what will happen in the absence of agreement). But the style of communication prized and promoted by conflict resolution professionals, mediators, and facilitators has strong affinities with deliberation (Susskind 2006). Deliberative democrats can allow that nondeliberative communication has its place. For example, partisan activism and boycotts may spur deliberation about injustices and pave the way for deliberation to occur on relatively equal terms (Dodge 2009; Fung 2005).

The question of deliberation's proper connection to collective decision is a thorny one. Some see deliberation as a problem-solving exercise (e.g., Levine, Fung, and Levine 2005), in contrast to mere dialogue in which individuals work toward mutual understanding. However as Kanra (2007) points out, it is better to think of two complementary phases of deliberation: social learning (covering what others would mean by dialogue) and decision making. Some writers believe that deliberation's primary home should be in a particular institution that actually makes collectively binding decisions. That institution might be a legislature (Bessette 1994) or a supreme court (Rawls 1993:231). Other writers believe that forums designed with deliberation in mind will (perhaps unsurprisingly) produce better deliberation, ideally with a strong influence on collective decision. Fishkin (2009) has these kinds of hopes for his deliberative polls. Most deliberative democrats are perhaps more open and expansive when it comes to the institutional location of deliberation. But they may still want to apply a relevance test. So, in clinging to some of the loftier ambitions of deliberative democracy to promote a very particular style of public reasoning, Thompson wants to distinguish "ordinary political discussion" from "decision-oriented deliberation," though he also believes that the relationship between these two sorts of communication merits examination (Thompson 2008:502). It is also possible to think of ordinary discussion, or what Mansbridge (1999) calls "everyday talk," as having its own rightful place in deliberative systems. Such talk need not necessarily involve reasoning about what is in the common good (Chambers 2003:309; Mansbridge 2006). However, she does not want to let just any talk into the system. In wrestling with this issue, Mansbridge (2006) suggests that the deciding factor should be whether the deliberative communication is politically relevant, that is, whether it involves the "authoritative allocation of values," in the language of Easton (1953). Much in the way of chitchat and gossip, even it is about politics, presumably fails this test.

As deliberative *democrats*, we also need to emphasize *inclusive* forms of public deliberation. A highly structured and formal deliberative process might disadvantage people accustomed to other modes of communication (Sanders 1997; Young 2000) or inadvertently induce strategic behavior (Button and Mattson 1999; Hendriks 2002). Democratically legitimate deliberation entails the right, opportunity, and capacity of all those affected by a collective decision—or their representatives—to participate in consequential decision about the content of that decision. If all those individuals cannot be physically present in a forum, then that raises some large issues of representation. Deliberative democracy should be able to accommodate the kind of pluralization of representation claims, and kinds of representatives (including unelected and self-appointed [self-authorized] ones), that are now stressed by democratic theorists (Montanero 2008; Saward 2008; Urbinati and Warren 2008). This pluralization is a matter of political practice, not just political theory. Deliberative democrats should also be able to identify the characteristics of a good representative in deliberative terms.

What Shapes How Deliberation Works?

Deliberative scholarship is rich with prescriptions on how to promote "good deliberation"; these contributions, however, tend to stem from normative theory (e.g., Fung 2003; Renn, Webler, and Wiedemann 1995) rather than empirical research. Some recent contributions offer "good design principles" for deliberative processes based on insights from deliberative practitioners. For example, in defining criteria for a "fully democratic deliberative process," Carson and Hartz-Karp suggest that in addition to influence and inclusion, a deliberative process must "provide open dialogue, access to information, respect, space to understand and reframe issues and movement toward consensus" (2005:122). Practitioners of deliberation tend to emphasize different aspects of deliberation than theorists. Mansbridge et al. find that facilitators generally believe that "good" deliberation entails "promoting an atmosphere that maintains a degree of 'gravitas' but is consistently comfortable, even friendly, so that participants feel safe enough to be humble, change their minds, and speak freely" (2006:15). Facilitators also judge deliberation in instrumental terms; a process is deemed deliberatively successful if the group makes progress on its set task. Emotions are also welcome, particularly if they aid "good reason-giving" (2).

There are also strong links here with the literature on participatory and consultative practice. For example, many of the core values of the International Association for Public Participation (IAP2 2007) emphasize not only that participation involves those potentially affected by decisions but also that those participating have access to information to assist meaningful participation (see also McCoy and Scully [2002] for useful design principles for public engagement processes).

Normative theory and insights from practitioners have their uses, but the danger is that they may degenerate into something like what Simon (1946) long ago denounced as "the proverbs of administration," a set of plausible but vague, inconsistent, and even contradictory prescriptions. We still know relatively little about what makes the actual process of deliberation work. As Rosenberg (2005) notes, intense studies of small-group interaction have been more the domain of social psychologists than of political scientists or policy analysts. This research suggests that the majority of people have a limited capacity to reflect on and reconsider their preferences in view of the arguments of others (Rosenberg 2005). When confronted with opposing views, most of us apparently dig our heels in or draw on other arguments to support our own position or take information shortcuts to make judgments (Ryfe 2005).

While findings from social psychology deserve to be taken seriously, they are not from forums designed with political deliberation in mind, so they should be applied with caution. These findings do not mean that many or most people are unable to deliberate, simply that "deliberation represents a disturbance of our everyday reasoning habits" (Ryfe 2005:56). Entering deliberation can make people feel uncomfortable, so the challenge is to find ways of enabling people to feel at home in deliberation.

The empirical literature on deliberative democracy is now so large and growing so fast that it defies easy summary (for surveys, see Bächtiger et al. 2010 and Thompson 2008). Some of it is a misdirected continuation of a long tradition in empirical political science that tries to discredit democracy of any depth (e.g., Hibbing and Theiss-Morse

2002). Some misconceptualize deliberation (e.g., Austen-Smith and Feddersen 2006). Some mistakenly want deliberative democracy to be a "falsifiable theory" rather than a normative project (e.g., Mutz 2008). Excising such studies does fortunately leave a substantial body of work from which useful lessons can be drawn, which we will focus on here in trying to assess how forum design affects the prospects for deliberative democracy. We recognize that there are limits to the degree deliberative democracy can and should be designed.

Among a host of possible topics, we focus our discussion on three key design issues:

Structure and rules
Participants and roles
Authority and legitimacy

Structure and Rules

Deliberation is not the dominant form of contemporary politics. To state the obvious, as does Shapiro (1999), politics is in practice often first and foremost about interest and power. Politics involves a host of activities that are nondeliberative, such as organizing, mobilizing, demonstrating, fundraising, and voting (Walzer 1999), although, as indicated earlier, these activities can sometimes prompt deliberation. To this we can add the pursuit of strategic advantage, media trivialization, mass deception, technocratic manipulation, populist prejudice, and occasional violence. Where then should we look for deliberation? The sites range from formal institutions such as legislatures and constitutional courts to the more informal sites of conversation on public issues to governance networks that join public and private actors to citizen forums. Each deliberative venue is likely to have its own "logic" of discourse, that is, informal understandings and formal rules governing the way deliberators interact (Rosenberg 2005).

These understandings and rules can affect the degree to which deliberation can occur. Consider, for example, the comparative work of Steiner et al. (2004), who have examined deliberative quality in parliaments in different kinds of liberal democracies. They applied a Discourse Quality Index (based on Habermas's theory of communication) to parliamentary debate and found that discourse is of a higher quality in parliaments in presidential systems compared to parliamentary systems and in parliaments in consensual democracies compared to majoritarian democracies, particularly where a second chamber is present. They also found that deliberation tends to be of higher quality when the issue has a low degree of polarization.

When we move beyond parliament into one-off forums involving either stakeholders or ordinary citizens, the influence of rules and structures becomes much harder to clarify. Part of the problem is the forums themselves, which are typically one-off exercises that differ substantially in their design details, even when a supposedly standard design is being used. Such variety is understandable given differences in policy problems, available opportunities, available funding, time constraints, and the agendas of sponsors. Forums vary substantially in size, types of participants, how they are recruited, how they interact, the length of time they spend on different kinds of tasks, whether or not they are asked to converge on policy recommendations, the relationship of the forum to other institutions, the availability of expert advice, and the role of advocates from different sides. Moving from forum design to research design, different pieces of research are informed by different views of what deliberation is, what it should achieve, and how it should be studied. This heterogeneity may provide a rich array of findings, but it makes empirical comparison that tests theoretical generalizations quite difficult (Thompson 2008). It gets in the way of making inferences about the effects of any particular factor, because there are too many variables. In this light, Fishkin's obsession with making sure that his basic deliberative poll design is not varied is actually a welcome exception, because it means it is possible to examine the influence of issue type or the political context in which the poll is applied.

That said, some preliminary observations can be made.

Time matters. It takes time for participants to feel at ease with and master a subject of any complexity and to realize that they can have something to say about it. Citizen forums in particular are sometimes convened for only an evening or a day; often this is not long enough. While practitioners stress the importance of giving participants enough time, we are aware of no empirical work that compares the relative quality of deliberative processes of different lengths.

Agenda matters. A broad charge with an open agenda means too many options on the table, and no time and no need for individuals to focus or to reflect on and address what others are saying about particular issues. On the other hand, excessive agenda control constricts the content of deliberation and prompts suspicion of preordained outcomes. The solution may be a reflexive process in which participants themselves can modify the agenda (Lang 2008).

Rules matter. Because deliberation is for many participants an unfamiliar activity, it is necessary to help participants learn to reason together and to help them form judgments and if necessary develop collective outputs (Mansbridge et al. 2006; Ryfe 2005). The rules can actually be designed by the participants themselves.

Facilitation matters. Impartial and skilled facilitation is necessary to ensure equal opportunities for meaningful participation (Carson 2002; Mansbridge et al. 2006). One way to help loosen the grip of problematic predispositions is to ensure that the deliberations are moderated or facilitated (Carson 2002; Fung 2006:164; Kosnoski 2005; Rosenberg 2005). With skillful facilitation, participants can learn about the issues under deliberation and be empowered to challenge arguments and reflect on the preferences and positions of themselves and others.

Task matters. Some forums (such as citizens' juries) give participants the task of producing a report or set of policy recommendations. Others (such as deliberative polls) just seek their opinion, for example, in answering items on a questionnaire. Grönlund, Setälä, and Herne (2010) find that a forum tasked with making a recommendation has a more positive effect on participants' civic dispositions than an otherwise identical forum concluding with a questionnaire.

Publicity matters—but in subtle ways. On the one hand, it seems that individuals process information more objectively when they are told they will have to discuss their perspective publicly (Tetlock 1983, cited in Ryfe 2005). On the other, secrecy means that participants can be more honest in what they say and can explore areas of convergence with those from the "other" side without being accused of betrayal by those on their "own" side (Chambers 2004). Steiner et al. (2004) find that, in parliamentary settings, publicity promotes common good justification, but that secrecy leads to better arguments being made. Naurin (2004) finds that publicity does not have any civilizing effect on business lobbyists. The resolution of conflicting demands of secrecy and publicity may lie in the need to attend to how moments of secrecy and moments of publicity are designed into the overall deliberative process.

Structural context matters. Seemingly identical forum designs will work out very differently in different kinds of political system. Dryzek and Tucker (2008) show that Danish-style consensus conferences play very different roles when inserted into different kinds of political systems. In the actively inclusive political system of Denmark itself, they are integrated into the process of policy making. In the more exclusive political system of France, consensus conferences are deployed as managerial tools and are expected to produce conclusions that support the general position of those who established them. In the passively exclusive United States, consensus conferences are just one kind of advocacy input among many others; at least when it comes to federal politics, they are organized by foundations and academics, not by the government itself. Within countries, there are also significant variations in how similar deliberative procedures play out (e.g., Hendriks 2005b). Exactly how specific contextual factors shape the quality of deliberation merits further exploration (Delli Carpini, Cook, and Jacobs 2004).

Size matters. Face-to-face deliberation cannot occur in any group larger than about twenty people (Gastil 1993; Parkinson 2003a:181). There are ways to organize larger numbers, normally by dividing them into smaller groups and then organizing communications between groups. The 21st Century Town meetings, as pioneered by the America-Speaks Foundation, do this through a sophisticated use of information technology, feeding back summaries from small group deliberations. Participants can also rotate across groups.

Participants and Roles

Deliberative forums can involve different sorts of participants, to very different effect. Variety of initial disposition across participants is generally desirable. For if participants share initial dispositions, their discussions may yield to Sunstein's (2002) "law of group polarization." The studies cited by Sunstein seem to show that if all individuals begin with a range of dispositions that lean in the same direction, then discussion will cause the average position to move toward the extreme. The consequences in situations characterized by deep social division look undesirable. But on other sorts of issues, what Sunstein calls polarization may also be described as the achievement of moral clarity (Goodin 2009). And enclave deliberation may give a group enough confidence subsequently to enter the larger public sphere without being disadvantaged. But if polarization is seen as a problem, the solution is obvious: select participants for deliberation from a variety of initial points of view. If that is the case, they are more likely in deliberation to be "more open-minded, to learn more from others, and to engage in a deeper consideration of issues—in short, to be more deliberative" (Ryfe 2005:52).

There are several different methods for recruiting participants for deliberative processes (Davies, Blackstock, and Rauschmayer 2005; Ryfe 2005). The three most common options are (1) to advertise and allow individuals to self-select; (2) to recruit participants in order to cover the pertinent range of substantive interests; and (3) to recruit in order to achieve a statistically representative sample. Opinion is divided on how these recruitment approaches influence the quality of deliberation.

Option (1) at first sight seems to be the most open recruitment strategy, for it enables any interested individual to participate. However, what can happen in practice is that self-selection means participants are typically highly competent and well resourced, with a history of interest and activism in the issue at hand. Inequalities of wealth and education are likely to be mirrored in forum composition. It is possible to correct for these problems by screening those who volunteer, which does of course mean denying participation to many who seek it. Smith points out that at least in the cases of participatory budgeting in Brazil and community policing in Chicago, self-selection "need not imply that traditional social distinctions will be replicated" and that in some cases the traditionally disadvantaged are more likely to want to participate (2009:71).

Option (2) is the selection procedure for stakeholder processes and advisory committees in which participants are selected to represent particular sectors, interests, or expertise. This option is particularly appropriate when the main aim of deliberation is conflict resolution or movement beyond an impasse in policy disputes (Susskind, McKearnan, and Thomas-Larmer 1999). Effective resolution here means that all parties to a dispute have to be at the table. Their strong initial commitments may mean that the reflection upon interests and preferences central to deliberation is impeded; but while it is unlikely that partisans will be induced to give up their core commitments, they may come to see issues in different ways and thus contribute to joint problem solving.

Mansbridge is optimistic here about what interest group representatives can offer, arguing that their involvement "produces information, generates innovation and changes preferences, creating gains not there before the process began" (1992:497). However, when it comes to the actual business of deliberating, there are obstacles to group representatives playing any deliberative role (Baber and Bartlett 2007; Talisse 2005; Williams 2000; Young 2001). They may struggle to be open-minded enough to be persuaded by the arguments of others (Williams 2000), or they might resist the very idea of deliberation with adversaries (Levine and Nierras 2007) and prefer to use more conventional political strategies to advance their agenda (Dodge 2009; Hendriks 2011).

Fung (2006:167) favors participants who have high stakes in the issue and have the capacity to affect the content of policy decisions. Such participants, he argues, can engage in "hot deliberation" that is likely to be more "rational" as the "participants have greater motivations to correctly align their ideas and views with their interests and values" (167). It is not clear that Fung has any evidence for this contention. A history of active involvement is likely to be carried through into the forum (Hendriks 2002). However, our own comparative study, together with that of Hunold (Hendriks, Dryzek, and Hunold 2007), has found that the quality of deliberative communication in "hot deliberation" is questionable because partisans are often unwilling to consider shifting their preferences and taking the views of others seriously.

Option (3) entails recruiting participants on the grounds that they are statistically representative of some larger community. The community in question is normally the citizenry of an established political entity such as a state or a city. Citizens' juries, consensus conferences, deliberative polls, citizens' assemblies, and planning cells all use stratified random sampling. The smaller the forum, the more the initial random sample will need to be tweaked to ensure that individuals across a broad range of the usual social characteristics and political dispositions are actually present in the forum. Random selection (plus stratification) means that elites, expert lobbyists, and the "articulate and incensed" are removed from the heart of deliberation (Carson and Martin 1999:130; see also Dienel and Renn 1995). Because participants have no obligations to a constituency and are relatively impartial, they can be more open to persuasion (Dienel 1997:104; Dienel and Renn 1995:126). Their deliberation may then be more easily drawn to collective purposes rather than partial interests (Carson and Martin 1999). They will be less likely than partisans to bargain because their relationships are not well established or likely to continue (Hörning 1999:357). Random selection also facilitates expression and consideration of the tacit forms of lay knowledge that ordinary citizens can offer: local perspectives and experiential knowledge (Epstein 1996; Fischer 2003; Wynne 1996). Many of these aspirations appear to be borne out in practice (Einsiedel, Jelsøe, and Breck 2001; Guston 1999; Hendriks 2005a; Joss 1995; Niemeyer 2004).

Skeptics here (e.g., Hibbing and Theiss-Morse 2002) would predict that the vast majority of citizens are not interested in participation and thus would have little enthusiasm for highly demanding deliberative participation. However, Neblo et al. (2010) demonstrate that given an opportunity to participate in a meaningful deliberative activity (in their case, deliberation involving their representative in Congress), most people jump at the chance. Enthusiasm is especially high among those turned off by more conventional political participation opportunities. Others worry that randomly selected citizens lack the capacity to master complex issues (Price 2000). The evidence suggests otherwise: it is precisely on complex issues featuring conflicting values that lay citizen forums have been used to best effect. The most popular issues that have been treated in such forums in many countries include genetically modified foods, human biotechnology, and nanotechnology.

A variant of option (3) (call it option [3b]) would draw the sample not from the citizenry in its entirety but from a subset of citizens. So, they might be young people deliberating on youth affairs (Carson 2010), or prostitutes deliberating on brothels (Wagenaar 2006), or public tenants deliberating on housing policy (BoL 2004).

Forums that place deliberating ordinary citizens at their center can also assign roles to partisan advocates, stakeholders affected by an issue, and experts (Hendriks, Dryzek, and Hunold 2007; Mendonça 2009). For example, in citizens' juries and consensus conferences, the task of deliberating is handed to lay citizens, while advocates and experts are given the more confined role of providing testimonies (Hendriks 2011). This role allocation requires these actors to present and defend their perspectives before a public forum and, according to Carson, frees them to get on with "what they do best—researching, campaigning, educating, lobbying, protesting, becoming experts" (2001:21). This division of labor may not, however, be attractive to actors worried about ceding authority to deliberating citizens (Hendriks 2011) or about the costs of time and effort required for a very uncertain result (Baber and Bartlett 2007).

Deliberation is also shaped by the different story lines and discursive practices of participants. These might be stories or a set of ideas about the issues under deliberation or about procedural matters such as the role of the state and ideas in democracy (Fischer 2006; Forester 1993; Hendriks 2005b). Ryfe suggests that effective deliberation needs to foster stories that help participants "feel accountable for the outcomes" and feel a sense of "civic identity" so that they stick with the process even when things get difficult (2005:63).

Authority and Legitimacy

Deliberative forums rarely possess anything like policy-making authority. Some are instigated by a government authority seeking public input and advice (what Carson [2008] refers to as an "invited space"). Others are created in the public sphere (what Carson [2008] terms an "insisted space"). In some cases, the latter location is a matter of necessity. For example, the federal government of the United States does not sponsor deliberative citizen forums; so, if they are to exist for federal issues, they need to be sponsored by foundations or academics. In other cases, this location is a matter of choice. Sometimes parties to a policy dispute may themselves initiate a dialogue after fighting with each other to exhaustion in adversarial processes. Sometimes it is a demonstration project for a different kind of politics (e.g., Kashefi and Mort 2004). Sometimes it is a matter of civic commitment on the part of organizers and funders.

Some experimental research suggests that individuals make more motivated deliberators when they perceive that their efforts will make a difference (Ryfe 2005). From this finding, we might infer that invited spaces—with their promise of advising decision makers—are more likely to induce engaged deliberation than insisted spaces. However, such an inference would be mistaken. To begin, the fact that a forum is initiated by the government does not mean that government will take any notice of its findings. The history of invited spaces is littered with ultimately meaningless or symbolic consultation exercises, conducted solely to buy some time, to divert critics, or to co-opt potential troublemakers. Observations of practice suggest that insisted spaces can do very well when it comes to the seriousness with which deliberation is approached by the participants (Dryzek 2009a; Hendriks 2006b). The fact that a forum is seen as independent from government may actually help here (perhaps even more so when trust in government is low, though we have no evidence on that). Drawing on experience with participatory budgeting, Baiocchi (2005) suggests that government-sponsored forums are more effectively deliberative to the degree they operate in conjunction with civil society organizations that work both within and outside the system.

Zapata (2009) finds that when forums are advisory (as opposed to having decision-making power), policy communication is less combative and more open to dialogue. It is at least plausible that better communicative conditions prevail when the forum is situated further from decision makers and thus less likely to be conditioned by their priorities (see Hendriks 2004). There is a long-running debate in democratic theory concerning whether the best place to seek authentic deliberation is in the public sphere at some distance from the state and its priorities (Dryzek 2000; Torgerson 1999). The potential cost of locating forums in the public sphere is a disconnect between deliberation and decision, since the deliberative process has little influence on collective decisions, a problem to which we return in the conclusion.

Deliberative forums remain for many participants in and observers of politics a very unfamiliar kind of practice that sits uneasily within more established sorts of processes. As such, they may struggle to achieve legitimacy (Connelly, Richardson, and Miles 2006; Parkinson 2003b; Wallington, Lawrence, and Loechel 2008). For some analysts of deliberative forums, legitimacy is mainly about the nature of the participants. So Warren (2009) argues that the reason the British Columbia Citizens' Assembly was regarded as legitimate and its recommendations taken on trust was that ordinary voters in the subsequent referendum were convinced that the assembly was composed of people like themselves. For other observers, legitimacy is about the quality of the content. Some apply tests of authorization and accountability drawn from electoral democracy, and of course deliberative forums look problematic in this light. Thus, the legitimacy of any particular forum can be challenged, especially after the fact, by those whose interests are challenged by the conclusions or recommendations of the forum. As one experienced deliberative practitioner explains:

If any step—determining who participates, how they deliberate, what information will be provided and by whom, how decisions will be made and the influence they will have—is judged to be insufficiently equitable by any of those involved or affected by the deliberation, the whole process tends to fall into disrepute. In a world where the outcome of a deliberation will matter, though, producing both the experience and the perception of an egalitarian process is far from simple. Despite attempts to include the key antagonists, protagonists, professional experts, and non-aligned community members throughout the process, the perceptions of different parties concerning what constitutes equity do not always align. (Hartz-Karp 2007:18)

Sometimes legitimacy and trust may grow with familiarity (McLaverty and Halpin 2008; Parkinson 2003a). So, in Denmark, consensus conferences are an accepted part of the political furniture, accepted as valid by all political parties. But legitimacy is rarely a given. There are steps that organizers can take to buy a little legitimacy, for example, by appointing an external advisory body (composed of engagement experts and stakeholders) to oversee key procedural decisions. These decisions might involve the development of the agenda, participant selection, the kind of information participants will receive, the selection of presenters, and how publicity will be organized (Hendriks 2011; Joss 2000; Lenaghan 1999).

Conclusions: Promoting Deliberation in the Deliberative System

Designing or achieving effective deliberation is far from straightforward, a fact suggested by the number of influences we have canvassed (as well as those we have not). A few of the influences have been subjected to systematic empirical study, others are part of the conventional wisdom of practitioners, and still others remain a matter of conjecture.

The requirements for good deliberation that we have identified do not converge on any single model of forum design. There is a place for forums that are part of the formal structure of government as well as those within the public sphere at varying distances from government, for those composed of representatives or partisans as well as those of lay citizens. Moments of publicity and moments of secrecy can both contribute to deliberative quality. Yet some general evaluations are possible. Deliberation benefits from sufficient time, effective facilitation, a focus on generating recommendations rather than simply registering opinions, and the effective management of forum size. Getting the design "right" does not necessarily guarantee effective deliberation. Sometimes the political context means that participants will be reluctant to take on the hard work that deliberation entails (Ryfe 2005).

There are also limits to the degree that deliberative democratic ideas can and should be sought within the confines of any particular forum, no matter how well designed and located. The theory of deliberative democracy has recently undergone a "systemic turn," in the wake of which the key question is that of the deliberative capacity of whole systems, not particular forums within systems. Any deliberative system features multiple sites, forums, discursive practices, and participants. (Contributors to the systemic turn include Dryzek 2009b; Goodin 2005; Hendriks 2006a; Mansbridge 1999; Parkinson 2006; earlier intimations can be found in Benhabib 1996; Habermas 1996.) Despite the gaps we have identified, we currently know a lot more about the conditions of effective deliberation in particular forums than we do about how effective deliberative systems can be promoted. The key task for future research is to consider the role of design in the larger deliberative system and its population of institutions, practices, discourses, and narratives.

We conclude with several ideas about what this kind of research might involve. To begin, it might be a good idea to work on the parts of the political system that are the *least* deliberative, where policy debates are highly exclusive, and where the rationale for decisions cannot easily be scrutinized. Sometimes exclusion here is a matter of the invocation of nonnegotiable priorities of government. When it comes to national security policy and economic policy in particular, there seems to be a large degree of immunity to open deliberation. National security is generally the preserve of top-down, executive branch policy making, and critics can be stigmatized as unpatriotic. When it comes to the economy, the main problem is the hegemony of the discourse of market economics, though this was undermined by global financial crisis in 2008 (without many obvious salutary deliberative consequences to date). National security and economic considerations can be invoked in many policy areas as a way to curtail deliberation. Exclusion can also occur with any issue in phases of policy making treated in technical terms, as the preserve of experts.

Second, there is a need to focus on what links the different parts of a deliberative system. Face-to-face deliberation is hard to sustain in larger deliberative systems, so rhetoric may play a much greater role in these larger systems (Chambers 2009).

A third possible focus is on the contribution of seemingly nondeliberative practices (to which we have already alluded). Uncompromising activism may get issues on the agenda and participants accepted as legitimate interlocutors. Enclave deliberation producing the group polarization feared by Sunstein may enable the group in question subsequently to enter the larger public sphere with confidence. We should not simply assume that deliberative parts will add up to deliberative wholes.

This nonadditiveness points to the importance of a fourth emphasis, what Thompson (2008) calls "meta-deliberation." Meta-deliberation is about the deliberative qualities of the system itself. It is a reflexive capacity to, for example, judge whether or not nondeliberative components such as enclaves are actually contributing to the deliberative capacity of the system as a whole.

Multiple deliberative sites and practices can contribute to policy making. But we should not assume that multiplicity and variety will necessarily yield an effective deliberative system; exactly how the parts interact matters a great deal.

References

Austen-Smith, D., and T. J. Feddersen. 2006. "Deliberation, Preference Uncertainty, and Voting Rules." *American Political Science Review* 100(2): 209–17.

Baber, W. F., and R. V. Bartlett. 2007. "Problematic Participants in Deliberative Democracy: Experts, Social Movements and Environmental Justice." *International Journal of Public Administration* 30:5–22.

Bächtiger, A., S. Niemeyer, M. Neblo, M. R. Steenbergen, and J. Steiner. 2010. "Disentangling Diversity in Deliberative Democracy: Competing Theories, Their Blind Spots and Complementarities." *Journal of Political Philosophy* 18(1):32–63.

Baiocchi, G. 2005. *Militants and Citizens: The Politics of Participatory Democracy in Porto Alegre*. Stanford: Stanford University Press.

Benhabib, S. 1996. "Toward a Deliberative Model of Democratic Legitimacy." In *Democracy and Difference: Contesting Boundaries of the Political*, edited by S. Benhabib, 67–94. Princeton: Princeton University Press.

Bessette, J. M. 1994. *The Mild Voice of Reason: Deliberative Democracy and American National Government.* Chicago: University of Chicago Press.

BoL (Brotherhood of St. Laurence). 2004. *Seeing Is Believing: The 2004 Victorian Southern Region Citizens' Panel.* Melbourne, Australia: Brotherhood of St. Laurence. Video recording.

Button, M., and K. Mattson. 1999. "Deliberative Democracy in Practice: Challenges and Prospects for Civic Deliberation." *Polity* 31(4):609–37.

Carson, L. 2001. "Innovative Consultation Processes and the Changing Role of Activism." *Third Sector Review* 7(1):7–22.

———. 2002. "Democratic Systems Sustained by Skilful Mediation." Paper presented at the International Sociological Association Conference, Brisbane, July 7–13.

———. 2008. "Creating Democratic Surplus through Citizens Assemblies." *Journal of Public Deliberation* 4(1), article 5, available on the web site of the *Journal of Public Deliberation*.

———. 2010. "Taking Control: Young People Convening Australia's First Youth Jury." In *Emancipatory Practices: Adult/Youth Engagement for Social and Environmental Justice*, edited by W. Linds, L. Goulet, and A. Sammel, 109–22. Rotterdam: Sense.

Carson, L., and J. Hartz-Karp. 2005. "Adapting and Combining Deliberative Designs: Juries, Polls and Forums." In *The Deliberative Democracy Handbook: Strategies for Effective Civic Engagement in the 21st Century*, edited by J. Gastil and P. Levine, 120–38. San Francisco: Jossey-Bass.

Carson, L., and B. Martin. 1999. *Random Selection in Politics.* Westport, Conn.: Praeger.

Chambers, S. 2003. "Deliberative Democracy Theory." *Annual Review of Political Science* 6:307–26.

———. 2004. "Behind Closed Doors: Publicity, Secrecy and the Quality of Deliberation." *Journal of Political Philosophy* 12(4):349–410.

———. 2009. "Rhetoric and the Public Sphere: Has Deliberative Democracy Abandoned Mass Democracy?" *Political Theory* 37(3):323–50.

Cohen, J. 1989. "Deliberation and Democratic Legitimacy." In *The Good Polity: Normative Analysis of the State*, edited by A. Hamlin and P. Pettit, 17–34. Oxford: Basil Blackwell.

Connelly, S., T. Richardson, and T. Miles. 2006. "Situated Legitimacy: Deliberative Arenas and the New Rural Governance." *Journal of Rural Studies* 22:267–77.

Conover, P. J., D. D. Searing, and I. Crewe. 2001. "The Deliberative Potential of Political Discussion." *British Journal of Political Science* 31:21–62.

Davies, B. B., K. Blackstock, and F. Rauschmayer. 2005. "'Recruitment,'

'Composition,' and 'Mandate' Issues in Deliberative Processes: Should We Focus on Arguments Rather Than Individuals?" *Environment and Planning C: Government and Planning* 23(4):599–615.

Delli Carpini, M. X., F. L. Cook, and L. R. Jacobs. 2004. "Public Deliberation, Discursive Participation and Citizen Engagement: A Review of the Empirical Literature." *Annual Review of Political Science* 7:315–44.

Dienel, P. C. 1997. *Die Planungszelle: Eine Alternative zur Establishment-Demokratie.* 4th ed. with Status Report '97 ed. Opladen: Westdeutscher Verlag.

Dienel, P. C., and O. Renn. 1995. "Planning Cells: A Gate to 'Fractal' Mediation." In *Fairness and Competence in Citizen Participation,* edited by O. Renn, T. Webler, and P. Wiedemann, 117–40. Dordrecht: Kluwer.

Dodge, J. 2009. "Environmental Justice and Deliberative Democracy: How Social Change Organizations Respond to Power in the Deliberative System." *Policy and Society* 28:225–39.

Dryzek, J. S. 2000. *Deliberative Democracy and Beyond: Liberals, Critics, Contestations.* Oxford: Oxford University Press.

———. 2009a. "The Australian Citizen's Parliament: A World First." *Journal of Public Deliberation* 5(1), article 9, available on the web site of the *Journal of Public Deliberation.*

———. 2009b. "Democratization as Deliberative Capacity Building." *Comparative Political Studies* 42:1379–402.

———. 2010. "Rhetoric in Democracy: A Systemic Appreciation." *Political Theory* 38(3):319–39.

Dryzek, J. S., and A. Tucker. 2008. "Deliberative Innovation to Different Effect: Consensus Conferences in Denmark, France, and the United States." *Public Administration Review* 68:864–76.

Easton, D. 1953. *The Political System: An Inquiry into the State of Political Science.* New York: Alfred A. Knopf.

Einsiedel, E. F., E. Jelsøe, and T. Breck. 2001. "Publics at the Technology Table: The Australian, Canadian and Danish Consensus Conferences on Food Biotechnology." *Public Understanding of Science* 10(1):83–98.

Epstein, S. 1996. *Impure Science: AIDS, Activism, and the Politics of Knowledge.* Berkeley: University of California Press.

Fischer, F. 2003. *Reframing Public Policy: Discursive Politics and Deliberative Practices.* Oxford: Oxford University Press.

———. 2006. "Participatory Governance as Deliberative Empowerment: The Cultural Politics of Discursive Space." *American Review of Public Administration* 36(1):19–40.

Fishkin, J. 2009. *When the People Speak: Deliberative Democracy and Public Consultation.* Oxford: Oxford University Press.

Forester, J. 1993. *Critical Theory, Public Policy and Planning Practice: Toward a Critical Pragmatism.* Albany: SUNY Press.

Fung, A. 2003. "Survey Article: Recipes for Public Spheres: Eight Institutional Design Choices and Their Consequences." *Journal of Political Philosophy* 11(3):338–67.

———. 2005. "Deliberation Before the Revolution: Toward an Ethics of Deliberative Democracy in an Unjust World." *Political Theory* 33(2):397–419.

———. 2006. "Minipublics: Deliberative Designs and Their Consequences." In *Deliberation, Participation and Democracy: Can the People Govern?* edited by S. W. Rosenberg, 159–83. Basingstoke: Palgrave Macmillan.

Gastil, J. 1993. *Democracy in Small Groups: Participation, Decision-Making and Communication.* Gabriola Island, B.C.: New Society.

Goodin, R. E. 2005. "Sequencing Deliberative Moments." *Acta Politica* 40:182–96.

———. 2009. "Rationalising Discursive Anomalies." *Theoria* 119:1–13.

Grönlund, K., M. Setälä, and K. Herne. 2010. "Deliberation and Civic Virtue: Lessons from a Citizen Deliberation Experiment." *European Political Science Review* 2:95–118.

Guston, D. H. 1999. "Evaluating the First U.S. Consensus Conference: The Impact of the Citizens' Panel on Telecommunications and the Future of Democracy." *Science, Technology and Human Values* 24(4):451–82.

Gutmann, A., and D. Thompson. 1996. *Democracy and Disagreement.* Cambridge, Mass.: Belknap.

Habermas, J. 1989. *The Structural Transformation of the Public Sphere: An Inquiry into a Category of Bourgeois Society.* Cambridge: MIT Press.

———. 1996. *Between Facts and Norms.* Translated by W. Rehg. Cambridge, England: Polity.

Hajer, M., and H. Wagenaar, eds. 2003. *Deliberative Policy Analysis: Understanding Governance in the Network Society.* Cambridge: Cambridge University Press.

Hartz-Karp, J. 2007. "Understanding Deliberativeness: Bridging Theory and Practice." *International Journal of Public Participation* 1(2), on the web site for the International Association for Public Participation.

Hendriks, C. M. 2002. "Institutions of Deliberative Democratic Processes and Interest Groups: Roles, Tensions and Incentives." *Australian Journal of Public Administration* 61(1):64–75.

———. 2004. "Public Deliberation and Interest Organisations: A Study of Responses to Lay Citizen Engagement in Public Policy." Ph.D. diss., Australian National University, Canberra.

———. 2005a. "Consensus Conferences and Planning Cells: Lay Citizen Deliberations." In *The Deliberative Democracy Handbook: Strategies for Effective Civic Engagement in the 21st Century,* edited by J. Gastil and P. Levine, 80–110. San Francisco: Jossey-Bass.

———. 2005b. "Participatory Storylines and Their Impact on Deliberative Forums." *Policy Sciences* 38(4):1–20.

———. 2006a. "Integrated Deliberation: Reconciling Civil Society's Dual Role in Deliberative Democracy." *Political Studies* 54(3):486–508.
———. 2006b. "When the Forum Meets Interest Politics: Strategic Uses of Public Deliberation." *Politics and Society* 34(4):1–32.
———. 2011. *The Politics of Public Deliberation: Citizen Engagement and Interest Advocacy*. London: Palgrave.
Hendriks, C. M., J. S. Dryzek, and C. Hunold. 2007. "Turning Up the Heat: Partisanship in Deliberative Innovation." *Political Studies* 55(2):362–83.
Hibbing, J. R., and E. Theiss-Morse. 2002. *Stealth Democracy: Americans' Beliefs about How Government Should Work*. Cambridge: Cambridge University Press.
Hörning, G. 1999. "Citizens' Panels as a Form of Deliberative Technology Assessment." *Science and Public Policy* 26(5):351–58.
IAP2 (International Association for Public Participation). 2007. "IAP2 Core Values of Public Participation." On the web site for the IAP2.
Joss, S. 1995. "Evaluating Consensus Conferences: Necessity or Luxury?" In *Public Participation in Science: The Role of Consensus Conferences in Europe*, edited by S. Joss and J. Durant, 89–108. London: Science Museum.
———. 2000. *Die Konsensuskonferenz in Theorie und Anwendung*. Stuttgart: Akademie für Technikfolgenabschätzung.
Kanra, B. 2007. "Binary Deliberation: The Role of Social Learning in the Theory and Practice of Deliberative Democracy." Paper presented at the Joint Sessions of the European Consortium of Political Research, Helsinki, May 7–12.
Kashefi, E., and M. Mort. 2004. "Grounded Citizens' Juries: A Tool for Health Activism?" *Health Expectations* 7(4):290–302.
Kosnoski, J. 2005. "Artful Discussion: John Dewey's Classroom as a Model of Deliberative Association." *Political Theory* 3(5):654–77.
Lang, A. 2008. "Agenda-Setting in Deliberative Forums: Expert Influence and Citizen Autonomy in the British Columbia Citizens' Assembly." In *Designing Deliberative Democracy: the British Columbia Citizens' Assembly*, edited by M. Warren and H. Pearse, 85–105. Cambridge: Cambridge University Press.
Lenaghan, J. 1999. "Involving the Public in Rationing Decisions: The Experience of Citizens' Juries." *Health Policy* 49:45–61.
Levine, P., A. Fung, and P. Levine. 2005. "Future Directions for Public Deliberation." In *The Deliberative Democracy Handbook: Strategies for Effective Civic Engagement in the 21st Century*, edited by J. Gastil and P. Levine, 271–88. San Francisco: Jossey-Bass.
Levine, P., and R. M. Nierras. 2007. "Activists' View of Deliberation." *Journal of Public Deliberation* 3(1), article 4, available on the web site of the *Journal of Public Deliberation*.

Mansbridge, J. 1992. "A Deliberative Perspective on Neocorporatism." *Politics and Society* 20(4):493–505.

———. 1999. "Everyday Talk in the Deliberative System." In *Deliberative Politics: Essays on Democracy and Disagreement*, edited by S. Macedo, 211–39. Oxford: Oxford University Press.

———. 2006. "'Deliberative Democracy' or 'Democratic Deliberation'?" In *Deliberation, Participation and Democracy: Can the People Govern?* edited by S. W. Rosenberg, 251–71. Basingstoke: Palgrave Macmillan.

Mansbridge, J., J. Bohman, S. Chambers, D. Estlund, A. Follesdal, A. Fung, C. Lafont, B. Manin, and J. L. Marti. 2010. "The Place of Self-Interest and the Role of Power in Deliberative Democracy." *Journal of Political Philosophy* 18(1):64–100.

Mansbridge, J., J. Hartz-Karp, M. Amengual, and J. Gastil. 2006. "Norms of Public Deliberation: An Inductive Study." *Journal of Public Deliberation* 2(1), article 7, available on the web site of the *Journal of Public Deliberation*.

McCoy, M. L., and P. L. Scully. 2002. "Deliberative Dialogue to Expand Civic Engagement." *National Civic Review* 91(summer):117–35.

McLaverty, P., and D. Halpin. 2008. "Deliberative Drift: The Emergence of Deliberation in the Policy Process." *International Political Science Review* 29(2):197–214.

Mendonça, R. F. 2009. "Challenging Subtle Forms of Power in Deliberation: A Case-Study on the Future of Hansen's Disease Colonies in Brazil." *Policy and Society* 28:211–23.

Montanero, L. 2008. "The Democratic Legitimacy of 'Self-Authorized' Representatives." Paper presented at the Workshop on Rethinking Representation: A North-South Dialogue, Bellagio, Sept. 29–Oct. 3.

Mutz, D. C. 2008. "Is Deliberative Democracy a Falsifiable Theory?" *Annual Review of Political Science* 11:521–38.

Naurin, D. 2004. *Dressed for Politics: Why Increasing Transparency in the European Union Will Not Make Lobbyists Behave Any Better Than They Already Do*. Göteborg: Göteborg University.

Neblo, M., K. M. Esterling, R. P. Kennedy, D. M. J. Lazer, and A. E. Sokhey. 2010. "Who Wants to Deliberate—and Why?" *American Political Science Review* 104(3):566–83.

Niemeyer, S. 2004. "Deliberation in the Wilderness: Displacing Symbolic Politics." *Environmental Politics* 13(2):347–72.

Parkinson, J. 2003a. "Legitimacy Problems in Deliberative Democracy." *Political Studies* 51(1):180–96.

———. 2003b. *The Legitimation of Deliberative Democracy*. Ph.D. diss., Australian National University, Canberra.

———. 2006. *Deliberating in the Real World: Problems of Legitimacy in Democracy*. Oxford: Oxford University Press.

Price, D. 2000. "Choices without Reasons: Citizens' Juries and Policy Evaluation." *Journal of Medical Ethics* 26(4):272–76.
Rawls, J. 1971. *A Theory of Justice.* London: Oxford University Press.
———. 1993. *Political Liberalism.* New York: Columbia University Press.
Remer, G. 1999. "Political Oratory and Conversation: Cicero versus Deliberative Democracy." *Political Theory* 27:39–64.
Renn, O., T. Webler, and P. Wiedemann, eds. 1995. *Fairness and Competence in Citizen Participation.* Dordrecht: Kluwer.
Riker, W. H. 1996. *The Strategy of Rhetoric: Campaigning for the American Constitution.* New Haven: Yale University Press.
Risse, T. 2000. "Let's Argue! Communicative Action in World Politics." *International Organization* 54:1–39.
Rosenberg, S. W. 2005. "The Empirical Study of Deliberative Democracy." *Acta Politica* 40:212–24.
Ryfe, D. M. 2005. "Does Deliberative Democracy Work?" *Annual Review of Political Science* 8:49–71.
Sanders, L. M. 1997. "Against Deliberation." *Political Theory* 25(3):347–76.
Saward, M. 2008. "Representation and Democracy: Revisions and Possibilities." *Sociology Compass* 2(3):1000–1013.
Shapiro, I. 1999. "Enough of Deliberation: Politics Is about Interests and Power." In *Deliberative Politics,* edited by S. Macedo, 28–38. Oxford: Oxford University Press.
Simon, H. A. 1946. "The Proverbs of Administration." *Public Administration Review* 6:53–67.
Smith, G. 2009. *Democratic Innovations: Designing Institutions for Citizen Participation.* Cambridge: Cambridge University Press.
Smith, G., and C. Wales. 2002. "Citizens' Juries and Deliberative Democracy." *Political Studies* 48(1):51–65.
Steiner, J. 2008. "Concept Stretching: The Case of Deliberation." *European Political Science* 7:186–90.
Steiner, J., A. Bächtiger, M. Spörndli, and M. R. Steenbergen. 2004. *Deliberative Politics in Action: A Cross-National Study of Parliamentary Debates.* Cambridge: Cambridge University Press.
Sunstein, C. 2002. "The Law of Group Polarization." *Journal of Political Philosophy* 10(2):175–95.
Susskind, L. 2006. "Can Public Policy Dispute Resolution Meet the Challenges Set by Deliberative Democracy?" *Dispute Resolution Magazine* (winter):506.
Susskind, L., S. McKearnan, and J. Thomas-Larmer. 1999. *The Consensus Building Handbook.* Thousand Oaks, Calif.: Sage.
Talisse, R. B. 2005. "Deliberativist Responses to Activist Challenges: A Continuation of Young's Dialectic." *Philosophy and Social Criticism* 31(4):423–44.

Tetlock, P. 1983. "Accountability and the Perseverance of First Impressions." *Social Psychology Quarterly* 46(4):285–92.
Thompson, D. 2008. "Deliberative Democratic Theory and Empirical Political Science." *Annual Review of Political Science* 11:497–520.
Torgerson, D. 1999. *The Promise of Green Politics: Environmentalism and the Public Sphere.* Durham: Duke University Press.
Urbinati, N., and M. E. Warren. 2008. "The Concept of Representation in Contemporary Democratic Theory." *Annual Review of Political Science* 11:387–412.
Wagenaar, H. 2006. "Democracy and Prostitution: Deliberating the Legalization of Brothels in the Netherlands." *Administration and Society* 38(2): 198–235.
Wallington, T., G. Lawrence, and B. Loechel. 2008. "Reflections on the Legitimacy of Regional Environmental Governance: Lessons from Australia's Experiment in Natural Resource Management." *Journal of Environmental Policy and Planning* 10(1):1–30.
Walzer, M. 1999. "Deliberation, and What Else?" In *Deliberative Politics*, edited by S. Macedo, 58–69. Oxford: Oxford University Press.
Warren, M., and H. Pearse, eds. 2008. *Designing Deliberative Democracy: The British Columbia Citizens' Assembly.* Cambridge: Cambridge University Press.
Warren, M. E. 2009. "Two Trust-Based Uses of Mini-Publics in Democracy." Paper presented at the Conference on Democracy and the Deliberative Society, York, U.K., June 24–26.
Williams, M. S. 2000. "The Uneasy Alliance of Group Representation and Deliberative Democracy." In *Citizenship in Diverse Societies*, edited by W. Kymlicka and W. Norman, 124–52. Oxford: Oxford University Press.
Wynne, B. 1996. "May Sheep Safely Graze? A Reflexive View of the Expert-Lay Knowledge Divide." In *Risk, Environment and Modernity: Towards a New Ecology*, edited by S. Lash, B. Szerszynski, and B. Wynne, 44–83. London: Sage.
Young, I. M. 2000. *Inclusion and Democracy.* Oxford: Oxford University Press.
———. 2001. "Activist Challenges to Deliberative Democracy." *Political Theory* 29(5):670–90.
Zapata, M. 2009. "Deliberating across Differences: Planning Futures in Cross-cultural Spaces." *Policy and Society* 28:197–209.

2. Performing Place Governance Collaboratively

Planning as a Communicative Process

In this chapter, I reflect on the concepts of communicative and collaborative planning as developed in my own work in the 1990s and situate these in the wider context of emerging social and political philosophies and practical experimentation. I argue that the ideas and practices associated with collaborative planning should not be treated as a coherent technical procedure to be inserted into a flow of practices to achieve specific ends. Instead, they express a philosophical and ethical perspective around which a bundle of discursive techniques and practices have gathered. The effects of calling up such a perspective and associated practices need to be evaluated not merely instrumentally for their immediate problem-solving capacity but for their wider contribution to the development of the political culture in which they are mobilized. This argument leads me to ask three questions. First, how can such a perspective be identified when invoked in specific situations? Second, how can the mobilization of such a collaborative perspective into actual practices be distinguished from mere rhetorical invocation? Third, how far do the ideas and practices associated with collaborative planning carry with them, from situation to situation, the particular social and political orientations associated more generally with the perspective? The main part of the chapter explores these questions through three core fields of collective action: managing neighborhood change, promoting major development projects, and making spatial development strategies.[1] I return to address the three questions at the end.

The Idea of Collaborative Planning

In my chapter in the *Argumentative Turn* (Healey 1993), I argued that a focus on the interactive dimensions of planning work would help to develop a better understanding of how such governance work was actually done. I suggested that such a focus was important with respect to both the design of governance interventions and their delivery. Understanding such interactions was a key aspect of explaining why governance outcomes emerged as they did. Informing this focus was an ontology and epistemology that emphasized the social relational dynamics through which identities are constructed and the interpretive dimensions through which knowledge and meanings are generated. Such an orientation also sought to avoid a polarization between a perspective on social life seen primarily in terms of structures and systems, and one focused on the aggregate behavior of autonomous individuals. Instead, it encouraged attention to the interactive, relational dynamics through which active agency shaped and was in turn shaped by structuring forces.

This orientation challenged the paradigms still dominant in planning and public policy at the time, as Frank Fischer and John Forester had done for some time (Fischer 1980; Fischer and Forester 1993). In the field of public policy, this different philosophical orientation implied that there were limits to the possibility of objective knowledge and universal expressions of value about which all could agree. What becomes accepted as valid knowledge and acknowledged values are struggled over through the rigors of scientific inquiry, through political struggles, and through all kinds of efforts where people work together (colabor) to address issues of collective concern.[2] This implies that the micropractices through which policy discourses are produced and governance activity is performed demand critical attention. I have referred to this orientation as "communicative planning theory" (Healey 1993).

In 1997, I developed this perspective to emphasize the collaborative dimensions of planning activity. This argued for attention to the relations through which planning ideas and strategies were formed and translated into activities that produced both material and mental outcomes (Healey 1997).[3] My particular concern was to encourage critical scrutiny of collaborative governance processes in order to assess ways in which more progressive outcomes could be encouraged and the resistances that might make this difficult. The focus on agency and social interaction in planning work led to a conclusion that a great deal of planning work was done not in a consultant's design studio, nor in some analytical back room, but in all kinds of discussions, meetings, workshops, council chambers, and confrontations in which people with diverse projects and sensibilities encountered one another and struggled to deal with issues about place futures. This perception brought to the forefront a concern with the communicative quality of such social interactions. This meant attention not just to texts—the words used and so on—but to the performative dimensions through which people work out meanings and intentions in social interaction. It centered attention on the meanings and understandings people brought into an interaction, and on how ideas and meanings are actively shaped through interchange in public, through forms of reasoning in public. In 1993, I called this quality "planning through debate."

The intellectual grounding of communicative planning theory, and the collaborative planning practices that draw from this trajectory of thinking, was linked to a much broader wave of ideas about how to conceptualize the dynamics of human life in interaction with natural forces. These ideas emphasized human creativity (agency) in interaction with complex institutions that shape and are also shaped by creative agency, situated in contexts with particular histories and geographies.[4] This approach spotlights relations of interaction and the microdynamics of social practices and their wider connections. It focuses attention on the situated and contingent properties of human existence, as a way of understanding how societies develop and change. It underlines the indeterminacy of the way futures evolve, the complexity of the relations through which future trajectories are shaped and the importance of understanding specific histories and geographies. It is thus closely linked to the more recent development in the planning field of ideas drawn from the analysis of the dynamics of complex adaptive systems and of evolutionary perspectives (Hillier and Healey 2010; Innes and Booher 2010).

Such ideas were also developing in parallel in the management field and in the field now known as international development.[5] Within the planning field, this intellectual wave was not just encouraged by a philosophical orientation, which itself was gathering momentum at the time. It also drew on practical experiences and research on the social interactions and reflections on practice of those doing planning work (Forester 1989; Friend and Hickling 1987; Innes and Booher 2010). By the mid-1990s, this intellectual turn to a communicative approach was given widespread recognition through Innes's account in the *Journal of Planning Education and Research* (Innes 1995).[6]

The interest in the communicative and performative dimensions of planning work was not just informed by an analytical interest. It was also infused with a concern with the power dynamics manifest in micropractices and in the consequent interaction between structuring forces and agency inventiveness. The project for many progressive planners has been to improve the livability and sustainability of the conditions of life of the diverse many and not just the few, in a world increasingly recognized in its complex multiplicities, with competing and conflicting structuring dynamics and power relations (Healey 2010). The recognition of the importance of micropractices implied that these are significant sites for transformative efforts. In this context, a progressive, normative meaning could be given to "collaborative planning," as planning activity centered on working interactively with stakeholders with diverse stakes and on place development problems and futures in ways that recognize and respect multiple perspectives and modes of engaging in governance work and that promote inclusive and richly informed public policy making. In the early 1990s, especially in the United Kingdom, this idea had attracted little attention, except in fields such as community development and some urban regeneration experiences. By the late 1990s, however, it was sweeping across the governance landscape.

This interest was fueled by the energetic initiatives to reconfigure governance practices in Western Europe generally, in an attempt both to make them more efficient and effective and, at the same time and in often contradictory ways, to make them more democratic.[7] This brought new groups into interaction with one another and demanded new ways of thinking as well as new ways of working. New forms of network governance were appearing in which creating new relations and new arenas were important.[8] It is in this context that all kinds of new institutional arrangements have been promoted to create new arenas for discursive encounter between those identified as stakeholders.

As an extension of communicative planning theory, collaborative planning as an idea has proved attractive to political leaders and policy advisers in many parts of the world, often as a new angle on participatory approaches to development activity, and sometimes as part of a general movement toward creating a more participatory polity.[9] This has encouraged organizational innovations in creating new arenas (also called forums or platforms) for policy development. Examples include the many partnership agencies set up in recent years, as well as participatory workshops for discussing the future of key sites (Hajer 2005). It has also encouraged an explosion of technologies for working collaboratively.[10] These have come from the management sciences, from work on conflict resolution and consensus building, from the design field, from work on participatory practices in international development, and from the urban and regional planning field. Collaborative working practices have been promoted as an alternative to the calculative techniques associated in a previous period with the logical calculus of option choices from initial goals and analytical studies.[11] Some critics have dismissed techniques associated with collaborative planning as just new kinds of instruments to make governance activity work better, a new process rationality for a neoliberal project.[12] This associated collaborative planning initiatives with the search for greater effectiveness, an instrumental value. The effectiveness benefit was to be achieved by enhancing knowledge and understanding and showing stakeholders how they were and could be engaged with issues, so that conflicts could be reduced and action options enhanced through shared resources, agendas, and actions.

Within the planning field, there has also been another dimension to the promotion of collaborative planning as an idea and a work practice. This is a development of the general normative orientation associated with the planning field. Collaborative planning practices are advocated not just for their instrumental value in making governance interventions in place development more effective, but also for their contribution to developing an inclusive polity in which the concerns of the many are considered. This is not just an idealistic value, but a discursive expression of real struggles going on in many parts of the world where citizens who are increasingly well informed demand more recognition of their perceptions, experiences, and values about the future.

In the context of such arguments, practices of collaborative planning can be understood as arising not just from an intellectual shift of focus, but as a response to citizen demands for governance programs more sensitive and responsive to their diverse concerns. Such practices should therefore be evaluated in terms of their progressive governance potential and, in particular, the extent to which they achieve greater recognition of multiple stakes in all their complex diversity and provide fairly distributed opportunities for diverse stakeholders to have a say in what happens in and to the places they care about. Any such evaluation involves getting beyond the rhetorical invocation of collaborative planning practices by politicians and officials seeking to legitimate some government activity. It involves examining critically whether the promotion of collaborative encounters in particular types of arena, using specific techniques, may actually suppress or ameliorate the conflicts that reflect the diversity of stakes people have in place development, rather than enriching the intelligence and pluralistic sensibility through which interventions are designed and implemented.[13]

Both advocates and critics have tended to discuss the idea and practice of collaborative planning as if it were a single package of coherent ideas that could be applied to a situation. Yet, as with any concept that is intellectual or involves policy and practice, the term "collaborative planning" refers to an evolving agenda of philosophically grounded concepts and specific practices. This means that researchers, policy advisers, and practical workers cannot expect to treat collaborative planning as a technical concept that can be introduced and applied in a specific situation. It is not a technique as such; rather, it is both a concept within an intellectual perspective and a bundle of discursive techniques and practices that may be called into use. So we need to look, as Forester advises us (1989, 1993), at the specifics of particular situations. Researchers and policy analysts need to evaluate the interaction technologies being used in specific instances and assess these according to their actual contribution to both the instrumental value of effectiveness (whatever the goal) and the sociopolitical value of attending to the concerns about the livability and sustainability of the conditions of life of the many, not just the few, and to the development of a polity capable of addressing such a challenge.

The rest of this chapter considers three fields of spatial planning practice to explore the three questions outlined initially. First, how can the interaction qualities and technologies to be found in particular contexts be identified? Second, how is it possible to distinguish when the invocation of collaborative planning is more than just a rhetorical flourish, or more than a tactic for achieving instrumental purposes rather than a contribution to wider, progressive aims? Third, are there *any* general qualities that inhere in the idea of collaborative planning, or is it better understood as an umbrella term given to an aggregation of discursive practices with certain process similarities, which get used for all kinds of purposes? The three fields of practice are the management of neighborhood change, promoting major projects, and making spatial development strategies.

Managing Neighborhood Change

There is a great deal of planning activity in urban areas that centers on the everyday work of managing small-scale changes to the built environment. Its role is partly a way of guiding change so that broader trajectories of place development are promoted. But it is also a mechanism for working out the balance between the public and private realms in specific instances of physical development change. Such activity involves regulation and enforcement practices, the active promotion of improvements to streets and squares, public facilities, and public spaces, and the provision of particular benefits, such as more affordable housing or the provision of neighborhood schools, health centers, day care facilities for children, and support for the elderly.

Such activities can be undertaken in different ways. Lawyers may draw up a set of rules and rights, which those promoting a development or improvement are expected to follow. In continental Europe, this is a dominant practice. Land use plans are a key mechanism through which such rules and rights are defined with respect to specific properties. These not only specify minimum standards, but also require attention to impacts on neighbors and local environments (Booth 1996). Where neighborhood improvement projects are pursued and in land use regulation systems such as in the United Kingdom, where planning officials make expert judgments about whether a development proposal conforms with wider principles intended to guide development change and performs appropriately with respect to its various impacts, the process can become more interactive, involving more discussion about particular proposals before a judgment is made. Planning officers in municipalities thus become key intermediaries, negotiating both between neighbors and between citizens and formalized government requirements.[14] In many cases, especially where conflicts are anticipated or already vigorous and where significant neighborhood improvement projects are proposed, those involved are drawn into more collaborative processes for policy deliberation, at least as proposals for change are shaped. Such practices are underpinned by the claim that, unless those affected accept, value, and trust what officials are doing and support the values embodied in the rules, hostility and grievances will build up. This may lead to social protests that may come to undermine the capacity of governments to deliver effectively on promises and projects. If they rumble on, such protests may in turn undermine the legitimacy of formal government activity itself. This affects the overall quality of the polity.

So, what does it take to perform collaborative processes that avoid such outcomes? Two examples illustrate interactive processes informed by a commitment to a sensitive, localized knowledge of local conditions and, in the first case, to giving voice to citizens about the future of their neighborhood and their city. In Vancouver, the practice of producing neighborhood design guidelines grew from a particular struggle to get affluent residents to recognize and accept some obligations to the wider city and political community they were a part of. Planning officials, with the support of politicians, were committed to an inclusive view of stakeholders, to encouraging people in different parts of the city to consider the city as a whole. This meant seeing the city not just as an aggregate of different parts but as an integrated system and polity. It encouraged the performance of governance activity grounded in deliberative participatory practices. Planning officials experimented with all kinds of ways of producing neighborhood guidelines: through shuttle diplomacy, design workshops, deliberative platforms, encouraging public debate, probing alternatives in discussion with affected parties, and other means. These processes became important arenas through which many stakeholders came to learn about how to perform planning activity in more collaborative ways. It all took time and experimentation, but the result was the creation of an interactive governance culture in which collaboration among an inclusive range of stakeholders became normal practice. Today, people across the city talk proudly of "their" planning tradition, whereas developers and their advisers have learned how to work within the participatory political culture that has been created. Some critics may think that Vancouver is an exceptional case in its history and political culture. But there are other cases in which a demanding public and an ethically committed band of planners, with political support, have moved in this direction.

My second case is from the United Kingdom, which, in the European context, is a highly centralized state, in which it is difficult for local governments to develop approaches that differ from those promoted at national level. At this national level, there has been much talk of the importance of public consultation, community engagement, and empowerment within planning processes, but this is combined with other demands for more efficient and speedy planning decision making. Principles governing how particular development situations should be approached are also repeatedly pronounced at the national level. These are supposed to cascade down to be implemented at the local level. This makes it hard for local politicians and planners to explain to local stakeholders what the basis for their decision making has to be. It also makes it difficult to find time both for collaborative discussion about proposals and to meet all the criteria that are needed if a local decision is to withstand a potential challenge mounted by an applicant for development.

In neighborhood regeneration generally in the United Kingdom, active networking and collaborative practices are well established, using a wide range of engagement techniques.[15] Some local authorities have found ways to combine a sensitive and ongoing engagement among neighborhood stakeholders with enabling people to get on with their own development projects, while paying attention to both local impacts and wider considerations articulated in urban and regional spatial plans and in national policy. Opportunities for residents to comment and deliberate on a development proposal are usually normal practice. Often, a special event will be organized to allow residents to discuss and probe a proposal and its implications. But just as important is the way planning officials are out and about in their "patches," talking, discussing, observing, gaining knowledge, and spreading it around. In doing so, they build up trust among local people that their views are important and will be heard. In parallel, there may be special forums for particular actors, such as the local agents who advise households and small firms about how to make planning applications and how to draw up the necessary planning documents. This helps to update the agents with the latest national and local policy advice and requirements. In a recent case I looked at in South Tyneside in northeast England, which has achieved excellent national ratings for the quality of its planning service, this interactive practice is valued by citizens, business people, and special interest groups (Healey 2010:ch. 5). This local authority is not an affluent place, but its local government is trusted by local people to pay attention to their concerns and to consult them where appropriate. Such a political culture takes time to build and even longer before it begins to perform. But through combining official requirements with a rich interaction between citizens, other stakeholders, and formal government, this local authority has avoided many of the conflicts, inefficiencies, and neglects found elsewhere in the United Kingdom.

These cases of the interactions between planners, citizens, and other stakeholders underline three important points about collaborative processes. First, the quality of such communicative interactions lies less in the specific techniques used within them than in the overall orientation that shapes the processes. In Vancouver, a whole range of methods was used to facilitate discussion, exchange, and knowledge building. In South Tyneside, interaction was underpinned by a combination of continual networking, through being around and about, and encounters dealing with specific projects, issues, and concerns of particular groups of actors, using formats for meeting that were familiar to participants, so they felt comfortable. Second, in both cases, people with planning expertise played a key role as intermediaries, circulating concerns, values, and knowledge among all stakeholders and, critically, between government arenas and everyone else. Third, in doing this interactive and in-between work, planning officials acted with an *ethics of commitment* to respect for stakeholders in all their variety. They were guided by an *ethics of attention* to all kinds of impacts near and far and to the way small changes to the urban fabric might impact wider systems. In this way, they maintained an awareness of the surrounding power dynamics and how this could be challenged. They acted with an *ethics of careful, transparent reasoning*, explaining why certain issues and impacts needed consideration and what might be done to address potential harmful impacts.

Managing neighborhood change in such an interactive, collaborative way helps to produce quality outcomes in a dual way. The richness of knowledge produced through ongoing discursive interaction helps to promote quality in the resultant changes to the urban fabric, contributing to the development and maintenance of future assets. The time taken in sensitive, knowledgeable, and respectful interaction in turn pays off further down the road, building up understanding of what managing neighborhood change involves. This makes addressing future challenges and changes less riddled by misunderstanding and the mobilization of media stereotypes.

Promoting Major Projects

Such major projects, whether of infrastructure investments or development projects, always require a great deal of collaboration. They typically involve mobilizing ideas and resources among several agents. Actions and resources have to be coordinated as a project moves from initial conception, to detailed design, and then to coordination of the development process. Such projects can never be just a building design on a large scale. Especially where development and redevelopment is concerned, developing such projects requires thinking not just about how a single building will function, but about how a new piece of urban fabric will evolve and change in relation to the wider urban area it is a part of. This means not merely mobilizing skilled capacity in design and coordination, but developing an awareness of the wider urban dynamics in which the fabric and the ambience in and around it will evolve. Collaborative ways of deliberating about projects and their impacts provide a range and richness that is difficult to obtain from technical analysis.

But such major projects typically generate intense conflict, especially where redevelopment is involved. This is partly because so much value is tied up in them. Much of this value is financial: the costs of any redevelopment and the potential increase in land and property values if a project succeeds as a desirable location within an urban context. Other kinds of value are involved too: the value that those displaced by a development project put on the place where they live and work, and the values people associate with a place as it used to be. As Altshuler and Luberoff (2003) have commented, the hostility generated by redevelopment projects in cities in the United States in the 1950s and 1960s encouraged a shift of development attention from inner-city residential locations to what they refer to as do-no-harm locations, such as redundant industrial and harbor areas. Another reason for conflict arises because it takes many stakeholders to get a project going. Landowners, future owners and tenants, developers, financiers, building companies, infrastructure providers, and public authorities are essential stakeholders, but they may often disagree among themselves. Other stakeholders —ranging from those threatened with displacement to those with concerns about how their city is evolving—are also likely to have views about whether a project should proceed and what it should be like.

Most projects are derailed if conflicts are too great. If conflicts are ignored, for example, by excluding attention to all but the necessary stakeholders, then hostility may build enough to reverberate into politicians' futures. Cities such as Vancouver, Amsterdam, Boston, and Portland, Oregon, all changed their political regimes and planning approach in response to such reverberations.[16]

Perhaps the most common collaborative processes found in the practice of producing major development projects involve forms of network building and shuttle diplomacy, interspersed with specific collaborative events, such as a project meeting or a design charette or discussion forums (these days perhaps organized through the web), accompanied by various forms of visualization. There may also be specific efforts at conflict mediation, consensus building, and negotiation that leads to a contract, especially where costs and benefits (pains and gains) are distributed among those considered as having a stake. The utility of different techniques depends on the particular context a project is being promoted in and the stage it has reached in its development. This means that careful attention to the overall institutional design of interactive processes is essential, with consideration of who to involve when and how and of the qualities of collaboration that such interactions are expected to develop.

More important than this, however, is where and how to consider the wider impacts of a project. It is all too easy for a project to be justified because it will create jobs and raise property values. But these advantages are likely to benefit the few rather than the many in a city. The urban fabric produced by the project may not contribute much to the overall future quality and dynamics of a city, whereas the costs and losses to many in an urban area may have been considerable. If we look at redevelopment projects that have created places later valued positively by immediate stakeholders, citizens, and visitors alike, we discover that somewhere in the interactive processes there were people who were ethically committed to producing high-quality developments that were likely to produce a wide range of public benefits. We have already seen how this was the case in Vancouver, where committed politicians and planners circulated an idea of the city around the neighborhoods, which also fed into work on major redevelopment projects and became, in time, part of the city's political culture. In Amsterdam, such a political culture has been in place for many years, shaping the way major projects are developed. But the locus of such a culture and its guardians are not just the city council and its planning office. In cases I have looked at in the United Kingdom, such guardians may be an informal group of committed professionals who network between the planning office and a development company. Or a special partnership agency may act with this commitment, maintaining an ongoing deliberative process that combines complex technical assessments and negotiations with developers along with collaborative forums with different stakeholder groups.[17] In a contentious and protracted case in London, the station redevelopment at Kings Cross, the perseverance and skill of a campaigning group made all the difference to the quality of the final development package that was eventually approved.[18]

Cases such as these emphasize how the outcome of planning activity and the process of its production are intertwined. Vigorous discussion and debate over project ideas, and even intense conflict, have a benefit in enlarging the appreciation of the impacts a project may have and the stakes that are affected. This in turn may feed into more imaginative designs and better negotiation over the balance between public and private benefit in a major project. Public debate and deliberation about projects helps to build a more knowledgeable political culture within which future major projects can be discussed and assessed. In evaluating the interactive processes through which any major project is produced, we should therefore not just look at whether there has been collaboration or whether particular techniques were used. All major projects proceed through some form of collaboration. Instead, it is important to look at where attention to wider public benefits is located in these collaborations and at the richness, inclusiveness, and knowledgeability of the interactions that shape a project. This implies not just an analysis of specific events and techniques that are deployed as a major project is being developed, but also an analysis of how these events and techniques are situated in the overall institutional ensemble and dynamics through which, over time, a project evolves.

Making Spatial Development Strategies

One of the most impressive changes that has occurred in planning methodology in the past half century has been in the area of spatial strategy making. In the mid-twentieth century, spatial strategies for cities and regions were drawn up in the design studios of planning consultants hired by municipal governments. By the 1960s, an approach based on social science took hold that emphasized analytical and research work in the research and intelligence section of a planning office. Pioneering work in the 1970s, exploring how planning strategies were actually produced, undermined these models and emphasized instead the complex networking processes and political bargaining through which spatial strategies evolved.[19] In this era of governance through complex networks, as one Amsterdam planner said, such strategy making is "95% talk" (quoted in Healey 2007). Interactive processes these days are not only evident in such bargaining and negotiation. They are also typically designed into the procedures through which strategy-making activity is undertaken. These include discursively mobilizing attention to key issues that need governance action in an urban area (known as scoping and scanning); visioning processes as strategic frames are discussed and developed; shaping the attention of the agencies whose activities will make a difference to what happens in the future; generating and discussing future scenarios; working out investment priorities and developing the strategic frame or vision (Albrechts 2004; Healey 2007; Hillier 2011). Neither the design studio nor the research office could, in themselves, mobilize sufficient knowledge about the dynamics and potentials of an urban area. Such arenas could neither predict nor leaven the complex and conflicting values people have about places in an urban area and the wider whole of the cities and regions where they live, work, and visit. Nor could they mobilize sufficient attention with the persuasive power to shape how key agencies act in the future. Collaborative ways of producing spatial development strategies have been encouraged for instrumental reasons to produce more informed and effective strategies. Whether intentionally or not, the use of such strategies then enlarges the repertoire of practices known within the wider polity.

Spatial strategies for urban areas are effective when they provide an integrative conception of key dimensions of an urban area and its dynamics. They create a sense of a whole into which specific parts—urban neighborhoods, particular projects, sectoral investment programs, and so on—can find a location. They involve work of synthesis, drawing together different perspectives, analyses of specific dimensions, and the outcomes of debates about future possibilities into a framing idea, or a frame of reference, about future potentials and directions. Such a framing idea works discursively by willing into being a particular conception of a place and its possible futures. This willing has sufficient resonance and coherence to convince and persuade many parties that it expresses what is important about an urban area.[20]

In many planning systems, formal procedures require the preparation of some kind of strategic, comprehensive, or overall development plan or strategy. But many of the resultant strategy statements and plan documents do not provide such a cohesive framing idea and do little strategic work. They may lack integrative capacity and persuasive power. They may fail to capture the imagination and interest of significant parties and be ignored. They may fail to take account of what key stakeholders are interested in doing or of the wider context in which the dynamics of an urban area are situated. The planning literature presents many examples of strategic planning exercises that have failed in one or more of these ways, even when prepared in interactive ways. Too few stakeholders may be involved in their preparation. Deliberative forums about urban futures may fail to include key actors. Where a strategy emanates from a nexus of those who wield significant power and resources, it may fail to have resonance with other stakeholders in an urban area and therefore may generate political hostility. So, spatial development strategies may fail because of a lack of interactive range or a lack of performative richness.

A spatial development strategy for a phenomenon as difficult to grasp and shape as the relations of a complex urban area needs such a broad range and richness if it is to command sustained attention and political support over time. Those promoting strategy making need to build a broad-based public that sustains the strategic ideas in many different institutional arenas within an urban context and that endures through time. The strategic frame needs to infiltrate and persuade into commitment all kinds of actors in many different parts of the urban institutional ensemble.[21] In this way, a strategy comes to act as the expression of a kind of social movement, sustaining particular values and strategic ideas about an urban area and its qualities. If such discursive mobilization is successful, it becomes a key piece of governance infrastructure. In this way, a spatial strategy can frame the work of neighborhood management and the promotion of major projects, as well as the way particular instruments, such as those of land use regulation, are used. Such strategies are not easy to create, and, in areas where little change is expected and conceptions of the "place of a city" are already well established and well supported, an explicit strategy may not always be needed. In such cases, a spatial strategy may be implicitly embedded in a political culture. But where there are new challenges, significant changes, and conflicting positions about future directions, the work to produce a spatial strategy and the existence of such a strategy once created can play an invaluable role. Examples of such situations illustrate the importance of the inclusive and collaborative nature of the interactive work involved in their production.

A good case in point is the city of Vancouver, which has built up the capacity to discuss the overall qualities of the urban area as a whole through discussing how particular neighborhoods relate to the wider "city as a whole." In Portland, planners and politicians worked in a different way, combining discussions about neighborhood futures with circulating information and research studies to encourage Portlanders to consider the urban region and how it was developing in their deliberations. In this way, they helped create a public for attention to the evolving dynamics of an expanding city.[22] Several French cities have been vigorously preparing spatial strategies through discussions in all kinds of arenas across an urban area (Motte 2007). Such discussions have helped in developing conceptions of the critical elements of an area and the selection of key projects. Similar efforts can be found in other cities in Europe, including the United Kingdom.

Not all of these strategies have succeeded in commanding sustained attention. Where a strategy does achieve this, it is often because a groundswell of public discussion combines with political support to create a climate and a frame of reference in which even powerful development companies and infrastructure agencies feel they have to position themselves, as in Vancouver. Once again, all kinds of different techniques may be deployed to cultivate the discussions and debates that can mobilize attention and gather knowledge about evolving urban dynamics and about what different stakeholders care about. The critical issue is how the different debates and discussions feed into the development of a strategic idea with persuasive coherence and resonance. If the strategic concepts are too diffuse, a strategy will not command attention. If they are too narrow in scope, for example, focusing merely on economic dynamics or solely on environmental threats in isolation, a strategy will generate hostility from those who see other dimensions as important and who see the significance of the interrelation of various dimensions of urban life. If the strategic idea is not connected to what resources are actually likely to become available, it may lose practical utility.

Those who promote a spatial development strategy for an urban area thus need to keep a continuously watchful eye on who is involved in the strategy-making process, how knowledge and proposals flow around the various institutional arenas, the discursive filtering that inevitably happens during such processes, and how far the framing concepts and ideas give an integrative coherence to conceptions of an urban area and its future. This requires not only careful attention to the way knowledge and concepts flow through interactive arenas; it demands an ethics of concern for attention to an urban area as a system, or complex of interacting systems, with multiple dimensions, multiple internal and external connections, and many different parts. It also requires a shrewd appreciation of the distinctive histories and geographies that have created the various pathways through which the urban present has been produced and an awareness of the pressures that will impact on and help to generate future possibilities. Spatial strategy making involves careful contextualizing and situating.

As for the technologies mobilized in spatial strategy making, some of those mentioned already are clearly important, especially the skills of networking and connecting different agencies and groups and drawing stakeholders with different backgrounds, knowledge, and interests into arenas where they are encouraged to focus attention on the dynamics of the urban area they are a part of. Such work also demands communicative skills in reasoning in public. This discursive capacity lies at the heart of an interactive, collaborative idea of planning with progressive intentions. It involves working from diverse claims and insights about particular issues, projects, and places to draw out the connections to the wider dynamics of an urban area. It demands continual and transparent testing of assumptions and theories about cause and effect in ways that are respectful to different points of view. The aim of such argumentation is not to integrate different perspectives and points of view, but to enrich the knowledge and understanding of urban dynamics and make it clearer how the gains and losses involved in key strategic choices are distributed. Transparent argumentation is also a key aspect of conveying how a strategic frame expresses these choices and how it relates an overall conception of an urban area to its many parts. Those involved in spatial strategy-making initiatives for complex urban areas thus need not only to monitor and assist the flow of concepts and knowledge around the various institutional arenas drawn into strategy-making processes. They also need to monitor and be prepared to adjust the institutional design of the processes through which a strategy evolves. This demands a shrewd sensitivity to the specific context a strategy is developing in and the work it is expected to perform. It also requires an ethical commitment to respect for a plurality of voices, to giving attention to multiple impacts, and to transparent reasoning.

Conclusion

The foregoing discussion of the technologies and ethical demands involved in these three fields of practice bring us back to the three questions raised at the start of this chapter. First, to identify the qualities of the interactions planning activity is performed through, researchers and policy analysts need to look at relational micropractices, both in specific arenas and in networking types of activity. Doing planning work in these multiple institutional sites and in the relational dynamics of network building and maintenance involves considerable knowledge and skill in performance. However, interactions cannot be reduced to specific techniques or procedures to be drawn from an expert manual and just applied in a particular situation. Instead, the quality of interaction reflects particular sensibilities. The collaborative planning idea promotes the significance of careful attention to the social and communicative relations through which any planning work is done and could be done. It advocates a capacity to appreciate the sociohistorical dynamics and potentialities of the particular context in which planning interventions are being undertaken. It demands an ethical commitment to pluralistic respect, to addressing impacts with a broad range of scales and dimensions, and to active and transparent argument and reasoning. When designing or evaluating a planning process that seeks to promote the progressive potential of collaborative planning processes, it is therefore important to focus on the quality of the social relations and communicative interactions through which such a planning process evolves, not just on the techniques being used and the rhetorical claims being made. And these relations and interactions need to be examined in the particular institutional specificities of the context of their use.

Second, it is this ethical orientation that helps to prevent the idea of collaborative planning being used as little more than a rhetorical flourish behind which business as usual carries on. Particular interactive techniques associated with collaborative planning can play a useful role, raising awareness about issues among those involved. But all too often these exercises do not feed into wider deliberative processes through which key decisions are made. Those committed to the progressive values of collaborative planning, both in its instrumental value of achieving more effective interventions and in the pursuit of distributive fairness with respect to the promotion of livability and sustainability, need to develop a situated awareness of how best to promote the mobilization of different forms of knowledge, how to give voice and attention to the plurality of the perspectives of the many, and how to promote honesty and transparency in presenting issues, arguments, possibilities, and solutions. Empty rhetoric can be countered by critical argument but also by the committed performance of the practice being invoked by the rhetoric, conducted with a shrewd awareness of the specific institutional context. This in turn helps to expand the capacity for more effective interventions, as complex urban polities learn to grasp and manage the urban worlds they live in reflexively and self-critically.

This leads to an answer to the third question. The idea of collaborative planning is more than just an empty signifier. And it is not just a label for an aggregation of interactive practices. It carries with it an ethics of attention and of conduct. Behind this ethics lies a social and a political philosophy. If shorn off, then invocations of collaborative planning ideas can be reduced to rhetorics or to a toolkit of techniques. The social philosophy draws on a relational, constructivist, and pragmatic understanding of social and communicative dynamics that emphasizes the situated, context-dependent nature of social life. Such a perspective anticipates that new possibilities creatively evolve in unpredictable ways from specific contexts, not by erasing or ignoring what is already "in presence," but by processes of emergence from the present. Such a philosophy also emphasizes the complex interactions between what is given policy attention and how policy attention is discursively mobilized. Substance and process coevolve. The political philosophy underlying the collaborative idea emphasizes an inclusive and rounded view of who and what deserves policy attention. It views us humans not just as economic individuals, but as creatures with many dimensions and attributes who exist in our relations with others, including nonhuman others. Planning activity for the future of urban areas that accepts such a viewpoint should therefore promote interventions that contribute to the flourishing of the many and not just the few, in many dimensions rather than in just one. This demands an attitude of tolerance and respect. Exactly what such interventions might be and what processes might help to identify them cannot be specified as a technology of collaborative planning. Much needs to be invented in situ. But without an ethics grounded in such a social and political philosophy, the invocation of collaborative planning and the use of specific techniques associated with the idea of collaborative planning may have limited leverage and may easily be subverted to narrower and more exclusive purposes. These may deal with short-term problems but, as emphasized at the beginning of this chapter, are likely to lead to resentments that impede future place development policy.

In conclusion, the art and craft of collaborative planning lies in maintaining critical attention to situated relational micropractices. As a discursively based practice, it involves using planning concepts and techniques in shrewd, situated ways, focused by ethical commitments to an inclusive and generous view of who and what gets to "count" in an urban area and by a capacious appreciation of what knowledge and understanding could help to promote urban futures that will provide sustainable contexts for the flourishing of future generations. This implies, for researchers and evaluators, careful analysis of the social and communicative dimensions of the specific relations through which practices are performed. For practitioners, it implies making context-specific, ethically informed judgments about the efficacy and legitimacy of using particular techniques associated with collaborative planning when undertaking planning work. With such sensitivity, discursive skills, and ethics, the collaborative microdynamics of planning practices can become important institutional sites for progressive innovation and transformation in the livability and sustainability of the places where we live, and in the culture of the polities through which we govern ourselves.

Notes

This chapter is adapted from a talk given at Hong Kong University in March 2010.

1. These examples draw on my discussion in Healey 2010.
2. See Callon, Lascoumes, and Barthe 2009 for an interesting discussion of the formation and circulation of scientific and political inquiries and ideas.
3. I set the discussion of such a collaborative approach to planning in the context of a relational approach to understanding the social, economic, and environmental dynamics through which places such as urban regions developed.
4. For relational ideas, see Graham and Healey 1999; Jessop 2008; Massey 2005.
5. For management ideas, see Huxham 1996, 2003; for public policy generally, see Lewis 2010. On international development, see Chambers 2005; Cornwall and Coelho 2007.
6. See Hillier and Healey 2010; Fischler 2000; and Fischer 2009 for a discussion of communicative planning theory, its proponents, and critics.
7. See Gualini 2010; Jessop 2008; Le Galès 2002; Sager 2009.
8. See Sorensen and Torfing 2007; Hajer 2009 on network governance; and Innes and Booher 2010.
9. On recent experiences in Brazil, see Briggs 2008; Fung and Wright 2003; Holston 2008.
10. By now, there are an array of handbooks on "how to do" collaborative problem solving, or "consensus building." See Sarkissian and Hurford 2010; Sarkissian et al. 2009; Susskind, McKearnan, and Thomas-Larner 1999 for a rich and critical compilation; and Wates 2000 for a useful handbook. See also the discussion in Innes and Booher 2010.
11. See Sager's (2007, 2009) work contrasting a calculative and a communicative approach.
12. See Hillier and Healey 2008 for contributions to, and a review of, these debates. See also Fainstein 2010.
13. See the discussion in Hillier and Healey 2008.
14. A recent TV series in the United Kingdom showed local planners going back and forth between applicants and affected neighbors to try to limit adverse impacts while helping the applicants to proceed with their projects (*After the Planners*, a BBC series in 2008–9).
15. See *Planning for Real* and accounts of urban regeneration practices and community development in the 1990s and 2000s (see Gilchrist 2009; for the United Kingdom, see Imrie and Raco 2003). *Planning for Real* is a neighborhood-planning technique where participants move cards and

simple models around on a layout plan, exploring problems and solutions together.

16. See Healey 2007 and Fainstein 2010 for Amsterdam; and Healey 2010 for Vancouver, Portland, and Boston.
17. See Healey et al. 2003.
18. See Edwards 2010.
19. See Friend, Power, and Yewlett 1974; Healey et al. 1988; Wannop 1985.
20. See Healey 2007, 2009.
21. Allen 2003 refers to such a persuasive capacity as the power of "seduction."
22. See Abbott 2001 and Healey 2010:ch. 7.

References

Abbott, C. 2001. *Greater Portland: Urban Life and Landscape in the Pacific Northwest.* Philadelphia: University of Pennsylvania Press.
Albrechts, L. 2004. "Strategic (Spatial) Planning Reexamined." *Environment and Planning B: Planning and Design* 31:743–58.
Allen, J. 2003. *Lost Geographies of Power.* Oxford: Blackwell.
Altshuler, A., and D. Luberoff. 2003. *Mega-Projects: The Changing Role of Urban Public Investment.* Washington: Brookings Institution Press.
Booth, P. 1996. *Controlling Development: Certainty and Discretion in Europe, the USA and Hong Kong.* Bristol, Pa.: UCL Press.
Briggs, X. d. S. 2008. *Democracy as Problem-Solving: Civic Capacity in Communities across the Globe.* Cambridge: MIT Press.
Callon, M., P. Lascoumes, and Y. Barthe. 2009. *Acting in an Uncertain World: An Essay on Technical Democracy.* Translated by Graham Burchell. Cambridge: MIT Press.
Chambers, R. 2005. *Ideas for Development.* London: Earthscan.
Cornwall, A., and V. S. P. Coelho, eds. 2007. *Spaces for Change? The Politics of Citizen Participation in New Democratic Arenas.* London: Zed.
Edwards, M. 2010. "King's Cross: Renaissance for Whom?" In *Urban Design and the British Urban Renaissance*, edited by John Punter. New York: Routledge.
Fainstein, S. 2010. *The Just City.* Ithaca: Cornell University Press.
Fischer, F. 1980. *Politics, Values and Public Policy: The Problem of Methodology.* Boulder, Colo.: Westview.
———. 2009. "Discursive Planning: Social Justice as a Discourse." In *Searching for the Just City: Debates in Urban Theory and Practice*, edited by P. Marcuse, J. Connolly, N. Johannes, et al., 52–71. New York: Routledge.
Fischer, F., and J. Forester, eds. 1993. *The Argumentative Turn in Policy Analysis and Planning.* Durham: Duke University Press.

Fischler, R. 2000. "Communicative Planning Theory: A Foucauldian Assessment." *Journal of Planning Education and Research* 19(4):358–68.

Forester, J. 1989. *Planning in the Face of Power*. Berkeley: University of California Press.

———. 1993. *Critical Theory, Public Policy and Planning Practice: Toward a Critical Pragmatism*. Albany: SUNY Press.

———. 2009. *Dealing with Differences: Dramas of Mediating Public Disputes*. Oxford: Oxford University Press.

Friend, J., and A. Hickling. 1987. *Planning under Pressure: The Strategic Choice Approach*. Oxford: Pergamon.

Friend, J., J. Power, and C. Yewlett. 1974. *Public Planning: The Inter-Corporate Dimension*. London: Tavistock.

Fung, A., and E. O. Wright, eds. 2003. *Deepening Democracy: Institutional Innovations in Empowered Participatory Governance*. London: Verso.

Gilchrist, A. 2009. *The Well-Connected Community: A Networking Approach to Community Development*. Bristol: Policy.

Graham, S., and P. Healey. 1999. "Relational Concepts in Time and Space: Issues for Planning Theory and Practice." *European Planning Studies* 7(5):623–46.

Gualini, E. 2010. "Governance, Space and Politics: Exploring the Governmentality of Planning." In *Ashgate Research Companion to Planning Theory*, edited by J. Hillier and P. Healey, 57–85. Farnham: Ashgate.

Hajer, M. 2005. "Rebuilding Ground Zero: The Politics of Performance." *Planning Theory and Practice* 6(4):445–64.

———. 2009. *Authoritative Governance: Policy-Making in the Age of Mediatization*. Oxford: Oxford University Press.

Healey, P. 1993. "Planning through Debate: The Communicative Turn in Planning Theory." In Fischer and Forester, *The Argumentative Turn in Policy Analysis and Planning*, 233–53.

———. 1997. *Collaborative Planning: Shaping Places in Fragmented Societies*. London: Macmillan.

———. 2007. *Urban Complexity and Spatial Strategies: Towards a Relational Planning for Our Times*. New York: Routledge.

———. 2009. "In Search of the 'Strategic' in Strategic Spatial Planning." *Planning Theory and Practice* 10(4):439–57.

———. 2010. *Making Better Places: The Planning Project in the Twenty-First Century*. London: Palgrave Macmillan.

Healey, P., C. de Magalhaes, A. Madanipour, and J. Pendlebury. 2003. "Place, Identity and Local Politics: Analysing Partnership Initiatives." In *Deliberative Policy Analysis: Understanding Governance in the Network Society*, edited by M. Hajer and H. Wagenaar, 60–87. Cambridge: Cambridge University Press.

Healey, P., P. McNamara, M. J. Elson, and J. Doak. 1988. *Land Use Planning*

and the Mediation of Urban Change. Cambridge: Cambridge University Press.
Hillier, J. 2011. "Strategic Navigation across Multiple Planes: Towards a Deleuzean-Inspired Methodology for Strategic Spatial Planning." *Town Planning Review* 82(5):503–28.
Hillier, J., and P. Healey, eds. 2008. *Contemporary Movements in Planning Theory: Volume III of Critical Readings in Planning Theory.* Aldershot, Hampshire: Ashgate.
———, eds. 2010. *Conceptual Challenges in Planning Theory.* Aldershot, Hampshire: Ashgate.
Holston, J. 2008. *Insurgent Citizenship: Disjunctions of Democracy and Modernity in Brazil.* Princeton: Princeton University Press.
Huxham, C., ed. 1996. *Creating Collaborative Advantage.* London: Sage.
———. 2003. "Theorising Collaborative Practice." *Public Management Review* 5(3):401–23.
Imrie, R., and M. Raco, eds. 2003. *Urban Renaissance? New Labour, Community and Urban Policy.* Bristol: Policy.
Innes, J. 1995. "Planning Theory's Emerging Paradigm: Communicative Action and Interactive Practice." *Journal of Planning Education and Research* 14(4):183–89.
Innes, J. E., and D. E. Booher. 2010. *Planning with Complexity: An Introduction to Collaborative Rationality for Public Policy.* New York: Routledge.
Jessop, B. 2008. *State Power.* Cambridge, England: Polity.
Le Galès, P. 2002. *European Cities: Social Conflicts and Governance.* Oxford: Oxford University Press.
Lewis, J. M. 2010. *Connecting and Cooperating: Social Capital and Public Policy.* Sydney: University of New South Wales Press.
Massey, D. 2005. *For Space.* Thousand Oaks, Calif.: Sage.
Motte, A., ed. 2007. *Les agglomérations françaises face aux défis métropolitaines.* Paris: Economica/Anthropos.
Sager, T. 2007. "Dialogical Values in Public Goods Provision." *Journal of Planning Education and Research* 26:497–512.
———. 2009. "Planners' Role: Torn between Dialogical Ideals and Neo-Liberal Realities." *European Planning Studies* 17(1):65–84.
Sarkissian, W., with N. Hofer, Y. Shore, S. Vajda, and C. Wilkinson. 2009. *Kitchen Table Sustainability: Practical Recipes for Community Engagement with Sustainability.* Sterling, Va.: Earthscan.
Sarkissian, W., and D. Hurford. 2010. *Creative Community Planning: Transformative Engagement Methods for Working at the Edge.* Washington: Earthscan.
Sorensen, E., and J. Torfing, eds. 2007. *Theories of Democratic Network Governance.* London: Palgrave Macmillan.
Susskind, L., S. McKearnan, and J. Thomas-Larner, eds. 1999. *The Consensus-Building Handbook.* Thousand Oaks, Calif.: Sage.

Wannop, U. 1985. "The Practice of Rationality: The Case of the Coventry-Solihull-Warwickshire Subregional Planning Study." In *Rationality in Planning*, edited by M. Breheny and A. J. Hooper, 196–208. London: Pion.

Wates, N., comp. and ed. 2000. *The Community Planning Handbook: How People Can Shape Their Cities, Towns and Villages in Any Part of the World*. London: Earthscan.

PART II
Discursive Politics and Argumentative Practices
INSTITUTIONS AND FRAMES

VIVIEN A. SCHMIDT

3. Discursive Institutionalism
Scope, Dynamics, and Philosophical Underpinnings

"Discursive institutionalism" is the term I use to cover the wide range of approaches in the social sciences that take ideas and discourse seriously. It has its origins in my desire to give a name to the very rich and diverse set of ways of explaining political and social reality which have been increasingly pushed to the margins in political science, in particular in the United States, by the growing domination of three older "new institutionalisms"—rational choice, historical, and sociological.[1] By adding a fourth new institutionalism to the other three, I seek to call attention to the significance of approaches that theorize about not only the substantive content of ideas—as in the "ideational turn" (Blyth 1997) or "ideational constructivism" (Hay 2006)—but also discourse and argumentation. And with discourse, I mean its theorization not just as the representation or embodiment of ideas—as in discourse analysis (following, say, Foucault 2000; Bourdieu 1990; or Laclau and Mouffe 1985)—but also as the interactive processes by and through which ideas are generated in discourse coalitions and discursive policy communities more generally (e.g., Haas 1992; Hajer 1993; Sabatier 1993) and communicated to the public (e.g., Dryzek 2000; Habermas 1989; Mutz, Sniderman, and Brody 1996; Wodak 2009; Zaller 1992). The institutionalism in the name, moreover, underlines the importance of considering both ideas and discourse in institutional context at the same time that it draws a line between this framework for analysis and those of the other neoinstitutionalisms.

Briefly defined, discursive institutionalism is an analytic framework concerned with the substantive content of ideas and the interactive processes of discourse and policy argumentation in institutional context. The ideas it elucidates may be developed through cognitive or normative arguments; may come at different levels of generality, including policy, programs, and philosophy, and in different forms, such as narratives, frames, frames of reference, discursive fields of ideas, argumentative practices, storytelling, and collective memories; and may change at different rates, either incrementally or in revolutionary shifts.

The discursive interactions may involve policy actors in discourse coalitions, epistemic communities, and advocacy coalitions engaged in a "coordinative" discourse of policy construction and political actors and the public engaged in a "communicative" discourse of deliberation, contestation, and legitimization of the policies (see Schmidt 2002a:ch. 5; 2006:ch. 5; 2008; 2010a). The directional arrows of these discursive interactions may come not only from the top down through the influence of the ideas of supranational or national elites but also from the bottom up through the ideas and discourse of local, national, or international "civil society," social movement activists, or ordinary people.

The institutional context, moreover, can be understood in two ways: first, in terms of the meaning context in which agents' discursive interactions proceed following nationally situated logics of communication; second, in terms of the formalized as well as informal institutions that inform their ideas, arguments, and discursive interactions (Schmidt 2008, 2010a). The institutions in the first sense of institutional context are above all dynamic, as structures and constructs of meaning internal to agents whose "background ideational abilities" enable them to create (and maintain) institutions while their "foreground discursive abilities" enable them to communicate critically about them and to change (or maintain) them. This kind of social construction of institutions skirts problems of relativism, moreover, because it recognizes differences in kinds of knowledge and certainty between agents' experiences in the world and their pictures of the world.

Institutions in the second sense are the formal (or informal) ones that are generally the objects of explanation of the three older neoinstitutionalisms: rationalist incentive structures, historical rules, or cultural frames that serve as external constraints to agents' action. In discursive institutionalism, these kinds of institutions may be treated as unproblematic background information, for example, to help elucidate why "simple" polities tend to have stronger communicative discourses and compound polities stronger coordinative ones. Or they may themselves be the objects of inquiry, in particular for those discursive institutionalists who emerge from and engage with any one of the older institutionalisms and are intent on showing the limits to explanations in terms of interest-based logics, historical path dependencies, or cultural framing. Agents' ideas, discourse, and actions in any institutional context, however, must also be seen as responses to the material (and not so material) realities which affect them, including material events and pressures, the unintended consequences of their own actions, the actions of others, the ideas and discourse that seek to make sense of any such actions, and the structural frameworks of power and position.

My purpose in developing what is essentially an umbrella concept for all such approaches to ideas and discourse is not simply definitional. It is also constitutive, in that it seeks to identify a discursive sphere within which practitioners of these varied approaches can discuss, deliberate, argue, and contest one another's ideas about ideas and discourse from epistemological, ontological, and methodological vantage points. And it is empirically oriented, in that in bringing together this wide range of interpretive approaches, it seeks to do a better job of theorizing the explanation of change (and continuity) in policy, politics, and institutions than the older three neoinstitutionalisms.

In what follows, I seek to build a systematic account of the range of ways in which discursive institutionalists deal with ideas, arguments, and discursive interactions in institutional context. To do so, we begin with ideas as the substantive content of discourse that comes in different forms, types, levels, and timing of change. Next, we consider the generators of ideas and discourse, that is, the "sentient" (thinking and speaking) agents who construct, articulate, communicate, argue, and contest ideas and arguments through discourse, with special attention to the philosophical questions regarding how such agents are constituted, how they constitute institutions, and what degree of knowledge and certainty about reality is possible given our definitions of agents and institutions. We then explore the dynamics of discourse in terms of the interactive processes of policy coordination and political communication, considering in detail the kinds of discursive policy communities through which ideas are generated and the political actors through which and forums in which they are communicated and argued. We end with the institutional contexts within which all discursive interaction takes place.

The Content of Ideas and Discourse

Discursive institutionalists tend to divide between those who concentrate on ideas and those who privilege discourse. The difference is primarily one of emphasis. Scholars concerned with ideas tend to focus on the substantive content of discourse while leaving the interactive processes of discourse implicit. Scholars who prefer discourse themselves divide into those who also emphasize its substantive content as the representation or embodiment of ideas and those who are more concerned with the discursive interactions through which actors generate, argue about, and communicate ideas in given institutional contexts (to be considered later). Among the scholars concerned most with the substantive content of ideas and discourse, differences abound with regard to the forms of ideas they identify, of which there are a vast array (see, e.g., Goodin and Tilly 2006:pt. 4). Such ideas may be cast as strategic weapons in the battle for "hegemonic" control (Muller 1995; see also Blyth 2002); "frames" that provide guideposts for knowledge, analysis, persuasion, and action through "frame-reflective discourse" (Rein and Schön 1994); narratives or discourses that shape understandings of events (e.g., Roe 1994); "frames of reference" that orient entire policy sectors (Jobert 1989; Muller 1995); "storytelling" to clarify practical rationality (Forester 1993); "collective memories" that frame action (Rothstein 2005); discursive "practices" or fields of ideas that define the range of imaginable action (Bourdieu 1994; Howarth, Norval, and Stavrakakis 2000; Torfing 1999); "argumentative practices" at the center of the policy process (Fischer and Forester 1993); or the results of "discursive struggles" that set the criteria for social classification, establish problem definitions, frame problems, define ideas, and create shared meaning on which people act (Stone 1988).

Scholars differ also with regard to the types of ideas and arguments they investigate. The literature of comparative politics and political economy tends to be more concerned with cognitive ideas that provide guidelines for political action and serve to justify programs through arguments focused on their interest-based logics and necessity (see Hall 1993; Muller 1995; Schmidt 2002a, 2008) than with normative ideas that attach values to political action and serve to legitimize the policies in a program through arguments based on their appropriateness, often with regard to underlying public philosophies (see March and Olsen 1989; Schmidt 2000, 2002a:213–17). By contrast, in international relations the focus is more on norms, defined as ideas about appropriate standards of behavior or desirable actions shared by members of a social entity (Finnemore 1996), and on the mechanisms by which ideas take hold and are diffused, such as learning, diffusion, transmission, and mimesis (Dobbin, Simmons, and Garrett 2007).

With regard to the timing of change in ideas, whether fast or slow, incremental or abrupt, differences among scholars have much to do with the level of ideas they consider (see Schmidt 2008, 2010a). Policy analysts have long tended to portray ideas and the arguments in which they are advanced as changing very rapidly, in particular when opportunities open in the face of events and as old policies no longer solve the problems or fit the politics for which they were designed (Kingdon 1984). But what remains unclear is whether events drive change in policy ideas or whether ideas open windows, creating new opportunities for policy change. Scholars who focus instead on policy programs mostly portray them as the objects of "great transformations" in periods of uncertainty (Blyth 2002) or as "paradigms," often building on Kuhn's (1970) approach in the philosophy of science. These are characterized as having a single overarching set of ideas for which a "paradigm shift" produces revolutionary, and incommensurable, change (e.g., Hall 1993; Jobert 1989; Schmidt 2002a:ch. 5, 2010b). Here, the problem is that although the concept of paradigm shift serves nicely as a metaphor for radical ideational change, it offers little guidance about how, when, or even why a shift takes place and rules out the coexistence of rival paradigms or the possibility that a paradigm shift can occur even without a clear idea behind it, as, say, the result of layering new policies onto the old in a given policy program (see Schmidt 2010a). Finally, philosophical ideas are generally portrayed as most long lasting, and less based on the policy sphere than on the political sphere, where the ideas and arguments tend to be broad concepts tied to normative values and moral principles (Weir 1992:169), ideologies (Berman 1998:21), or "global frames of reference" (Muller 1995). Here, the danger is assuming that they never change at all rather than looking to the ways in which public philosophies may be created and recreated over time, which is often the focus of more historically minded political scientists (e.g., Berman 1998) or historians (e.g., Hunt 1984; Nora 1989).

As for scholarly analyses of change in ideas over time, most political scientists go directly to empirical studies, both quantitative and qualitative. Among qualitative studies, process-tracing methods are the most prevalent. These show how ideas and arguments are tied to action by serving as guides for public actors on what to do and as sources of justification and legitimation for what such actors do (see Berman 1998; Blyth 2002). In addition to tracing empirically the ideas central to the processes of transformation, such processes can also serve to demonstrate the causal influence of ideas. This could involve providing matched pairs of cases in which everything is controlled for except the discourse, as in demonstrating the success of neoliberal discourse in economic reform (Schmidt 2002b) or in elucidating the ways in which ideas trap or capture agents, whether through rhetorical traps (Schimmelfenig 2001) or previous diplomatic agreements that agents find themselves bound to follow, whether they like it or not (Parsons 2003).

Another approach that takes us deeper into the theorization of the content of ideational change—this time from public administration—is provided by Bevir and Rhodes (2003), whose theory of meaning focuses on the incremental changes around a "web of beliefs" that over time constitute political traditions. These political traditions are (re)created through individuals' narratives, arguments, and story lines about how what they are doing fits with the tradition even as they alter it.

For in-depth philosophical theorizing about how the content of the ideas themselves change, however, one generally needs to turn to more postmodernist or poststructuralist approaches to policy change following discourse analyses that build on the work of Bourdieu, Foucault, and Laclau and Mouffe. These theoretical concepts—once translated from the sometimes difficult to access and internally referential language—can provide great value to the analysis of the content of ideas and how they change (and continue) over time. And here, there is no need to buy into their specific ontological and epistemological views in order to benefit from their theorizations of how ideational concepts change through discourse (Schmidt 2010a, 2010b). For example, discourse analyses that build on Michel Foucault can offer insights into how to investigate the archaeology of what was acceptable in a given discursive formation over time, from one period's *episteme* to the next, through examination of networks of rules establishing what is meaningful at any given time (see Pedersen 2011). Conversely, discourse analyses built on Laclau and Mouffe (1985) can point to different ways in which concepts may be employed, such as by serving as "nodal points" from which all other ideas take their meanings in an ideological system, showing, for example, how communism in Central and Eastern Europe served to distinguish between "real" (communist) democracy and "bourgeois" democracy (Howarth, Norval, and Stavrakakis 2000).

Sentient Agents and Discursive Practices

Ideas, naturally, do not "float freely" (Risse-Kappen 1994). They need to be carried by agents. But even where agents are treated as carriers of ideas, the connection between ideas and collective action remains unclear. The missing link is discourse not as representation but as interaction, and the ways in which ideas conveyed through discursive argumentation lead to action. But discourse also cannot be considered on its own, since it requires agents who articulate and communicate their ideas through discourse in exchanges that may involve discussion, deliberation, negotiation, and contestation. These agents can be defined as sentient (thinking and speaking) beings who generate and deliberate about ideas through discursive interactions that lead to collective action.

Focusing on sentient agents is important, because it emphasizes the fact that "who is speaking to whom about what where and why," or the interactive practices of discourse, makes a difference. Importantly, it is not just that agents are thinking beings who have ideas and arguments but that they are also speaking beings who share their ideas through discursive interactions that can lead to collective action. What makes agents sentient is that they are possessed not only of what I call their "background ideational abilities," which underpin their ability to make sense of as well as act within a given meaning context, that is, in terms of the ideational rules or rationality of that setting. It is that they also have "foreground discursive abilities" that enable them to communicate, argue, and deliberate about taking action collectively to change their institutions (see Schmidt 2008:314–16). This means that institutions are socially constructed. What ensures that we don't end up in complete relativism as a result of agents' background and foreground abilities to (re)construct their institutional structures has to do with the fact that there are differences in kinds of knowledge (on a continuum from more universal to more culturally bound) and certainty (on a continuum from more certain because based on agents' experiences in the world to less so because based on agents' pictures of the world) (Schmidt 2008: 318–19).

Agency through Background Ideational Abilities and Foreground Discursive Abilities

It is useful to elaborate on this briefly in ontological terms, not only to deepen our consideration of the ways in which sentient agents constitute or are constituted by institutions in the world, but also as a way to bridge divides between analytic and continental philosophies.[2] Most scholars who take ideas and discourse seriously intuitively assume that agents acting within institutions are simultaneously structure and construct (agency), but they rarely articulate this, especially those whose work is largely empirical. The exceptions are scholars influenced by the work of continental philosophers and macrosociologists such as Pierre Bourdieu (1994), Michel Foucault (2000), Jürgen Habermas (1989), and Anthony Giddens (1984). But there are also clues in the work of a philosopher in the analytic tradition, John Searle, to which I turn mainly to show that one need not only go to continental philosophy to gain similar kinds of insights on the construction of social reality.

Searle (1995) defines "institutional facts" as those things that exist only by way of collective agreements about what stands for an institution, such as property, money, marriage, governments, human rights, and cocktail parties. Although such facts are consciously created by sentient agents through words and action, once they are constituted people lose sight of this not only because they are born into them but also because they use them as part of a whole hierarchy of institutional facts, in which they may be conscious of this or that institution but not of the whole architecture. Moreover, as they use them in speech and practice, the institutions themselves may evolve, whether unconsciously, as people change how they use them, or consciously, as people decide to use them differently or not to use them at all, at which point the institution itself ceases to exist, as in the case of property rights during a Marxian revolution. In consequence, as Searle (1995:57) insists, institutions are process rather than product.

But where, then, is agency? That is, how do we situate human action within institutions, as process rather than product? For Searle (1995: 140–45), the whole hierarchy of institutional facts makes up the structure of constitutive rules to which agents are sensitive as part of their "background abilities" that encompass human capacities, dispositions, and know-how related to how the world works and how to cope with the world. Such background abilities are thus internal to agents, enabling them to speak, argue, and act without the conscious or unconscious following of rules external to the agent assumed by the rationalist calculations, historical path-dependencies, or the normative appropriateness of the older neoinstitutionalists.

Searle's concept of background abilities is not unique, as he himself acknowledges. He sees it as the focus of Wittgenstein's later work and also notes that it is present in Bourdieu's notion of the "habitus" (Searle 1995:127–32). Bourdieu's "habitus" resembles Searle's "background abilities" in that Bourdieu sees human activity as neither constituted nor constitutive but both simultaneously, as human beings act "following the intuitions of a 'logic of practice' which is the product of a lasting exposure to conditions similar to those in which they are placed" (Bourdieu 1990:11). In psychology, the theory of cognitive dissonance also comes close to what we are talking about here, at least insofar as it refutes assumptions about the rule-following nature of behavior, because it shows that people generally act without thinking of any rules they may be following, but then check what they are doing against the various rules that might apply, with consciousness about the rules coming into play mainly where cognitive dissonance occurs, that is, when the rules are contradictory (Harmon-Jones and Mills 1999).

The ideational processes by which agents create and maintain institutions, whether we ground these in Searle, Bourdieu, or cognitive psychology, can be summarized by the concept of "background ideational abilities." This generic concept is useful in signifying what goes on in individuals' minds as they come up with new ideas or follow old ones. But it does not explain much about the processes by which institutions change, which is a collective endeavor. It also underemphasizes a key component in human interaction that helps explain such change: discourse.

We undersell discursive institutionalism if we equate the ontology of institutions with background ideational abilities alone, neglecting what I call sentient agents' "foreground discursive abilities." This is people's ability to think and argue outside the institutions in which they continue to act, to talk about such institutions in a critical way, to communicate and deliberate about them, to persuade themselves as well as others to change their minds about their institutions, and then to take action to change them, individually or collectively. Even though Searle does not talk about any such "foreground abilities," one could argue that they are implicit in his view of the importance of language, in particular "speech acts," and in his insistence that institutional change not only can be unconscious, as agents start to use the institutions differently, but also can be conscious, when they "decide" to use them differently. Such "deciding" leaves the way open for our argument, which says that discourse as an interactive process is what enables agents to consciously change institutions, due to its deliberative nature allowing them to conceive (ideas) of and talk (discourse and argue) about institutions as objects at a distance and to dissociate themselves from them even as they continue to use them. This is because discourse works at two levels, at the everyday level of generating and communicating about institutions and at a metalevel, as a kind of second-order critical communication among agents about what goes on in the institutions.

By calling this interactive externalization of our internal ideational processes "foreground discursive abilities," I offer a generic term close to Habermas's (1989) view of "communicative action" (although without the normative prescriptions). It is also in line with much of the underlying assumptions of the literature on "discursive democracy" and "deliberative democracy" (e.g., Dryzek 2000), which is all about the importance of discourse and deliberative argumentation in breaking the elite monopoly on national and supranational decision making while ensuring democratic access to such decision making. As such, the concept of "foreground discursive abilities" also provides a direct response to macrosociologists and philosophers like Michel Foucault (2000), who sees little escape from the ideational domination of the powerful, or Pierre Bourdieu (1994), who argues that the *doxa* or vision of the world of elites who dominate the state creates the "habitus" that conditions people to see the world in the way they (the dominant) choose. "Foreground discursive abilities" are what ensure that Foucault, Bourdieu, and colleagues are able to step outside the *doxa* through their own writings, and that the public more generally is able to do so through discourse and debates. These are the abilities that ensure that people are able to reason, argue, and change the structures they use, a point also brought out by Antonio Gramsci (1971), who emphasizes the role of intellectuals in breaking the hegemonic discourse. But beyond even Gramsci, this term points to the importance of public debates in democratic societies in serving to expose the ideas which serve as vehicles for elite domination and power or, more simply, the "bad" ideas, lies, and manipulations in the discourse of any given political actor or set of actors. An approach that takes ideas and discourse seriously, in short, assumes that the clash in ideas and discourse is just as important in building, maintaining, and changing "institutions" as any ultimate compromise, consensus, or even imposition related to one set of ideas, arguments, or discourses.

The ontology of discursive institutionalism, in sum, combines the "background ideational abilities," which answer the questions "how are institutions created?" and "how do they persist?" with the "foreground discursive abilities," which answer the question "why do they change (or continue)?" But this then sends us on to another set of questions, focused on epistemological issues about the kinds of knowledge and certainty possible in a world in which sentient agents could be said to construct the structures by which they are structured.

Knowledge and Certainty Based on Experiences in the World vs. Pictures of the World

The epistemological questions raised by our answers to the ontological questions are mainly "how can we be sure that we know what we know?" and "what is reality in a world in which structure and agency are as one?" These questions often lead to accusations against those who come down on the agency side of the agency-structure debate, such as the claim that they cannot know anything for certain once they see everything as socially constructed, that they turn reality itself into a social construction, and that they therefore are on the slippery slope of relativism.

Fears of relativism have led some discursive institutionalists to stay on the materialist side of the materialist-constructivist divide. They tend to hold to a correspondence view of the world, that is, that material reality is out there for agents to see and that scholars are in the business of discovering it. Wendt (1999:109–10), for example, maintains a kind of "rump materialism" determining a hierarchy of needs in economic life. Others (e.g., Gofas and Hay 2010) try to straddle the divide between materialism and constructivism through "critical realism," worried that if there is no "truth," no "objective" reality, then there is no way to protect contextualized (social) "scientific" explanation from the radical relativism of "anything goes," in which power and subjectivity could trump truth and objectivity. Critical realism traces its roots back to the ambivalence of philosophers of science such as Bhashkar (1998) and others in choosing between, on the one hand, beliefs in proximate truths established through standards of empirical verification or falsification of (objective) explanations and, on the other hand, beliefs in relative truths established through standards of evaluation based on the success, progress, or creativity of (subjective) ideas (as elaborated in the work of Kuhn, Lakatos, Feyerabend, and Polanyi). Critical realists, in other words, remain on the fence, trying to reconcile what are essentially nonreconcilable approaches grounded in different ontological and epistemological presuppositions. It is therefore questionable enough an approach when applied to science. But for the social sciences, it could very well end up in the radical relativism critical realists fear most, since it starts with a definition of reality based on science and then goes from particles to people, rather than starting with a philosophy more focused on society that goes from people to particles (see Schmidt 2010b).

Moving to the constructivist side of the divide between materialists and constructivists need not lead to radical relativism. Constructivists tend to assume that most of reality is constructed by the actors themselves beyond a very basic level, but they do not deny the "materiality" of that most basic level.

However, to ask if material reality exists (correspondence vs. noncorrespondence) is in any event the wrong question: We do better to ask what is material and "real" and what is real even if it is not "material." The latter is particularly the case with institutions that may be "real" because they constitute interests and cause things to happen even though they are socially constructed and thus not material in a visible, "put your hand or rest your eyes on it" kind of concrete sense. Searle (1995) can prove helpful in elucidating this point when he distinguishes between "brute facts" like mountains, which exist regardless of whether sentient (intentional) agents acknowledge their existence or have words for them, and "social facts," of which "institutional facts" are a subset, and which do not exist without sentient agents. Thus, while brute facts define a basic material reality, social facts may not be material even though they are "real," while institutional facts are real to the extent that the collective agreements by which they are constituted continue to hold, which is often very real indeed if we think about the institution of property or of money, even though it is a "social construction" (see Ingham 2008).

To get clearer about questions of certainty or uncertainty related to such "social facts," from a different vantage point, we could turn to Wittgenstein who, in *On Certainty* (1972), suggests answers to our questions by differentiating between different kinds of knowledge and certainty based on different "forms of life," as expressed through "language games."[3] Here, he makes a little-noticed but important distinction between language games based on our experience in the world, for which radical uncertainties rarely occur, and those based on our pictures of the world, which involve knowledge closer to the kind found in (social) science, and which can involve radical uncertainty akin to shifts in "paradigms" and "cosmologies."

Language games based on our everyday experiences in the world ordinarily admit of no doubts and mistakes, such as knowledge of one's own name, address, actions, and history; of the number of hands and toes one has; and of the meaning of the words one uses. If doubts occur, they suggest exceptional circumstances (e.g., I doubt that this is my name because I have amnesia; Wittgenstein 1972). Similarly, we don't doubt that the step will be there as we step down, or that the mountain we see out of our window will disappear if we look away. If there is no reasonable explanation for such doubts, we might assume that the individual expressing doubts does not know the meaning of the words themselves or is not rational in any everyday sense of the word.

By contrast, language games based on our pictures of the world, which often follow from our (social) scientific interpretations of the world—such as belief in the existence of the earth one hundred years ago, in the events of history, in the temperature at which water boils—always allow for doubts, mistakes, and even gestalt switches, although much less often for those at the "foundation" of our picture of the world, which "stand fast" because they are part of the very "scaffolding" of our thoughts (Wittgenstein 1972:211, 234). In science, we could add the existence of subatomic particles—molecules, quarks, neutrinos, and so on—along with theories of relativity, which exist for us today in the way that the humors and gases or the four elements of earth, wind, fire, and water existed for the Ancients, at the very foundations of our scientific explanations of the world.

The experience games of everyday life, in other words, are so certain that they are not to be doubted; but picture games may always be doubted, although some may be more uncertain than others depending upon their place in the overall system of picture games. Moreover, while knowledge derived from picture games always allows for a radical conversion process, as in revolutionary changes in scientific paradigms à la Kuhn, experience games do not (see Schmidt 1986). Radical relativism, as a result, could be much more of a danger for picture games, in particular if they are far removed from the "scaffolding" of our own pictures of the world, than for experience games, which tend to be more universal. As Wittgenstein has noted elsewhere, "The common behavior of mankind is the system of reference by means of which we interpret an unknown language" (1968:206). And although this need not mean that we will have words for everything, such as with the Hopi Indian's understanding of time or the Eskimo's many words for snow (see Whorf 1956), we can translate these into our own language and experience. This ensures a high degree of certainty not only for common behavior (knowing one's name) but also commonly experienced material realities—what we see, like mountains and buildings—even if their significance may be more uncertain for us depending upon where they fit against our pictures of the world. One could even argue that there are certain bases to human rationality that allow for universalism, as illustrated in Wittgenstein's (1968:xi, 223) famous observation that "if a lion could talk, we would not understand him." And it is also the case that if all ideas are "constructed," it is possible, although not easy, to construct international ideas about interests and norms—what is the modern notion of human rights about, after all, if not that (see Risse, Ropp, and Sikkink 1999)?

In the social sciences, approaches based on historical and interpretive analytic frameworks tend to be closer to everyday experience in the phenomena they seek to explain than the more systemic and lawlike social science frameworks, which produce explanations that are often closer to picture games. For example, in historical explanation, the "facts" about agents' experiences are usually not in dispute even if the interpretations are, and those facts are not likely to change radically even if there may be some question about which facts to take into account in the interpretation of events. By contrast, the "facts" deduced through the mathematical models of the economists—with their pictures of a world in which rational actors are in the business of rationally calculating their interests to maximize their utility—can vanish entirely, in particular when the models fail to predict, as in the massive financial market crash of 2008. As Taleb (2007) has argued, all such probabilistic models mistakenly assume that this is a world of risk (read: world of experience) and is therefore predictable, rather than one of uncertainty, in which unpredictable "black swan" events happen with much greater regularity than probabilistic theories (i.e., pictures of the world) expect. The further complicating factor here, as Mackenzie (2006) argues with regard to performativity in financial markets, is that social agents employing probabilistic "pictures of the world" to measure market performance actually alter the market (and the picture), because their models act as an "engine" transforming the environment, not a "camera" recording it. Note that where bankers went wrong is when they ignored what they knew from their everyday experience of lending and assessing the reliability of risk, credit-worthiness, and the likelihood of repayment over time, placing their faith instead in probabilistic (picture of the world) models and packaged credit default swaps on loans they knew from everyday experience were major credit risks (Schmidt 2010b).

Even in the natural sciences, moreover, we can differentiate between knowledge based on pictures of the world and those closer to everyday experience. For example, changes in the theories of physics (say, from Newtonian mechanics to Einsteinian relativity) are very different from those in natural history (say, between Linnaeus and Darwin). Whereas in physics the very nature of the phenomena described may change—from the elements of the Greeks to subatomic particles—much as in Kuhn's (1970) duck-rabbit picture (first you see a duck, then a rabbit), they do not in natural history. An eagle remains an eagle for Darwin and Linnaeus. Only if the characterization of an eagle perched on a cliff turned into a "cleagle" would the change in explanation be similar (Schmidt 1988:184–85).

The distinction between matters of experience and pictures of the world is thus a crucial one for our discussion of epistemological questions related to knowledge and certainty, since it helps us avoid the risks of radical relativism. It suggests that social scientists' explanations have varying degrees of certainty, depending on their objects of knowledge and explanation. It demonstrates that social agents in any given culture and time can generally understand other cultures and times based on common experiences through translation and interpretation, even if they may have greater difficulty with their pictures of the world. Finally, with regard to sentient agents, it shows that knowledge and certainty are collectively constructed within given institutional contexts. And for such collective construction, we need to examine more closely the range of discursive actions in which sentient agents engage.

Discursive Interactions: Discourse Coalitions, Discursive Communities, and Communication with the Public

Discursive interactions generally fall into one of two domains in the public sphere: the policy sphere characterized by a "coordinative" discourse among policy actors engaged in creating, deliberating, arguing, bargaining, and reaching agreement on policies, and the political sphere characterized by a "communicative" discourse between political actors and the public engaged in presenting, deliberating, arguing over, contesting, and legitimating those policy ideas (see Schmidt 2002a:ch. 5, 2006:ch. 5, 2008).

The agents in the coordinative discourse are generally the actors involved in the policy process, including "policy makers" or government officials, policy consultants, experts, lobbyists, business and union leaders, and others. They generate policy ideas and arguments with different degrees and kinds of influence. And they organize themselves in a variety of groupings as discursive communities to influence the generation, shaping, and adoption of policies, often activated by entrepreneurial or mediating actors and informed by experts.

"Discourse coalition" is arguably the most general way of conceiving of such discursive communities. Maarten Hajer (1993:45) uses the concept to combine the analysis of a "discursive production of reality," or "social construct," with the extradiscursive practices from which social constructs emerge and in which the groups of policy actors who construct the new social idea or narratives engage. He uses the concept of discourse coalitions in particular to illustrate how a social construct, in his case acid rain in Britain, came increasingly to be used by competing coalitions that sought to control the construction and implementation of acid rain policy in the country. Discourse coalitions are also used by Gerhard Lehmbruch to identify the policy actors who share ideas across extended periods of time, as in the rise of ordo-liberalism in Germany and of the idea of a social market economy, developed in early postwar Germany by Alfred Müller-Armack, the entrepreneurial actor responsible for leading the discourse coalition that developed the arguments that convinced policy actors, political actors, and then the public of the necessity and appropriateness of this idea (Lehmbruch 2001).

The members of the discourse coalitions themselves need not share all the same ideas, beliefs, or goals, or share them to the same degree, to promote a common policy program. Instead, they may be united by agreement on certain policy objectives or the use of certain policy instruments. They may agree on the cognitive arguments to justify a policy program but disagree over aspects of the normative arguments to use in legitimization. They may agree on an overall policy program but disagree over the nature and range of its sectoral applications. Their interests may naturally be different, but they may nevertheless agree on the institutional arrangements to be set up to arbitrate among those interests (see Jobert 2003). Importantly, discourse coalitions are themselves engaged in constant argumentation in their efforts to develop the arguments that they hope policy actors will ultimately take as their own as they generate policies.

When discourse coalitions are conceived of mainly as linking actors on the basis of their shared ideas, they have also been called "epistemic communities" to call attention to the loosely connected transnational actors who hold the same cognitive and normative ideas about a common policy enterprise that they seek to promote (Haas 1992). Another subset of discourse coalitions are "advocacy coalitions," a term that tends to be used for more closely connected individuals who don't just share ideas but also have access to policy making (Sabatier 1993). In addition, particular agents in discourse coalitions may themselves be cast as policy "entrepreneurs" (Kingdon 1984) or "mediators" (Jobert 1989; Muller 1995) who serve as catalysts for change as they articulate the ideas of the various discourse coalitions or of discursive communities more generally.

Discursive communities, including discourse coalitions, often generate their own information, although increasingly the technical experts to whom they turn are organized in think tanks, often separate from the discursive communities. Fischer (1993), for example, notes that in the United States, the Democratic Party first used policy analysts in think tanks as a way to legitimize their "new class liberal arguments" by disguising them as technocratic discourse, with cognitive arguments that, because they came from purportedly apolitical experts, were to supplant "the everyday, less sophisticated opinions of the common citizen." He then shows that the Republican discourse coalition went farther than their rival's liberal and technocratic reform strategy by politicizing expertise via the conservative, politically engaged think tanks that had been proliferating since the 1970s. Rich (2004) updates this with his own study of Washington think tanks, in which conservative think tanks that produce unabashedly political and value-laden research have had much greater impact than more progressive think tanks, which seek to be (or at least appear to be) more value-neutral and objective. Campbell and Pedersen (2010) have recently shown that a similar phenomenon has been developing in Europe, in which only in the past five years or so have think tanks proliferated in national capitals and in Brussels.

In the communicative discourse, the agents of change consist not only of the usual suspects: political leaders, elected officials, party members, policy makers, spin doctors, and the like who act as "political entrepreneurs" as they attempt to form mass public opinion (Zaller 1992), engage the public in debates about the policies they favor (Mutz, Sniderman, and Brody 1996), and win elections. They also include the media, interest groups acting in the specialized "policy forums" of organized interests (e.g., Rein and Schön 1994), public intellectuals, opinion makers, social movements, and even ordinary people through their everyday talk and argumentation, which can play an important role not just in the forum of "opinion-formation" but also in that of "will-formation" (Mansbridge 2009). In other words, all manner of discursive publics engaged in "communicative action" (Habermas 1989) may be involved, with communication going not only from the top down but also from the bottom up.

The spheres of coordinative policy construction and communicative policy legitimation are of course interconnected both in the substantive content and in the interactive process. To begin with, the policy ideas in the coordinative discourse—often more heavily weighted toward cognitive justification—are generally translated by political actors into language and arguments accessible to the general public as part of a communicative discourse that also adds normative legitimation to ensure that the policy and programmatic ideas resonate with the philosophical frames of the polity (see Schmidt 2006:255–57). The process itself is one in which the coordinative discourse can be seen to prepare the ground for the communicative. In the United Kingdom, for example, the ground was prepared for Thatcher's monetarist paradigm change before her election by the ideas developed in a coordinative discourse consisting of a small group of the "converted" from the Conservative party, financial elites, and the financial press (Hall 1993). But Thatcher herself was the political entrepreneur who put these ideas into more accessible language through a communicative discourse to the general public, as we saw earlier (Schmidt 2002a:259–66).

But the coordinative and communicative discourses don't always connect with one another. Policy ideas may remain in the policy sphere, either because the public might not approve, as has sometimes been the case with more progressive policies, or because the public is not interested, as in the case of highly technical reforms of banking and finance. But there may also be cases where politicians argue for one thing in the coordinative policy sphere and another in the communicative political sphere, as has often been the case with the European Union, where the perceived democratic deficit is due in part to the blame shifting of national political leaders who agree to one thing in the coordinative discourse of the Council of Ministers but, fearful of negative public reaction, say something very different in the communicative discourse to the general public (see Schmidt 2006:36–45, 2008).

We still have a problem, however, because this discussion remains focused primarily on the discourse of elites, whether in a top-to-top coordinative discourse or in a top-down communicative discourse. Mostly, however, in addition to any formalized, elite processes of coordinative consultation, and whatever the elite-led processes of communicative deliberation are, the public has a whole range of ways of arguing about and responding to policies produced by elites. The media, for example, are often key to framing the terms of the communicative discourse, creating narratives, arguments, and images that become determinant of interpretations of a given set of events. In the case of the financial market crises, we could mention the Barings bank debacle, when the British bank spectacularly collapsed as a result of the unauthorized trading of Nick Leeson. This crisis was personalized in terms of a "rogue trader" as opposed to being generalized as a deeper critique of the internationalized banking system (Hudson and Martin 2010), just as

Martha Stewart became the poster child for the financial crisis of the early 2000s, and Bernie Madoff for the 2008 crisis.

Social movements are also significant forces in a "bottom-up" communicative discourse. Scholars who focus on "contentious politics" demonstrate the many ways in which leaders and social movement activists, along with everyday actors, spur change through ideas that contest the status quo, which are conveyed by discourse that persuades others to join in protest, in turn generating debate and argumentation (e.g., Aminzade et al. 2001; Della Porta 2009). Charlotte Epstein's (2008) account of how "Moby Dick" became "Moby Doll" is a clear demonstration of the way in which social movements coalesced against the whaling industry and, determined to save the whale, were able to change ideas through a communicative discourse that led to radically altered policies negotiated in the transnational coordinative sphere.

Social movements are best categorized as part of the communicative discourse because they are at least initially removed from the policy world and rely on pressure from the outside, through media coverage of their protests and actions, rather than from the inside, through policy influence. But often, as social movements develop, the outside communicative practices are accompanied by inside coordinative ones. In some cases, as social movements become institutionalized, which was particularly the case with regard to the environment or women's issues, the coordinative discourse with policy actors becomes predominant, and the kind of activity engaged in makes the social movement one in name only except for the moments when a mobilizing issue comes up and the social movement returns to protest and argumentation in the streets.

Finally, the general public of citizens and voters to whom this communicative discourse is directed also contribute to it and thereby spur policy change. They do this as members of civil society, not just through grass-roots organizing, social mobilization, and demonstrations, but also as members of "mini-publics" in citizen juries, issues forums, deliberative polls, and the like (see Goodin and Dryzek 2006), as, more simply, members of the electorate, whose voices are heard as the subjects of opinion polls, surveys, focus groups and, of course, as voters, where actions speak even louder than verbal arguments. Not to be neglected in this, however, are the everyday practices of ordinary people, even in cases where ideas are unarticulated and change is individual, subtle, and slow, as they articulate their protest through sanctioning politicians in votes or by not voting at all (Seabrooke 2007).

The Context of Ideas and Discourse

Institutional context also matters. If sentient (thinking and speaking) agents are the drivers of change, and their ideas (what they think about what to do) and discourse (what they say about what to do) are the vehicles of change, then the institutional context is the setting within which their ideas have meaning, their discourses have communicative force, and their collective actions make a difference (if they do what they say and think about what to do).

Three elements—ideas, discourse, and institutions—all need to be considered in the institutional context. That context is first of all the "meaning context" in which ideas, arguments, and discourse make sense, such that speakers "get it right" in the ideational rules or rationality of a given setting by addressing their remarks to the "right" audiences at the "right" times in the "right" ways. This is why even where a term may be disseminated internationally, when it is taken up nationally, it is likely to be used very differently, given differences in meaning context and all that that entails in culture—economic, political, and social. Ideas and discourse about globalization, for example, are very different from country to country, even between countries with seemingly similar liberal public philosophies like the United Kingdom and Ireland, where leaders sought to present it as a challenge to rise to (Hay and Smith 2005), let alone between these countries and a country like France, in which leaders argue more about the virtues of resisting globalization (Schmidt 2007).

The context, however, may also refer to the "forum" within which the discourse proceeds, following a particular logic of communication. Thus, for example, Stephen Toulmin (1958) shows that in any given "forum of argumentation" or discourse, the procedural rules create a common set of understandings even when speakers lack trust or consensus, as in the adversarial arguments that take place in a courtroom. Moreover, in international negotiations where the rules are not pre-established and the "forum" is an ad hoc creation dependent upon the players and the circumstances, prenegotiations are the context within which the rules of discursive interaction are set, even though the actual process involves other kinds of discursive interactions outside the negotiating context, such as with domestic constituencies and other international actors (Stein 1989). Here we could also mention differences, as understood by the *référentiel* school, between the forums in which deliberative argumentation is more open and those arenas in which bargaining is the focus (Jobert 1989). Finally, formal institutions—as elaborated in historical and institutionalist explanations—also constitute the institutional context and give shape to discursive interactions. Formal arrangements affect *where* discourse matters by establishing who talks to whom about what, where, and when. For example, although all countries have both coordinative and communicative discourses, one or the other tends to be more important due to the configuration of their political institutions. Political institutional setting helps explain why simple polities like France and the United Kingdom, where authority tends to be concentrated in the executive and reform agendas are generally decided by a restricted elite, tend to have more elaborate communicative discourses to the public—so as to legitimate those reforms—than in compound polities like Germany and Italy, where authority tends to be more dispersed. These countries tend to have more elaborate coordinative discourses among policy actors—so as to reach agreement among the much wider range of actors involved in arguing about and negotiating reform (Schmidt 2000, 2002a, 2006).

The formal institutional context, however, is not neutral with regard to its effect on politics. But one cannot therefore simply map power onto position, as is often done in rationalist and historical and institutionalist analyses that assume we know an agent's interests and power to serve those interests if we know their position (Schmidt 2010a). In discursive institutionalism, by contrast, there is always the recognition that ideas and discourse can also provide power, as actors gain power from their ideas and as they at the same time give power to their ideas (see also Wodak 2009:35–36). This results, for example, when agents are able to "set the agenda" as "policy entrepreneurs" who build coalitions for reform or as "political entrepreneurs" who gain public support for reform (Baumgartner and Jones 1993; Kingdon 1984). Moreover, actors can gain power from their ideas even where they may lack the power of position—as in the case of discourse coalitions that manage to have their own social construct adopted, such as in the case of acid rain

(Hajer 1993), or of social movements in which their arguments become predominant, such as in the case of whales (Epstein 2008).

But actors also gain (or lose) power to the extent that their ideas, arguments and discourse have meaning for their audience. Because power itself derives not only from position (i.e., actors' ability to wield power) but also purpose, actors' ideas and discourse about how they can and should wield that power may reinforce or undermine the power they derive from their position, depending upon the responses of their audience to their stated purposes. This is the essence of political leadership.

Ideational power can also come from a position *qua* position, however, since ideas and values infuse the exercise of power and perceptions of position (Lukes 2005). Theories about the structures and practices of elite ideational domination abound among continental philosophers and macrosociologists (e.g., Bourdieu 1994; Foucault 2000; Gramsci 1971). But as we have already seen, the importance of discourse means that regardless of the power of the background ideational context, in which people may very well be socialized into a certain manner of thinking and arguing through ideas dominated by elites, foreground discursive abilities enable those selfsame people to reason about and critique those ideational structures. But this is not to suggest that therefore simply recognizing, arguing about, and thereby seeking to delegitimize the power of elites' ideas necessarily changes the structures of power and the power of position. Structural power is also the power not to listen.

Conclusion

In discursive institutionalism, we focus attention not only on the content of the ideas and discourse, which comes in a wide variety of forms and types at different levels and different degrees of change, but also on the interactive processes of discursive argumentation. The "sentient" agents in such processes engage in coordinative policy discourses and communicative political discourses that may go in many directions, whether from top to bottom or bottom to top, or may even stay at the bottom. The institutional context in which they interact is also important. It is constituted not only by the meaning-based logics of communication in any given setting that agents navigate through their background ideational abilities and maintain or change through their foreground discursive abilities. That context is also defined by their (in)formal institutions, since power and position also matter for ideas and discourse as well as structural constraints.

But once we have constituted the field that discursive institutionalists occupy, what is next? Learning from one another as well as debating and argumentatively contesting one another's conceptions of ideas and discourse. First in line could be my own ontological and epistemological arguments, such as the argument that relativism need not be a problem so long as we recognize that certainty is split between things we can't really doubt involving matters of experience, and those we can always doubt, although we often don't, involving our pictures of the world. Beyond this, however, it would also be useful to engage with other approaches in social science—in particular, the other neoinstitutionalisms—in order to see to what extent their results can provide useful background information for the discursive institutionalist enterprise and what needs to be contested. Most importantly, however, I developed discursive institutionalism not to make it stand alone, but rather to demonstrate that it, too, is a key component in the social sciences' methodological toolbox.

Notes

1. Rational choice institutionalism focuses on rational actors who pursue their preferences following a "logic of calculation" within political institutions, defined as structures of incentives. Historical institutionalism details the development of political institutions, described as regularized patterns and routinized practices subject to a "logic of path-dependence." Sociological institutionalism concentrates on social agents who act according to a "logic of appropriateness" within political institutions, defined as socially constituted and culturally framed rules and norms. See Schmidt 2010a.
2. The following discussion expands on Schmidt 2008.
3. The following builds on discussions in Schmidt 2008, 2010b.

References

Aminzade, Ronald R., Jack A. Goldstone, Doug McAdam, Elizabeth J. Perry, William H. Sewell Jr., Sidney Tarry, and Charles Tilly. 2001. *Silence and Voice in the Study of Contentious Politics*. New York: Cambridge University Press.

Baumgartner, Frank R., and Bryan D. Jones. 1993. *Agendas and Instability in American Politics.* Chicago: University of Chicago Press.

Berman, S. 1998. *The Social Democratic Movement: Ideas and Politics in the Making of Interwar Europe.* Cambridge: Harvard University Press.

Bevir, Mark, and R. A. W. Rhodes. 2003. *Interpreting British Governance.* London: Routledge.

Bhashkar, Roy. 1998. *The Possibility of Naturalism.* 3rd ed. London: Routledge.

Blyth, Mark M. 1997. "'Any More Bright Ideas?' The Ideational Turn in Comparative Political Economy." *Comparative Politics* 29(2):229–50.

———. 2002. *Great Transformations: Economic Ideas and Institutional Change in the Twentieth Century.* New York: Cambridge University Press.

Bourdieu, Pierre. 1990. *In Other Words: Essays towards a Reflexive Sociology.* Stanford: Stanford University Press.

———. 1994. *Raisons Pratiques.* Paris: Le Seuil.

Campbell, John L., and Ove K. Pedersen. 2010. "Knowledge Regimes and Comparative Political Economy." In *Ideas and Politics in Social Science Research,* edited by Daniel Béland and Robert H. Cox, 167–90. New York: Oxford University Press.

Della Porta, Donatella, ed. 2009. *Democracy in Social Movements.* Basingstoke: Palgrave Macmillan.

Dobbin, Frank, Beth Simmons, and Geoffrey Garrett. 2007. "The Global Diffusion of Public Policies: Social Construction, Coercion, Competition or Learning?" *Annual Review of Sociology* 33:449–72.

Dryzek, John. 2000. *Deliberative Democracy and Beyond.* Oxford: Oxford University Press.

Epstein, Charlotte. 2008. *The Power of Words in International Relations: Birth of an Anti-Whaling Discourse.* Cambridge: MIT Press.

Finnemore, M. 1996. "Norms, Culture, and World Politics: Insights from Sociology's Institutionalism." *International Organization* 50(2):325–47.

Fischer, Frank. 1993. "Policy Discourse and the Politics of Washington Think Tanks." In Fischer and Forester, *The Argumentative Turn in Policy Analysis and Planning,* 21–42.

Fischer, Frank, and John Forester, eds. 1993. *The Argumentative Turn in Policy Analysis and Planning.* Durham: Duke University Press.

Forester, John. 1993. "Learning from Practice Stories: The Priority of Practical Judgment." In Fischer and Forester, *The Argumentative Turn in Policy Analysis and Planning,* 186–212.

Foucault, Michel. 2000. *Power.* Vol. 3 of *Essential Works of Foucault, 1954–1984.* Edited by J. D. Faubion. New York: New Press.

Giddens, A. 1984. *The Constitution of Society: Outline of a Theory of Structuration.* Cambridge: Polity.

Gofas, A., and C. Hay. 2010. "Varieties of Ideational Explanation." In *The Role of Ideas in Political Analysis: A Portrait of Contemporary Debates*, edited by A. Gofas and C. Hay, 13–55. London: Routledge.

Goodin, Robert, and John Dryzek. 2006. "Deliberative Impacts: The Macro-Political Uptake of Mini-Publics." *Politics and Society* 34(2):219–44.

Goodin, Robert, and Charles Tilly, eds. 2006. *Oxford Handbook of Contextual Political Analysis*. Oxford: Oxford University Press.

Gramsci, Antonio. 1971. *Selections from the Prison Notebooks*. New York: International.

Haas, P. M. 1992. "Introduction: Epistemic Communities and International Policy Coordination." *International Organization* 46:1–35.

Habermas, Jürgen. 1989. *The Structural Transformation of the Public Sphere*. Translated by T. Burger and F. Lawrence. Cambridge: MIT Press.

Hajer, Maarten. 1993. "Discourse Coalitions in Practice: The Case of Acid Rain in Great Britain." In Fischer and Forester, *The Argumentative Turn in Policy Analysis and Planning*, 43–76.

Hall, Peter. 1993. "Policy Paradigms, Social Learning and the State: The Case of Economic Policy-Making in Britain." *Comparative Politics* 25: 275–96.

Harmon-Jones, E., and J. Mills. 1999. *Cognitive Dissonance: Progress on a Pivotal Theory in Social Psychology*. Washington: American Psychological Association.

Hay, C. 2006. "Constructivist Institutionalism." In *The Oxford Handbook of Political Institutions*, edited by R. A. W. Rhodes, S. Binder, and B. Rockman, 56–74. Oxford: Oxford University Press.

Hay, Colin, and Nicola J. Smith. 2005. "Horses for Courses? The Political Discourse of Globalisation and European Integration in the UK and Ireland." *West European Politics* 28(1):125–59.

Howarth, D., A. J. Norval, and Y. Stavrakakis, eds. 2000. *Discourse Theory and Political Analysis*. Manchester: Manchester University Press.

Hudson, David, and Mary Martin. 2010. "Narratives of Neoliberalism: The Role of Everyday Media Practices and the Reproduction of Dominant Ideas." In *The Role of Ideas in Political Analysis*, edited by Andreas Gofas and Colin Hay, 97–117. London: Routledge.

Hunt, Lynn. 1984. *Politics, Culture, and Class in the French Revolution*. Berkeley: University of California Press.

Ingham, Geoffrey. 2008. *The Nature of Money*. Cambridge: Polity.

Jobert, Bruno. 1989. "The Normative Frameworks of Public Policy." *Political Studies* 37:376–86.

———. 2003. "Europe and the Recomposition of National Forums." *Journal of European Public Policy* 10(3):463–77.

Kingdon, John. 1984. *Agendas, Alternatives and Public Policies*. New York: Longman.

Kuhn, Thomas. 1970. *The Structure of Scientific Revolutions*. 2nd ed. Chicago: University of Chicago Press.

Laclau, Ernesto, and Chantal Mouffe. 1985. *Hegemony and Socialist Strategy: Towards a Radical Democratic Politics*. Oxford: Blackwell.

Lehmbruch, G. 2001. "Institutional Embedding of Market Economies: The German Model and Its Impact on Japan." In *The Origins of Nonliberal Capitalism*, edited by W. Streeck and K. Yamamura, 39–93. Ithaca: Cornell University Press.

Lukes, Stephen. 2005. *Power: A Radical View*. 2nd ed. Basingstoke: Palgrave Macmillan.

MacKenzie, Donald. 2006. *An Engine Not a Camera: How Financial Models Shape Markets*. Cambridge: MIT Press.

Mansbridge, J. 2009. "Deliberative and Non-Deliberative Negotiations." Harvard Kennedy School Working Papers, *HKS Working Paper No. RWP09-010*, on the web site of the Social Science Research Network.

March, James G., and Johan P. Olsen. 1989. *Rediscovering Institutions*. New York: Free Press.

Muller, P. 1995. "Les politiques publiques comme construction d'un rapport au monde." In *La Construction du Sens dans les Politiques Publiques*, edited by Alain Faure, Gielles Pollet, and Philippe Warin, 153–79. Paris: L'Harmattan.

Mutz, Diana C., Paul M. Sniderman, and Richard A. Brody. 1996. *Political Persuasion and Attitude Change*. Ann Arbor: University of Michigan Press.

Nora, Pierre. 1989. "Between Memory and History." *Representations* 26: 11–12.

Parsons, Craig. 2003. *A Certain Idea of Europe*. Ithaca: Cornell University Press.

Pedersen, Ove. 2011. "Discourse Analysis." In *Encyclopaedia of Political Science*, edited by Bertrand Badie, Dirk Berg-Schlosser, and Leonardo Morlino. Thousand Oaks, Calif.: Sage.

Rein, Martin, and D. A. Schön. 1994. *Frame Reflection Toward the Resolution of Intractable Policy Controversies*. New York: Basic.

Rich, A. 2004. *Think Tanks, Public Policy, and the Politics of Expertise*. New York: Cambridge University Press.

Risse, Thomas, Stephen Ropp, and Kathryn Sikkink. 1999. *The Power of Human Rights: International Norms and Domestic Change*. Cambridge: Cambridge University Press.

Risse-Kappen, Thomas. 1994. "Ideas Do Not Float Freely: Transnational Coalitions, Domestic Structures, and the End of the Cold War." *International Organization* 48(2):185–214.

Roe, E. 1994. *Narrative Policy Analysis: Theory and Practice*. Durham: Duke University Press.

Rothstein, Bo. 2005. *Social Traps and the Problem of Trust.* Cambridge: Cambridge University Press.
Sabatier, Paul. 1993. "Policy Change over a Decade or More." In *Policy Change and Learning: An Advocacy Coalition Approach*, edited by H. C. Jenkins-Smith. Boulder, Colo.: Westview.
Schimmelfennig, F. 2001. "The Community Trap: Liberal Norms, Rhetorical Action, and the Eastern Enlargement of the European Union." *International Organization* 55(1):47–80.
Schmidt, Vivien A. 1986. "Four Approaches to Scientific Rationality." *Methodology and Science* 19(3):207–32.
———. 1988. "Four Models of Explanation." *Methodology and Science* 21(3):174–201.
———. 2000. "Values and Discourse in the Politics of Adjustment." In *Welfare and Work in the Open Economy*, vol. 1, edited by Fritz W. Scharpf and Vivien A. Schmidt, 229–309. Oxford: Oxford University Press.
———. 2002a. *The Futures of European Capitalism.* Oxford: Oxford University Press.
———. 2002b. "Does Discourse Matter in the Politics of Welfare State Adjustment?" *Comparative Political Studies* 35(2):168–93.
———. 2006. *Democracy in Europe: The EU and National Polities.* Oxford: Oxford University Press.
———. 2007. "Trapped by Their Ideas: French Elites' Discourses of European Integration and Globalization." *Journal of European Public Policy* 14(4):992–1009.
———. 2008. "Discursive Institutionalism: The Explanatory Power of Ideas and Discourse." *Annual Review of Political Science* 11:303–26.
———. 2010a. "Taking Ideas *and* Discourse Seriously: Explaining Change through Discursive Institutionalism as the Fourth New Institutionalism." *European Political Science Review* 2(1):1–25.
———. 2010b. "On Putting Ideas into Perspective: Schmidt on Kessler, Martin and Hudson, and Smith." In *The Role of Ideas in Political Analysis: A Portrait of Contemporary Debates*, edited by Andreas Gofas and Colin Hay, 187–204. London: Routledge.
———. 2011. "Speaking of Change: Why Discourse Is Key to the Dynamics of Policy Transformation." *Critical Policy Studies* 5(2):106–26.
Seabrooke, Leonard. 2007. "The Everyday Social Sources of Economic Crises." *International Studies Quarterly* 51:795–810.
Searle, John 1995. *The Construction of Social Reality.* New York: Free Press.
Stein, Janice. 1989. *Getting to the Table.* Baltimore: Johns Hopkins University Press.
Stone, Deborah. 1988. *Policy Paradox and Political Reason.* Glenview, Ill.: Scott Foresman.

Taleb, Nassim Nicholas. 2007. *The Black Swan: The Impact of the Highly Improbable.* New York: Random House.
Torfing, J. 1999. *New Theories of Discourse: Laclau, Mouffe and Žižek.* London: Blackwell.
Toulmin, Stephen. 1958. *The Uses of Argument.* Cambridge: Cambridge University Press.
Weir, Margaret. 1992. *Politics and Jobs.* Princeton: Princeton University Press.
Wendt, Alexander. 1999. *Social Theory of International Politics.* Cambridge: Cambridge University Press.
Whorf, B. L. 1956. *Language, Thought and Reality: Selected Writings of Benjamin Lee Whorf.* Cambridge: MIT Press.
Wittgenstein, Ludwig. 1968. *Philosophical Investigations.* Oxford: Basil Blackwell.
———. 1972. *On Certainty.* New York: Harper and Row.
Wodak, Ruth. 2009. *The Discourse of Politics in Action.* Houndmills, U.K.: Palgrave.
Zaller, J. 1992. *The Nature and Origins of Mass Opinion.* New York: Cambridge University Press.

MARY HAWKESWORTH

4. From Policy Frames to Discursive Politics

Feminist Approaches to Development Policy and Planning in an Era of Globalization

As a policy that promises to improve the quality of life through economic expansion and poverty reduction, development has had near universal appeal for more than a century. Despite enormous differences that distinguish colonial powers from newly independent states, and liberal democratic regimes from state socialist systems, all states have embraced the "project of development" as a means to modernize society and economy and cultivate industrial infrastructure and educational capacities, while also rationalizing legal and administrative systems and forging national identity. As specified in the latest global articulation, the Millennium Development Goals, there has been impressive continuity in the contours of development, which has called for a global partnership to eradicate extreme poverty and hunger, achieve universal primary education, promote gender equality and empower women, reduce child mortality, improve maternal health, combat malaria and other diseases (including HIV/AIDS), and ensure environmental sustainability.[1] Since the mid-nineteenth century, developmentalists—an alliance of international agencies, national governments, policy experts, and private foundations—have worked in consort to attain these worthy goals.

Despite the near-universal assent to the project and the growing transnational alliance involved in the effort, development policies have consistently failed to achieve their stated objectives. According to the United Nations Development Program (UNDP) Human Development Reports, the economies of the majority of the world's nations worsened during the last two decades of the twentieth century. More than one hundred nations were worse off in 2005 than they had been in 1980. More than 1.5 billion people continue to live in extreme poverty, defined by the UNDP as living on less than $1.25 a day. The exponential growth in wealth over the past thirty years has been matched by a meteoric rise in inequality. The assets of the three wealthiest people in the world ($153 billion in 2010) are greater than the combined gross national product (GNP) of the forty-nine least-developed nations; and the assets of the two hundred richest persons in the world are greater than the combined income of 42 percent of the world population (Beneria 2003: xiii). While the wealthiest 20 percent of the world population controls 86 percent of world income, the poorest 20 percent controls only 1.1 percent (Moghadam 2005:41). Explicit commitments to poverty alleviation for the past half century have locked poor nations into a debt spiral where each year they pay $50 billion *more* in interest than the original sums they borrowed and have long since paid off.

How are we to make sense of the gulf between explicit commitments by national and international policy makers and institutions to improve the human condition and decades of development policies, which they have promoted, that heighten inequalities while doing little to reduce poverty? One strategy might be to proclaim development an unmitigated policy failure and to begin to probe the factors contributing to that failure such as inadequate resources, ineffective policy instruments, and the role of extraneous forces such as corrupt regimes, rival political factions, and violent conflict in derailing development efforts. This chapter takes an alternative approach. By undertaking a discursive analysis of development policies, I suggest that, contrary to explicit claims, the central project of development has not been poverty reduction, but the production, circulation, and naturalization of hierarchical power relations that figure the political economy of the North as the telos of economic development for the global South, while also positioning policy experts trained in the North as possessors of vital knowledge essential for the social transformation of the South. In addition to consolidating a geopolitical regime that accredits capitalism as the only alternative, development policy and planning produce and naturalize hierarchies of gender, race, and class even as they deploy a rhetoric of progress that proclaims development itself the remedy to such archaic forms of inequality.

To advance this alternative interpretation of development policy and planning, this chapter situates its methodology in a long tradition of "frame" and "discourse" analysis that seeks to illuminate representational practices that make particular configurations of power make sense. It then contrasts standard accounts of development policy and planning with several policy frames drawn from feminist political economy—Women and Development (WAD), Women in Development (WID), and Gender and Development (GAD)—which enable us to see development differently. By taking the lives of women and men at markedly different sites around the globe into consideration, these feminist frames illuminate power dynamics omitted from dominant development discourses. By contesting the presumption that development benefits everyone, these feminist frames demonstrate dynamics of class, gender, race, indigeneity, and region that differentially distribute the benefits and burdens of development within and across global sites. In contrast to development's narrative of progress, this chapter shows that racial and gender hierarchies are not remnants of "premodern" life: they are produced and sustained by development processes themselves. It also explores other ways of understanding what development policy has accomplished in relation to the accreditation of a form of policy expertise, the naturalization of the national economy as a unit of analysis, the comparative ranking of the world's nations on the basis of statistical indicators, and the legitimation of policy interventions that position the North as perpetually coming to the aid of the global South. By calling attention to representational practices that mask the operation of power, I suggest that feminist analysis demonstrates the importance of discursive politics both within the discipline of policy studies and to address structures of inequality integral to development processes.

Policy Frames

Like many concepts in political science, the notion of a "policy frame" has been used in multiple analytical contexts for very different purposes. Policy framing has been discussed in the policy process literature in relation to agenda setting, in the public opinion literature in relation to media "priming" and framing of particular policies, and in the social movement literature as "conscious strategic efforts by groups of people to fashion shared understandings of the world and of themselves that legitimate and motivate collective action" (McAdam, McCarthy, and Zald 1996:6). Within these literatures, framing is understood instrumentally, as a tool deployed by policy makers, analysts, or activists: "A 'frame' refers to the perspective or point of view on a policy issue that politicians, the public, or analysts use to make sense of it. It sets the issue within a context of values and beliefs that call attention to some facts rather than others and delimits the types of actions that would be appropriate for addressing the issue" (Zundel 1995:423; see also Gamson and Modigliani 1989; Snow and Benford 1992; Steinberg 1998).

The conception of a policy frame that surfaces in these contexts is thoroughly compatible with the scientific study of political behavior. As a methodological approach that gained popularity in the 1960s, "behavioralism" in political science assumed that it is possible to make a hard-and-fast distinction between facts and values. Seeking to describe and explain the facts of political life, the trained political analyst adheres to strict methodological guidelines to control for individual bias in observation, operationalization of terms, data collection, and analysis. Within the context of behavioral approaches to the study of politics, policy frames were construed as tools to generate testable hypotheses about political perception and misperception, the formation of and competition among advocacy coalitions, and the relationship of the mobilization of particular interests to policy outcomes (Sabatier and Jenkins Smith 1993).

A second approach to the conception of policy frames takes issue with behavioralist assumptions about the ease with which facts can be separated from values, challenging the conceptions of perception, cognition, and the relation between words and things embedded in the behavioralist paradigm (Hawkesworth 1988). Acknowledging that language is far more than a neutral medium through which the political world is described and explained, postbehavioralists suggest that politicians, policy makers, citizens, and policy analysts live within linguistic and symbolic systems that structure perception and understanding in ways that are always theoretically mediated and value-laden (Fischer and Forrester 1993). Rather than aspiring to a misguided notion of analytical neutrality, interpretive policy analysis suggests that policy frames provide insights into the complex ways that cognitive categories organize, shape, and classify experience (Brandwein 2006; Gottweis 2003; Hajer 1995; Schön and Rein 1994, 1996; Yanow 1995, 1996; Yanow and Schwartz-Shea 2006). Taking issue with social science methodologies that claim the possibility of neutral or unmediated observation, interpretive approaches to frame analysis suggest that claims about the world are constructed in relation to a range of partial perspectives, problematic assumptions, and determinate interests. Interpretive approaches to frame analysis offer a methodology tailored to the postpositivist recognition of the role that theoretical presuppositions play in cognition. Interpretive frame analysis expands the sphere of research to encompass tacit theoretical frameworks that support competing empirical claims. By exploring the impact of particular theories on the organization of perception, the operationalization of concepts, the selection of evidence, and the construction of explanations, interpretive frame analysis can illuminate questionable assumptions, foster recognition of the intricacy and complexity of "facts," and identify the structure of bias in particular accounts, contributing to more sophisticated policy analyses. Attentive to multiple sources of error and power dynamics within knowledge production, interpretive frame analysis encourages researchers to interrogate that which seems least contestable in order to engage complexity, plurality, and fallibility.

Situating their work within a long hermeneutic tradition, some interpretive policy theorists analyze policy frames in relation to cultural and linguistic practices, historical traditions, and philosophical frameworks to provide explanations consistent with the meaning of a policy to those involved in its creation and implementation. Although the meanings discerned by these interpretive policy analysts may go well beyond individual or shared conscious intentions, they illuminate and are consistent with key policy actors' intellectual horizons. Hermeneutic frame analysis seeks to capture the systems of meaning that enable particular constructions of policy problems, dynamics of political contestation, intractable policy dilemmas, and acceptable policy solutions.

While acknowledging the partiality of all perspectives and the role that contentious presuppositions play in the constitution of facticity (i.e., what comes to be perceived and accredited as a "fact"), interpretive policy analysts also recognize that policy frames are neither closed nor fixed. On the contrary, contestation over the conceptualization of a political "problem," negotiation over accredited policy meanings, and struggles over the institutionalization of particular policy frames are part and parcel of everyday politics—dimensions of politics rendered invisible by analytic approaches that presume unmediated perception, fixed interests, or stable, rationally ordered value preferences.

Acknowledging a space for critical reflexivity within policy frames is central to interpretive approaches to policy studies for several reasons.

It not only affords an account of policy change and identifies dimensions of political conflict that contribute to change, but also helps explain the role of the policy analyst. In the words of Maarten Hajer and David Laws, "To the extent a policy analyst can adopt a reflexive position *outside* the cognitive domain of the policy makers, he or she can get analytic leverage on how a particular discourse (defined as an ensemble of concepts and categorizations through which meaning is given to phenomena) orders the way in which policy actors perceive reality, define problems, and choose to pursue solutions in a particular direction" (2006:261). In this sense, the policy analyst contributes to knowledge of the political world by demonstrating how policy makers make sense of a complex world under conditions of uncertainty, and devise, or in some circumstances fail to devise, creative policy solutions. Although this approach does not claim value neutrality for policy analysts, it does suggest that the interpretive policy analyst is uniquely positioned to provide "practical insights into key policy dilemmas and produce meaningful knowledge that can help us understand controversy, resolve conflicts, and innovate" (Hajer and Laws 2006:265). In this sense, the interpretive policy analyst continues to contribute to Lasswell's (1951) vision of science in service to democracy.

A third approach to the discursive analysis of policy frames is less sanguine about the likelihood that policy analysts can gain critical purchase on the theoretical presuppositions structuring their work. Following Foucault's insight that scientific knowledge itself is productive, this approach suggests that policy analysts do more than explain the political world, they generate new representations, discourses, and practices that promote specific modes of political life. In keeping with poststructuralist understandings of the constitutive power of language, this approach suggests that policy "discourse"—structures of statements, concepts, categories, and beliefs specific to particular sociohistorical formations—is productive: it constitutes us as subjects in a determinate order of things (Derrida 1980, 1981a, 1981b; Foucault 1973, 1977, 1980; Scott 1988). Emphasizing that every scientific discourse is productive, generating determinate effects within its investigative domain, this approach cautions that policy planning and analysis must also be understood as a productive force that creates a world in its own image, even as it employs conceptions of passivity, neutrality, detachment, and objectivity to disguise and conceal its role (Foucault 1973, 1977).

The following analysis draws insights from both hermeneutic and poststructuralist approaches to demonstrate that development planning and policy has indeed created a world understood according to concepts of their own making. Statistical indicators, comparative measures, and models of growth devised to facilitate development planning have become the perceptual default in the twenty-first century. Precisely because the worldview naturalized through development policy is permeated by assumptions that privilege the most affluent while disadvantaging the poor, the final section of this chapter advocates *discursive politics*, that is, an attempt to disrupt and transform hegemonic discourses, sets of assumptions, and frameworks of analysis so thoroughly inured in the dominant worldview that they have been "naturalized," taken as given, inevitable, and unalterable.

As a social change strategy, discursive politics seeks to disrupt widely accepted understandings of the world by challenging established definitions, categories, and conceptions; demonstrating the shortcomings of the received view; showing that alternative understandings are possible; and mobilizing support for significant changes in accepted meanings or "discursive regimes." Several policy frames developed by feminist political economists, which illuminate the unintended but pervasive raced and gendered nature and effects of development policies, provide the means to analyze and subvert hegemonic development discourses.

Development: Modernization Theory as Policy Practice

Within policy and planning circles, development is typically discussed as a strategy to improve "quality of life." National governments, international agencies, and philanthropic foundations have launched various initiatives, short-term and long-term, to produce measurable improvement in the quality of life for people living in conditions of extreme adversity. Incorporating a belief in progress through rational planning and policy implementation, development has involved interventions to reorganize and relocate human communities, introduce mechanization of farming or "scientific agriculture," generate hydroelectric power, and foster industrialization and urbanization. It has also involved systemic campaigns to alter land use and property ownership, diversify the economy and the range of occupations, expand literacy, limit fertility, and provide law reform. Contrasting itself to "backwardness," "ignorance," and the corruption of "old ways," development is future-oriented, deploying rational planning, technocratic expertise, and means-ends calculations to promote human progress.

As one version of modernist discourse, development tells a story of linear progress, of movement from traditional modes of agricultural life to modern industrial and service economies. Embracing visions of modernization, both capitalist and socialist states have assumed that humans possess the ability to control and improve natural and social environments and have devised intricate projects to transform "traditional" agrarian subsistence economies to industrial, urbanized modern economies.

In *Seeing Like a State*, James Scott (1998) demonstrates that strategic interventions to improve the human condition require manifold preconditions—the creation of appropriate measures of progress, the determination of manageable units of analysis for comparison, the demarcation of normal patterns of change from anomalous episodes, and the identification of legitimate vehicles for social change. As Arturo Escobar (1992, 1995) has pointed out, the discovery of "underdevelopment" as a policy problem ushered in a host of new technologies of governance, which created a partnership between science and state that profoundly influenced the experience of development across the global South. In the decades following the Second World War, as economic development was transformed from the most neglected to the most popular subfield of economics, development expertise was constructed as apolitical, a new scientific specialization that takes the "national economy" as its object of inquiry (Bergeron 2006). Borrowing concepts created within industrial corporations, the discipline of economics, and the emerging field of comparative politics, development was construed as a marriage of science and state "to secure the basis of social harmony through national development" (Cowen and Shenton 1995:445). As Keynesian economic theory gained ascendency in the aftermath of the Depression, the borders of the nation-state were naturalized as the appropriate frame for analyses of production, circulation, and consumption, which could guide national policy makers in their efforts to stimulate growth (Bergeron 2006).

By creating and deploying measures of income, earnings, labor force participation in the formal economy, GNP, and GDP—indicators drawn largely from the "developed" economies of the North, all nations could be compared in terms of "economic growth." GNP, a new statistical indicator of national well-being, for the first time in history allowed whole nations "to be seen (and to see themselves) as poor" (Rahnema 1992:161). As an average that collapses the range of difference in a statistical array, per capita GNP renders vast class differences invisible, even as it enables comparisons across nations. Development experts defined nations with GNP lower than $100 per capita as poor and designated them suitable targets of development (Bergeron 2006:41). They relied on modernization theory to provide the rationale for development interventions, suggesting that a coherent development strategy required poor nations to emulate rich nations by industrializing.

Models for growth developed in Western industrialized nations assumed that the problem of underdevelopment could be traced to a lack of investment capital. For this reason, the earliest development models prescribed strategies "to fill the savings gap" by shifting labor from subsistence agriculture to the industrial sector, where higher wages would allow increased savings (Bergeron 2006:39). Although development experts argued that capital investment would increase GNP, providing benefits for all members of the national community in the long run, they also noted that efficient development strategies required skewed distribution of income that benefited the affluent because only "the saving class" could provide funds for investment (Bergeron 2006: 40). Like the classical economists who preceded them and the neoliberals who followed them, developmentalists in the era after the Second World War embraced a model of economic growth that required and legitimated significant income differentials. With the advent of econometrics, development experts devised complex mathematical models to measure the maturity of a nation's economy and to prescribe steps to foster growth. Emphasizing aggregate wealth and average GNP, these models did not make reduction in mass poverty a test of economic development, a point made by Jacob Viner as early as 1953 (Bergeron 2006:41–42).

In its *Measures for Economic Development of Underdeveloped Countries* (1951), the United Nations attributed underdevelopment to the internal economic structures of countries in the global South and advocated comprehensive development plans to apply scientific management to foster dramatic social, economic, and cultural transformations. Although the language of the report embraced monetarization and marketization, hallmarks of capitalist economic development, it also enthusiastically promoted planned industrialization that shared marked similarities to strategies developed within command economies. In the 1950s, the United Nations encouraged all developing countries to form national planning institutes staffed by Western-trained development economists and distributed planning manuals designed to help nations close the savings gap and enhance capital investment (Staudt 1991). The World Bank used the same planning tools in their investment programs, devising ever more sophisticated econometric models to foster investment and industrialization. And the United States government restricted aid through Alliance for Progress to those countries that had adopted approved national development plans. Planning based on claims of scientific expertise was thereby institutionalized as a critical precondition for both development and development aid.

By carving out the national economy as the unit of analysis and suggesting that factors internal to nations determined the stage of economic development, developmentalists effectively erased the role of colonialism, imperialism, and neocolonialism in producing and sustaining underdevelopment. By settling on GNP and GDP as viable indicators of national well-being, development experts also naturalized a conception of national well-being markedly insensitive to distributive inequities within a nation. And by positioning all nations within a modernizing dynamic, they fostered the optimistic notion that development experts possessed objective knowledge about "the level of investment, savings, imports, and external borrowings requisite to meet target rates of national growth. . . . The vagaries of social and economic life, the complexity of agents and the dynamics of social systems that might not fit this calibration" disappeared as topics of debate (Bergeron 2006:114).

Feminist Critiques of Development

The economic indicators used to measure growth were drawn not only from the experiences of industrialized nations in the North; they were also drawn from economic sectors dominated by male workers with profound consequences for women, who make up 80 percent of the world's poor. Precisely because these aggregate indicators were designed to measure distance from subsistence agriculture, they grossly undervalued the economies of the majority of nations in the South structured on the basis of informal, subsistence, and care economies.[2] Because women's labor fell largely within informal, subsistence, and care sectors, it was rendered invisible by these quantitative measures. As Lourdes Beneria (1997) demonstrates, national accounting measures devised to track progress in development underestimate women's work in four areas: subsistence production, informal paid work, domestic production and related tasks, and volunteer work within the community. Some of the kinds of labor omitted from econometric computations include production of food via hunting, fishing, gathering, and kitchen gardening; pounding, husking, and grinding foodstuffs; slaughter of animals, house cleaning, and child care; production of home crafts such as clothing, baskets, clay pots, and calabashes; and services provided by women, including fuel collection, funerals, haircuts, entertainment, and traditional medicine (Waring 1988). When the indicators used to measure development are drawn from practices in Western industrial economies, informal and subsistence economies—the kinds of economies where 70 percent of the world population continues to work—are actively distorted. As Irene Tinker (1976) points out, in East Africa, for example, where women do the bulk of farm and market work, feeding their families and communities, official economic measures indicate that only 5 percent of women are "in the labor force." Despite such systemic distortions, neglect of subsistence and informal sectors has been central to development strategies across the world, including prescriptions designed to address issues concerning women and development.

Having rendered women's waged and unwaged labor invisible by placing it outside standardized econometrics, development experts constructed women variously as backward or lazy, but in either case as a "problem" for development. With impressive unanimity, capitalist, Chinese Marxist, Soviet Marxist, and economic nationalist approaches to modernization converged on a singular solution for "the Woman Question." Women should enter the formal labor force both for the sake of the nation's economic development and for the sake of their own emancipation. According to this development logic, integrating women into the labor force within the formal sector would contribute to economic growth and elevate women's status, while also changing outmoded patriarchal mindsets as modern methods of production generated modernist belief systems.[3] Adoption of modern machine technologies was expected to promote norms of rationality, universalism, and egalitarianism, which in turn would engender mobility and achievement. The norms of "modern" society were expected to negate ascription standards—including gender—as determinants of the individual's socioeconomic status. As technological innovation made production less dependent on physical strength, opportunities for women would expand. Greater employment opportunities would contribute to higher aspirations as women began to recognize their own economic power. Inclusion of women in the modern industrial economy would thereby contribute to greater open-mindedness, resulting in the destruction of patriarchal ideologies that had justified women's exclusion from the "socially valued" productive sphere and from participation in all aspects of social and cultural life including the institutions of state.

The policy frames WAD, WID, and GAD have been developed by feminist scholars working in the fields of international political economy and development studies to shift from speculation about "the Woman Question" to theoretical and empirical analyses of the gendered dimensions and effects of development policies (Moser 1993; Parpart, Connelly, and Barriteau 2000; Staudt 1985, 1991, 1997). From their earliest articulation, feminist scholars have devised policy frames both to capture the complexity of women's and men's lives in the context of various development regimes, while also examining the world produced through policies that privilege particular conceptions of modernization. Through their interrogation of neo-Malthusian assumptions about poverty, ahistorical and decontextualized assumptions about male breadwinners, and gender dynamics embedded within national and international development strategies, these feminist policy frames afford markedly different insights into the nature and practices of development.

Women and Development: Reproduction and "Welfare"

In the benign formulation of Carolyn Moser (1993), the first initiatives of international development agencies aimed at women were "welfarist." Incorporating race- and class-based assumptions about women drawn from certain European and North American contexts, developmentalists assumed that women were exclusively mothers, that is, that their social roles and contributions were defined solely by reproduction. Modernizing nationalist regimes across the global South reinforced these assumptions by circulating discourses emphasizing that the family was key to the well-being of the nation and that women were the key to the well-being of families. Early development partnerships were forged between national governments and international agencies to provide "welfare," including nutrition projects for women and children and for pregnant and lactating mothers and medical interventions to address the high maternal and infant mortality rates of rural, agricultural workers. The development initiatives of the era after the Second World War, however, also contained language drawn from a much older antipoverty discourse, calling for intervention to address "overpopulation" (Briggs 2002) and to reduce large families and the number of "irregular marriages" in rural areas as crucial to improving the economy (Rai 2002:75).

For the English political economist Thomas Robert Malthus (1766–1834), population growth was a key factor in the explanation of poverty. From the mid-nineteenth century, the British Malthusian League helped popularize the idea that excessive reproduction caused poverty, constructing overpopulation as a timeless problem that contributes to hunger, homelessness, lack of educational opportunity, unemployment, and substandard housing. As Laura Briggs has documented, the idea of overpopulation as the primary cause of poverty gained popularity in the 1920s through the work of two groups, "reformers associated with the birth control movement and academic demographers and population experts associated with eugenics movement" (2002:83). Accepting the Malthusian premise that poverty results when population grows faster than wealth, population experts characterized the problem of overpopulation "as a matter of simple arithmetic," a statistical relation between rising birth rates and falling death rates as life expectancy increased, and between the growth of the population and the constancy of resources, such as land and agricultural production. The racial and class bias of this diagnosis was blatant as neo-Malthusians insisted not only that the "global population was growing alarmingly," but that "the segment that was increasing was of the worst sort" (Briggs 2002:83).

Within the geopolitical context of the Cold War, as the superpowers of the United States and the Soviet Union carved the world into their respective spheres of influence, development assistance assumed a familiar form, combining foreign aid, industrialization, import substitution, and population control. Whether dispensed by international agencies, philanthropies, or affluent nations, technical development assistance included "international family planning" as key to development. The language of "social hygiene" was deployed in ways that combined sanitation, infant and maternal health, and efforts to "improve the race" by "preventing degradation of the population" (Dore 2000:48). The Rockefeller Foundation used its Bureau of Social Hygiene to fund contraceptive programs in India, China, the Near East, Latin America, and the Caribbean, constructing the "undeveloped world" as a site in need of eugenic assistance as well as social reform (Briggs 2002).

When expert, scientific, and managerial knowledge were unleashed to solve the problem of overpopulation, "improving the race" was defined as a condition of development. As Kathleen Staudt (2008) has pointed out, no effort was made to mask the racism of early development efforts. Implying movement from a lower to a higher stage, development policies were initially designed to transform "uncivilized countries" into "civilized nations," a project that legitimized both colonial domination and the containment of "inferior" races. Proudly proclaiming that endeavor, the leading journal of international relations in the United States, *Foreign Affairs*, initially chose the title *Journal of Race Development* (Staudt 2008:140).[4] This civilizing mission used women's bodies as their proving ground. The global South became a laboratory for experimentation with contraceptive methods (spermicidal foams and jellies, Depo-Provera, intrauterine devices, and various forms of birth control pills).[5] Racist notions about the "dull-wittedness" of indigenous peoples led some development experts to counsel against the use of the diaphragm as a birth control method, encouraging adoption of far less reliable foams and jellies (Briggs 2002:105–7). Focusing on control of population rather than the reproductive wishes of individual women, development experts manifested greater concern with "acceptance rates" (calculated by numbers willing to try contraception) than failure rates of particular contraceptive methods or harmful side effects of particular products. The zeal to address overpopulation also motivated development experts to launch sterilization campaigns. In some nations, "eugenic sterilization laws" were passed that included poverty as a legitimate reason for sterilization (Briggs 2002:107). Sterilization abuse, along with experimentation on human subjects, became a hallmark of the "welfarist" approach to WAD. One United Nations Children's Fund (UNICEF) study documented an increase in sterilization rates of women in Brazil from 11 percent in the 1960s to 45 percent in the 1990s.

Indeed, in one rural area in northeastern Brazil, Maranhão, 79.8 percent of the women had been sterilized (Purewal 2001:113). In Puerto Rico, more than one-third of women of childbearing years had been sterilized by the 1970s (Briggs 2002).

Concerns about "the population bomb" (Goldstone 2010) have remained a staple of development discourse, so it is useful to consider what this account of poverty omits from the explanatory frame. When poverty is blamed on overpopulation, the maldistribution of global resources is conveniently elided from the analytic frame, as are all questions about patterns of ownership of the means of production (Rai 2002:57). The complex systems of resource extraction associated with colonialism and neocolonialism that have fostered underdevelopment and dependency disappear from the explanatory framework. In the words of Laura Briggs, Malthusian assumptions about overpopulation are like "a bulldozer that leveled all counterevidence in its path . . . although it failed utterly as an explanation of poverty . . . it had sufficient force that it persisted even in the face of evidence that flatly contradicted it" (2002:85).

Claims about overpopulation attribute poverty to the behavior of the poor themselves. "Uncontrolled reproduction" positions women in the global South as in need of a kind of technical assistance that only advanced science can remedy. Thus, it legitimates neocolonial projects to rescue poor women from dangers posed by their own bodies. The population control strand of development discourse is as much about preserving high modernism in the developed world as it is about modernizing developing nations. For central to the project of modernism is the rhetoric of "protecting" women and children from various evils, including self-induced harms. In undertaking this work, developmentalists purport to have the best interests of women at heart at the same time that they abridge women's reproductive freedom, subject their bodies to dangerous experimentation, and initiate programs that deprive women of their traditional livelihoods.

Women in Development: The Virtues of Waged Labor in the Formal Sector

In the early 1970s, critiques of failed development policies began to surface from several sectors. In her classic study, *Women's Role in Eco-*

nomic Development, Ester Boserup (1970) demonstrated that agricultural development projects in Africa were directing resources and training programs toward men, when women had traditionally been and continued to be the majority of farmers. Allowing Western gendered assumptions about traditional roles to govern policy, women's agricultural expertise was being ignored with dire consequences for agricultural production and for the environment as well as for women and their families. Westerners implementing development projects were replicating Western patterns of male dominance in their choice of trainees and employees in both industrial and agricultural development projects. Far from improving women's status and condition, Boserup showed that development policies were creating new forms of gender inequality, eroding the bases of women's power within traditional communities and exacerbating poverty.

Triggered by Boserup's recognition that the condition of women was being made worse by development policies that separated women's labor from agricultural labor, feminist scholars and policy makers began conceptualizing a new approach that emphasized the importance of women's labor to development, which became known in the field as WID. Construing women as partners in development who possessed needed expertise, WID endorsed the expansion of opportunities for women on dual grounds. Increasing women's participation in development efforts would heighten efficiency, thereby benefiting women as well as development itself.

Viewing the absence of women from development plans and policies as the major problem, WID sought to promote more efficient development by integrating women fully in the development process. Emphasizing that excluding women effectively wasted half the available development resources, WID proponents endorsed three strategies to solve the problem: creating separate women's projects that would capitalize on women's spheres of expertise; adding women's components to long-standing projects; and integrating women fully into development projects, particularly those involving the mechanization of agriculture and industrialization (Kabeer 1994; Moser 1993; Rai 2002).

Feminists working in the field of development studies successfully lobbied national governments and international institutions to shift to the WID focus. In 1973, for example, the United States Foreign Assistance Act was amended to include incorporation of women in national economies as part of its agenda. The United States Agency for International Development (USAID) created the Women in Development Office to implement this goal. Where earlier development efforts had targeted men exclusively, and collected no data on women, the USAID WID program specified that women be funded proportionate to their traditional participation in a particular activity or according to their presence in the population, whichever was greater (Poster and Salime 2002). The United States government also introduced changes in its tax codes, which encouraged offshore production, while also pressing firms in the United States to employ a largely female labor force (Bayes 2006; Briggs 2002). In the export processing zones that grew up across the global South, women constitute 70 to 90 percent of the factory workers producing textiles, leather goods, toys, electronic goods, and pharmaceuticals (Wichterich 2000).

As a policy frame, WID did not contest the assumptions of modernization theory. Assuming that modernization was inevitable, WID proponents sought to extend the benefits of modernization to women as well as to men. Ignoring class differences among women, WID programs placed a high premium on efforts to improve women's education and skills so they could compete more vigorously with men in the labor market. But they failed to consider the toll on women who tried to combine waged work in the formal sector with their unwaged work in the home. Even when employed in the formal sector, women continue to work unwaged second and third shifts devoted to the production of subsistence foods in small garden plots, food preparation, child care and elder care, early childhood education, and nursing care for the ill and infirm, as well as household cleaning and maintenance. One study in Mexico, for example, demonstrated that 90.5 percent of the economically active women were working a double shift *in the formal sector* compared with 62 percent of the men (Purewal 2001:106). The demands of unwaged work in the home had to be met over and above the hours devoted to waged labor in the market. The assumption that women's time is infinitely elastic and could expand indefinitely to absorb added responsibilities failed to consider the limits of human exhaustion (Bedford 2009; Elson 1995). Evidence of the harmful physical effects of overwork has become increasingly clear. Since the early 1980s, infant and child mortality rates have increased, reproductive tract infections have increased, and sterility has increased as women's health is taxed beyond endurance (Purewal 2001:101). Moreover, across the global South women have turned to their daughters for assistance in unwaged work. As a consequence, the number of girls in school has decreased and female illiteracy is rising.

The costs associated with WID strategies have also become increasingly clear. Long hours at work in the formal sector impose strains upon family life as women workers have little time to perform the domestic chores expected of them. Some families find it difficult to withstand such strains. In Salvador, for example, 80 percent of the married women in textile production are living without their husbands (Brooks 2007; Wichterich 2000). The strains associated with women's double and triple shifts have been changing family formations: 52 percent of poor households across the global South are now headed by women, compared with 20 percent in the 1990s, and 10 percent in the 1970s (Poster and Salime 2002:211). The health effects of employment in export processing zones, where workdays are long and working conditions are hazardous, are also palpable. Women working in export processing zones have twice the normal rate of miscarriages and deliver twice as many underweight babies. Poor lighting, eyestrain, and repetitive stress syndrome combine to impair the performance of women factory workers after a comparatively short period. The average work life for women factory workers in Thailand, for example, is five years. Job-induced problems with hand-eye coordination provide managers with a reason for firing workers. In Central America, a woman factory worker is let go after an average of seven years (Wichterich 2000). As capital has become increasingly mobile, factories have opened and closed with unexpected speed, as owners have moved in search of cheaper labor forces. All of these factors have resulted in formal-sector employment being far less dependable than WID proponents expected.

By emphasizing mechanisms to increase women's productivity in the formal sector, while also expecting women to contribute to the economic well-being of their households, WID recruited women as "partners in development" on markedly unequal terms. The inequality stems from the continuing failure to perceive women's unwaged labor in their homes and communities as "work." The UNDP has calculated that 70 percent of the work performed by women globally is unwaged and conservatively estimates the economic value of women's unwaged labor at $11 trillion annually. Ingrid Palmer characterizes women's unwaged labor as a "reproductive tax," created as the market "externalizes the costs of reproduction and life sustenance and entrusts it to women" (1992:69). The reproductive tax imposes an exacting toll on women in the global South, who are already working a triple shift in subsistence, productive, and reproductive labor.

By relying on the core assumption of modernization theory—that work in the formal sector is the key to women's liberty and equality—WID ignored structural forces that produce inequality. Although WID called attention to certain gendered problems within development, it ignored gender power within and across cultures. WID accredited formal sector norms grounded in men's employment experiences without attending to how poorly these norms suit women's complex responsibilities in the informal and subsistence sectors and within the household and community. WID also incorporated the unwarranted assumption that employment in the formal sector would generate linear progress for women across multiple gendered terrains. These assumptions of modernization theory have not been borne out in development projects across the global South (or for that matter in the industrialized nations). Inclusion of women in industrial production coexists with traditional belief systems and traditional patterns of women's subordination. A modicum of progress in one aspect of social life can be offset by setbacks in other areas of life. Increases in violence against women and divorce are more highly correlated with women's increasing economic independence than is elimination of patriarchal traditions or male gender privilege.

Gender and Development

Concern that the WID frame was perpetuating development strategies detrimental to women, families, and communities spurred the creation of an alternative analytic framework, known as Gender and Development (GAD), that was designed to focus on the unequal relations between men and women and their naturalization as a problem in and for development. Advocating analysis of the complex hierarchies of power grounded in the intersections of race, class, gender, sexuality, indigeneity, ethnicity, and nationality, GAD sought to investigate socially produced subordination and unequal power relations, which prevent equitable development and women's full participation within it. To envision equitable development, feminist proponents of GAD argued that rather than treating men and women across the global South as "target populations" (Schneider and Ingram 1993), they should be incorporated as full participants in decision making. Thus, GAD identified empowerment of the disadvantaged (including women) as integral to development. Rather than replicating gender and global inequalities in development planning and implementation, GAD suggested creation of strategies to allow the poor to identify their needs and recommend tactics to improve their condition.

The people-centered development envisioned by feminist GAD proponents drew insights from critiques of development advanced by the International Labor Organization (ILO), which pointed out that economic growth defined in terms of income generation in the formal sector was an inadequate conception of development because it ignored a host of basic human needs (Rai 2002). As early as the 1970s, the ILO argued that "trickle-down development" had reduced neither poverty nor unemployment, because poverty was not an "end" that could be eliminated by means of higher income alone. To remedy poverty in all its complexity required far more than the employment of able-bodied adults. For development to be effective, the needs of children, the elderly, and the disabled would have to be incorporated into the development agenda. According to this "basic needs" or "capacities" approach, poverty eradication required satisfaction of an "absolute level of basic needs" for everyone, which included physical needs (food, nutrition, shelter, health), as well as "agency achievements" such as participation, empowerment, and involvement in community life (Sen 1987). Successful approaches to poverty eradication also required a shift from a focus on household consumption to an understanding that people need infrastructure and services (sanitation, safe drinking water, public transportation, and health and educational facilities). Within this frame, individual and collective self-determination were as central to development as the satisfaction of physical needs and construction of adequate infrastructure. Thus, successful development required development agencies to shift from technocratic administration to fostering democratic deliberation in which the poor participated fully in setting and achieving development goals.

While advocating a focus on empowerment, capacity building, and need satisfaction, feminist proponents of GAD also advanced a critique of critical omissions from earlier articulations of a needs-based approach. Although basic needs advocates had used collective nouns, referring to families and households rather than individuals as their unit of analysis, they did not disaggregate households by gender. On the contrary, they ignored gender relations and gendered distributions of power and goods within families. As Naila Kabeer (1994) points out, households were imagined to be altruistic, benignly governed, and characterized by equitable distributions across age and gender, an image altogether at odds with empirical evidence. In cultivating methodologies to analyze GAD, feminist scholars sought to illuminate gendered divisions of labor in households and workplaces, gendered access to and control over resources and benefits, and critical differences in the material and social positions of women and men in various contexts. Keenly aware that taking women's empowerment seriously within GAD would challenge gender subordination and inequality, feminist development scholars pointed out that deliberations over needs and capacities would likely be confrontational and pose serious risks for women who serve as agents of social change (Madhok and Rai 2012).[6]

In efforts to improve development policies on the ground, feminist development scholars pressed international agencies such as UNDP, United Nations Development Fund for Women (UNIFEM), the World Bank, and the International Monetary Fund (IMF) to adopt a GAD framework. Although they have achieved impressive success in this effort, the outcomes have been far from what they had hoped. As Kathleen Staudt (2008:147–48) has demonstrated, the shift to GAD has moved scarce resources from WID units to men's programs, while substituting notions of equal treatment of men and women in development projects for analyses of gender power and redress of gender inequities. The operationalization of gender outside of feminist contexts has also suffered, as disaggregating data by sex is substituted for complex intersectional analyses that examine changing power relations among men and women in different ethnic, national, class, and race contexts.

The adoption of "women's empowerment" by the World Bank (2000) as a core commitment in its development agenda provides a useful example of what is lost in translation when an international institution appropriates a feminist policy frame (Vas Dev and Schech 2003). The World Bank's decision to include women's empowerment within its development objectives was the result of years of feminist efforts to influence the Bank's policies (Bedford 2009). In 2002, the World Bank issued new policy guidelines, *Integrating Gender into the World Bank's Work: A Strategy for Action*, which requires "gender mainstreaming," including gender impact analyses of all its programs as well as the promotion of women's economic development. To groom women as agents of their own empowerment, the World Bank has turned to microfinance. Adapted from a model of women's pooled savings and incorporated into the business model of the Grameen Bank, microfinance has been hailed as a form of economic salvation, embraced with "evangelical zeal" by governments, donors, and nongovernmental organizations as well as the World Bank (Tamale 2001:75).[7]

Microcredit provides very small loans to individuals to enable them to launch profit-generating business ventures. Multiple studies have shown that women are far better than men at repaying their loans. With repayment rates near 90 percent, microcredit programs for women have been demonstrated to be sound capital investments. In advocating microcredit, the World Bank follows a long-established development script, emphasizing that microcredit enables individual women to engage in market competition via microenterprise, promoting self-confidence and economic achievement, while fostering economic growth and promoting community development. Lending individual women investment capital, which they repay from their successful economic ventures, is an equitable means to economic development as well as a strategy for empowering women. "Empowering women" within this frame becomes a means to the expansion of capitalist markets, economic growth, and the protection of capital investments.

Feminist critics have pointed out that the meaning of women's empowerment is distorted when transplanted to a neoliberal context. Although microcredit programs can assist some women in meeting their most immediate subsistence needs, this falls far short of eliminating poverty. Unlike the loans made within women's informal financial solidarity groups, microloans from capitalist lenders are restricted to profit-generating business ventures and cannot be used to cover other expenses that burden the poor, such as those for funerals, health care, food, and fuel. Within the scope of capitalist institutions, microcredit programs focus on individual women rather than on prevailing gender and class and caste relations. Emphasizing changes in individual attitudes to promote self-confidence and economic achievement, they ignore structural inequalities. In addition, microcredit programs increase the debt of poor women, imposing new levels of stress as well as responsibility on individual women.

In contrast to the glowing descriptions of microcredit schemes, feminists have called attention to the "onerous terms of these loans," which are seldom publicized. In Uganda, one of the twenty poorest nations in the world, for example, the interest rate on microcredit loans is 18 percent, far higher than prevailing commercial rates in the country. The interest is compounded monthly. The borrower is allowed no grace period on interest payments; indeed, the first payment is due within seven days. To mobilize peer pressure to encourage repayment, each loan must be cosigned by two to three individuals who are not relatives of the borrower and who face financial liability if the borrower defaults (Tamale 2001:75–78). Microfinance rules specify that only one loan is allowed per family; only one person within the family may borrow microcredit funds. Thus, at the same time that microcredit fosters women's microenterprises, it also restructures family relations, precluding equal financial involvement of men and women in family businesses. Under "constant pressure to repay their loans, women have no time for literacy, health, job training, or seminars on political rights" (Tamale 2001:78). Development strategies grounded in women's microenterprise may help expand capitalist markets and foster economic growth, but they also heighten the economic responsibilities of women, magnifying their burden as providers for family subsistence. Thus, gender disadvantage is intensified for women, who already work longer hours than men, earn less, and are restricted to lower quality employment (Buvinic 1999:570).

World Bank discourses frame women's empowerment through microfinance in terms of individual self-help. But rhetoric about self-help as a means of poverty alleviation can also legitimate the government's abandonment of collective responsibility to meet the most basic needs of the people at the very moment that structural adjustment policies require governments to cut back on health, education, and welfare provision. Although World Bank strategies to "engender development" put women at the center of development policy, they do so in decidedly nonfeminist ways. Promoting self-employment through microfinance as the paradigm for poverty alleviation shifts responsibility for household income support from men to women, while also shifting the responsibility for "development" from the nation-state to the market. Operating squarely within the privatizing imperatives of neoliberalism, the World Bank deploys the language of GAD to favor private lending associations over public service agencies without necessarily improving the condition or status of women (Poster and Salime 2002:191–92). A new alliance of private microfinance providers, including Citibank and Deutsche Bank, now seek to "financialize" development, turning the poor into a financial asset. Suggesting that the risk in microfinance accrues to the lender, not the borrower, they have secured support from governments and international financial institutions to subsidize their corporate risk (Moodie 2012).

In the current era of globalization, GAD has been subsumed within a neoliberal framework that closes off approaches to women's empowerment that emphasize structural constraints circumscribing the conditions in which women and men live and work. Legacies of colonialism and the continuing depredations of neocolonialism are excluded from this approach to development, as is the maldistribution of resources and risk consolidated by capitalism.

In *Our Common Future*, the report of the World Commission on Environment and Development (1987), chaired by Gro Harlan Brundtland, introduced the language of sustainable development, suggesting new directions in development policy and planning. Pledging to reorient development toward questions of justice and ethics rather than unrelenting growth, the Brundtland Commission emphasized "needs" and "limits to growth" to sustain the environment's capacity to meet future need. Indeed, the commission insisted that development must meet the needs of the present without compromising the ability of future generations to meet their needs. Despite its strong commitment to ecological issues as a means to change the terms of the development debate, *Our Common Future* also operates within a liberal frame committed to market-led development. The primary policy instrument embraced by proponents of sustainable development is *persuasion* designed to mobilize development partnerships that link the private sector to policy activism on the part of states and international institutions.

Like so many mainstream approaches, sustainable development tends to separate women from core questions of economic, social, and political processes (Rai 2002). And while persuasion is the sole means legitimated to redress poverty, legally binding contracts have been deployed to facilitate public-private partnerships that protect new modes of extraction, variously labeled bioprospecting or biopiracy. Under the rubric of sustainable development, pharmaceutical, medical, and agricultural corporations have been appropriating indigenous knowledge of plants and animals as well as the biogenetic resources of indigenous peoples, patenting them for commercial purposes, and "transforming nature's bounty into commodities of global economic value" (Isla 2007:324). Rather than fostering economic justice, "sustainable development and natural capital have intensified the theft of Latin American conditions of production and survival" (327). In the words of Michael Goldman, "as long as the commons is perceived as only existing within a particular knowing, called development, with its unacknowledged structures of dominance ... [corporate environmental groups] will continue to serve the institution of development, whose *raison d'être* is restructuring Third World capacities and social-natural relations to accommodate transnational capital expansion" (1998:47).

Toward a Discursive Politics

Maxine Molyneux has suggested that gender analysis has the capacity to revolutionize development policy debates.[8] By demonstrating that national and international development agencies and actors are "affected by and in turn affect race and gender relations," feminist analysis dispels once and for all mistaken notions about the neutrality of technical expertise (Molyneux 2000:34). Although development institutions are far from unified expressions of intentionality, they nonetheless "create, perpetuate and enforce inequality of status and means" (39). Far from being models of disembodied rationality, development planning and implementation are better understood as sites of struggle in which competing interests vie for power. As the feminist critiques of development discussed in this chapter make clear, feminist analyses illuminate crucial facets of struggle neglected by mainstream approaches.

The feminist policy frame analysis presented here is informed by a postpositivist conception of knowledge, which emphasizes that theoretical presuppositions structure perception, the definition of an appropriate research question, the nature of acceptable evidence, the data collection and analysis, and the interpretation of research findings. By requiring the investigation of multiple interpretations of the same phenomenon, this methodology illuminates theoretical assumptions that frame and accredit the constitution of facticity within each explanatory account. By explicating alternative development frames, feminist analysis makes visible social and political values in need of critical assessment. Juxtaposing divergent accounts creates a context in which to engage questions concerning the adequacy and internal consistency of theoretical presuppositions, the standards of evidence, and the models of explanation accredited by the competing accounts (Hawkesworth 1988, 2006). As a postpositivist methodology that is attuned to multiplicity and complexity, interpretive frame analysis recognizes that knowledge claims are produced and accredited within specific intellectual communities (including feminist communities) and provides a mechanism for comparatively assessing accounts that emerge within markedly different communities.

Feminist frame analysis might also be construed as a "self-consciously derived theoretical tool in service of a politics" (Grant 1993:119).[9] In this view, feminist analytical frames serve as a bridge between intellectual inquiry and transformative politics. On this account, a central question concerning the utility of feminist frame analysis is whether it makes development policy debates more intelligible and more actionable. If comparisons of alternative feminist frames—WAD, WID, and GAD— illuminate inequitable dimensions of development masked by hegemonic development discourses, then they can help devise political strategies to resist domination and oppression.

The juxtaposition of multiple development frames in this chapter suggests that it is a mistake to take the explicit claims of developmentalists at face value. Contrary to their rhetoric, the central project of development has not been poverty reduction, but the production, circulation, and naturalization of hierarchical power relations. Development policy and planning efforts have institutionalized modernization theory in ways that situate the political economy of the North as the telos of economic development for the global South, while also positioning policy experts trained in the North as possessors of vital knowledge essential for the social transformation of the South. Under the guise of objective scientific expertise, they have consolidated a geopolitical regime that accredits capitalism as the only alternative, enshrined the nation-state as the only viable mode of governance, and rendered invisible systemic inequalities within contemporary political systems. They have produced and naturalized hierarchies of gender, race, and class even as they deploy a rhetoric of progress that proclaims development itself the remedy to such archaic forms of inequality.

Rather than a century of policy failure, developmentalists have succeeded in producing a world that privileges waged labor in the formal economy, mechanization, industrialization, and capitalist social relations. Envisioning *homo economicus* as the telos of human progress, they have legitimated massive interventions in worklife, the organization of physical space, and mental habits and attitudes, while professing commitment to laissez-faire modes of governance. By attributing underdevelopment to the internal logic of national economies in the global South, they have masked longer histories of colonial and patriarchal domination that structured inequities across systems of governance, education, and economic organization (plantation and slave systems), facilitated particular modes of resource extraction, and contributed to the construction of trade routes and markets within a "center-periphery" frame. Like colonialism, development discourses have also produced raced and gendered patterns of skilling and deskilling, differences in political rights and economic opportunities, political visibility and invisibility, and subtle and unsubtle manipulations of life through eugenic strategies of population control and callous experimentation on human subjects. Despite unprecedented increases in inequality within and across nations, developmentalists have also succeeded in producing an impressive transnational consensus that capitalism is the only viable economic alternative.

Discursive politics attempt to disrupt and transform hegemonic discourses, sets of assumptions, and frameworks of analysis so thoroughly inured to the dominant worldview that they have been "naturalized," taken as given, inevitable, and unalterable. Feminist frame analysis suggests that development—narrowly construed in terms of capitalist strategies to promote economic growth—is sorely in need of disruption and transformation. If poverty is to be reduced, much less eradicated, then trickle-down theories must be supplemented with serious attention to redistribution. To the extent that feminist interpretive frame analysis illuminates the power dynamics of development discourses and their critical erasures and occlusions, as well as their remarkably productive effects, it contributes to critical modes of discursive politics, forms of democratic political argumentation and struggle that may produce more equitable policies in the future.

Notes

1. In September 2000, leaders of all the nations of the world convened at the United Nations to launch a new global partnership to reduce extreme poverty by 2015. They committed their nations to the achievement of these eight Millennium Development Goals and created timetables for their achievement. Under the auspices of the United Nations, World Summits were held in 2005 and 2010 to assess progress and reinvigorate commitments to meet these goals by 2015.

2. Emphasizing relation to markets, paid remuneration, and production (typically for profit), national economic statistics incorporate a procapitalist bias precisely because capitalism concentrates attention on the market as the heart of economic activities. As early as 1947, Kuznets called this bias to the attention of the United Nations, noting that these statistical indicators put agricultural societies, where the majority of the population was involved in subsistence agriculture, at a disadvantage. In 1960, a working group of African statisticians recommended including subsistence production in agriculture, forestry, and fishing in the computation of national statistics, a strategy endorsed by International Conference of Labor Statisticians in 1966 (Waring 1988:114).

3. It is worth noting that this kind of economic determinism was every bit as prevalent in liberal democratic discussions as in state socialist and nationalist economic discussions of development. For more extensive discussion of these similarities see Rai 2002.

4. In a classic act of historical revisionism, *Foreign Affairs* has masked this history. Its web site claims its heritage only to 1922, when the name *Foreign Affairs* was adopted; but library catalogues indicate that the journal was founded in 1910 as the *Journal of Race Development*. The name was changed to the *Journal of International Relations* in 1919, then to *Foreign Affairs* in 1922.

5. Depo-Provera was an injectable birth control drug disbursed across the Caribbean, Latin America, and Africa before adequate clinical trials, causing harmful side effects for thousands of women and their offspring.

6. The nature of these risks range from ostracism and rape to murder; for a full discussion, see Madhok and Rai 2012.

7. Simel Esim (2001) provides an overview of these "informal financial solidarity groups," including *roscas* in Latin America, *tontines* and *oususus* in West Africa, and *gamayes* in the Middle East. The most widely discussed of these efforts, however, is that developed by the Self-Employed Women's Association (SEWA), which was founded in Ahmedabad, Gujarat, India, in 1972, and which culminated in the creation of SEWA Bank using the deposits and shared capital of its members to give women access to small

loans. Funded by the pooled resources of women's collectives, these programs afford their members decision power in loan approval, hands-on practice in participatory governance, capacity-building opportunities in collective microenterprises, and innovative strategies for political mobilization and electoral accountability. Access to loans also enables members to meet immediate needs.

8. Molyneux advanced her claim about the revolutionizing effects of gender analysis in a slightly different context, the analysis of state institutions. In extending her argument to development discourses, I believe that I am being faithful to the tenor of her claims.

9. Grant's explicit focus was feminist standpoint claims rather than feminist frame analysis. But her insights are helpful in assessing the utility of feminist frame analysis, for she illuminates the bridge between intellectual inquiry and discursive politics.

References

Bayes, Jane. 2006. "The Gendered Impact of Globalization on the United States." In *Women, Democracy, and Globalization in North America: A Comparative Study*, edited by Jane Bayes, Patricia Begné, Laura Gonzalez, Lois Harder, Mary Hawkesworth, and Laura MacDonald, 145–71. New York: Palgrave.

Bedford, Kate. 2009. *Developing Partnerships: Gender, Sexuality and the Reformed World Bank*. Minneapolis: University of Minnesota Press.

Beneria, Lourdes. 1997. "Accounting for Women's Work: The Progress of Two Decades." In *The Women, Gender and Development Reader*, edited by N. Visvanathan, Lynn Duggan, Laurie Nisonoff, and Nancy Wiegersma, 114–20. London: Zed.

———. 2003. *Gender, Development and Globalization: Economics as If All People Mattered*. New York: Routledge.

Bergeron, Suzanne. 2006. *Fragments of Development: Nation, Gender, and the Space of Modernity*. Ann Arbor: University of Michigan Press.

Boserup, Ester. 1970. *Women's Role in Economic Development*. New York: St. Martin's.

Brandwein, Pamela. 2006. "Studying the Careers of Knowledge Claims." In *Interpretation and Method*, edited by D. Yanow and P. Schwartz-Shea, 228–43. Armonk, N.Y.: M. E. Sharpe.

Briggs, Laura. 2002. *Reproducing Empire: Race, Sex, Science and U.S. Imperialism in Puerto Rico*. Berkeley: University of California Press.

Brooks, Ethel. 2007. *Unraveling the Garment Industry: Transnational Organizing and Women's Work*. Minneapolis: University of Minnesota Press.

Buvinic, Mayra. 1999. *Promoting Gender Equality*. Oxford: Blackwell/UNESCO.

Cowen, Michael P., and Robert Shenton. 1995. *Doctrines of Development.* New York: Routledge.
Derrida, Jacques. 1980. *The Archaeology of the Frivolous.* Pittsburgh: Duquesne University Press.
———. 1981a. *Dissemination.* Translated by Barbara Johnson. Chicago: University of Chicago Press.
———. 1981b. *Positions.* Translated by Alan Bass. Chicago: University of Chicago Press.
Dore, Elizabeth. 2000. "One Step Forward, Two Steps Back: Gender and the State in the Long Nineteenth Century." In Dore and Molyneux, *Hidden Histories of Gender and State in Latin America,* 3–28.
Dore, Elizabeth, and Maxine Molyneux, eds. 2000. *Hidden Histories of Gender and State in Latin America.* Durham: Duke University Press.
Elson, Diane. 1995. "Male Bias in Macro-Economics: The Case of Structural Adjustment." In *Male Bias in the Development Process,* edited by Diane Elson, 164–90. Manchester: University of Manchester Press.
Escobar, Arturo. 1992. "Planning." In *The Development Dictionary,* edited by Wolfgang Sachs, 132–45. London: Zed.
———. 1995. *Encountering Development: The Making and Unmaking of the Third World.* Princeton: Princeton University Press.
Esim, Simel. 2001. "Sisters' Keepers: Economic Organizing among Informally Employed Women in Turkey." In *An International Feminist Challenge to Theory,* edited by Vasilikie Demos and Marcia Texler Segal, 163–78. Amsterdam: Elsevier Science.
Fischer, Frank, and John Forester, eds. 1993. *The Argumentative Turn in Policy Analysis and Planning.* Durham: Duke University Press.
Foucault, Michel. 1973. *The Order of Things: An Archaeology of the Human Sciences.* New York: Vintage.
———. 1977. *Discipline and Punish: The Birth of the Prison.* Translated by Alan Sheridan. New York: Vintage.
———. 1980. *The History of Sexuality.* Vol. 1. New York: Vintage.
Gamson, William A., and Andre Modligliani. 1989. "Media Discourse and Public Opinion on Nuclear Power: A Constructionist Approach." *American Journal of Sociology* 95(1):1–37.
Goldman, Michael. 1998. "Inventing the Commons: Theories and Practices of the Commons' Professional." In *Privatizing Nature: Political Struggles for the Global Commons,* 20–51. New Brunswick, N.J.: Rutgers University Press.
Goldstone, Jack A. 2010. "The New Population Bomb: The Four Megatrends That Will Change the World." *Foreign Affairs* 89(1):1.
Gottweis, Herbert. 2003. "Theoretical Strategies of Post-Structuralist Policy Analysis: Towards an Analytics of Government." In *Deliberative Policy Analysis: Understanding Governance in the Network Society,* edited by

Maarten A. Hajer and Hendrik Wagenaar, 247–65. Cambridge: Cambridge University Press.
Grant, Judith. 1993. *Fundamental Feminism: Contesting Core Concepts of Feminist Theory.* New York: Routledge.
Hajer, Maarten. 1995. *The Politics of Environmental Discourse: Modernization and the Policy Process.* Oxford: Oxford University Press.
Hajer, Maarten, and David Laws. 2006. "Ordering through Discourse." In *The Oxford Handbook of Public Policy*, edited by Michael Moran, Martin Rein, and Robert E. Goodin, 251–68. Oxford: Oxford University Press.
Hawkesworth, Mary. 1988. *Theoretical Issues in Policy Analysis.* Albany: SUNY Press.
———. 2006. *Feminist Inquiry: From Political Conviction to Methodological Innovation.* New Brunswick, N.J.: Rutgers University Press.
Isla, Ana. 2007. "An Ecofeminist Perspective on Biopiracy in Latin America." *Signs: Journal of Women in Culture and Society* 32(2):323–32.
Kabeer, Naila. 1994. *Reversed Realities: Gender Hierarchies in Development Thought.* London: Verso.
Lasswell, Harold. 1951. "The Policy Orientation." In *The Policy Sciences*, edited by Harold Lasswell and Daniel Lerner. Stanford: Stanford University Press.
Madhok, Sumi, and Shirin Rai. 2012. "Agency, Injury and Transgressive Politics in Neoliberal Times." *Signs: Journal of Women in Culture and Society* 37(3).
McAdam, Doug, John McCarthy, and Mayer Zald. 1996. *Comparative Perspectives on Social Movements: Political Opportunities, Mobilizing Structures, and Cultural Framings.* Cambridge: Cambridge University Press.
Moghadam, Valentine. 2005. *Globalizing Women: Transnational Feminist Networks.* Baltimore: Johns Hopkins University Press.
Molyneux, Maxine. 2000. "Twentieth-Century State Formations in Latin America." In Dore and Molyneux, *Hidden Histories of Gender and State in Latin America*, 33–83.
Moodie, Megan. 2012. "Microfinance and the Gender of Risk." *Signs: Journal of Women in Society* 38(1).
Moser, Carolyn. 1993. *Gender Planning and Development: Theory, Practice, Training.* New York: Routledge.
Palmer, Ingrid. 1992. "Gender Equity and Economic Efficiency in Adjustment Programmes." In *Women and Adjustment Policies in the Third World*, edited by Haleh Afshar and Carolyn Dennis, 69–83. Basingstoke: Macmillan.
Parpart, Jane, Patricia Connelly, and Eudine Barriteau, eds. 2000. *Theoretical Perspectives on Gender and Development.* Ottawa: International Development Research Centre.
Poster, Winifred, and Zakia Salime. 2002. "The Limits of Micro-Credit:

Transnational Feminism and USAID Activities in the United States and Morocco." In *Women's Activism and Globalization: Linking Local Struggles to Transnational Politics*, edited by N. Naples and M. Desai, 189–219. New York: Routledge.
Purewal, Navtej. 2001. "New Roots for Rights: Women's Responses to Population and Development Policies." In *Women Resist Globalization: Mobilizing for Livelihood and Rights*, edited by Sheila Rowbotham and Stephanie Linkogle, 96–117. London: Zed.
Rahnema, Majid. 1992. "Poverty." In *The Development Dictionary*, edited by Wolfgang Sachs, 158–76. London: Zed.
Rai, Shirin. 2002. *Gender and the Political Economy of Development*. Cambridge, England: Polity.
Sabatier, Paul A., and Hank C. Jenkins Smith, eds. 1993. *Policy Change and Learning: An Advocacy Coalition Approach*. Boulder, Colo.: Westview.
Schneider, Ann, and Helen Ingram. 1993. "Social Constructions and Target Populations: Implications for Politics and Policy." *American Political Science Review* 87(2):334–47.
Schön, Donald A., and Martin Rein. 1994. *Frame Reflection: Toward the Resolution of Intractable Policy Controversies*. New York: Basic.
———. 1996. "Frame Critical Policy Analysis and Frame Reflective Policy Analysis." *Knowledge and Policy: The International Journal of Knowledge Transfer and Utilization* 9(1):85–104.
Scott, James. 1998. *Seeing Like a State: How Certain Schemes to Improve the Human Condition Have Failed*. New Haven: Yale University Press.
Scott, Joan. 1988. "Deconstructing the Equality vs. Difference Debate: Or the Uses of Poststructuralist Theory for Feminism." *Feminist Studies* 14(1):575–99.
Sen, Amartya. 1987. *On Ethics and Economics*. Oxford: Basil Blackwell.
Snow, David A., and Robert D. Benford. 1992. "Master Frames and Cycles of Protest." In *Frontiers in Social Movement Theory*, edited by A. D. Morris and C. McClurg Mueller, 133–55. New Haven: Yale University Press.
Staudt, Kathleen. 1985. *Women, Foreign Assistance and Advocacy Administration*. New York: Praeger.
———. 1991. *Managing Development: State, Society and International Contexts*. Newbury Park, Calif.: Sage.
———. 1997. *Women, International Development and Politics: The Bureaucratic Mire*. Philadelphia: Temple University Press.
———. 2008. "Gendering Development." In *Politics, Gender, and Concepts: Theory and Methodology*, edited by Gary Goetz and Amy Mazur, 136–56. Cambridge: Cambridge University Press.
Steinberg, Marc W. 1998. "Tilting the Frame: Considerations on Collective Framing from a Discursive Turn." *Theory and Society* 27:845–72.

Tamale, Sylvia. 2001. "Between a Rock and a Hard Place: Women's Self-Mobilization to Overcome Poverty in Uganda." In *Women Resist Globalization: Mobilizing for Livelihood and Rights*, edited by Sheila Rowbotham and Stephanie Linkogle, 70–85. London: Zed.

Tinker, Irene. 1976. *Women and World Development*. Washington: Overseas Development Council.

United Nations. 1951. *Measures for Economic Development of Underdeveloped Countries*. New York: United Nations Publications.

Vas Dev, Sanjugta, and Susanne Schech. 2003. "Gender Justice: The World Bank's New Approach to the Poor." Paper presented at the XIX World Congress of the International Political Science Association, Durban, South Africa, June 29–July 4.

Visvanathan, Nalini, Lynn Duggan, Laurie Nisonoff, and Nan Wiergersma, eds. 1997. *The Women, Gender, and Development Reader*. London: Zed.

Waring, Marilyn. 1988. *If Women Counted: A New Feminist Economics*. San Francisco: Harper and Row.

Wichterich, Christa. 2000. *The Globalized Woman: Reports from a Future of Inequality*. London: Zed.

World Bank. 2000. *Advancing Gender Equality: World Bank Action since Beijing*. Washington: World Bank, Gender and Development Group.

———. 2002. *Attacking Poverty: World Development Report 2000/01*. New York: Oxford University Press.

World Commission on Environment and Development. 1987. *Our Common Future*. Oxford: Oxford University Press.

Yanow, Dvora. 1995. "Practices of Policy Interpretation." *Policy Sciences* 29:111–26.

———. 1996. *How Does a Policy Mean? Interpreting Policy and Organizational Actions*. Washington: Georgetown University Press.

Yanow, Dvora, and Peregrine Schwartz-Shea, eds. 2006. *Interpretation and Method*. Armonk, N.Y.: M. E. Sharpe.

Zundel, Alan. 1995. "Policy Frames and Ethical Traditions: The Case of Homeownership for the Poor." *Policy Studies Journal* 23(3):423–34.

PART III

Policy Argumentation on the Internet and in Film

STEPHEN COLEMAN

5. The Internet as a Space for Policy Deliberation

This chapter explores three aspects of the policy process in contemporary representative democracies that seem particularly ripe for reconfiguration. These relate to ways of defining policy problems; ways of gathering, organizing, and making sense of the knowledge that underpins policy; and ways of debating policy options. Empirical accounts of how the Internet is implicated in changes to the policy-making process abound in the recent policy literature; they focus on new means of interdepartmental, agency, and national policy transfer (Drake, Steckler, and Koch 2004; Stone 1999; Wolman and Page 2002); innovations in evidence gathering and knowledge management (Foss 2007; Pawson 2006; Sanderson 2002); and attempts to connect hybrid policy issues (Koppenjan, Kars, and van der Voort 2009; Papadopoulos 2003; van Kersbergen and van Waarden 2004). These shifts in practice are all worthy of note but do not address the central question of this chapter, which is how the Internet might provide the kind of discursive space that could engender and coordinate forms of experientially and affectively framed deliberation consistent with the "argumentative turn" in policy studies.

A key characteristic of the "argumentative turn" has been its emphasis on what Warren (1992) refers to as "expansive democracy": "increased participation, either by means of small-scale direct democracy or through strong discursive linkages between citizens and broad-scale institutions by pushing democracy beyond traditional political spheres, and by relating decision-making to the persons who are affected" (Hajer and Wagenaar 2003:3). Drawing attention to new spaces of the political, theorists of the "argumentative term" have not had a great deal to say about new information and communication technologies. There has been a sense in which the mushrooming literature on e-democracy has tended to ignore policy outcomes. While excitedly focusing on the potential for civic connection, deliberative policy theorists have paid wise attention to new practices of policy formation and decision making, without giving sufficient thought to the empirical manifestations of communicative networks. The question to be addressed in this chapter is whether the democratic potential of the Internet and the turn toward more participatory and deliberative governance are mutually reinforcing.

But before we are in a position to reflect on that critically important question, we need to be sure that they are not lost in a mist of hyperbolic rhetoric that all too commonly surrounds discussion of the Internet. Let me attempt to outline the sense in which the policy-making context is changing.

A prevalent characteristic of contemporary policy making has been the diffusion of innovative ideas and practices through interdependent but uncoordinated networks. Castells suggests that we are witnessing "the transformation of the sovereign nation-state that emerged throughout the modern age into a new form of state," which he refers to as "the network state," characterized by "shared sovereignty and responsibility between different states and levels of government; flexibility of governance procedures; and greater diversity of times and spaces in the relationships between governments and citizens compared to the preceding nation-state" (2008:40). Even if one is not persuaded that there has been such a radical transformation in the morphology of state power, few would disagree that an unprecedentedly diverse range of globally expansive and temporally synchronous communicative networks have emerged within late modernity, precipitating enlarged opportunities for casual linkage between dispersed social actors. Granovetter's important observation that "whatever is to be diffused can reach a larger number of people, and traverse greater social distance (i.e. path length), when passed through weak ties rather than strong" is important here; networks generate interpersonal connectivity by creating bridges between dispersed nodes—and "all bridges are weak ties" (1973:1366, 1364).

Unleashed by innovations in microelectronics and communication technologies, the emergent ubiquity of weakly linked networks that exceed state boundaries has coincided with a decentering of political power and an escalation of new patterns of dispersed and unorthodox collective action (Bennett 2003; Diani and McAdam 2003; Flinders 2004; Kooiman 2003; Rhodes 2002). To be a powerful network actor in the early twenty-first century, capable of accessing and even influencing policy debates, entails a capacity to disseminate information, to appear to others on one's own terms, and to address others who do not necessarily share one's own characteristics. Those who possess dexterity in techniques of switching between networks and exploiting weak links have an advantage in an era of distributed governance. The Internet—which is in reality a network of communication networks linked by codified programs that determine metacommunication—has emerged as an axial zone of appearance and influence. It may not be where policy is *made* (whatever form that might take), but it is increasingly the space in which it is shaped, announced, contested, and evaluated.

Scholars have devoted much speculative attention to the implications of social networks in general, and the Internet in particular, for democratic policy making. At the risk of oversimplifying perspectives, conjecture seems to have fallen into three categories. First, there are those who see the rise of the Internet, with its low cost of entry to public communication, its inherent capacity for interactive feedback, and its tendency to facilitate dispersed virtual networks, as a precursor to the demise of representative democracy. The rhetoric is rich. Morris has asserted that "the internet offers a potential for direct democracy so profound that it may well transform not only our system of politics but our very form of government. . . . Bypassing national representatives and speaking directly to one another, the people of the world will use the internet increasingly to form a political unit for the future" (2001). Similarly, Grossman claims that "in kitchens, living rooms, dens, bedrooms, and workplaces throughout the nation, citizens have begun to apply . . . electronic devices to political purposes, giving those who use them a degree of empowerment they never had before. . . . By pushing a button, typing on-line, or talking to a computer, they will be able to tell their president, senators, members of Congress, and local leaders what they want them to do and in what priority order" (1995:146). In anticipating the redundancy of political representation as we have known it, writers such as these seem to have subscribed to a dizzy form of technological determinism. It is not my intention to engage in much detail with this category of argument, as empirical evidence for such a political revolution remains elusive.

A second response by scholars has been to dismiss with some skepticism the likelihood that "networked politics" will have much impact on established patterns and practices of power. Culture, they have argued, is more powerful than communicative technologies, and, over time, entrenched configurations of socioeconomic interest will assert themselves, appropriate the new modes of interaction, and reinforce their hegemony (Hindman 2009; Margolis and Resnick 2000). Compelling empirical research has indeed shown how vested political interests have utilized, exploited, and sought to control the new communications ecology, adapting their repertoires of domination to survive and indeed augment their legitimacy. Governments, parliaments, political parties, and politicians have adopted a wide range of e-communication strategies, but these have generally amounted to little more than the replication of long-standing institutional practices within a virtual setting (Coleman and Moss 2008; Gibson, Nixon, and Ward 2003). Contra Castells, the characterization of "politics as normal" suggests that networks are simply another terrain that must be negotiated by wielders of state power.

A third category of scholarly response acknowledges the enduring nature of political representation and the deep socioeconomic disparities that underlie most institutional policy making, while arguing that, faced by the ubiquity of networked relationships, actors within the policy process are having to adapt to new modes of democratic accountability and expectations for civic efficacy (Coleman and Blumler 2009). Pressure arises from the compression of distances that once seemed to justify a thin and irregular communicative relationship between political representatives, who "speak for" the public, and the remote and vicariously spoken-for citizens. As scope for both instantaneous and asynchronously stored interactive exchanges between representatives and the represented has emerged, the right of the former to speak for, but not with, the latter has diminished. An expectation that democracy entails more than the occasional election of elite actors and that policies are most effective when they are shaped, implemented, and evaluated in coproduction with those likely to be affected by them has stimulated calls for more direct forms of representation (Coleman 2005; Coleman and Blumler 2009). At the same time, the problem of coordination, which is a traditional barrier to collective action, has been partially overcome by the relative convenience and low cost of virtual mobilization. Whereas traditionally it was much easier for well-resourced, organized, and confident people to find others who share their interests, preferences, and values than for those who have little money, time, or self-efficacy to do so, the Internet enables dispersed citizens to form networks that are potentially capable of intervening in the policy process. As representatives are forced into more dialogical relationships with the people they had hitherto spoken for as surrogates, and as citizens establish profuse relations of lateral sociability, scholars are beginning to ask whether the conventional dynamics of policy making can be sustained.

Making sense of the reconfigurative role of networks calls for a rejection of the seductive belief that the architectonics of hyperlinkage are in themselves a means of ensuring that hitherto marginalized or excluded actors can engage in meaningful and consequential policy discourse. Three critical factors need to be acknowledged.

The first factor is that networks consist in more than abstract nodal linkages. As with all communicative relationships, networks are contextually and contingently enacted by complex human beings. Network analyses too often assume a reductive form, endlessly plotting internodal linkages, but failing "to explore the ways in which they are made and remade through the activities of particular individuals" (Rhodes 2002:400). Rhodes's exhortation to put "people back into networks" (400) should be taken very seriously, for the alternative would be a drift toward an arid policy cartography in which policy outcomes would seem to be a consequence of spatial position and propinquity rather than of motive and affinity.

Second, policy networks engage in agonistic relationships with one another. That is, they represent interests, preferences, and values that—given that politics is about the allocation of values under conditions of scarcity—inevitably compete with one another. Networks do indeed sometimes coalesce and converge, but they more frequently collide with and encroach on one another. Networks are warlike as well as consensual or creative. They endeavor to outwit and misrepresent other networks. And, in policy influence, they work for successful outcomes by disabling other networks as well as by entering into reflexive deliberation with them.

Third, as is the case throughout the political sphere, policy networks possess asymmetrical resources, both materially and in cultural capital. It may be that network governance makes power more porous and institutions more accessible, but it remains the case that the policy-making citadel is more fortified against some social actors than against others. Each of these three points underlines a central argument of this chapter, which is that, although the Internet might render the policy process more open and responsive to citizens who have tended to find themselves outside of the policy loop, this does not eradicate the contingencies of *habitus,* asymmetries of power, or pragmatics of *realpolitik*.

Multivocal Narratives

Stories are at the heart of policy discourse. As Tilly says of standard stories, "They lend themselves to vivid, compelling accounts of what has happened, what will happen, and what should happen. They do essential work in social life, cementing people's commitments to common projects, helping people make sense of what is going on, channeling collective decisions and judgments, spurring people to action they would otherwise be reluctant to pursue" (2002:27).

As Fischer puts it, "narratives create and shape social meaning by imposing a coherent interpretation on the whirl of events and actions around us" (2003:162). They do so in a particular way that jars the rationalistic positivism of political science; for narratives and stories are expressions of subjective experience and perception and cannot be boiled down to the kind of univocal ascriptions produced by opinion polling or a national census. Relying on storytelling as a source of problem framing or problem solving is to acknowledge that experience can never be translated into simple data; there is a messiness and ambiguity about life as it is lived that is rarely captured by life as it is measured.

Stories are social phenomena that gain momentum through circulation. In this sense, they are intersubjective and dialogical, entangling the tellers, the told, the retellers, and the respondents in a dynamic interplay of claims, counterclaims, and occasional syntheses of accounting. In elite policy making, narratives have long served an important purpose, both as transmitters of ideological positions and ways of packaging complex arguments for public consumption. While the public might not have confidence in politicians who appear to be "telling them stories," they are unlikely to even pay attention to those who don't have a compelling story to tell.

But some social actors have far greater opportunities to articulate, circulate, and gain legitimacy for their stories than others. People who have access to the civil service, the mass media, think tanks, and political parties are in a relatively small minority and tend to possess atypical combinations of cultural capital. For most citizens, although they have stories to tell and a wish to exercise influence on policies that will affect them, their scope for intersubjective account sharing is limited. Widespread access to the Internet "provides the means to distribute more widely the capacity to tell important stories about oneself—to represent oneself as a social, and therefore potentially political agent—in a way that is registered in the public domain" (Couldry 2008:386). A number of scholars, such as Lundby (2008), Hardy (2007), Burgess (2006), Thumin (2006), and Lambert (2007), have come to regard "digital storytelling" as a way of broadening not only the communicative space, but the expressive mode, of public narrating. As the most intersubjective medium in the history of communication technology, the Internet has opened up a vast arena for almost unrestricted storytelling.

A particular role for digital storytelling within the policy process relates to problem definition. Determining what constitutes a social problem, who is affected by it, and how it is normatively apprehended is best not left to political elites, who tend to inhabit an exclusive and unrepresentative social world. An illustration of how problem definition can be illuminated by lay voices was the British Parliament's online consultation with women survivors of domestic violence (Coleman 2004). The power of the approximately one thousand messages posted on the consultation forum derived from experiential authenticity rather than from technical expertise. In speaking for themselves, the terms of representation were altered: politicians were no longer left to speak *for* an absent constituency, but to respond *to* a vocal community of experience. The political consequences of this compression of distance between storytellers and policy makers are significant, with the potential to undermine Burkean principles of indirect representation (Coleman and Blumler 2009:ch. 3); but equally important, from a more microempirical perspective, is the impact of such virtual testifying on the delineation of the policy problem.

Consider a later online consultation organized by the Hansard Society in September and October 2004 on behalf of the Northern Ireland Affairs Committee, which had launched an inquiry into hate crime in Northern Ireland.[1] The consultation was publicized via a range of mainstream and digital media outlets. Although there were only eighty-one registered participants in the consultation, they represented a broad range of communities and third-sector organizations in Northern Ireland. In reporting the findings from the online consultation, the Northern Ireland Affairs Committee explained that it saw this as a way of helping "the Committee to gather evidence beyond official statistics." Some of the qualitative richness of the evidence gathered can be gleaned from the following excerpts:

> I live in south Belfast, an area that has had much media coverage re: racist incidents. I have noticed an increase in the number of people from "visible minorities" in the area and indeed in my children's school. It is easy to condemn the people who find this threatening or objectionable. Of course, I live in a valuable house, have a well-paid, stable job and am pleased to see this increased diversity—it doesn't feel threatening to me. But I cannot speak for people who feel they get nothing but the crumbs off the table of this society.

> Many gay people do not report "low level" homophobic attacks (from a stone through your window to being verbally or physically harassed in the street) because they think nothing will be done, for fear of incurring more prejudice from the police and authorities, and for fear of attracting more attention to themselves from the community around them. Many adopt a low profile, in the hope that people harassing them will get bored and eventually leave them alone.

> The constant focus on South Belfast tends to conceal the fact that racism affects foreign nationals and migrant workers across the Province, and not just in the working class loyalist community of South Belfast. It also suggests, and falsely so, that working class loyalists are inherently racist. To stigmatise a whole community because of the racist activities of a minority simply mirrors the prejudice displayed by the racists themselves. By all means let's highlight the problem of racism, but let it be highlighted right across the Province, and let us do it in a strictly non-sectarian manner.

These messages (and several others like them posted in the online forum) exemplify the sense in which online networks of what Lambert (2007) calls "storycatching" are populated by real people facing complex experiences that cannot be captured through webmetric mapping. They come to narrative with histories, values, and claims that inevitably inflect the political form and tone of what they have to say. And they bring to their storytelling a reflexive awareness of how others might think of them even before they utter their first word. These implicit sensibilities add nuance to the activity of problem definition, thereby compelling policy makers to think beyond simplistic, binary accounts of culpability and victimhood.

Tensions between the style of digital storytelling and the norms of Habermasian discursive will-formation raise important questions about the extent to which an expanded sphere of policy making is compatible with the lofty demands of consensus-building rationalism. Habermas famously dismisses forms of speech such as irony, humor, and parody as "parasitic"; they distort the "ideal speech situation" by undermining reason and transparency. When political elites have invited citizens to give them evidence, there has tended to be an explicit or tacit expectation that they should adopt a rationalist tone, stripped of affective excitement and excess. A strength of digital storytelling is its abandonment of such constraints, an openness to the raw authenticity of the first-person singular, an acknowledgment of the local and quotidian, and a willingness to embrace existential ambiguity. Digital storytelling is, in this sense, more Bakhtinian than Habermasian;[2] its legitimacy derives from the situated contingency and multivocal understanding of fragmented polyphony rather than the sober articulation of a formally reasoning public.

According to Bakhtin, it is the "eventness" of speech, realized at the very point of intersubjectivity, that generates the kind of wisdom that can sustain pluralistic perspectives: "It is quite possible to imagine and postulate a unified truth that requires a plurality of consciousnesses, one that in principle cannot be fitted within the bounds of a single consciousness, one that is, so to speak, by its very nature full of event potential and is born at a point of contact among various consciousnesses" (1984:81).

By refusing to accommodate the notion of a singular problem definition or policy solution, the multiple-narrative approach to the gathering of public values highlights a key motive for the argumentative turn in policy making, prompted by a desire to see the world and its contradictions panoramically and multiperspectivally, in contrast to the univocal rationalism that too often constrains both the reach and aura of the public sphere. In this sense, multivocalist dialogism casts doubt on Foucauldian claims that "control society" tends to be prone to a tight discursive grip on public talk.

Policy Networking

Policy networks, through which clusters of actors with common areas of expertise, experience, or values come together within loose structures of mutual learning, are now a pervasive feature of governance. In contrast to the centralized and hierarchical rigidity of institutionally embedded administrative bureaucracies, policy networks tend toward organizational agility and flexibility. However, maintaining policy networks has traditionally been much easier for well-resourced networks, whose members have easy access to international travel, conference facilities, and telecommunication, than for poorer, dispersed groups. Consider, for example, the International Working Men's Association (IWMA)—the First International—which met between 1864 and 1876. As a global network of socialists, anarchists, and trades unionists, the organization claimed to represent eight million members. It met in various European cities—and finally in New York—but few of its members could hope to participate, and reports of its congresses were not disseminated until weeks or months after the meetings.

The Internet has made policy networking more feasible in three ways. First, there are networks that operate predominantly online, as virtual policy communities. For example, a group of British mothers formed Netmums, an online group with a view to sharing information and influencing policy related to parenting. The nature of the pressures facing its participants makes online communication an appropriate means of mobilizing their dispersed energies. Its cofounder, Sally Russell, takes the view that operating online allows participants "to work as a cooperative rather than just providing information to parents one-way." In addition to providing mutual support for parents, Netmums campaigns on policy issues such as better support for postnatal depression, teen knife crime, and junk food advertising. Russell argues that "what we do does allow parents to engage with politics, on issues that affect them, both locally and nationally. We get complaints in about local council services and then we forward them to the council, then they reply, and they do take notice of them, increasingly . . . they write long replies and take an interest in what we're doing."

Quite clearly, Netmums could not have achieved this degree of daily interaction between its members by running seminars or conferences. As a group of people who might easily have been marginalized by the policy process, Netmums seems to have defied the assumption that collective action needs to be physically rooted. Other examples of virtual policy networks include campaigners on climate change (McNutt 2008), the World Social Forum (Kavada 2005), and a coalition of Muslim feminists in the Middle East (Moghadam 2000). Not only do such networks expand the range of issues on the policy agenda and the number of voices addressing them, but they change the way in which policy work is conducted, first through a distributed division of labor that undermines the scope for centralized hierarchy, and second by maintaining loose boundaries, so that participants within Netmums can share their work with other online networks addressing related issues. While virtual networks often lack the tight-knit solidarity of traditional policy communities, the scope for synergistic fusion resulting from open borders can make for more coherent and imaginative approaches to policy.

A second form in which policy networks can emerge is through sites designed to capture distributed knowledge, such as wikis.[3] Such networks depend largely on floating participants rather than the quasi members who identify with the kind of virtual policy communities described earlier. For example, Mambrey and Doerr have surveyed users of city wikis in Germany, which they describe as "social platforms created by citizens to inform and communicate about local affairs within a certain geographical boundary" (2009:5). Asked to explain their objectives in participating in a city wiki, survey respondents identified the following: "Interactive knowledge collection and communication platform, creation of collective thoughts augmented by pictures and videos, information platform with serious arguments and new mass media in its early stage" (11, 12). Similarly, e-petitions, as a means of submitting policy proposals to parliaments, governments, and local councils, provide an opportunity for like-minded citizens to cluster together. (In some cases, as with the German Bundestag and the Scottish Parliament, these embryonic networks are nurtured by providing spaces for policy discussion, whereas in other cases, as with the British government's e-petition site, opinion-formation is limited to silent aggregation.) Nonetheless, these adventitious encounters can at least stimulate citizens to think of themselves as part of a potentially collaborative community. The ethos of the wiki, the e-petition, and the recommender system are ones in which civic identities and viewpoints emerge out of a messy process of collective becoming. As Fairclough has put it, "people's individual identities, their collective identities as members of particular and diverse groups, and their universal identities-in-common as citizens and human beings are collectively constituted simultaneously through a complex weaving together of different facets of the self" (1998:32). In this sense, policy networking of this kind can be characterized neither by the amorphous univocality evoked by technologies of "public opinion" research, nor by the notions of individualized attachments on which traditional membership organizations depend.

Taking this notion of uncoordinated policy networks emanating from casual hyperspatial relationships a step further, some scholars argue that the most important influences on contemporary policy thinking arise out of linkages *between* virtual networks, identifiable by the semantic patterns that unite them. Rogers and Marres argue that "information provided by organizations stands not alone in space (as a public relations folder or an annual report) but potentially in immediate relation to other organizations' information in hyperspace" (2000:142). Shumate and Lipp regard hyperlinkage as "evidence of a symbolic relationship between entities" (2008:181). While there is surely a danger of such accounts coming dangerously close to the abstract, culturally decontextualizing position criticized earlier, there is empirical evidence to suggest that some policy alliances comprise actors and networks that are not aware of or familiar with one another, but at the same time operate in ways that are mutually reinforcing. For example, risky online networking between human rights dissidents in countries as different as Iran, China, and Saudi Arabia have the overall effect of a global network that exceeds the terms of their specific demands. Even if they are not directly linking to one another as content producers, if those accessing them decide to tag them as being issue related—or, even less directly, to search for them on Google using common key words—a policy connection will become apparent. Similarly, if policy networks about global poverty invoke arguments based on social justice and quite separate networks dedicated to opposing state aid to the banks utilize similar terms, this semantic connection will become manifest and the two networks might reasonably be described as a symbolically convergent entity. The extent to which such discrete hyperlinkages are reconstructing the policy sphere is a subject for empirical research. Debatescaping applications such as Rogers's Issue Crawler could perform an important role in illuminating the unintended entanglements and fortuitous opportunities presented by virtual propinquities.

Girard and Stark, who state that in some policy situations "we can come to know the question only in the process of making active steps toward solutions" (2007:149), have identified an important benefit of these forms of online collaboration. Considering the example of a series of discretely connected activities initiated by a range of groups in Lower Manhattan after September 11, they analyze three types of collaborative action that led, sometimes indirectly, to the formulation of policy positions: "sensing (e.g., gathering, collecting, sampling) . . . 'sense making' (articulating, contrasting, discussing, re-cognizing) and . . . demonstrating (showing, confronting, constituting)" (152).[4] Out of these quasi policy-making gestures, there sometimes emerge more elaborate forms of problem diagnosis and strategy that no one actor or organization alone could have devised. These dividends of networked adaptation can serve to redress asymmetries of resources, influence, and confidence that have traditionally skewed the policy process in favor of elites.

Online Deliberation

From the earliest days of the Internet, much writing has been devoted to its potential as a space for public deliberation. There are two reasons for this: the conspicuous absence of opportunities for public deliberation in modern democracies, long lamented by a range of theoretical and empirical scholars (Delli Carpini, Cook, and Jacobs 2004), and the apparent scope afforded by interactive, asynchronous, polyphonous online communication for the elimination of some of the most indomitable barriers to inclusive deliberation (Price and Cappella 2002; Shane 2004). A more deliberative democracy could bring five benefits to policy making. First, the more that public arguments and disagreements are rehearsed and recognized, the easier it will become to devise policies that directly address them. Second, as citizens become involved in deliberating policy options, they will have a greater incentive to seek information that will help them to arrive at considered views. Third, deliberating citizens will develop skills of arguing, listening, weighing positions, and negotiating trade-offs. Fourth, the experience of engaging in deliberation could lead to enhanced political trust and efficacy, resulting from a sense of inclusion in a process that might otherwise seem exclusive and suspicious. Finally, by bringing a broad range of experiences, values, and voices to the deliberative forum, key perspectives are less likely to be missed, so the quality of policy is thereby enhanced. If online connections between citizens could be structured in ways likely to promote ideal deliberative conditions, this could have a decidedly invigorating effect on the democratic nature of policy making.[5]

Opportunities presented by the Internet for more open and inclusive modes of defining policy issues and collaborative policy making, as discussed earlier, are dependent upon the speed and fluidity of symbolic circulation, which makes it possible for loose networks characterized by weak ties to flourish. Deliberation, it might be argued, depends on precisely the opposite: temporal and spatial contexts that allow for enduring attention and unhurried reflection. Wolin writes of how "political time, especially in societies with pretensions to democracy, requires an element of leisure" because of the need for "political action to be preceded by deliberation and deliberation, as its 'deliberate' part suggests, takes time because, typically, it occurs in a setting of competing or conflicting but legitimate considerations" (1997:156). He argues that the political "zone of time" is out of kilter with economic and cultural time. While the latter tends to be characterized by an incessantly innovatory mood of "replacement through obsolescence," the effectiveness of democratic politics depends on the existence of room for measured rumination (ibid.). As Lupia has rightly pointed out,

> For a deliberative endeavor to increase participation, or affect how a target audience thinks about an important political matter, its informational content must, at a minimum: attract the audience's attention and hold it for a non-trivial amount of time; affect the audience's memories in particular ways (not any change will do) and cause them to retain subsequent beliefs—or choose different behaviors—than they would have had without deliberation. (2002:59)

Could the accelerated pace and hyperlinked geography of online communication, which prove so positive in affording more heterogeneous expression and miscellaneous collaboration, attenuate the scope for deliberative intercourse by weakening the maintenance of attention?

If we define deliberation as "a dialogical process of exchanging reasons for the purpose of resolving problematic situations that cannot be settled without interpersonal coordination and cooperation" (Bohman

1996:27), and if we agree that a test of its success is the capacity of deliberators to understand the values and preferences of others and be open to revising their own, it is quite clear that online policy deliberation must amount to more than pervasive chatter about political options. This rules out much online discussion, which takes the form of partisan position taking or casual and inconsequential sociability. The relatively few examples of online policy deliberation that have taken place have fallen into three categories: specific experiments, usually initiated by deliberative theorists to test the potential of the setting; real-world policy consultations, initiated by governments or other institutions, usually with a view to replicating offline deliberative exercises online; and innovative attempts to structure naturally occurring public talk so that the more challenging aspects of deliberating might be made more accessible and meaningful to inexpert citizens.

Fishkin's recent experimentation with running his deliberative polls online have been enlightening, because they have taken a well-tested and sophisticated method of engendering rational public debate with a view to drawing comparative conclusions. In an offline deliberative poll, participants are first surveyed to discover their views on a particular policy issue; then exposed to balanced information about the issue; then allocated to random groups in which the issue is discussed; and then, after a weekend of such debate, asked to fill in the initial survey again. Repeatedly, the results of the second (postdeliberative) survey have differed significantly from those of the initial one: public judgments have changed because of direct exposure to new information and other people's perspectives. In several replications of this methodology online, Fishkin and his colleagues have found that, despite participants not sitting down together over a lengthy period and having the benefit of physical fellowship, the conditions of dispersed online participation did not detract from the desired outcome. On the contrary, "if anything, the participants' changes of attitude seemed *more* information driven online than face to face. In particular, the information based model, which we have used to explain change in other Deliberative Polls, worked extremely well in the online case—explaining change for five of the six indices for which there was significant change" (Luskin, Fishkin, and Iyengar 2003:24). Given the relatively low cost of conducting online deliberative experiments, it is somewhat surprising that more have not taken place, perhaps testing key variables, such as ideal discussion group size, the effects of particular rules or moderation styles, and the differences resulting from textual, audio, and visual presentations of information. There are clearly many ways of thinking about what it means to be a deliberative citizen and which technological applications can best facilitate civic efficacy (Coleman and Blumler 2010). And, as the Internet evolves into a diversified media system, scholars need to be able to offer more than sweeping statements that online communication is—or is not—compatible with deliberation. What kind of deliberative outcomes are being measured? What kinds of technologies are evaluated as "online communication"?

Most cases in which online deliberation has played a significant role in policy making have involved elite networks (such as transnational agencies or parties) addressing issues that exceed territorial jurisdiction, require multistakeholder trade-offs, and cannot await the luxury of extensive physical copresence. It has been rare for governments to engage citizens in genuine opportunities to deliberate online about policy options. The few examples that have been studied are notable for the consistency of their findings: while participation remains dominated by citizens who tend to be already closer to the policy process, a number of traditionally excluded voices are added to the mix; citizen-deliberators have generally been prepared to respond tolerantly to views that oppose their own; and the process of online deliberation does seem to encourage more informal, vernacular styles of policy talk (Albrecht 2006; Coleman 2004; Milioni 2009; Monnoyer-Smith 2008; Papacharissi 2004; Polletta and Lee 2006; Schifino 2006). However, the complexities of policy discourse should not be underestimated; most examples of citizen-based online deliberation have involved relatively simple issues that directly affect participants. The most politically contentious policy questions, such as going to war, determining national budgets, or responding to failing banks, are not put to citizens, partly because of a will by elites to monopolize "hard-core" decision making, and partly because the challenge of designing inclusive discursive processes has been regarded as insurmountable. The danger here is that deliberative stakeholder exercises are relegated to the level of "soft" politics and tokenistic outcomes, with unpropitious consequences for democratic efficacy.

Beyond Online Deliberation

The rather limited and unambitious outcomes of online deliberation to date have led some scholars and practitioners to think about ways that the Internet might facilitate forms of policy deliberation that benefit from its specific affordances. French (2007), for example, has attempted to devise a methodology that would allow large, dispersed groups meeting online to make decisions that are not thwarted by Savage's (1954) subjective expected utility (SEU) paradigm. The key to this has been to devise ways for participants to reveal their interests and preferences to one another and to act transparently throughout the communication process. The design of web interfaces could play an important part in making deliberative exchanges more—or less—accessible and effective (Wright and Street 2007).

Others have gone further, arguing that the mapping of arguments as they are stated within a deliberative process and the visualization of positions, exchanges, and decision flows could be generated online in a far more sophisticated way than can be achieved within face-to-face settings (Donath 2002; Mancini and Buckingham-Shum 2006; Renton and Macintosh 2007; Sack 2000). One of the most promising attempts to make complex and contentious policy issues amenable to online public deliberation is the Debategraph system, pioneered by David Price and Peter Baldwin. This tool seeks to represent within a visual structure all pertinent issues, positions, arguments, evidence, and scenarios relating to a policy debate and to open this process to anyone wishing to explore or interact with the ongoing discursive mapping. The process entails three stages, each of which follows dynamically from the emerging contours of the policy deliberation: the policy issue is broken down into meaningful parts; discursive relationships between these different parts are plotted; and the parts and their relationships are represented visually. A large Debategraph map typically shows a vast number of thought boxes, each of which can be edited and rated by debate participants, who can also add new boxes (issues, arguments, and positions, and the like) to the map. Underlying each box is an in-depth display to which images, charts, tables, full-length essays, free-form comments, and links to external documents can be added. In addition to forming part of a vertical tree structure, the boxes can be semantically linked to any other box, so that patterns of discursive connection are revealed. Wiki-like collaborative editing of the maps across the web makes it possible for the collective knowledge and insights distributed across the entire community of interested participants to be disclosed. The idea is that, in accordance with the norms of public deliberation, initial seed maps evolve (and can be seen to evolve) toward mature and comprehensive accounts of available positions, their rationales, and their connections.

While argument mapping and visualization tools offer important opportunities for greater transparency in position-taking, the nurturing of mutual trust between participants, and the assemblage of intellectual and political affinities, they do not—and should not try to—overcome the material conflicts of interests and values that underlie most policy deliberation. However valuable such epistemic tools may be, they do not solve two problems: that policy decisions cannot escape agonistic contestation and that real-world policy decisions are made in conditions of power inequality. If we take seriously Fischer's (2003:30) call for a new policy epistemics that recognizes the need to interpret knowledge as it is situated within contingent social contexts and Mouffe's (2005) concern that deliberation should not be regarded as a search for universal commensurability of interests and values, it is vital that space for contestation and mobilization is not crowded out by a naive quest for universal consensus.

Considering the three areas of reconfiguration that have been outlined earlier (multivocal policy definition, collaborative networking, online deliberation), we might argue that each contributes a particular strength to the broad objective of making public policy debate epistemically accessible and meaningful and at the same time agonistically authentic and equitable. The expansion of policy narratives might be seen as helping to expose the experiential basis of incommensurable discourses, compelling democratically committed policy makers to avoid setting agendas or devising solutions that can only "succeed" by neglecting the presence of actors they would prefer to be invisible. Collaborative networking augments collective action opportunities, thereby making it more possible for promoters of nonhegemonic policy options to mobilize around counterstrategies. And online deliberation, while often framed by normative commitments to "ideal speech situations," at its best provides scope for forms of animated rhetorical exchange that cut across traditional social barriers.

Making a Difference

By focusing on the Internet as a discursive space, rather than a producer of technical effects, one is forced to confront two real-world challenges that cannot be obfuscated by the heady hyperbole of the technocratic sublime. These challenges relate to the tangible consequences of online policy making and the efficacy of online policy makers. While accepting that both variables are notoriously difficult to measure, a conspicuous absence of either material effects or enhanced efficacy within the online policy sphere should surely be grounds for some skepticism.

A first challenge arises from consistent findings across all evaluations of government-managed online policy processes acknowledging the negligible extent to which they have had any impact on policy outcomes (Abelson et al. 2003; Culver and Howe 2008; Halseth and Booth 2003; Martin and Sanderson 1999; Rowe and Frewer 2005). Governments have been accused of running online policy exercises after they already made their decisions; of failing to interact with citizens who take the trouble to deliberate online; of being insensitive to informal, vernacular, quotidian testimony that does not conform to official language; and of selectively interpreting the views of deliberators and consultees. Online policy making seems to have been thus far dominated by process and neglectful of outcomes.

Matthew Taylor, who was chief strategic adviser to British Prime Minister Tony Blair, sums up the discursive mismatch that characterizes most policy consultation:

> As long as the conversation we have about society is government-centric rather than citizen-centric, consultation cannot work because it is based upon an inadequate description of what the problem is. Most of the social problems we have to solve are as much to do with what I do as a citizen as they are to do with what you do as a politician, but that is not how most consultations are framed. They do not start with, "What are we as a community going to do to make our community safer? Let us spend a day talking about that together and from that we will derive some things that the council should do as well as a rich amount of things that we are going to do." It starts from a group of people on the panel saying, "What do you think about the way in which we are policing your community?" You create a language of

disempowerment as a consequence of which you feel quite rightly that people are just shouting at you because you almost invite the public to make a set of incommensurate demands to you. The room is full of people demanding this, that and the other. You do not give them the responsibility of trying to reconcile these conflicting demands. You invite them to be unreasonable to you and as a consequence you say, "This did not work. I am not going to do this any more." (House of Commons Public Administration Committee 2007:Q394; quoted in Coleman and Blumler 2009:196)

Taylor rightly emphasizes that obstacles to democratic policy making emanate from elite dispositions that simply cannot come to terms with the capacity of ordinary citizens to think and act in reasonable, imaginative, and constructive ways. Communicative interaction can be stymied before any word is uttered or gesture made if the discrete anxieties, resentments, and expectations that the political class bring with them to encounters with citizens are so power-laden that they suffocate meaningful exchange (Levinas 1969). The effectiveness of any inclusive policy process, online or offline, is dependent upon the genuine goodwill of all who are involved. Hollow commitments to political dialogue invariably become apparent and lead inevitably to further declines in public efficacy and trust.

A second challenge arises from the democratic habits that are emerging through online networks. In a survey of British Internet users who protested against the invasion of Iraq, Coleman, Morrison, and Yates (2011) found that although very few of them believed that their actions had any affect on policy makers, they were optimistic about their capacity to reach and influence other citizens. As a vertical path to established authority, the Internet was not trusted; but as a lateral means of finding and connecting with like-minded others, the Internet was regarded as a space of potential empowerment. Could it be that the interdependent but uncoordinated networks of diffusion that have come to characterize the Internet are not only broadening the range of potential policy actors, but recasting the terms of political efficacy by diminishing public reliance on institutional recognition? Hajer has rightly observed that "there are important policy problems for which political action either takes place *next to* or *across*" traditional state institutions (2003:175, original emphasis). This does not imply that the latter have vanished, but that "the norms of the respective participants" are challenged. The Internet offers a vital space for such challenges to be mounted, a site of democratic disruption in which political monopolies might be evaded and counteracted. The empirical evidence suggests that there is a contemporary disjuncture between the institutional machinery of the state and the emerging habits of networked democracy. Three things could happen in response to this emerging tension: state institutions could continue to make policy in routine ways while engaging in endless e-governmental schemes and gimmicks; or they could adapt radically to the coproductive potential offered by online networks; or they could become increasingly marginalized, as citizens come to the view that states lack technologies of listening and hearing and that the spaces around them are where power flows. Appealing though the third option might seem, in pitting the electoral legitimacy of institutional governance against the deliberative richness of grass-roots networks, it risks undermining the efficiency of democratic coordination.

If, on the one hand, the vertical path between citizens and representative government is rendered hazardous by the suspicion and lack of confidence of the former and the defensiveness and inertia of the latter and, on the other hand, horizontal paths within and across publics are prone to fragmentation and political irrelevance, there must surely be a way that the representative force of government as a coordinating allocator of values and the experiential energy of discursive publics can be creatively combined. Metler and Soss have astutely argued that "political scientists ought to be able to explain why some policies draw citizens into public life and others induce passivity. We should have a sense of how living under a given policy regime affects citizens' goals, beliefs and identities—and hence, the possibilities for future political action" (2004:56).

If the potential of the Internet as a discursive space for policy deliberation is to be taken seriously, the ways in which new civic practices can be mediated and promoted must themselves become a focus of policy attention. Not only do we have scant information about the types of citizens who participate in online policy making, the quality of their participatory experience, the extent to which political officials take them seriously, or the precise ways in which their policy recommendations are integrated within existing processes, but we also know very little about how governments imagine citizens, how far they normatively accommodate them within their conceptions of democracy, and whether, in Metler and Soss's terms, they see online policy making as a way of drawing citizens into the very center of governance or as a means of inducing passivity.

The starting point here should be an investigation of motives. Why are some governments choosing to involve citizens in the work of policy making? If the aim is to promote policy coproduction, as outlined by Ostrom (1991), the criteria of success will be very different from those entailed by a more Foucauldian project of mollifying collusion, as described by Cruikshank (1999), Rose (1999), and Dean (1999). In short, any strategy, technology, or technique designed to advance a particular conception of democratic behavior will be dialectically enmeshed in the task of both working with and working on norms of citizenship. The Internet, in this sense, should be understood less as a space within which already-formed citizens come to make policy than a site for the construction of civic habits. The Internet's potential to become a democratic space in which the dispersed energies, self-articulations, and aspirations of citizens can circulate relatively freely, enabling publics to see themselves, their preferences, and their values for what they are, depends on how far the tension between actually existing and creatively emerging citizenship are played out.

The Turn to Communication Networks and the Argumentative Turn

I have argued in this chapter that there is an intimate connection between the emergence of communicative networks and the kind of "expansive democracy" on which the "argumentative turn" depends; that the most useful way to think about these networks is as contingent, peopled, agonistic, and asymmetrical entities; that the multivocality of the narratives that emerge from these networks undermine endeavors to reach singular problem definitions; that networks facilitate policy linkages, sometimes even despite the intentions of dispersed actors; and that they enable rehearsals of public reason that strengthen the position of the demos. However, I have argued at the same time that we know too little about how political elites imagine, evade, and resist the networked public or about what the consequences might be if and when citizens counterevade or counterresist elite centers. All of this, I have suggested, has profound implications for our conception of democratic citizenship. Long inscribed in political discourse as passive recipients of other people's policy narratives, strategies, and deliberations, citizens have been conceived as the objects of policy. As new modes of networked intersubjectivity emerge, the very notion of policy making calls for redefinition, focusing on spaces and practices of civic subjectivity.

First, as access to the field of policy-related discourse expands to include hitherto silent or neglected constituencies, positivist conceptions of policy making as a search for scientific truths must give way to new practices of capturing and reflecting pluralistic and diverse perspectives. As Gottweis puts it, "Every instance of policymaking can be described as an attempt at social and political ordering: to manage a field of discursivity, to establish a situation of stability and predictability within a field of differences, to maintain a specific system of boundaries such as between the state, science and industry, and to construct a center that fixes and regulates the dispersion of a multitude of cominable elements" (Hajer and Wagenaar 2003:261).

The management of discursivity across national, professional, socioeconomic, and generational boundaries is beyond most state governments and has rarely been attempted by global bodies, such as the United Nations. It is an approach to ordering social knowledge that is more likely to be successful within a visible and mappable network of networks such as the Internet than via elaborate efforts to calibrate public knowledge and experience across national boundaries, state agencies, and invisible borders of cultural exclusivity.

At stake here is the potential to create a sphere of empathy in which public preferences and values can be openly compared and contrasted. Much attention has been paid to aspects of online communication that encourage group herding and tribal indifference, but this should not be allowed to obscure the sense in which the emergence of crosscutting networks open up ethical spaces in which meaning making and truth seeking can transcend parochial walls.

Second, it follows from this multidiscursive notion of policy making that fetishistic methodological attempts to anchor policy making in the certainties of "objectivity" are bound to fail. For, as Fischer has suggested, "Social meaning is an integrated ensemble of connections among images and ideas that appear in various modes of presentation, such as perception, remembrance, and imagination. Meaning operates in a complex of interaction involving different levels of awareness, abstraction, and control. Complex social patterns, folding back on each other through processes of symbolic displacement and condensation, interconnect the interpretive elements in ways that make it difficult to empirically investigate the realm of meaning" (2003:139).

In contrast to the "final vocabulary" (Rorty 1990) of positivist social science, which claimed to establish a precise correspondence between truth and description, the task for postpositivist policy analysts is to investigate the vast array of messages, testimonies, conversations, claims, and refusals that constitute everyday communication with a view to making intersubjective understandings legible. As a communicative space, the Internet is more like a poetic stream of consciousness, made intelligible through its hypertextual interconnections and conspicuous thematic gaps, than a database of manifest meanings. Characterized by ongoing and always incomplete redescription rather than any final and incontrovertible vocabulary, the Internet is best understood as a site of irony: a space in which the instability of truth claims is a source of analytical strength rather than weakness.

To understand social reality ironically is not to abandon notions of truth or objectivity, but to inflect them with a respectful regard for the ambiguities of everyday sense making. The production of social meaning is both a structural and cultural enterprise; the neglect of structural constraints makes for naive policy analysis; the neglect of cultural critique all too often results in an approach to policy that comprehends everything except its human effects and affects. In resisting both determinist and subjectivist assumptions about the meanings underlying policy, analysts in the tradition of the argumentative turn have insisted on engaging with the dialectical interplay between context and agency that shapes the policy imagination. Thinking about policy in this way calls for attention to the mediated environments within which ideas circulate. Given the extensive literature devoted to the particularities and affordances of the Internet as a communication medium, the role of virtual mediation in the formation, dissemination, and evaluation of policies remains surprisingly understudied.

Third, as governance comes to rely increasingly on technologies of connection—citizen-representative, citizen-citizen, government-citizen, and business-citizen—it makes sense to revisit some of the dreams and experiments of communicative togetherness that have for so long been dismissed and disparaged by the hardheaded empiricists of policy science (Coleman 2007; Simonson 1996). The almost irrepressible sociability of online communication raises questions about the hyperrationalism of much political and communication theory. A tendency to dismiss and diminish emotional expression and to assume that intelligent policy reflection calls for modes of argumentation that resemble the seminar room more than the living room has been responsible for a serious empirical neglect among policy analysts of the mundane conversations and demonstrations that characterize a great deal of street-level policy talk. In turning to the Internet as a source of such talk, it would be futile to spurn the affective; to do so would be like trying to decode cinema movies by only taking note of the spoken word. Indeed, one of the most important ways in which the Internet might engender and coordinate forms of experientially and affectively framed policy deliberation depends on its reconstruction of the notion of democratic togetherness. Abandoning the utopian quest for spatiotemporal compression, in which whole publics appear as microcosmic entities existing in simultaneous time and space, the Internet, as a network of networks, embraces not only spatiotemporal but also cultural and epistemological incongruity, acknowledging that the recognition of difference is the first step toward apprehending a common public.

Notes

1. The Hansard Society is an independent, nonpartisan organization that aims to strengthen parliamentary democracy and encourage greater public involvement in politics. As a declaration of interest, I should state that as director of the society's e-democracy program I organized and evaluated the first online policy consultations run by Parliament.

2. While Habermas's more rationalistic early writings might seem to be in conflict with Bakhtin's focus on the force of spontaneous and intersubjectivity, in his later writings, such as *Between Facts and Norms: Contribution to a Discourse Theory of Law and Democracy*, he revises this position, arguing that "systemic deficiencies are experienced in the context of individual life histories; such burdens accumulate in the lifeworld. The latter has the appropriate antennae, for in its horizon are intermeshed the private life histories of the 'clients' of functional systems that might be failing in their delivery of services" (1996:365).

3. A wiki is an online site that allows users to add and update content by

using their own web browser. Wiki content is created by the collaborative effort of the site users rather than by a single producer or designer.

4. Examples of "sensing" cited by Girard and Stark include tools for making the reconstruction of the attacked area more transparent. They refer to the circulation of online maps identifying the subterranean remains of cables, pipes, and electricity lines beneath the destroyed streets, information about environmental pollutants around the site, the erection of a virtual viewing platform so that the area could be looked at by people planning its future, and the establishment of a web-based sonic archive of sounds from the World Trade Center. As an example of "sense making," they describe how Listening to the City assembled an array of technologies to bring together otherwise disparate and fragmented deliberations that were taking place across New York. An example of "demonstrating" cited by Girard and Stark was the online protest by New Yorkers in response to the false information being given to them about environmental risks following September 11, 2001.

5. Coleman and Gotze (2001) set out the following seven ideal deliberative conditions: access to balanced information; an open agenda; time to consider issues expansively; a rule-based framework for discussion; participation by a representative sample of citizens; scope for free interaction between participants; recognition of differences between participants, but rejection of status-based prejudice.

References

Abelson, J., P.-G. Forest, J. Eyles, P. Smith, E. Martin, and F.-P. Gauvin. 2003. "Deliberations about Deliberative Methods: Issues in the Design and Evaluation of Public Participation Processes." *Social Sciences and Medicine* 57(2):239–51.

Albrecht, S. 2006. "Whose Voice Is Heard in Online Deliberation? A Study of Participation and Representation in Political Debates on the Internet." *Information, Communication and Society* 9(1):62–82.

Bennett, W. L. 2003. "New Media Power: The Internet and Global Activism." In *Contesting Media Power: Alternative Media in a Networked World*, edited by N. Couldry and J. Curran, 17–37. New York: Rowman and Littlefield.

Bohman, J. 1996. *Public Deliberation: Pluralism, Complexity and Democracy.* Cambridge: MIT Press.

Burgess, J. 2006. "Hearing Ordinary Voices: Cultural Studies, Vernacular Creativity and Digital Storytelling." *Continuum* 20(2):201–14.

Castells, M. 2008. "The New Public Sphere: Global Civil Society, Communication Networks, and Global Governance." *Annals of the American Society of Political and Social Science* 616:78–93.

Coleman, S. 2004. "Connecting Parliament to the Public via the Internet: Two Case Studies of Online Consultations." *Information, Communication and Society* 7(1):1–22.

———. 2005. *Direct Representation: Towards a Conversational Democracy.* London: Institute for Public Policy Research.

———. 2007. "E-Democracy: The History and Future of an Idea." In *The Oxford Handbook of Information and Communication Technologies*, edited by D. Quah, R. Silverstone, R. Mansell, and C. Avgerou, 362–82. Oxford: Oxford University Press.

Coleman, S., and J. G. Blumler. 2009. *The Internet and Democratic Citizenship: Theory, Practice and Policy.* Cambridge: Cambridge University Press.

———. 2010. "Political Communication in Freefall: The British Case—and Others?" *International Journal of Press/Politics* 15(2):139–54.

Coleman, S., and J. Gotze. 2001. *Bowling Together: Online Public Engagement in Policy Deliberation.* London: Hansard Society.

Coleman, S., D. E. Morrison, and S. Yates. 2011. "The Mediation of Political Disconnection." In *Political Communication in Postmodern Democracy: Challenging the Primacy of Politics*, edited by K. Brants and K. Voltmer, 215–30. London: Palgrave.

Coleman, S., and G. Moss. 2008. "Governing at a Distance: Politicians in the Blogosphere." *Information Polity* 10(3):373–92.

Coleman, S., and P. Shane, eds. 2011. *Connecting Democracy: Online Consultation and the Future of Democratic Discourse.* Cambridge: MIT Press.

Couldry, N. 2008. "Mediatization or Mediation? Alternative Understandings of the Emergent Space of Digital Storytelling." *New Media and Society* 10(3):373–92.

Cruikshank, B. 1999. *The Will to Empower: Democratic Citizens and Other Subjects.* Ithaca: Cornell University Press.

Culver, K., and P. Howe. 2008. "Calling All Citizens: The Challenges of Public Consultation." *Canadian Public Administration* 47(1):52–75.

Dean, M. 1999. *Governmentality: Power and Rule in Modern Society.* London: Sage.

Delli Carpini, M., F. Cook, and L. Jacobs. 2004. "Public Deliberation, Discursive Participation, and Citizen Engagement: A Review of the Empirical Literature." *Annual Review of Political Science* 7:315–44.

Diani, M., and D. McAdam, eds. 2003. *Social Movements and Networks: Relational Approaches to Collective Action.* Oxford: Oxford University Press.

Donath, J. 2002. "A Semantic Approach to Visualizing Online Conversations." *Communications of the ACM*, 45(4):45–50.

Drake, D., N. Steckler, and M. Koch. 2004. "Information Sharing in and across Government Agencies: The Role and Influence of Scientist, Politician, and Bureaucrat Subcultures." *Social Science Computer Review* 22(1):67–84.

Fairclough, N. 1998. "Democracy and the Public Sphere in Critical Research on Discourse." Paper delivered at conference on Discourse, Politics and Identity in Europe, Vienna.

Fischer, F. 2003. *Reframing Public Policy: Discursive Politics and Deliberative Practices.* Oxford: Oxford University Press.

Flinders, M. 2004. "Distributed Public Governance in the European Union." *Journal of European Public Policy* 11(3):520–44.

Foss, N. 2007. "The Emerging Knowledge Governance Approach: Challenges and Characteristics." *Organization* 14(1):29–52.

French, S. 2007. "Web-enabled Strategic GDSS, e-Democracy and Arrow's Theorem: A Bayesian Perspective." *Decision Support Systems* 2007:1476–84.

Gibson, R., P. Nixon, and S. Ward, eds. 2003. *Net Gain? Political Parties and the Internet.* London: Routledge.

Girard, M., and D. Stark. 2007. "Socio-Technologies of Assembly: Sense Making and Demonstration in Rebuilding Lower Manhattan." In *Governance and Information: The Rewiring of Governance and Deliberation in the 21st Century*, edited by D. Lazer and V. Mayer-Schoenberger, 145–82. Oxford: Oxford University Press.

Granovetter, M. 1973. "The Strength of Weak Ties." *American Journal of Sociology* 78(6):1360–80.

Grossman, L. 1995. *The Electronic Republic: Reshaping Democracy in the Information Age.* New York: Viking.

Habermas, J. 1996. *Between Facts and Norms: Contributions to a Discourse Theory of Law and Democracy.* Translated by W. Rehg. Cambridge: MIT Press.

Hajer, M. 2003. "Policy without Polity? Policy Analysis and the Institutional Void." *Policy Sciences* 36(2):175–95.

Hajer, M., and H. Wagenaar, eds. 2003. *Deliberative Policy Analysis: Understanding Governance in the Network Society.* New York: Cambridge University Press.

Halseth, G., and A. Booth. 2003. "What Works Well; What Needs Improvement: Lessons in Public Consultation from British Columbia's Resource Planning Processes." *Local Environment* 8(4):437–56.

Hardy, P. 2007. "An Investigation into the Application of the Patient Voices Digital Stories in Healthcare Education: Quality of Learning, Policy Impact and Practice-Based Value." MSc thesis, University of Ulster, available on the Pilgrim Projects web site.

Hindman, M. 2009. *The Myth of Digital Democracy.* Princeton: Princeton University Press.

Kavada, A. 2005. "Exploring the Role of the Internet in the Movement for

Alternative Globalization: The Case of the Paris 2003 European Social Forum." *Westminster Papers in Communication and Culture*, available on the University of Westminster web site.
Kooiman, J. 2003. *Governing as Governance*. London: Sage.
Koppenjan, J., M. Kars, and H. van der Voort. 2009. "Vertical Politics in Horizontal Policy Networks: Framework Setting as Coupling Arrangement." *Policy Studies Journal* 37(4):769–92.
Lambert, J. 2007. "Digital Storytelling: Capturing Lives, Creating Community." *Futurist* 41(2).
Levinas, E. 1969. *Totality and Infinity*. Pittsburgh: Duquesne University Press.
Lundby, K. 2008. *Digital Storytelling, Mediatized Stories: Self-Representations in New Media*. New York: P. Lang.
Lupia, A. 2002. "Deliberation Disconnected: What It Takes to Improve Civic Competence." *Law and Contemporary Problems* 65:133–50.
Luskin, R., J. Fishkin, and S. Iyengar. 2003. "Considered Opinions on U.S. Foreign Policy: Face-to-Face versus Online Deliberative." Paper presented to the annual meeting of the American Political Science Association, Philadelphia, August 27–31.
Mambrey, P., and R. Doerr. 2009. "Local Encyclopedias beyond Mass Media and Government: City Wikis." In *Electronic Government: 8th International Conference, EGOV 2009, Linz, Austria, August 31–September 3, 2009, Proceedings*, edited by Maria A. Wimmer et al., 123–30. New York: Springer.
Mancini, C., and S. Buckingham-Shum. 2006. "Modelling Discourse in Contested Domains: A Semiotic and Cognitive Framework." *International Journal of Human-Computer Studies* 64(11):1154–71.
Margolis, S., and D. Resnick. 2000. *Politics as Usual: The Cyberspace "Revolution."* Thousand Oaks, Calif.: Sage.
Martin, S., and I. Sanderson. 1999. "Evaluating Public Policy Experiments Measuring Outcomes, Monitoring Processes or Managing Pilots?" *Evaluation* 5(3):245–58.
McNutt, K. 2008. "Policy and Politics on the Web: Virtual Policy Networks and Climate Change." *Canadian Political Science Review* 2(1):1–15.
Metler, Suzanne, and Joe Soss. 2004. "The Consequences of Public Policy for Democratic Citizenship: Bridging Policy Studies and Mass Politics." *Perspectives on Politics* 2(1):55–74.
Milioni, D. 2009. "Probing the Online Counterpublic Sphere: The Case of Indymedia Athens." *Media, Culture and Society* 31(3):409–31.
Moghadam, V. 2000. "Transnational Feminist Networks: Collective Action in an Era of Globalization." *International Sociology* 15(1):57–86.
Monnoyer-Smith, L. 2008. "Deliberation and Inclusion: Framing Online Public Debate to Enlarge Participation: A Theoretical Proposal." *I/S: Journal of Law and Policy* 87.

Morris, D. 2001. "Direct Democracy and the Internet." *Loyola of Los Angeles Law Review* 34(3).
Mouffe, C. 2005. *On the Political*. London: Routledge.
Ostrom, E. 1991. *Crossing the Great Divide: Coproduction, Synergy, and Development*. Institute of Research Studies, University of California, Berkeley.
Papacharissi, Z. 2004. "The Virtual Sphere: The Internet as a Public Sphere." *New Media and Society* 4(1):9–28.
Papadopoulos, Y. 2003. "Cooperative Forms of Governance: Problems of Democratic Accountability in Complex Environments." *European Journal of Political Research* 42(4):473–502.
Pawson, R. 2006. *Evidence-Based Policy: A Realist Perspective*. London: Sage.
Polletta, F., and J. Lee. 2006. "Is Telling Stories Good for Democracy? Rhetoric in Public Deliberation after 9/11." *American Sociological Review* 71(5):699–723.
Price, V., and Joseph N. Cappella. 2002. "Online Deliberation and Its Influence: The Electronic Dialogue Project in Campaign 2000." *IT and Society* 1(1):303–29.
Renton, A., and A. Macintosh. 2007. "Computer Supported Argument Maps as a Policy Memory." *Information Society* 23(2):125–33.
Rhodes, R. A. W. 2002. "Putting People Back into Networks." *Australian Journal of Political Science* 37(3):399–416.
Rogers, R., and N. Marres. 2000. "Landscaping Climate Change: A Mapping Technique for Understanding Science and Technology Debates on the World Wide Web." *Public Understanding of Science* 9(2):141–64.
Rorty, R. 1990. *Contingency, Irony and Solidarity*. Cambridge: Cambridge University Press.
Rose, N. 1999. *Powers of Freedom: Reframing Political Thought*. Cambridge: Cambridge University Press.
Rowe, G., and L. Frewer. 2005. "Public Participation Methods: A Framework for Evaluation." *Science Technology and Human Values* 25(1):3–29.
Sack, W. 2000. "Conversation Map: An Interface for Very-Large-Scale Conversations." *Journal of Management Information Systems* 17(3):73–92.
Sanderson, I. 2002. "Evaluation, Policy Learning and Evidence-Based Policy Making." *Public Administration* 80(1):1–22.
Savage, L. J. 1954. *The Foundations of Statistics*. New York: John Wiley and Sons.
Schifino, L. 2006. "Engaging Vernacular Voices: Exploring Online Public Spheres of Discourse for Everyday Citizens." PhD diss., Duquesne University.
Shane, P., ed. 2004. *Democracy Online: The Prospects for Political Renewal through the Internet*. New York: Routledge.

Shumate, M., and J. Lipp. 2008. "Connective Collective Action Online: An Examination of the Hyperlink Network Structure of an NGO Issue Network." *Journal of Computer-Mediated-Communication* 14(1):178–201.

Simonson, P. 1996. "Dreams of Democratic Togetherness: Communication Hope from Cooley to Katz." *Critical Studies in Mass Communication* 13(4):324–42.

Stone, D. 1999. "Learning Lessons and Transferring Policy across Time, Space and Disciplines." *Politics* 19(1):51–59.

Thumin, N. 2006. "Mediated Self-Representations: 'Ordinary People' in 'Communities.'" *Critical Studies* 28:255–74.

Tilly, C. 2002. *Stories, Identities and Political Change*. Lanham, Md.: Rowan and Littlefield.

van Kersbergen, K., and F. van Waarden. 2004. "'Governance' as a Bridge between Disciplines: Cross-Disciplinary Inspiration Regarding Shifts in Governance and Problems of Governability, Accountability and Legitimacy." *European Journal of Political Science* 43(2):143–71.

Warren, M. 1992. "Democratic Theory and Self-Transformation." *American Political Science Review* 86(1):8–23.

Wellman, B., A. Quan-Haase, J. Boase, W. Chen, K. Hampton, I. de Diaz, and K. Miyata. 2003. "The Social Affordances of the Internet for Networked Individualism." *Journal of Computer-Mediated Communication* 8(3).

Wolin, S. 1997. "What Time Is It?" *Theory and Event* 1(1).

Wolman, H., and E. Page. 2002. "Policy Transfer among Local Governments: An Information-Theory Approach." *Governance* 15(4):477–502.

Wright, S., and J. Street. 2007. "Democracy, Deliberation and Design: The Case of Online Discussion Forums." *New Media and Society* 9(5):849–69.

LEONIE SANDERCOCK AND GIOVANNI ATTILI

6. Multimedia and Urban Narratives in the Planning Process
Film as Policy Inquiry and Dialogue Catalyst

This chapter explores some of the potential applications of multimedia in the urban policy and planning fields.[1] This is an epistemological as well as a pragmatic exploration, probing the capacities of multimedia as a mode of inquiry, as a form of meaning making, as a tool of community engagement, and as a catalyst for public policy dialogues. Although this is not a totally new epistemological excavation, we are trying out new tools and developing a new approach, which we describe as *digital ethnography* (Attili 2007; Sandercock and Attili 2010a), a qualitative inquiry using film and multimedia languages to create a polyphonic narrative.

Our chapter is a critical reflection on a three-year action research project that began in 2005 as a dual inquiry: it is both policy-oriented and methodologically and epistemologically experimental. In policy terms, we were interested in how Canada's liberal approach to immigration, and the accompanying national multicultural philosophy, actually translated from the national policy-making level to the streets and neighborhoods where diverse cultures face the daily challenges of coexistence. What kinds of sociological and political imagination, at the local level, could make for peaceful coexistence? How were anti-immigrant and racist sentiments being addressed? What would an in-depth study of one culturally diverse neighborhood in Vancouver reveal? Methodologically, could we use film as both a mode of inquiry and as a means to disseminate research findings? And what were the epistemological underpinnings of such a methodology?

We begin with an account of our postpositivist epistemological orientation, particularly our emphasis on polyphonic narrative analysis through the medium of film as an antidote to the typically bidimensional, cartographic, and quantitative biases of urban policy and planning research. We then proceed with a sketch of the back story of Canada's evolving approach to immigration policy, followed by our case study, a thick description of the role of one local institution in one culturally diverse neighborhood in Vancouver, asking "how do strangers become neighbors?" Interwoven with this inquiry is the account of the making of our documentary *Where Strangers Become Neighbours* and an evaluation of its effectiveness as a catalyst for policy dialogue.

Epistemological Shifts

The beginnings of an epistemological shift in the field of planning were foreshadowed in the early 1970s in the works of J. Friedmann (1973) and C. W. Churchman (1971). Friedmann outlined a "crisis of knowing" in which he skewered the limitations of "expert knowledge" and advocated a new approach that he called "mutual learning" or "transactive planning," an approach that could appreciate and draw on local and experiential knowledge in dialogue with expert knowledge. At the same time, Churchman's inquiry into knowing was exploring the value of stories. "The Hegelian inquirer is a storyteller, and Hegel's Thesis is that the best inquiry is the inquiry that produces stories" (Churchman 1971:178). Over the next several decades, the termites kept eating away at the Enlightenment foundations of modernist planning, anchored as it was in an epistemology that privileged scientific and technical ways of knowing. Accompanying a broader postpositivist movement in the social sciences (Bourdieu 1990; Flyvbjerg 2002; Rabinow and Sullivan 1987; Stretton 1969), which was pushed further along by feminist and postcolonial critiques (hooks 1984; Kelly 1984; Lerner 1997; Said 1979; Sandercock 1998; Trinh 1989), planning scholars began to see the need both for an expanded language for planning and for ways of expanding the creative capacities of planners (Landry 2000, 2006; Sandercock 2005a, 2005b; Sarkissian and Hurford 2010). An "epistemology of multiplicity" (Sandercock 1998) would nurture these other ways of knowing, without discarding or dismissing more traditional forms of scientific or technical reasoning.

The "story turn" in planning has been one response to this epistemological crisis. In the past two decades a growing number of planning scholars have been investigating the relationship between story and planning (Attili 2007; Eckstein and Throgmorton 2003; Forester 1989; Mandelbaum 1991; Sandercock 2003a). These investigations highlight how planning is performed through stories, how rhetoric and poetics are crucial in interactive processes, how the communicative dimension is central to planning practices, and how story can awaken energies and imaginations, becoming a catalyst for involving urban conversations and for deep community dialogues.

Elsewhere we have argued that multimedia is becoming "a new frontier" in the urban policy and planning fields (Sandercock and Attili 2010a), providing not only multiple forms of voice and thus participation but also opportunities for stimulating dialogue, opening up a public conversation and influencing policy. There are diverse ways in which multimedia can nurture community engagement and community development as well as oppositional forms of planning. Multimedia tools create the opportunity for urban researchers to discover new realities, to expand the horizons of qualitative and quantitative research, and to represent the city in multidimensional and polyphonic ways. And multimedia products can offer transformative learning experiences, "educating the heart" through mobilizing "a democracy of the senses" (Back 2007). In this chapter, we outline our approach and reflect on our first attempt at applying it.

From Bidimensional Surfaces to Ethnographic Polyphonies

The language of film can give expression to a dense qualitative analysis of social phenomena in a territorial context. It can be used to give thick and complex accounts of the city focused on stories, interviews, and narration. Qualitative analysis succeeds in expressing what lies beyond the surface of maps, physical objects, classifications, and aggregate quantitative data. It intentionally focuses on individual lives in urban settings made up of changing densities, memories, perceptions, and aesthetics. It is an attentive, extremely focused analysis of urban space, where existence, intersections, languages, and interstitial freedoms delineate controversial and palpitating urban landscapes.

The goal of this kind of analysis is to probe deeply into inhabitants' lived practices, conflicts, and modalities of space appropriation that will reveal principles, rationalities, and potential writings that interrogate the ordered text of the planned city. Capturing these multiform practices means to listen to the city's murmurs, to catch stories, and to read signs and spatial poetics, all of which are generative of new meanings.

Using film is a way of researching what normally remains invisible in planning (though not in life) and ends by questioning the way planners typically explore, analyze, and represent urban space.

Bypassing the ideology of the Archimedean observer who stands outside the observed, the qualitative approach privileges collaborative contexts that produce a collective invention of interconnected stories. In this perspective, there is no longer a single eye that encompasses "everything" in its vision, but a multiplicity of stories told by the inhabitants of specific neighborhoods (or villages or organizations) who no longer can be thought of as isolated monads (as, for example, in survey research), and whose stories must be understood as an interconnected web. Through in-depth interviews and the confrontation of diverse visions of the world, this approach becomes a powerful tool for a deeper comprehension of what animates the many souls, conflicts, and resources of the city.

The result is a film narrative built on the intersection of multiple narratives captured by the ethnographer. It is a story that doesn't pretend to represent "the truth"; rather, it is explicitly subjective, even partial. The key words to comprehend the fulcrum of digital ethnographic analysis is "to evoke," that is, to create a plausible world—one of many such worlds—taken from everyday life. Digital ethnography becomes an interconnected patchwork of evocative images whose full comprehension escapes the researcher's intentionality, as the film creates a dynamic field that is open to diverse interpretations and possibilities. This level of interpretive openness transforms a digital ethnography into a potential catalyst for participatory planning. In other words, digital ethnographies represent a new way of provoking dialogue in decision-making contexts. It is a way of starting a public conversation (Attili 2010a).

Learning from our predecessors in visual anthropology (see Asch 1992; Banks 2001; Ruby 1995, 2000), we are very aware, in our practice of digital ethnography, of ethical issues and power relations. Digital ethnographies are self-reflexive analytical practices aimed at portraying lives and stories, transgressing objectified urban representations, and creatively expressing meaningful narratives. The polyphonic ethnographic narrative is the result of a series of in-depth interviews, acquired after a process of building rapport and trust, an activity based on a deep interaction with people who entrust their stories to us. It is an interpretive practice, the aim of which is to make sense of phenomena in terms of the meanings people bring to them (Denzin and Lincoln 2005).

Narrative Analysis

The ethnographic approach is an in-depth exploration of people's stories. These stories are the contextualized product of a complex dialogical process (a situated relationship) between the researcher and his or her interlocutor. In this process, things are in constant relation to each other, acting on and being acted on at the same time. There are not rigid and dichotomous boundaries that set the subject against the object, the researcher against the researched, the stimulus against the answer, or the causes against the effects. This dialogical process can be described as "I never react to you but to you-plus-me; or to be more accurate, it is I-plus-you reacting to you-plus-me. *I* can never influence *you* because you have already influenced me; that is, in the very process of meeting, by the very process of meeting, we both become something different" (Follett 1924:62–64). In other words, there is a coevolving relational dynamic in which the different activities are deeply and circularly interpenetrated, a conversational dynamic in which the involved subjectivities reciprocally influence and transform each other.

Therefore, narration is not a solipsistic act: it is a sense-making practice that involves the other and the relationship with the other. This discursive interaction constantly deals with identity issues (Weick 1995). Through the process of narration, we locate ourselves and try to delineate who we are. This means building a sense of identity, framing our actions, making sense of our projects, and defining our place in the world. In the construction of a story, the narrator is a sense maker who selects an appropriate self, among the many selves who coexist within each person (among the many identities that are part of an intricate "parliament of selves"; Mead 1934), and offers this identity to his or her interlocutor. From this perspective, the narrative construction of an identity is always relational and expositive (Arendt 1958; Nancy 1990) and often strategically and politically built. It is rooted in a dialogical process that transgresses an essentialist, substantial, and objective interpretation of identity. Identity is not something stable and unmodifiable: it is not given before and outside the encounter with the other. Rather, it constantly reshapes itself in this very same encounter, in a process that is ambiguous, fluid, and problematic.

Narratives produced in an ethnographic study have other characteristics that need to be outlined. Narratives are always built in retrospect: they refer to something that has already happened, so narrating something implies that something already occurred. But the narrative reconstruction of what happened is not a faithful account; rather, it is an inevitably distorted interpretation. Weick (1995) uses an interesting image to portray a retrospective sense-making process: a light cone that is projected toward the past and whose vertex is located *hic et nunc* (here and now: a specific point in time and space). This particular configuration implies that what we see of the past is influenced by the placement of the vertex: that is, our present. Everything that is affecting our present (projects, ideas, emotions) will consequently affect how we make sense of the past. Making sense doesn't simply refer to the selection of specific elements of the past, but also to their reconstruction according to an "interested" present. In this process, the resulting narrative often erases events, simplifies uncertainties, justifies past experiences, and reelaborates action sequences. It can only make "the past clearer than the present or future; it cannot make the past transparent" (Starbuck and Milliken 1988). The unfaithfulness of memory is not simply a lack of objectivity. It reveals the presence of the narrator, of his or her current concerns and values. As a result, Weick's cone of light selectively illuminates particular things and not others. In this process the light doesn't simply reveal; rather, it colors, deforms, and distorts.

In *Out of Africa*, Karen Blixen (1937) tells the story of a man who lives close to a pond. One night this man is awakened by a terrible noise coming from the pond and leaves his house to find the cause of it. It's very dark. The man walks. At various times he stumbles, falls down, gets up, and stumbles again. Finally, he realizes that the noise is coming out of a big leak in the dam. The man succeeds in repairing the hole. Now he can go to bed. When the next morning the man looks out of his little window, he recognizes in the sets of footprints he left the previous night in the sand the design of a stork. This little story is metaphorically very dense. The stork is the meaning the man recognizes in what he has lived. The disorganized events of his life, the confused footprints left in the sands, are now seen and interpreted in an organized and meaningful perspective. His life path, in which intentionality and accidents are mixed together, is now precisely lighted. The stork can be seen and appreciated only retrospectively. The man needs to wait for the following day and can value the figure of the stork only from his window. From a distanced place: from the perspective of one who doesn't participate in the events anymore or observe the ground without trampling on it. The stork saves the man from the confused events of his life. The stork is the story he tells to himself. A story that is not accurate, even completely false, may still be useful and plausible for the one who produced it.

Narratives, in fact, distance themselves from a logical-deductive rationality. They imperfectly refer to facts and are based on selected and incomplete information. The process of constructing meanings is not primarily a pursuit of truth, accuracy, or objectivity. People need to distort and filter in order to distinguish the signal from the background noises if they don't want to be overcome by detailed data. If we consider the interactive and interpersonal context in which narratives are built, it becomes clear how this form of knowledge is fluid and mutable. In this dimension, there is no constancy in the perception of external stimulus. The same personal identity is plural, evolving, different in space and time. The unsteadiness of relationships and interpersonal perceptions makes no room for accuracy. From this perspective, narratives can be interpreted as delicate arts that try "to reveal the meaning without defining it" (Cavarero 1997). To narrate means to circumscribe without closing or labeling, to create borders and transgress them: "Like a space that contains and opens at the same time" (Melucci 2000). In a narrative, what is needed is plausibility, internal coherence, and social acceptance rather than accuracy. Plausibility makes things comprehensible and potentially more able to stimulate actions.

From a constructive perspective, narratives not only interpret the world, they also create it. Or, in other terms, narratives create what they interpret. A sense-making narrative shapes, transforms, and establishes a world. Narratives institute a set of constraints and possibilities that will influence projects and actions. Whenever people say something, they create rather than describe a situation (Winograd and Flores 1986). For instance, when something is labeled and narrated as a problem, that same problem comes to life. In doing this, a story creates a field for possible actions, a theater in which new things can potentially occur. As in the Veda, in which Vishnu, through his steps, creates a space for the warlike action of Indra (cited in de Certeau 1990:185), a story is capable of building and founding meaningful contexts that shape what people might do. A circularity marks this process: people create what they interpret, but at the same time what is created and narrated influences people. People enact the environments of their narratives and different worlds are created by being talked about. But these worlds shape the subjects of the same narratives.

After considering all these things, it appears clear that a careful and attentive narrative analysis can focus not on stories as fixed and objectified products, but rather on narratives as a result of complex dialogical processes. This kind of analysis tries to understand not only the content of what is narrated (thematic analysis), but also the process through which that particular story has been built (interactional analysis). From this perspective, storytelling must be interpreted as a process of co-construction, where teller and listener are mutually and circularly interconnected: a process in which the complex relationship between interviewer and interviewee influences and shapes the narrative; a process rooted in a specific space and time, where retrospective views do not mirror but refract the past; a process in which current imagination and strategic interests influence how narrators choose to select and connect events and make them meaningful for others (Kohler Riessman 2004). It is a process of "enactment" (Weick 1995).

From this perspective, the narrative analysis deals not only with texts but even with how those texts are built: it focuses on the interpretation and on the construction at the same time. Emphasizing how and why a narrative is built helps provide further elements to contextualize the narrative itself. It also involves self-reflection regarding the role of the researcher, who can no longer be seen as an external and neutral entity. The whole process amounts to a shift from things as they are (ontology) to things as we know them (epistemology).

Moreover, the levels of reflexivity increase if we consider that an ethnographic analysis is characterized by a double-hermeneutical approach. People interpret their worlds by building narratives. Researchers build a polyphonic "text" out of these narratives (a narration of narrations), through further interpretive processes. In other words, ethnography's attempt is to make sense (the work of researcher) of various sense-making processes (the narratives of the interviewees). And every level of interpretation requires an in-depth reflexive practice that is potentially able to scan products and processes, texts, and the conditions of their existence.

These levels of reflexivity led us to consider ourselves as part of the phenomenon being studied (Flyvbjerg 2001:132): our presence and the relationships we built in the research process profoundly shaped the inquiry. Throughout this project, we constantly analyzed our own role: we were always aware that we were acting as engaged researchers rather than neutral policy analysts or social technicians. We became very engaged with this community and its struggles to overcome anti-immigrant sentiments that were prevalent in the 1970s and 1980s. And at a certain point we realized that we were becoming advocates for their particular policy approach to integrating immigrants. But before that story unfolds...

The Back Story

Almost a century ago, the Liberal government led by Prime Minister Wilfred Laurier decided that immigration was Canada's destiny and proposed an answer to the question of immigration and identity: "Let them look to the past, but let them also look to the future: let them look to the land of their ancestors, but let them also look to the land of their children." These words happen to capture succinctly the tightrope that Canadian multicultural policy has teetered along as it has sought to adjust to new waves of immigration since 1967 from predominantly non-Anglo-European source countries. Canada, then, can be seen as a remarkable social and political experiment in constructing a nation that is not—or rather is no longer—based on assumed cultural homogeneity as the foundational citizenship criterion. Precisely *how* national immigration policies propelled by an economic and geopolitical rationale translate into ways of actually living together in cities and neighborhoods is the underlying fascination of and curiosity behind our film and this text.

Canada's immigration policy has always been driven opportunistically as well as ideologically: on the one hand, by the need to populate and develop a country of vast and challenging geographic scale; on the other, by the desire to reproduce European civilization. From the late nineteenth century onward, immigration quotas were racist: Europeans were welcome; non-Europeans were not. The single most significant change in this approach to immigration policy did not come until the passage of the Immigration Act of 1967, which, in response to the labor shortages of the postwar boom, explicitly ended the racially and culturally based criteria for immigration.

Over the next twenty years or so, the long-standing global pattern of migration to Canada was turned almost completely upside down. The combined proportion of immigrants admitted from Europe (including the United Kingdom) and the United States fell from 85 percent in 1966 to 50 percent in 1975, to 30 percent in 1985, to 22 percent in 1995, and was just over 21 percent in 2004 (Hiebert 2006:7). In 2004, 47 percent of immigrants landing in Canada came from the Asia-Pacific region, 22 percent from Africa and the Middle East, and 9 percent from Latin America. In other words, almost four-fifths of recent immigrants have arrived from nontraditional source countries, presenting significant challenges in both economic and social integration.

In 1971, Liberal Prime Minister Pierre Trudeau's multiculturalism policy was invented to acknowledge the increasingly diverse demographic profile of the postwar period (Fleras and Elliot 1999; Hiebert, Collins, and Spoonley 2003). Beginning in 1971, when Canada became the first country in the world to introduce an official policy embracing the idea of multiculturalism, this new self-understanding became permanently embedded in political discourse and the Canadian imagination (Canadian Heritage 2006a, 2006b). As the idea of multiculturalism evolved, it came to encompass the rights of individuals to retain their cultural practices (as opposed to the idea of assimilation to the dominant culture, or the "melting-pot" approach of the United States), the provision of social services to new immigrants, and antidiscriminatory policies (Hiebert, Collins, and Spoonley 2003). Multiculturalism thus became deeply embedded in a broad range of laws, policy statements, and international agreements, including the Employment Equity Act (1986), the Pay Equity Act (1985), and the Multiculturalism Act (1988). As a central tenet of Canadian society, it was finally enshrined in the Charter of Rights and Freedoms (1982; Canadian Heritage 2006c). The Charter and the Multiculturalism Act have been particularly important. The legislative and charter frameworks established in the 1980s now require all federal institutions to formally adopt multicultural policies as part of their working mandates, and the Ministry of Citizenship and Immigration Canada (CIC), which implements multiculturalism policy, is supported by the minister of state for multiculturalism. Since the federal government sets policy and establishes funds to implement policies, provincial governments have been forced to follow suit, establishing their own ministries to oversee multicultural affairs. Over the past twenty years, a thick institutional infrastructure supporting the integration of immigrants has evolved, connecting federal, provincial, and municipal governments along with an increasingly important role for nongovernmental organizations, all of which is evidence of Canada's commitment to actively creating a multicultural society.

The Research Question and Collaborative Research Protocols

But how does this work in streets and shops and schools, on public transit, in recreational pursuits, in everyday language and body language? How does a multicultural society become a lived experience? That was our research question, which we captured in the phrase "how do strangers become neighbors," and we set about looking for sociological as well as political answers.

We chose Collingwood as our research site; it is one of the most culturally diverse neighborhoods in Vancouver, and we wanted to pay special attention to the role of one local institution in that neighborhood, the Collingwood Neighbourhood House (CNH), which came into existence in 1985 as a sort of modern-day incarnation of the nineteenth-century settlement house tradition.[2] Actually, CNH had approached us about a partnership between the community and the university that might assist them in their funding challenges, so there was always a reciprocal relationship at play.

From the very beginning, there was both an advocacy and collaborative dimension of our film-research project. Our research agenda, as we expressed it to CNH, was twofold. We wanted to understand how this neighborhood of forty-five thousand people had overcome the anti-immigrant sentiment that existed there (and in the city at large) in the 1970s and 1980s and succeeded in becoming a remarkably integrated intercultural community. How had a once predominantly Anglo-European population adapted to the arrival of a large number of newcomers from East and Southeast Asia, the Middle East, Latin America, and Africa? How did this process of immigrant integration actually work?

How did immigrants begin to establish a new life and develop a sense of belonging to a new place? How did strangers become neighbors? How important was CNH's role in this? And we also wanted to experiment by using film as both a mode of inquiry and as a way of communicating research results and stimulating policy dialogue. There was thus always an action component of our research agenda, in that we believed that the CNH story was a potentially inspirational one that deserved to be told not only across Canada but perhaps also in European and now Asian countries experiencing similar unsettlings as a result of immigration from culturally diverse source countries.

CNH folks were comfortable with our research objectives, which they found compatible with their own desire to document their achievements (in community building broadly, and in the integration of immigrants more specifically) for fundraising purposes and for the sharing of institutional learning.

We believed (as researchers), but had yet to do the research to prove, that the CNH's work over its almost twenty-year life span had resulted in transformational social changes at the neighborhood scale. We needed to find out as much as we could about what they had done and how. We also believed that the best way to do this was to work with CNH, developing relations of trust with them, seeking their advice and feedback throughout the research and especially through the film editing process. Broadly speaking, we were embracing an approach to policy research that sought to incorporate the learning of service providers (CNH) and service users (the residents of this neighborhood) and to capture "evidence" of policy effectiveness in a qualitatively rich way rather than in the currently fashionable and supposedly objective systematic reviews and feedback questionnaires of evidence-based practice.

Research, Filming, and Postproduction

We spent a lot of time (and had a whole class of graduate students assisting us with) interviewing neighborhood residents, both oldtimers and newcomers, as well as staff, volunteers, and members of the CNH board. We also interviewed residents, city planners, and politicians who had been involved in the initial community planning process that had resulted in the residents' desire to create the CNH as a gathering place and as a facility that could provide services for families and children.

Close to a hundred people were interviewed, using a video camera to collect their voices.

Once the interviewing work was finished, we embarked on the next phase, identifying further research and reflecting on the shape and content of the story we wanted to tell: the story of a neighborhood that, just twenty years earlier, had been locking its doors, was afraid of change, and was telling immigrants to go back where they came from, but that is now a totally welcoming place. We spent three more months in the neighborhood, talking with many people in an ever-widening web of relations, and consolidating our relationship with CNH. At a certain point, we realized that people recognized us as we walked around the streets with our camera and tripod, were friendly and welcoming toward us, and were curious about how our project was coming along. In other words, we were developing a sense of identification with and affection for this amazing neighborhood and were, on a number of occasions, moved to tears by the stories we were being told and the passionate intensity of the lived experiences of upheaval, arrival, struggle, and achieving a new sense of belonging. At the same time, we were also trying to think critically and analytically about what we were absorbing and how to interpret it, always aware that our own voices would ultimately mingle and dialogue with those of our interviewees, both implicitly, in the way that we chose to edit, and explicitly, in the narration that Leonie was beginning to write.

The decision to use voice-over narration came about in the postproduction stage. When we began the project, our reflections on the "politics of voice" (who is speaking, on behalf of whom?) suggested to us that we wanted this community and this organization to tell their own story, in their own words, rather than our speaking for them. But once we began to edit sequences (pieces of the overall story), we began to realize that a narrative voice was necessary not only to thread these pieces together, but also to connect some of the microstories with the larger sociocultural and political economic forces at play in Canada and globally. We were, always consciously and reflectively, trying to be in and out at the same moment, walking a tightrope between empathic compassion, admiration, and distanced observation. And rather than posing as objective documentary filmmakers, we found that the voice-over narration made our role as interpreters more transparent.

Research Findings

We have written at length elsewhere about the answers we found to our research questions, specifically concerning the community development approach to the integration of immigrants (Sandercock and Attili 2009). Here, we focus on the second and third parts of our research agenda: the experimental use of film as a research tool and as a communicative device.

Our approach to making the documentary was actually a two-stage process, in the first of which we were asking several questions: What is the story we want to tell? What is the answer to our initial question ("how do strangers become neighbors?")? What is the best way to tell that story? So the first challenge was how to tell the story in a powerful way, as narrative, using as much as possible the voices of the actual community. At the end of that stage, we had a "talking heads" story. The second stage was the visual storytelling, the layering in of all the digital material we had been collecting (photographs, old video footage, newspaper clippings, posters, location footage, statistics, and so on), and the creative invention of visually stimulating ways of placing all this on a screen, often telling multiple stories in one frame through the use of multiple images alongside and around a talking head or voice-over narration.

The theme that emerged most powerfully from the multiple interviews was how this neighborhood had been transformed over a twenty-year period, from initial fear and anxiety and even hostility toward the new immigrants, to eventual acceptance and working together to build a community where none had previously existed. It was clear that the central actor in this story was the Neighbourhood House itself, but the story of the CNH was in turn a story about the people who founded it, their vision and mission, and their ongoing efforts at outreach and social inclusion. We also realized that it was important to explain how and why this particular local institution was established in 1985, since that story reflected something about the planning culture in Vancouver (in other words, a larger contextual element of explanation). The short answer to the question of how strangers had become neighbors in Collingwood is the community development approach of the CNH (as opposed to being simply a service and program delivery agency) and the vision of social inclusion. Our challenge was how to explain this community development process and the gradual shift in attitudes that it produced.

We decided to construct the narrative both as a "then-and-now" story and as a sequence of stories around themes, programs, and events that illustrated the community development approach. Beginning with the origins story of how the CNH came into being, we then constructed sequences focusing on the growth of the CNH, both physical and programmatic. These included the development of a Community Leadership Institute that helped local residents acquire leadership skills to take on important roles in the community; the development of the Buddy Program, which involved matching local youth with newcomers and then developing programs taught by youth themselves about antiracism and violence-bullying; the unearthing of local artistic skills through the Arts Pow Wow, a community cultural development process that began with an inventory of residents' skills and then involved mobilizing those skills in an array of community development activities led by these local artists (from gardening to music and dance to lantern making, puppetry, storytelling, and so on, all of which are used to enhance local celebrations); the story of the reclamation (from drug dealers and gangs) of a local park and its transformation through a participatory design process led by local residents; and the story of the annual celebration of cultural diversity in Multiweek, a week in February during which the many cultures that coexist in this neighborhood come together to share traditions and customs.

As we reviewed our digital interviews, we realized that there were five women whose personal stories of leaving, arrival, struggle to find their place, and achieving a sense of belonging through the CNH could drive the narrative forward and provide a very involving emotional dimension. We used their voices to convey through life stories what the CNH had been able to achieve. Finally, we realized that to weave some of these sequences together, we needed a voice-over narration, which could also convey analytical and thematic information such as "the age of migration" and the global forces operating on a neighborhood, as well as the national political philosophy of multiculturalism that shaped federal and provincial funding and enabled the CNH to access resources for the kinds of programs it was inventing. So, our own interpretive voice was added to provide these additional contextual dimensions.

As we worked on the film, it became more and more evident to us that we were making a documentary that advocated a particular policy approach to the social integration of immigrants. We were hoping to raise awareness of the importance of a local, place-based, community development approach in fostering the social integration of immigrants through demonstrating the achievements of the CNH. In other words, we understood that we were acting politically in making this film, in assuming the responsibility of narrating an inspiring story, and in showing how a local institution managed to help a neighborhood to overcome its fear of strangers and in the process to do remarkable community building work.

Every single choice we made during the editing process was connected with these emerging objectives that affected not only the construction of the story itself, but the way it was told visually. From this perspective, what we produced was a multistratified visual layout, a complex web of images and information that were interconnected and displayed on the same screen. The documentary thus featured not merely talking heads, but an intricate tangle of images potentially able to allow the spectator to dive into the story's depth. What we pursued was the possibility of creating aesthetic connections intended as different ways of learning through visual, narrative, and musical languages.

Dissemination of the Film and Research

There were three audiences of equal significance to us as we constructed the film: the neighborhood residents themselves, other communities who may be inspired by the CNH story, and people in various policy-making arenas (local, provincial, and federal). The local community was the first to see the film, at the twentieth birthday celebration of the CNH in late November 2005. On that occasion, CNH rented a huge screen and professional sound equipment to convert the gym into a movie theater that could hold three to four hundred people. At the reception before the screening, there was a lot of excitement and anticipation in the air. We stood at the back of the gym in the dark, feeling anxious. At this first official projection of the documentary, the audience's reaction was incredible. Many people were in tears after the screening, positively moved by the inspiring story. Most of the people we had interviewed now saw their own story as part of something much larger, as a web of connections and actions that amounted to a heroic story of human achievement. There was incredible pride as people realized what they had accomplished and understood the bigger picture of a complex story of which they only knew the small segments in which they had personally been involved. The consciousness of being part of a larger story was both empowering and an important step toward a renewed sense of belonging. This was something we had not fully anticipated as filmmakers: the way the film could contribute to this ongoing process of creating a sense of community and belonging. For many, it was akin to a ritual passage that enabled them to make sense of the history of this institution over the last twenty years. It was both energizing and an occasion, subsequently, for further reflection by CNH staff and board about the future.

In addition to the local residents at this screening, there were also some local politicians and city planners who had been involved in the community planning process that resulted in the establishment of CNH, as well as folks from other Neighbourhood Houses in Vancouver. The screening generated a lot of interest in the film, and shortly after this we began to receive a lot of requests for further screenings. We now had to think about the distribution issue: how could we get the film out there, without ourselves traveling with it everywhere? Obviously, we wanted to get the film shown as widely as possible because of its educational value and policy relevance. We needed a distributor, and CNH agreed with us that the ideal distributor would be the National Film Board (NFB) of Canada.[3]

While we waited for the NFB to review the film, Leonie worked with CNH Executive Director Paula Carr on a grant application, with the idea of producing a manual to accompany the film, and then taking both film and manual on the road in workshops in different Canadian cities. We won the grant from the Metropolis research network and hired Val Cavers, who had just retired as settlement services coordinator at CNH, to research and write the manual.[4] We agreed that the manual would convey more of the details of the "how"—how the CNH had done what it had done—and also that the manual would be written as much as possible through stories.

Our Metropolis grant funding enabled Paula and Leonie to visit four cities (Edmonton, Halifax, Moncton, and Toronto) to run half-day workshops using the film as a catalyst for community dialogue about immigration and integration, and leaving participants with manuals to take back to their organizations. The collaboration with the Metropolis research network was important strategically at this stage of the project. Each of the Centres of Excellence advertised our workshops through their local networks, so we were able to reach exactly the audiences we hoped to reach: local organizations involved with immigrants and refugees, nonprofits and faith-based organizations, and municipalities that were becoming increasingly concerned about the challenges of the arrival of significant numbers of newcomers. Provincial and federal policy makers also attended in each city, as well as university researchers and people from the arts sector. In Toronto, we had an audience of between seventy and eighty people. In the other three cities, attendance was between thirty and fifty. We used the same format for each, a brief introduction about why we had made the film, followed by a screening, followed by ninety minutes or so of facilitated discussion, tailored to the interests and concerns of the specific audience. Workshop attendees were given a copy of the manual, *How Strangers Become Neighbours: Constructing Citizenship through Community Development* (Cavers, Carr, and Sandercock 2007), which tells how the CNH developed its unique approach to community development through building relationships, what kinds of programs and services it offers, where it gets its funding, how it trains staff and volunteers, how its outreach programs work, how the resident-run board operates, how they develop community leadership, why its approach is intercultural rather than multicultural, and above all, the values that have shaped this very special place.

These workshops had diverse goals: creating dialogue in each city between different actors in the policy sector concerned with immigration and integration; discussing the intercultural philosophy at the heart of CNH work; raising awareness of the importance of a focus on the neighborhood level as a policy domain; demonstrating the value of a community development approach to active citizenship; understanding what brings about positive changes in attitudes toward immigrants; and empowering of other communities through the example of this one.

Discussions were extraordinarily animated, and the response was extremely positive. In all postworkshop evaluations, 90 percent of attendees rated the workshops in the top category (on a scale of one to five) and rated the value of the film at the same level. In addition, an interesting dynamic emerged in the course of these workshops as people working in the same field and in the same city discovered each other for the first time, thus establishing new networks concerned with the social integration of immigrants.

Two other pieces of the dissemination process are worth mentioning. We have received many invitations to screen the film and facilitate discussion, from government agencies to community meetings to keynotes at academic conferences, as well as screenings at several international film festivals.[5] Social issues, immigration policies, planning themes, the media, and communications became the subjects of intense discussion wherever we have shown the film. Perhaps the single most gratifying experience was the use of the film as the "evidence" submitted by CNH in nominating itself for the BMW Award for Intercultural Learning in the Practice category in 2007. CNH was awarded first prize, and the executive director and the chairman of the board of CNH were flown to Munich to receive the award, with a lot of attendant publicity. It was the first time in the ten years of this award that an organization outside of Europe had received the prize.

The third and final stage of our project was to reach an audience in European cities. Talking that through with each other and with CNH, we concluded that for the film to have any significant impact in Europe, we would need to write a book to accompany and contextualize the film, setting it in its metropolitan planning context as well as the national political, legal, and philosophical context (Sandercock and Attili 2009). The book (which includes the DVD) was again a collaborative enterprise between the two filmmakers-researchers and two CNH staffers (the executive director and the coordinator of settlement services).

Evaluation

How can we gauge the successes and weaknesses of this project? Given the intent expressed earlier, the project could be assessed by the community dialogue it produced, by the range of organizations currently using the film for education and training, by the number of invited screenings and awards, and, in the longer term, by community and government responses. Outcomes are hard to identify and even harder to measure in this kind of research, but here is what we have observed, evaluated, and heard over the four years since the film was finished and the three years since its official release by the NFB.

Impact on the Local Community

One more or less immediate (but unexpected) impact was the sense of psychological empowerment experienced by local residents and the CNH. Even those interviewees who had been involved with the CNH from its inception or over many years had a kind of epiphany about the scope and achievement of the organization and the way it had transformed so many lives. Among those interviewees who were less frequent users of programs or had been volunteers at a certain stage of their lives in the neighborhood, there was an eye-opening sense of the larger history of which they had been a part. This realization, and the enormous pride it engendered, has been energizing and renewing for the staff, the volunteers, and the board, as well as the local residents.

It was something of a surprise to us, as filmmakers, that the film encouraged the local community (and their politicians) to reflect about themselves and to begin to strategize the next twenty years and helped to further motivate and empower people. The subsequent publicity and attention focused on CNH, both nationally and internationally, especially as a result of the BMW Award for Intercultural Learning, has brought an enormous sense of recognition and generated new opportunities. In late 2008, Executive Director Paula Carr put forward a proposal to the board to start a social enterprise within CNH, offering their acquired expertise to other nonprofits and government agencies as consultants in "creating welcoming communities." The proposal is currently being implemented, and the film has a central ongoing role as a catalyst and training tool.

Wider Impact

As word has spread about the film through screenings, conference presentations, and keynotes, a number of organizations have purchased the film and are using it in training with their staff. These organizations include the municipalities of Halifax, Nova Scotia, and Richmond and Vancouver, British Columbia; the planning department of the City of Auckland, New Zealand: the City of Oslo and the Police Department of Oslo; the Norwegian National Housing Authority; the Race Relations Office of the Northern Ireland Housing Executive; and the Salem-Keizer Community Development Corporation in Salem, Oregon. This is a random sample, known to us only because these organizations approached us for copies rather than going to the NFB.

There has certainly been great interest and lively debate at all of the screenings of the film that we have attended, whether in universities or communities. Anecdotal and experiential evidence from these occasions shows that the film works well as a stimulator of dialogue, as an inspiration and a learning tool that demonstrates the effectiveness of community development approaches to particular issues. But the only systematic evidence that we have is from the aforementioned four workshops organized through our Metropolis research grant. The 90 percent approval rating for both the workshop and the film after each of these workshops seems to confirm both the power of the story itself and the power of film as the storytelling medium.

Beyond these outcomes, there are a few other interesting strands worth a brief mention, which suggest an ongoing influence in the policy realm in diverse arenas. In 2008, Paula Carr was seconded part-time to the province's Government and Non-Profit Initiative as a member of an advisory group on the contributions made by the nonprofit sector to community well-being and to the implementation of government policy. Later that year, the province released Can$750,000 in funding for twelve Neighbourhood Houses to continue "welcoming communities" programs, suggesting that awareness of neighborhood-based approaches is spreading. CNH is also in discussions to pilot a new provincial government initiative showcasing the benefits of a multisectoral approach to integration.

There is also new interest at the federal government level in local, place-based approaches to social policy issues. The Community Approaches and Initiatives Division of Human Resources and Social Development Canada initiated a Round Table discussion in November 2008 (to which Leonie was invited) on place-based policy, research, and initiatives with the intention of developing a national policy framework and learning network. Leonie was also invited to Ottawa in March 2009 to address and have a dialogue with federal public servants in a series known as the Armchair Discussion, organized by the Multiculturalism Branch of the federal department of Citizenship and Immigration Canada, a discussion that is also web cast. In the audience was the director-general of multiculturalism, who became very interested in the CNH story.

Critical Reflections

In developing our approach to digital ethnography as policy inquiry and as planning praxis, our intent is both to evoke and to provoke: to evoke the richness and diversity of urban life through a polyphonic multimedia approach, and to provoke both policy conversation and community dialogue about the subject matter. There is always an action research agenda, which is context specific and affects how we "frame" the project, ethically and politically. What follows is a self-evaluation, bearing in mind these intentions.

On reflection, we realized that there were a number of failures and omissions in the narrative analysis, some of which only became apparent through dialogues with various audiences. Perhaps the most frequently asked question at screenings concerns the relative absence of conflict in the story. Our answer conveyed our own frustration at not succeeding in getting interviewees to tell those stories on camera. We heard a lot more in informal conversation with residents about the levels and forms of racism and xenophobia that had existed in the 1980s than we were able to capture on camera. Most people were reluctant to recall such troubles, especially since they thought these problems had pretty much been overcome in the past two decades, thanks to the work of CNH; but they were also reluctant because they were still working and living alongside people with whom they had once been in conflict but who now had changed their attitudes toward newcomers.

The relative absence of conflict is a problem in filmic terms, resulting in less tension and less of a sense of what was at stake here in the past two decades. It is even more of a problem for social learning. Other communities could learn more from the film if they had a better understanding of how great the challenges were in the 1980s. We should have given much more emphasis, in the film, to the extensive and ongoing antiracism training conducted by CNH for board members, staff, and volunteers and their many proactive efforts involving antiracism work, for example, in the immediate aftermath of September 11. As we became aware of this shortcoming, we sought to address it in the manual and the book, foregrounding stories of specific conflicts and providing a detailed description of how these conflicts were handled by CNH.

The second most frequently asked question concerned the apparent dominance of women in CNH activities. This was because we obtained more animated interviews from the women than from most of the men we interviewed, resulting in selection and editing processes that give an inaccurate portrayal of the levels of involvement of men in CNH programs and governance. Reflecting on what we learned from this, for future projects, we would either spend more time preparing interviewees who are intimidated by the camera, or we would record them on audio tape and create audio montages of voices, to not exclude people because they are less articulate. Interestingly, though, we found that people's level of articulation and animation was not closely related to class and education. This is a low to moderate income neighborhood in which 73 percent of the population does not speak English as their first language, yet most people were in fact wonderfully engaging interviewees, irrespective of their English-language fluency.

A third omission is the absence of voices from the First Nations (indigenous) residents of the neighborhood. A related shortcoming was that our voice-over narration goes straight into the story of late-twentieth-century immigration to Canada, without acknowledging First Nations as the original inhabitants of this land. Because we were worried about the length of the film and felt that a couple of sentences on this topic could easily be regarded as tokenism, we chose not to mention it at all, a decision we later regretted. In Canada, First Nations peoples are still locked in struggle with provincial and federal governments over land and sovereignty. The history of colonization and the attempted cultural genocide of First Nations peoples is not well known within Canada, let alone beyond, and remains the dark side of Canadian history.[6]

We started from a theoretical position critical of the dominant forms of representation of the city (the cartographic anxiety) and the kinds of knowledge and experience regarded as legitimate. We feel an urgency to invent new descriptive and analytical tools that can give centrality to people, focusing on not only individual practices but also the collective practices through which inhabitants create their own meaningful life spaces in the face of large social and historical forces. From this perspective, we decided to explore tools that not only capture such everyday experiences of meaning making, but also give citizens more opportunities to participate in conversations about their cities and communities and more influence in shaping, improving, and protecting them.

But, like most policy researchers, we also wanted to have some impact in the policy realm. A major lesson in this respect is the importance of identifying, at the outset of a project, one's desired audience or audiences and developing a plan for getting the film to those audiences. In other words, it's not enough to make a film and then simply hope that it reaches the desired audiences. One has to actively pursue opportunities for screenings in policy forums and strategize about avenues of influence. We were partially successful in this respect because of our multiple-city workshops, co-organized with the Metropolis research network, and because we energetically pursued screening opportunities in diverse settings and locations. But one would be hard-pressed to point to direct policy changes as a result of the message of a documentary film, even one as commercially successful as, say, Al Gore's *An Inconvenient Truth*, at least in the short term. Ultimately, then, a longer time frame is needed for evaluation, along with a recognition that one's voice is just that: one voice among many influences in a public policy conversation, albeit a voice emerging from a medium a little more seductive than the standard research monograph.

Notes

1. *Multimedia* refers to the combination of multiple contents (both traditional and digital: texts, still images, animations, audio and video productions) and interactive platforms (offline interactive CD-ROMs, online web sites and forums, digital environments) in the urban policy and planning fields.

2. For more details about CNH, see Sandercock and Attili 2009.

3. The NFB has a proud history of pioneering a participatory film and video tradition dedicated to the pursuit of social change. In December 2006, the National Film Board of Canada agreed to distribute our film, which was released through the NFB web site in late 2007.

4. The Metropolis Research Network is funded jointly by the Canadian government (through the Department of Citizenship and Immigration) and the Social Sciences and Humanities Research Council (SSHRC) and in 2010 was in its third five-year funding cycle. Each of the five Centres of Excellence involves a collaboration between universities, government agencies, and NGOs in the city in which the center is located. We were funded through Metropolis BC (British Columbia). Information is available on the Metropolis BC web site.

5. We personally screened the film at thirty-four venues between November 2005 and November 2009. The film was awarded an Honourable Mention (International Federation of Housing and Planning, Interna-

tional Film and Video Competition, Geneva, 2006) and a Special Mention (Berkeley Video and Film Festival, 2006).

6. Our current documentary project tells this story through the eyes of two First Nations communities in north-central British Columbia (see Sandercock and Attili 2010b).

References

Arendt, H. 1958. *Human Condition.* Chicago: University of Chicago Press.
Asch, T. 1992. "The Ethics of Ethnographic Film Making." In *Film as Ethnography*, edited by P. I. Crawford and D. Turton, 98–115. Manchester: Manchester University Press.
Attili, G. 2007. "Digital Ethnographies in the Planning Field." *Planning Theory and Practice* 8(1):90–98.
———. 2008. *Rappresentare la citta dei migranti.* Milan: Jaca.
———. 2010a. "Beyond the Flatlands: Digital Ethnographies in the Planning Field." In Sandercock and Attili, *Multimedia in Urban Policy and Planning*, 39–54.
———. 2010b. "Representations of an *Unsettled* City: Hypermedial Landscapes in Rome." In Sandercock and Attili, *Multimedia in Urban Policy and Planning*, 177–208.
Attili, G., and L. Sandercock. 2007. *Where Strangers Become Neighbours: The Story of the Collingwood Neighbourhood House and the Integration of Immigrants in Vancouver.* Montreal: National Film Board of Canada. Documentary, 50 minutes.
Back, L. 2007. *The Art of Listening.* Oxford: Berg.
Banks, M. 2001. *Visual Methods in Social Research.* London: Sage.
Barbash, I., and L. Taylor. 1997. *Cross-Cultural Film Making: A Handbook for Making Documentary and Ethnographic Films and Videos.* Berkeley: University of California Press.
Blixen, K. 1937. *Out of Africa.* London: Putnam.
Bourdieu, P. 1990. *In Other Words: Essays towards a Reflexive Sociology.* Cambridge, England: Polity.
Canadian Heritage. 2006a. *Canadian Multiculturalism: An Inclusive Citizenship*, on the web site for Canadian Heritage.
———. 2006b. *Diversity in Our Urban Centres: Canada's Ethnicities*, on the web site for Canadian Heritage.
———. 2006c. *Policy and Legislative Framework*, on the web site for Canadian Heritage.
Cavarero, A. 1997. *Tu che mi guardi, tu che mi racconti. Filosofia della narrazione.* Milan: Feltrinelli.
Cavers, V., P. Carr, and L. Sandercock. 2007. *How Strangers Become Neigh-*

bours: *Constructing Citizenship through Neighbourhood Community Development*. Vancouver, B.C.: School of Community and Regional Planning, on the Metropolis BC web site.

Churchman, C.W. 1971. *The Design of Inquiring Systems*. New York: Basic.

de Certeau, M. 1990. *L'invention du quotidien*. Paris: Gallimard.

Denzin, N. K., and Y. S. Lincoln, eds. 2005. *The Sage Handbook of Qualitative Research*. Thousand Oaks, Calif.: Sage.

Eckstein, B., and J. Throgmorton, eds. 2003. *Story and Sustainability*. Cambridge: MIT Press.

Fleras, A., and J. H. Leonard Elliott. 1999. *Multiculturalism in Canada: The Challenge of Diversity*. Scarborough, Ont.: Nelson Canada.

Flyvbjerg, B. 2002. *Making Social Science Matter*. Cambridge: Cambridge University Press.

Follet, M. P. 1924. *Creative Experience*. New York: Longmans Green.

Forester, J. 1989. *Planning in the Face of Power*. Berkeley: University of California Press.

Freire, P. 1970. *Pedagogy of the Oppressed*. New York: Herder and Herder.

Friedmann, J. 1973. *Retracking America*. New York: Doubleday Anchor.

Geertz, C. 1988. *Works and Lives: The Anthropologist as Author*. Stanford: Stanford University Press.

Hiebert, D. 2006. *Beyond the Polemics: The Economic Outcomes of Canadian Immigration*. RIIM Working Paper Series, 06-15.

Hiebert, D., J. Collins, and P. Spoonley. 2003. *Uneven Globalization: Neoliberal Regimes, Immigration, and Multiculturalism in Australia, Canada, and New Zealand*. Research in Immigration and Migration Working Paper, 03-05.

Hindess, B. 1996. *Discourses of Power: From Hobbes to Foucault*. Cambridge, Mass.: Blackwell.

hooks, b. 1984. *Feminist Theory: From Margin to Center*. Boston: South End.

——. 1990. "Marginality as Site of Resistance." In *Out There: Marginalization and Contemporary Cultures*, edited by R. Ferguson et al. Cambridge: MIT Press.

Kelly, J. G. 1984. *Women, History, and Theory*. Chicago: University of Chicago Press.

Knight, L. W. 2005. *Citizen: Jane Addams and the Struggle for Democracy*. Chicago: University of Chicago Press.

Kohler Riessman, C. 2004. "Narrative Analysis." In *Encyclopedia of Social Science Research Methods*, edited by M. S. Lewis-Beck, A. Bryman, and T. Futing Liao, 705–9. London: Sage.

Landry, C. 2000. *The Creative City*. London: Earthscan.

——. 2006. *The Art of City Making*. London: Earthscan.

Lerner, G. 1997. *Why History Matters*. Oxford: Oxford University Press.

Mandelbaum, S. 1991. "Telling Stories." *Journal of Planning Education and Research* 10(1):209–14.

Mead, G. H. 1934. *Mente, sé e società*. Firenze: Giunti Barbera.

Melucci, A. 2000. *Culture in gioco: Differenza per convivere*. Milan: Il Saggiatore.

Nancy, J. L. 1990. *La Communauté désoeuvrée*. Paris: Bourgeois.

Rabinow, P., and W. M. Sullivan, eds. 1987. *Interpretive Social Science: A Second Look*. Berkeley: University of California Press.

Ruby, J. 1995. "The Moral Burden of Authorship in Ethnographic Film." *Visual Anthropology Review* 11(2):77–82.

———. 2000. *Picturing Culture: Explorations of Film and Anthropology*. Chicago: University of Chicago Press.

Said, E. 1979. *Orientalism*. New York: Vintage.

Sandercock, L. 1998. *Towards Cosmopolis: Planning for Multicultural Cities*. Chichester: John Wiley and Sons.

———. 2003a. *Cosmopolis 2: Mongrel Cities of the 21st Century*. London: Continuum.

———. 2003b. "Out of the Closet: The Importance of Stories and Storytelling in Planning Practice." *Planning Theory and Practice* 4(1):11–28.

———. 2005a. "A Planning Imagination for the 21st Century." *Journal of the American Planning Association* 70(2):133–41.

———. 2005b. "A New Spin on the Creative City: Artist/Planner Collaborations." *Planning Theory and Practice* 6(1):101–3.

Sandercock, L., and G. Attili. 2009. *Where Strangers Become Neighbours: The Integration of Immigrants in Vancouver, Canada*. Heidelberg: Springer.

———, eds. 2010a. *Multimedia in Urban Policy and Planning: Beyond the Flatlands*. Dordrecht: Springer.

———. 2010b. *Finding Our Way*. Vancouver: Moving Images. Documentary, 90 minutes.

———. 2010c. "Digital Ethnography as Planning Praxis." *Planning Theory and Practice* 11(1).

Sarkissian, W., and D. Hurford, with C. Wenman. 2010. *Creative Community Planning: Transformative Engagement Methods for Working at the Edge*. London: Earthscan.

Scott, J. C. 1998. *Seeing Like a State*. New Haven: Yale University Press.

Starbuck, W. H., and F. J. Milliken. 1988. "Executives' Perceptual Filters: What They Notice and How They Make Sense." In *The Executive Effects: Concepts and Methods for Studying Top Managers*, edited by D. C. Hambrick, 35–65. Greenwich, Conn.: JAI.

Stretton, H. 1969. *The Political Sciences*. London: Routledge.

Trinh, T. Minh-Ha. 1989. *Woman Native Other: Writing Postcoloniality and Feminism*. Bloomington: Indiana University Press.

Weick, K. E. 1995. *Sensemaking in Organizations.* Thousand Oaks, Calif.: Sage.
Winograd, T., and F. Flores. 1986. *Calcolatori e conoscenza: Un nuovo approccio alla progettazione delle tecnologie dell'informazione.* Milan: Mondadori.
Young, I. M. 1997. *Intersecting Voices: Dilemmas of Gender, Political Philosophy and Policy.* Princeton: Princeton University Press.

PART IV

Policy Rhetoric, Argumentation, and Semiotics

7. Political Rhetoric and Stem Cell Policy in the United States

Embodiments, Scenographies, and Emotions

In 2006, during the midterm election, Missouri was a crucial state for the Democratic Party's attempt to win a majority in the United States Senate. The contest between incumbent Republican senator Jim Talent and his Democratic challenger Claire McCaskill was one of the most closely watched Senate races in the country.

A few weeks before the election, a thirty-second video appeared on local TV and was soon available on the Internet, featuring the Hollywood star Michael J. Fox with the following message: "As you might know, I care deeply about stem cell research. In Missouri, you can elect Claire McCaskill, who shares my hope for cures. Unfortunately, Senator Jim Talent opposes expanding stem cell research. Senator Talent even wanted to criminalize the science that gives us a chance for hope. They say all politics is local, but that's not always the case. What you do in Missouri matters to millions of Americans—Americans like me." Fox's message was followed by a statement of the Democratic Party's candidate for Missouri's Senate seat:[1] "I'm Claire McCaskill, and I approve this message."[2]

From its beginnings in the late 1990s, human embryonic stem cell research has been a broadly debated and highly divisive issue in politics in the United States. In Missouri, stem cells were one of the biggest issues during the Senate race in 2006 because of a state initiative on the ballot that year to allow human embryonic stem cell research. The general assessment was that an approval of stem cell research by voters in Missouri, a state with a strong tradition of religious groups opposed to abortion participating in politics, would send a strong message to the nation's political leadership.

Michael J. Fox's support for stem cell research came at a crucial moment for the future of stem cell research in the United States, but it also played a role in a close contest for the majority in the United States Senate. It aimed to influence an election but also tried to tip the balance in a crucial battle over the direction and regulation of biomedical research in the United States.[3]

Hollywood stars using their public fame to influence elections is a common feature of politics. But the Michael J. Fox video did not just constitute a simple endorsement of a politician: it operated and gained its power of persuasion through the subtlety and complexity of its intervention. It demonstrates in just thirty-eight seconds why rhetoric must be seen as an essential moment in the process of policy making.

Michael J. Fox, to start with, was not just another Hollywood star taking a position in a political campaign. After being diagnosed with Parkinson's disease in the early 1990s, he eventually reduced the acting roles he accepted and became an advocate for Parkinson's disease research. The star of *Back to the Future*, known to most viewers as a youthful and humorous actor, in his message in support of Claire McCaskill is sitting in a dimly lit room, his head and upper torso incessantly and strongly shaking from side to side as he speaks. He looks serious, but also worn and desperate. He confronts the viewers with the somehow unsettling situation in which he, the obvious victim of long-lasting, crippling disease, implores his audience to vote for a politician who wants to help people like him, people who suffer badly under a devastating disease that they could be healed of if only important research were not banned for political reasons. Fox's clear message for his audience is in essence "help stem cell research through your vote." But to some extent, *he is also* this message: his suffering body is inseparably connected with what he says. This is not a role he plays; instead, he embodies Parkinson's. Not only does he appeal to the viewers' sense of logical reasoning, but he also elicits an emotional response. Fox sends a verbal message to his viewers and also communicates through his body, producing a complex situation of exchange and involvement in which he enacts his disease before his audience so they can see and feel what it means to have Parkinson's disease.

None of the rhetorical forms applied in the Michael J. Fox video were new, unlike the technologies that were used to disseminate it. Since its posting on YouTube, it has been viewed about 3.4 million times worldwide.[4] Rhetoric is always in policy making, but, stunningly enough, while the importance of the mass media in policy making is commonsense knowledge today, the role of rhetoric is not broadly acknowledged in the field of policy studies. Public policy is, to paraphrase John Dewey about the public and its problems, about the ways that issues and problems are defined and enter the political and the policy agenda (Dewey [1927] 1991; Parsons 1995). Rhetoric is a key force in this context. The concept of rhetoric directs our attention to the centrality of persuasion in policy making. What it helps us to understand is *how* policy-making processes—the definition of policy issues and problems—come about and are settled, or not. Many policy-making processes from stem cell research to global warming are never-ending, fraught by struggles that at no time seem to end or that only temporarily see closure. Many intractable policy conflicts either do not lend themselves to processes of frame-reflection and reconciliation (Schön and Rein 1994), or cannot be stabilized through hegemony or tamed by imposing procedural rules. But they are always—if openly in public or secluded in back rooms—characterized by processes of persuasion enacted with the purpose of defining, influencing, and reaching decisions and policy outcomes: in short, with the idea of influencing and shaping political judgment, or, in Bryan Garsten's words, "the mental activity of responding to particular situations in a way that draws upon our sensations, beliefs and emotions without being dictated by them in any way reducible to a simple rule" (2006:7). These processes of persuasion involve not only good arguments but also emotions and those who do the arguing, through words and emotions. With persuasion, people try to influence and change one another's mind by appealing not only to reason but also to passions or even prejudice (Garsten 2006:3). The politics of persuasion is a politics of disagreement and controversy that goes beyond the exchange of arguments, a politics that counts on the free play of persuasion rather than on the taming of judgment through the imposition of rules of deliberation, as is typically suggested in deliberative policy analysis in the Habermasian tradition (Habermas 1985). Rhetorical analysis in policy research pays attention to the irreducible complexity of policy making and views the wealth of practices in persuasion as essential in the process of democratic decision making (Gottweis 2007).

Rhetoric and Argumentation

Rhetoric is broadly acknowledged as an important feature of the political process. Often associated with "the art of persuasion," rhetoric is typically defined as an integral moment of policy making, pointing to the necessity of convincing, persuading, and communicating efficiently in the context of shaping and implementing public policies. A highly publicized speech "to the nation" by a president of a country or a video message by a well-known actor in an electoral campaign can set the agenda in a policy field, push decision making into particular direction, or put pressure on policy makers of all parties.

As Michel Meyer points out, rhetoric appears forcefully in times of crisis because of a lack of directing principles for settling questions that are being submitted and receiving controversial answers. In the absence of leading principles that could offer definitive, unequivocal answers, problems are bound to be disputed and solved "equivocally." Just as in ancient Greece when the Peloponnesian War led to a collapse of well-established values and modes of thought and the rise of rhetoric, the upheavals of our times have led to a new reconsideration of rhetoric, argumentation, persuasion, and their relationship to logic and communication (Meyer 1994:36–37).

Although the power of rhetorical presentation in politics is hardly contested, the term "rhetoric" suffers from an image problem: while rhetoric is widely seen as closely linked with politics, it nevertheless often has a pejorative connotation, thought of as describing intellectually vacuous statements that mainly serve to manipulate, obfuscate, or distract from the real sequences of events. As I argue, this image problem of rhetoric dates back to Plato and has played a major role in the relative negligence of rhetoric in policy research. It is time to restore the place of rhetorical analysis in policy studies so we can cast an analytical light on highly important aspects of the policy-making process. Rhetoric is genuinely linked to the idea of persuasion, but it also has a much-neglected performative dimension: in the play of language, not only are signs communicated, but "things are being done."

Argumentation theory and rhetoric thus share a long history that dates to pre-Aristotelian philosophy. They are connected to considerations and reconsiderations of the notions of logic, communication, and persuasion. Mobilizing, positioning, and transmitting arguments also requires appropriate sociopolitical conditions. Argumentation is the antithesis of revelation; it does not concern itself with revealing a truth but instead attempts to convince (Breton and Gauthier 2000:3–5). The Sophists emphasized the importance of rhetoric in politics and embraced the idea that we are persuaded by facts (Danzinger 1995).

Plato accused the Sophists of only dealing with the *appearance* of truth, whereas philosophy's role was to deal with establishing the true and the good (Meyer 1994:50–51). Likewise, "embodied" positions were excluded from considerations of "truth" and later from "scientific objectivity" (Wilson and Lewiecki-Wilson 2001:6). In the Platonian tradition, the discipline of rhetoric has had to live with its image problem of superficially dealing with surface phenomena and deceit, instead of serving the establishment of the good and the true.

Aristotle, by contrast, attempted to accord a positive place to rhetoric by positioning rhetoric as part of dialectic, along with poetics and the study of topics (Meyer 1994:119–23). Classical rhetorics found its culmination in his work. According to Aristotle:

> Rhetoric may be defined as the *faculty* of observing in any given case the available means of persuasion. . . . Of the modes of persuasion furnished by the spoken word there are three kinds. The first kind depends on the personal character of the speaker (ethos); the second on putting the audience into a certain frame of mind (pathos); the third on the proof, or apparent proof, provided by the words of the speech itself (logos). Persuasion is achieved by the speaker's personal character when the speech is so spoken as to make us think him credible. We believe good men more fully and more readily than others: this is true generally whatever the question is, and absolutely true where exact certainty is impossible and opinions are divided. This kind of persuasion, like the others, should be achieved by what the speaker says, not by what people think of his character before he begins to speak. It is not true, as some writers assume in their treatises on rhetoric, that the personal goodness revealed by the speaker contributes nothing to his power of persuasion; on the contrary, his character may almost be called the most effective means of persuasion he possesses. (1991)

In contemporary times, the theory of argumentation and rhetoric was taken up and further developed in the late 1950s by Stephen Toulmin and, in particular, by Chaïm Perelman in his "New Rhetoric," and the work of both had a lasting influence in the field of political science (Perelman 1977; Perelman and Olbrechts-Tyteca 1958; Toulmin 1958). One of the key texts in contemporary policy analysis, Giandomenico Majone's *Evidence, Argument, and Persuasion in the Policy Process*, explicitly defines the ancient tradition of rhetoric as the obvious and necessary point of departure for modern policy analysis: "The centuries-old tradition of humanistic disciplines, from history and literary criticism to moral philosophy and law, proves that argumentative skills can be taught and learned. Thus, if the crucial argumentative function of policy analysis is neglected in university departments and schools of public policy, this is due less to a lack of suitable models than to serious misconceptions about the role of reason in human affairs and about the nature of the 'scientific method'" (1989:xii). Majone discusses in great detail the virtues of rhetoric for policy analysis and the argumentative character of the policy process itself, which calls for systematic attention to the role and function of words and the ways of "doing things with words" (7). As he observes, "its crucial argumentative aspect is what distinguishes policy analysis from the academic social sciences on the one hand, and from problem-solving methodologies such as operations research on the other" (7). In a similar way, James A. Throgmorton, in his chapter in *The Argumentative Turn in Policy Analysis and Planning*, has pointed to the importance of rhetoric in planning and policy making (1993; see also Throgmorton 1991).

But both Majone's and Throgmorton's texts reduce the notion of rhetoric to the idea of persuasion via the argument itself, to the process of demonstrating that something either is the case or is not, as determined by induction and deduction. Aristotle has called this form of reasoning "argumentation through logos." While emphasizing the fact that policy analysts themselves are part of a process of argumentation that ties the observer to the observed, Majone and Throgmorton focus on rhetoric as constitutive of the meaning of policy and planning, without elaborating further on the analytical instruments of rhetoric. Thus, the notion of rhetoric remains closely tied to the idea of logos, or the appeal to reason by means of words, deduction, and induction, which, already in the classical tradition of Aristotle was seen as only one among other "rhetorical proofs."

Rethinking Ethos, Pathos, and Logos in Rhetoric and Policy Making

This brings us back to the central rhetorical notions of ethos and pathos, which take us far beyond the usual confinements of deliberative policy analysis, which basically operates with an understanding of the policy process characterized by the operation of logos, communicative rationality, and the normative commitment of the political or democratic need to establish rules and procedures that "tame" the process of political judgment. While logos in the Aristotelian tradition convinces by itself, pathos and ethos are tied to specific circumstances and, above all, to the persons implied in those situations (Eggs 1999:45). It is important to distinguish between two understandings of ethos. In its broadest sense, *ethos* refers to the presentation of the self and its connection to one's personality, ideology, status, and milieu. In a (second) sense, this ethos, or image of oneself, implies a certain mode of argumentation (logos), a certain way to express emotions, and a certain way to present oneself as a speaker (ethos in the second sense) (1999:41). Following the tradition of the New Rhetoric as developed by Chaïm Perelman, Ruth Amossy, and Dominque Maingueneau (Amossy 2009; Maingueneau 1999; Perelman 1977), I suggest that the notion of ethos must be understood as something discursive and material rather than as particular qualities of a speaker, and I want to emphasize generally the procedural nature of rhetoric. In the perspective of what has been called the New Rhetoric, rhetoric is seen as something dynamic that links the concepts of the actor, language, and institutions in a theoretically novel manner. Besides logos, ethos, and pathos, key concepts are scenography, narrative, and discourse. These concepts allow us to rethink the notion of persuasion as a key element in policy making.

Where there is policy, there is persuasion, which is an interactive and material process that takes place with particular actors at a particular time and place. This interpretation of policy seems obvious, but it is not always practiced in discourse analysis, which too often seems to be interested exclusively in the play of language, quite often leading to analytical abstractionism. Simply put, we understand persuasion as a performative process and interactive process. J. L. Austin's performative speech act theory, most famously developed in his *How to Do Things with Words* (1962), interprets sentences as forms of actions. Performative utterances do not refer to an extralinguistic reality but instead enact or produce what they refer to. In contemporary constellations of policy making, this means that a multitude of actors operates at multiple places at different times in loosely structured networks that attempt to shape and implement policies in relationship to the public and to bring events and structures into existence (Hajer 2009; Weick 1988).

Following the work of Dominique Maingueneau (1999), we suggest that the operation of the ethos in rhetoric be defined as a process of interlocution in which a self-image of a speaker or actor is being constructed. In this context, we need to differentiate between what Beneviste (1972) has called enunciation and the enounced. The enounced is the corpus realized by the speaking subject, presented from his point of view as a homogeneous unity resulting from his enunciation. Both elements of the speech—enunciation and the enounced—have to be taken into consideration. They are indispensable for each other and for the speech. In his rhetorical analysis, Maingueneau focuses on the speaker, analyzing the way in which he or she enters into the interlocution as an appropriate self-image is constructed. The discursive ethos is built at the level of uttering. In the example cited at the beginning of this chapter, Michael J. Fox projects an image of his Self through his respective style, as well as at the level of the utterance, through what he explicitly highlights in his self-presentation. The construction of an ethos in the discourse often aims to displace or modify the prior image of the speaker. In the TV ad, Fox emphasizes the image of the Parkinson's patient and patient activist rather than that of the glamorous Hollywood actor, though this image exists in the background. Michael J. Fox presents himself as the likable actor but also as a patient and as a fellow citizen, as an American "like you" who lets the people in Missouri know that how they vote matters for America and for him, Michael J. Fox.

At the same time, Fox operates through the specific presentation of his Self as an emotional mode of persuasion. It is important to recognize that this emotional mode has nothing to do with eliciting irrationality; in fact, for Aristotle there was no contradiction between reason and emotion. He construed thought and belief as the cause of emotion and showed that emotional response is intelligent behavior that is open to reasoned persuasion. As William W. Fortenbaugh puts it in his classical study *Aristotle and Emotion*, "When men are angered, they are not victims of some totally irrational force. Rather, they are responding in accordance with the thought of unjust result. Their belief may be erroneous and their anger unreasonable, but their behavior is intelligent and cognitive in the sense that it is grounded upon a belief which may be criticised and even altered by argumentation" (1975:17). In contrast, emotions could also be conceptualized as a discursive practice. Emotions belong to the repertoire of rhetoric, and emotional display and the language of passion may very well coexist with argumentative and ethical discourse. This rhetorical view of emotions allows us to explore how speech and language provide the means by which local views of emotions have their effects and take on significance. Thus, this view emphasizes the interpretation of emotions as pragmatic acts and as communicative performances, and thus as modes of argumentation. Emotions should not be seen as "things" being carried by the vehicle of discourse and rhetoric, but as a form of rhetorical praxis that creates effects in the world (Abu-Lughod and Lutz 1990; Lutz and White 1986). Emotions can be "argumentative" in the sense that they function as an adjuvant to argumentation. In addition, the construction of emotion can be called argumentative when emotion becomes the object of argumentation: "In this respect, speakers argue in favor of or against an emotion: they give reasons supporting why they feel (or do not feel) this emotion and why it should (or should not) be legitimately felt. What comes into play here is the arguability of emotions. Emotions may become matters of dispute during interaction and their adequacy may be challenged. In such cases, the argumentative process bears not so much upon dispositions to believe or to act as upon dispositions to feel" (Micheli 2010: 13). Thus, not only does Michael J. Fox embody Parkinson's disease and not only is his visible suffering meant to contribute to the persuasion of the viewers to cast their votes for senatorial candidate Claire McCaskill, but his message implicitly also communicates that it is acceptable to be moved by his appearance.

A key notion in this framework for rhetorical analysis is the concept of scenography, which connects linguistic analysis with a social science approach and points to the dimension of the enactment of rhetoric. A scenography is a specific kind of constitution and composition of the speech of a subject and has great importance for the analysis of policy processes as it helps to discover the most important elements of the discursive strategies (Adam 1999) of the speaking subject (Maingueneau 2002). As already pointed out, the enounced is the corpus realized by the speaking subject, presented from his or her point of view as a homogeneous unity resulting from his or her enunciation. Both elements of the speech—enunciation and the enounced—have to be taken in consideration. Speakers freely choose a scenography, such as Michael J. Fox chose communication through a video message with his audience. He, his advisers, and the McCaskill campaign team could have chosen any other scenographies. In his video message, he speaks from what seems to be a home, a living room, as many Americans have, and from there he speaks intimately to his fellow citizens, at a critical moment in stem cell research, and his goal is to persuade Missourians toward a particular voting decision. His message is brief but full of direct and indirect references to a much larger discourse: the political discourse and controversy around stem cell research. He creates a scenography that should not be seen as a frame, a scenery, or a stage, as if discourse occurs within an already fixed place, independent of discourse. Scenography must be understood simultaneously as frame and process. A scenography is about a particular scene, such as a video message to an audience, and the making of this scene in a process. Scenographies are transformative and determined according to the content of discourse: discourse implies a given scenography (a speaker and an addressee, a place and a moment, a given use of language) through which a certain world is shaped, and in turn that world must validate the scenography through which it is shaped. Scenography is both what discourse comes from and what discourse generates. It is transformative, interactive, and connects somebody who speaks and who argues with others. Michael J. Fox draws on a larger political discourse on stem cell research, but he also produces this discourse. This discourse legitimizes a text that, in return, must show that the scenography from which the speech is proceeding is the pertinent scene for what it is speaking of. In a scenography, a decision is made for a particular genre of discourse: a press conference, a sermon, a political speech, or a contribution of expert knowledge. Depending on the selected genre of discourse, certain rules apply for how to argue and reason (Amossy 2001; Maingueneau and Angermüller 2007). Fox chose the scenography of a video message with its multiple implications, such as who constitutes his audience (not only the voters of Missouri, but also a much larger potential public in Web 2.0, which actively engaged in lively debate and exchange in the YouTube commentary section on the video) and the medium for distribution, namely, TV channels or the Internet. In the political world of the twenty-first century, with its multiplicity of sites of politics and policy making and networked structures of governance, the concept of scenography is also important to help us grasp the proliferation of sites of policy making.

    A scenography is embedded and at the same time productive of larger discourse structures, in particular of narrative and discourse (Maingueneau 1984). Related to the concepts of the enounced and of enounciation is the concept of the narrative, a type of organizing of enunciations that gives them order and structure and that plays an especially important role in policy making (Adam 1999). Policy narratives are the frames or plots used in the social construction of the fields of action for policy making, for governmental activities from environmental to technology policy. In the stem cell field, the argument that regenerative medicine will be essential in dealing with increasingly aging societies is such a policy. On the most general level, narrativity is the representation of real events that arises out of the desire to have real events display the coherence, integrity, fullness, and closure of an image of life that is and can only be imaginary (White 1981:23). Narratives bring elements of meaning, clarity, stability, and order into what usually tends to be the complicated and contradictory world of politics. This power to create order is an attractive quality that makes narratives essential for the shaping of policies, the settling of conflicts, and the securing of legitimacy for political action. A related concept is discourse, which, in its most basic definition, describes any level of language organization above the phrase. Again, for our purpose, narrativizing discourses are of special importance, as Hayden White puts it (1987:218). Narrativizing discourse refers to the numerous kinds of narratives that every culture can draw on for those of its members (such as administrators) who might wish to use them for the encodation and transmission of messages (for example, about pollution control). People bring narratives into the world. But these individuals give birth to narratives only within the confines of the available discursive possibilities. Actors cannot freely choose the narratives they deploy. The given discursive possibilities describe the large reservoir of narratives, which can be mobilized for political purposes.

Let me now return to this larger discourse on stem cell policy in the United States. Michael J. Fox's role in the Missouri Senate race was part of a much longer political battle dating back to 1998. At that time, two research teams, one headed by John Gearhart of Johns Hopkins University, the other lead by James Thomson at the University of Wisconsin, reported on a number of breakthroughs in the culturing of human embryonic stem cells. While Gearhart's team had isolated embryonic germ cells from aborted fetuses, Thomson and his collaborators obtained embryonic stem cells from embryos created by in vitro fertilization (IVF) and had grown them each for about five days. Their research was widely interpreted as a crucial step in the development of new strategies to grow human tissue and even organs. At the same time, from the very beginning it was clear that human embryonic stem cell research operated on ethically and morally difficult grounds. It was thematically connected to abortion and embryo research, and soon a line of conflict developed between those who supported stem cell research and experimental medical research with embryos and those, often religiously motivated, who opposed it, often as part of the opposition to abortion in the United States. During the Clinton administration, which was in office during the breakthrough in human embryonic stem cell research, the United States government was supportive of this line of research and had approved funding it through the National Institutes of Health (Gottweis, Salter, and Waldby 2008).

Then President George W. Bush took office in January 2001. At that time, there were already rumors that the new president would change the government's stem cell policy and adopt a more restrictive approach toward funding and regulation. In a much-publicized nationally televised speech on August 9, 2001, held at the Bush Ranch in Crawford, Texas, President Bush outlined in about ten minutes the federal government's new policy.

Tackling some of the key issues in stem cell research, the president started his speech by defining stem cell research as a key issue for his presidency:

> Good evening. I appreciate you giving me a few minutes of your time tonight so I can discuss with you a complex and difficult issue, an issue that is one of the most profound of our time....
>
> As I thought through this issue, I kept returning to two fundamental questions: First, are these frozen embryos human life, and therefore, something precious to be protected? And second, if they're going to be destroyed anyway, shouldn't they be used for a greater good, for research that has the potential to save and improve other lives?
>
> I've asked those questions and others of scientists, scholars, bioethicists, religious leaders, doctors, researchers, members of Congress, my Cabinet, and my friends. I have read heartfelt letters from many Amer-

icans. I have given this issue a great deal of thought, prayer and considerable reflection. And I have found widespread disagreement. . . .

My position on these issues is shaped by deeply held beliefs. I'm a strong supporter of science and technology, and believe they have the potential for incredible good—to improve lives, to save life, to conquer disease. Research offers hope that millions of our loved ones may be cured of a disease and rid of their suffering. I have friends whose children suffer from juvenile diabetes. Nancy Reagan has written me about President Reagan's struggle with Alzheimer's. My own family has confronted the tragedy of childhood leukemia. And, like all Americans, I have great hope for cures.

I also believe human life is a sacred gift from our Creator. I worry about a culture that devalues life, and believe as your President I have an important obligation to foster and encourage respect for life in America and throughout the world. And while we're all hopeful about the potential of this research, no one can be certain that the science will live up to the hope it has generated. . . .

Embryonic stem cell research offers both great promise and great peril. So I have decided we must proceed with great care.

As a result of private research, more than sixty genetically diverse stem cell lines already exist. They were created from embryos that have already been destroyed, and they have the ability to regenerate themselves indefinitely, creating ongoing opportunities for research. I have concluded that we should allow federal funds to be used for research on these existing stem cell lines, where the life and death decision has already been made. . . .

This allows us to explore the promise and potential of stem cell research without crossing a fundamental moral line, by providing taxpayer funding that would sanction or encourage further destruction of human embryos that have at least the potential for life. . . .

I will also name a President's council to monitor stem cell research, to recommend appropriate guidelines and regulations, and to consider all of the medical and ethical ramifications of biomedical innovation. . . .

As we go forward, I hope we will always be guided by both intellect and heart, by both our capabilities and our conscience.

I have made this decision with great care, and I pray it is the right one.[5]

Bush's speech is first of all a text with an argument developed step by step. It intervenes in a complex policy constellation by offering a new interpretation of the meaning and nature of the ongoing conflict. Bush employs the scenography of a presidential speech, posing in front of the national flag, a symbol of his power, but then chooses to speak not from the White House but from his home, his ranch in Crawford, Texas. He does not speak just to the United States Congress or to voters, but to "Americans," and wants to engage them "to discuss with him" a difficult topic. He builds an "intimate" scenography linking himself with "Americans" in a "discussion." While Michael J. Fox's statement attempted to persuade the voters of Missouri to cast their votes for a senator in support of stem cell research, President Bush had to convince all Americans that he had made the "right" decision. In the logic of Bush's narrative, the central conflict in stem cell policy is not between medical research and the rights of the unborn, but between those who want to develop new cell lines and those who are satisfied working with already existing lines of embryonic stem cells. President Bush does not just speak, he also presents himself to his audience as the president of the United States, always in touch with the nation and in some way the embodiment of the nation, in power, ready to decide when necessary and to take action as needed. He, the newly elected president, also operates strongly through his institutional position and the degree of authority that this position confers upon him, and he thus elicits what Maingueneau calls the "prior ethos" (Maingueneau 1999:78). Thus, the presidential decision and the new regulations offer simultaneously to protect the rights of the unborn and the freedom of research and to foster medical progress in America.

A televised speech to the nation by a United States president is neither a philosophical lecture nor an internal discussion paper: it is a much more interactive process. President Bush did not only develop an argument, he also engaged in a process of exchange with an evoked audience, the American public. And he used his personal ethos in this exchange, as well as the ethos of his office, the presidency of the United States, which he embodies as the elected president. Michael J. Fox had no office to speak from: he just had his persona, which encompassed not only a well-known actor but also someone suffering from, in essence, embodying, Parkinson's disease. In President Bush's speech, emotions also have their place; the strong emotions of people who have suffered under a disease like Alzheimer's are addressed. At the same time, Bush contends with these emotions, understandable as they might be for him, and balances them against the emotions of people who fear that stem cell research will lead the way into a new brave world and the termination of human life. At the end of the speech, he tells America that he prays he has made the right decision. Obviously, he is not sure if he has made the right decision: he has weighed argument against argument, emotions against emotions, and then announced his decision. His speech, then, attempts to persuade that he has made the "right decision," not just by putting forward good arguments for the presidential decision, but by operating the ethos of the president to give weight to his reasoning and balancing of the emotions in the stem field controversy.

Rhetoric in Texts and Deliberation

Policy texts are often composed by hundreds, if not thousands, of authors. It is not just in high-profile public appearances that we see rhetoric operate; we also see it in the much less spectacular world of daily-life policy controversy, on the level of administrative agencies and their clients and the lobby groups interacting with them, and in the field of policy deliberation. Such controversies proceed through debate, narrative, visual display, television, or Web 2.0. The ubiquity of controversy refers to its appearance across the diverse forums and interactions of our everyday lives, as well as its emergence across a range of topics. As temporally pluralistic, controversies endure over varying periods of time, exhibiting more and less active periods of engagement (Asen 2010:130). Policy making, such as in the stem cell or the global warming fields, operates across a multiplicity of sites that are more or less networked; persuasion does so as well, which can be observed across these many sites in a variety of scenographies in which policy actors attempt to shape the course of decision making.

Returning to the subject of stem cell research in the United States, it is important to see that the intervention of Michael J. Fox and President Bush's decision to slow the pace of human embryonic stem cell research were preceded by a long political battle dating back to the 1990s, when the question first surfaced of whether or not the National Institutes of Health (NIH) should and could support research in this field. At the core of this battle was a struggle over the meaning of what constitutes an embryo and what constitutes acceptable research with embryos. Since the 1990s this struggle has been enacted in a multitude of locations, and untold numbers of policy makers have engaged in a process of persuasion, attempting to advance their interpretations, definitions, and feelings into legislation, regulation, and policies (Gottweis, Salter, and Waldby 2008).

One site of struggle has been the field of invited consultation on the guidelines issued by the NIH to regulate both human embryonic stem cell research and its funding. In 1993, the NIH formed the Human Embryo Research Panel (HERP), which suggested that researchers be allowed to create embryos for certain research purposes. This position was rejected by President Clinton, and Congress took the opportunity afforded by the Department of Health and Human Services (DHHS) appropriations process to stipulate that an activity involving the creation, destruction, or exposure to risk of injury or death to human embryos for research purposes may not be supported with federal funds. Coauthored by Republican Jay Dickey and later called the Dickey Amendment, a rider, attached to the appropriations bill in 1995, said that any research posing a risk to an organism derived by fertilization was prohibited.[6] Congress has annually passed a similar ban since that time. The original congressional ban stated that federally appropriated funds could not be used for the creation of a human embryo or embryos for research purposes or for research in which a human embryo or embryos are destroyed, discarded, or knowingly subjected to risk of injury or death greater than that allowed for research on fetuses in utero. In light of the presidential and legislative bans, the NIH requested a legal opinion from the general counsel of DHHS on whether federal funds could be used to support research on human stem cells derived from embryos or fetal tissue. Harriet Rabb, DHHS general counsel, concluded that then-current law prohibiting the use of DHHS appropriated funds for human embryo research would not apply to research using stem cells "because such cells are not a human embryo within the statutory definition." General Counsel Rabb determined that the statutory ban on human embryo research defines an embryo as an "organism" that when implanted in the uterus is capable of becoming a human being. The opinion stated that pluripotent stem cells are not and cannot develop into an organism, as defined in the statute. DHHS concluded that the NIH could fund research that uses stem cells derived from the embryo through private funding. But, because of the language in the rider, the NIH could not fund research that had used federal funds to derive the stem cells from embryos.[7] This legal opinion—that NIH could fund research with already existing cells that were, with other funds, derived from embryos, but not fund the creation of new stem cell lines—was precisely what moved into the center of interpretations and contestations connected with the approval of federal funding for stem cell research in the United States (Gottweis, Salter, and Waldby 2008).

In the late 1990s, efforts to develop a government position on the federal support of embryonic stem cell research had culminated in the NIH draft guidelines issued December 2, 1999, for research using human pluripotent stem cells. As part of established NIH policy to invite comments on its draft proposal, in this particular consultation it received approximately fifty thousand comments from members of Congress, patient advocacy groups, scientific societies, religious organizations, and private citizens. In that manner, an engaged public emerged that attempted to take an active part in shaping the new NIH guidelines (Gottweis, Salter, and Waldby 2008).

In this "commenting scenario," the roles of all participants were relatively clearly predetermined, but each commentator had the opportunity to present himself or herself or his or her institution in the context of stating a case about the proposed guidelines. On one side of the spectrum of comments were many positive reactions to the NIH draft guidelines, an expression of a powerful alliance of groups and actors coming into existence that rallied behind human embryonic stem cell research; on the other side of the spectrum was condemning rejection.

There was a strong mobilization of biomedical research organizations across the United States to support stem cell research with the full weight of their institutional ethos as spearheads of medicine stem cell research. For example, the National Coalition for Cancer Research (NCCR), a coalition of twenty-six national organizations of cancer researchers, patients, and research advocates wrote: "The NCCR believes that the NIH should fund and fully support research on human pluripotent stem cells and strongly opposes any attempts to ban this very promising research. . . . The possibilities are astounding and could unlock the doors to understand, treat, and cure many diseases. Further research is required to unlock the doors, and the financial support of the NIH to fund stem cell research is the key to ensure progress."[8]

Not only should embryo research become permissible, but it would also ensure the maintenance of high bioethical standards. The American Association of Medical Colleges (AAMC) wrote on behalf of the nation's 125 medical schools and 400 teaching hospitals about the NIH guideline proposal: "We recognize that these guidelines have been developed in an environment in which federal monies may not be legally be used for the creation of embryos for research purposes. . . . The federal support should not only be viewed as permissible, but also as highly desirable. . . . In the absence of this proposal, stem cell work would undoubtedly occur, but in a very limited private context without the benefit of public scrutiny and ethical oversight that this proposal affords."[9]

Another powerful voice in the discussions came from patient organizations, which spoke for all those patients suffering under crippling and life-threatening diseases and were pushing for stem cell research. The McCaskill senatorial campaign TV ad featuring Michael J. Fox is just one example of this kind of contribution, but there were many others, such as that of the Alzheimer's Association.

To be sure, the many opponents of embryonic stem cell research had attacked this line of research using a counternarrative related to the abortion debate that attempted a different structuring of the space of human embryonic stem cell research. The focus of this counternarrative was on the representation of embryos as human beings (not a formation of cells), their rights, and the duty of the law to protect them, as well as on graphic descriptions and evocations of the atrocities of stem cell research. The National Conference of Catholic Bishops wrote in one of its submissions: "The guidelines, for the first time in our national history, authorize the federal government to approve and regulate destruction of innocent human life for research purposes. They instruct researchers in how to harvest versatile 'stem cells' from living week-old human embryos, a procedure which kills embryos."

Or, as Orange County Right to Life in California stated in a letter to the NIH: "You will be known as the cannibals of the twenty-first century if you use human pluripotent stem cells . . . for research and experimentation."[10] The voices of the critics ranged from letters of well-established organizations, including churches, to countless e-mails, many of similar content. As one of these mails stated: "Please hear the voice of a mother of 3 healthy children—Do not commit this atrocity! Please do not disturb the aborted who have already endured the most horrifying torture anyone can imagine by being ripped from the only safe, warm home they have ever known—their mother's womb! I hope you realize there is ONE who is concerned for the lives of these little ones and He watches your every move. Consider He who formed their tiny parts with purpose and loves them enough to die from them as you contemplate your work. It is He to whom you will one day give an account."

While the supporters and the critics of stem cell research all wove their positions into the genre of a comment on a government document, there is great variety of strategies of persuasion enacted: There was a tendency of voices from the research establishment to give weight to their argument by presenting themselves as the arbiters of science, medicine, and reason and thus eliciting their prior ethos. Patient and religious groups, viewing themselves as "voices of the patients," cooperated with well-known public figures such as Christopher Reeves or Michael J. Fox and put strong emphasis on articulating the emotional dimensions of the decision, the suffering of the patients, or the atrocity of killing human life, as the mainly religious groups typically were putting it.[11]

The final guidelines were published on August 25, 2000 (U.S. National Institutes of Health 2000). At the core of the new guidelines was the decision to extend the scope of government support for embryonic stem cell research and to create a framework for regulatory oversight. These guidelines, most importantly, permitted the use of cells derived from spare IVF embryos for research purposes and constituted a forceful, unambiguous statement of support for embryonic stem cell research. The NIH guidelines opened the possibility for NIH funding of stem cell research. The guidelines constituted an attempt to shape a "reasonable compromise" that would satisfy both supporters and opponents of stem cell research and, further, incorporated opponents' desired ban of therapeutic cloning. The central arguments of opponents focused on the "rights of the embryo" and the duty of the law to protect human life from further potential abuses. The new guidelines remained in force until 2001, when the recently elected President George W. Bush gave his speech in Texas that reversed the Clinton administration's supportive course of action toward human embryonic stem cell research in favor of a much more cautious approach. The discourse across a variety of positions on stem cell research that was dominant during the Clinton administration and that had endorsed stem cell research and created legitimacy for federal funding had collapsed in the wake of a highly emotionalized controversy after the passing of the NIH regulations. Human embryonic stem cell research continued to be an emotional battleground in which the pain and suffering of patients fighting for cures clashed with the horrors of "killed babies" instrumentalized as research materials. Stem cell research had been high on the agenda of the presidential race in 2000, and Bush reversed his predecessor's decision in one of the first major political acts in his presidency.

Conclusion

On March 9, 2009, the newly elected President Barack H. Obama issued Executive Order 13505: *Removing Barriers to Responsible Scientific Research Involving Human Stem Cells.* The order stated that the secretary of Health and Human Services, working with the director of NIH, may support and conduct responsible, scientifically worthy human stem cell research, including human embryonic stem cell (HESC) research, to the extent permitted by law.[12] But it took just over five months before, on August 23, a United States district court issued a preliminary injunction stopping federal funding of human embryonic stem cell research, a slap to the Obama administration's new guidelines on the sensitive issue. The court ruled in favor of a suit filed that June by researchers who said that human embryonic stem cell research involved the destruction of human embryos. Judge Royce C. Lamberth ruled that the executive order violated the Dickey Amendment, which prohibits the federal funding of research that destroys human embryos.[13]

This account of stem cell research is revelatory about policy making, and in particular about the importance of a rhetorical perspective in policy making. Stem cells and cloning can mean very different things to different people, cultures, or actors. Fields such as HESC research are located at the fuzzy intersection between science, society, and politics. Policy making in such areas tends to operate under conditions not only of substantial uncertainty but also of ambiguity with respect to its key notions. For example, the meaning of phenomena such as "stem cells" and "embryos" is by no ways fixed or stable. Phenomena such as human embryonic stem cells are not simply "objective data" for regulatory decision making. Rather, for human embryonic stem cells to become relevant in the policy process, they need to be transformed from something that is "out there" into something that is socially and politically signified. Political and scientific narrative and discourse play critical roles in this process (Fischer 2003).

But apart from the fact that discourse matters, this case also highlights some other important, often neglected aspects of the analysis of public policy. Not only does discourse matter, but persuasion, persons, and emotions also play a central role in policy making. This might be an unsurprising insight, but, oddly enough, these aspects often are missing in policy analysis. I have pointed out that argumentation is not necessarily persuasion (even though persuasion is always argumentation) and that the perspective of rhetoric brings in a key dimension to the policy process: when there is policy making, there is persuasion.

Stem cell policy making in the United States since the late 1990s offers an extended illustration of this aspect, with thousands of actors involved in persuading others of the importance of going ahead with this research in a multitude of locations and spaces or of stopping it. But persuasion does not just work through referencing narratives and discourse supportive or critical of stem cell research, or by forging semantic coalitions for the purpose of making solutions that compromise. While such processes are important, they need to be enacted by persons and bodies who, in their attempt to persuade, present themselves and their qualities or needs in the policy process. Of course, these actors are not free-floating, utility-optimizing individuals, but operate in complex scenographies that connect them with institutions and the discursive economy. Policy making is not only about persuasion and done through persons; it is always, so I argue, emotional. Michael J. Fox's TV ad for the Democratic candidate Claire McCaskill tipped the balance in a close Senate race; it was a referendum on the candidate and the agenda Fox supported. There was no complicated narrative in his message: he was the message itself through his moving appearance. But additionally, in deliberation processes such as that of the NIH consultation and in written texts, institutions, groups, and individual actors actively engage in a process of presenting themselves and their cause in an advantageous manner, giving them weight in the decision-making process. They do this not just by exchanging arguments driven by logos, but also by appealing to and arguing emotions, such as fear, anger, and disgust.

One might be tempted to stipulate that stem cell policy is just a special case of policy in which emotions play a role because of the very nature of the issue, which deals with sensitive areas. While there is no question that emotions play a special role in the context of embryo research, it does not seem to be clear why social or financial policy should be detached from expressing and arguing emotions such as anger, fear, excitement, or jealousy.

Stem cell policy in the United States demonstrates that policy-making processes often seem to be protracted, unsolvable, and without closure. Obviously, this has much to do with the narrativization of the stem cell debate and how constituencies differ in creating the meaning of stem cell research, either as project about the future of regenerative medicine, or as a slippery slope toward an inhuman and godless world. But this policy-making process would be only very partially understood if we did not pay attention to interventions such as those by Michael J. Fox or by antiabortion groups in Orange County, whose main contribution was not a particularly important framing or reframing of the stem cell debate, but its emotionalization. President George W. Bush did not just hold a speech in which he announced new, restrictive regulations for stem cell research, he also used the ethos, the weight of his office, and his persona as the United States president to establish the legitimacy of the new regulations, which was important for their implementation. Compared with other countries, the stem cell debate in the United States seems to be especially "emotionalized" (Gottweis, Salter, and Waldby 2008). This might, to some extent, explain why both regulations remained comparatively restrictive in this country, as well as why attempts toward compromise seemed to be futile: when emotions come into play and are argued, it might be difficult to arrive at an "emotional compromise." This is neither bad nor good but simply a fact. It would be futile to try to change this situation by any kind of political engineering. The political costs of emotions in politics, such as the presence of demagoguery and manipulation, must be weighed against the benefits of emotions, such as their supportive role in the process of political judgment. Apart from the fact that there seems to be little real politics without emotions—whether we like it or not—emotions are not simply obstacles to reasonable decision making and judgment; they have a number of important functions in the process of judging, from directing our attentions toward particular topics to helping us to move from thought to thought in a coherent manner (Garsten 2006:195). Hence, there is little reason to follow the path of reflection in the tradition of

Rawls and Habermas, who argue that all citizens can be convinced by the same arguments about what constitutes a deliberate argument and search for "rules of the game" that are meant to bring reason into the world, but end up taming judgment in an effort to sanitize it from passions. When we face up to the reality that there is no policy making without persuasion in its broadest sense, this will open up the space for a much richer argumentative policy analysis (Gottweis 2006).

Notes

1. As it is requested by law.
2. The video is available on YouTube.
3. Claire McCaskill won the Missouri Senate seat in a close contest, and the state ballot on human embryonic stem cell research resulted in a majority supporting human embryonic stem cell research.
4. There were 3.4 million views as of September 15, 2010.
5. Available on the archived web site of the George W. Bush White House.
6. FY 1996, section 128, P.L. 104-99.
7. Harriet Raab, letter, January 15, 1999.
8. C. R. Aldige, president of NCCR, letter to the NIH on stem cell guidelines, January 31, 2000.
9. Castro, January 19, 2000.
10. Orange County Right to Life, letter to the NIH, "Comments on Stem Cell Guidelines, by Orange County Right to Life," January 16, 2000.
11. Christopher Reeves, most prominent for his film role as Superman, was paralyzed after an accident and became one of the main spokespersons and activists in support of human embryonic stem cell research.
12. Available on the Stem Cell Information page of the NIH web site.
13. Available on the *Washington Post* web site.

References

Abu-Lughod, L., and C. A. Lutz. 1990. "Introduction: Emotion, Discourse and the Politics of Everyday Life." In *Language and the Politics of Emotion*, edited by L. Abu-Lughod and C. A. Lutz, 1–23. Ithaca: Cornell University Press.

Adam, J.-M. 1999. *Linguistique textuelle et analyse des pratiques discursives*. Paris: Nathan.

Amossy, R. 2001. "Ethos at the Crossroads of Disciplines: Rhetoric, Pragmatics, Sociology." *Poetics Today* 22(1):1–23.

———. 2009. "The New Rhetoric's Inheritance: Argumentation and Discourse Analysis." *Argumentation* 23:313–24.
Aristotle. 1991. *On Rhetoric: A Theory of Civic Discourse.* Edited by G. A. Kennedy. New York: Oxford University Press.
Asen, R. 2010. "Reflections on the Role of Rhetoric in Public Policy." *Rhetoric and Public Affairs* 13(1):121–43.
Austin, J. L. 1962. *How to Do Things with Words.* Cambridge: Harvard University Press.
Benveniste, E. 1972. *Problémes de linguistique générale.* 2 vols. Paris: Gallimard.
Breton, P., and G. Gauthier. 2000. *Histoire des théories de l'argumentation.* Paris: La Découverte.
Danzinger, M. 1995. "Policy Analysis Postmodernized: Some Political and Pedagogical Ramifications." *Policy Studies Journal* 23(3):435–50.
Dewey, J. (1927) 1991. *The Public and Its Problems.* Athens: Ohio University Press.
Eggs, E. 1999. "Ethos aristotélicien, conviction et pragmatique moderne." In *Images de soi dans le discours: La construction de l'ethos,* edited by R. Amossy, 31–59. Lausanne: Delachaux et Niestlé.
Fischer, F. 2003. *Reframing Public Policy: Discursive Politics and Deliberative Practices.* Oxford: Oxford University Press.
Fortenbaugh, W. W. 1975. *Aristotle on Emotion: A Contribution to Philosophical Psychology, Rhetoric, Poetics, Politics, and Ethics.* New York: Barnes and Noble.
Garsten, B. 2006. *Saving Persuasion: A Defense of Rhetoric and Judgement.* Cambridge: Harvard University Press.
Gottweis, H. 2006. "Argumentative Policy Analysis." In *Public Policy Handbook,* edited by J. Pierre and E. G. Peters, 461–79. London: Sage.
———. 2007. "Rhetoric in Policy Making: Between Logos, Ethos, and Pathos." In *Handbook of Public Policy Analysis. Theory, Politics, and Methods,* edited by F. Fischer, G. J. Miller, and M. S. Sidney, 237–50. Boca Raton, Fla.: CRC.
Gottweis, H., B. Salter, and C. Waldby. 2008. *The Global Politics of Human Embryonic Stem Cell Science: Regenerative Medicine in Transition.* London: Palgrave Macmillan.
Habermas, J. 1985. *The Theory of Communicative Action.* 2 vols. Translated by T. McCarthy. Boston: Beacon.
Hajer, M. A. 2009. *Authoritative Governance: Policy Making in the Age of Mediatization.* Oxford: Oxford University Press.
Lutz, C., and G. M. White. 1986. "The Anthropology of Emotions." *Annual Review of Anthropology* 15:405–35.
Maingueneau, D. 1984. *Genèses du discours.* Bruxelles: P. Mardaga.
———. 1999. "Ethos, scénography, incorporation." In *Images de soi dans le*

discours: La construction de l'ethos, edited by R. Amossy, 75–101. Lausanne: Delachaux et Niestlé.

———. 2002. *Analyser les textes de communication.* Paris: Nathan.

Maingueneau, D., and J. Angermüller. 2007. "Discourse Analysis in France. A Conversation." *Qualitative Social Research* 8(2). Available at http://www.qualitative-research.net.

Majone, G. 1989. *Evidence, Argument and Persuasion in the Policy Process.* New Haven: Yale University Press.

Meyer, M. 1994. *Rhetoric, Language, and Reason.* University Park: Pennsylvania State University Press.

Micheli, R. 2010. "Emotions as Objects of Argumentative Constructions." *Argumentation* 24:1–17.

Parsons, W. 1995. *Public Policy: An Introduction to the Theory and Practice of Policy Analysis.* Cheltenham: Edward Elgar.

Perelman, C. 1977. *L'Empire rhétorique: Rhétorique et argumentation.* Paris: J. Vrin.

Perelman, C., and L. Olbrechts-Tyteca. 1958. *Traité de l'argumentation, la nouvelle rhétorique.* Paris: Presses Universitaires de France.

Schön, D. A., and M. Rein. 1994. *Frame Reflection: Toward the Resolution of Intractable Policy Controversies.* New York: Basic.

Throgmorton, J. A. 1991. "The Rhetorics of Policy Analysis." *Policy Sciences* 24:153–79.

———. 1993. "Survey Research as Rhetorical Trope: Electric Power Planning Arguments in Chicago." In *The Argumentative Turn in Policy Analysis and Planning,* edited by F. Fischer and J. Forester, 117–44. Durham: Duke University Press.

Toulmin, S. 1958. *The Uses of Argument.* Cambridge: Cambridge University Press.

U.S. National Institutes of Health. 2000. *Guidelines for Research Using Human Pluripotent Stem Cells.* Federal Register 51976.

Weick, K. 1988. "Enacted Sensemaking in Crisis Situations." *Management Studies* 25(4):305–17.

White, H. 1981. "The Value of Narrativity in the Representation of Reality." In *On Narrative,* edited by W. J. T. Mitchell, 1–23. Chicago: University of Chicago Press.

———. 1987. *The Content of the Form: Narrative Discourse and Historical Representation.* Baltimore: Johns Hopkins University Press.

Wilson, C. J., and C. Lewiecki-Wilson, eds. 2001. *Embodied Rhetorics: Disability in Language and Culture.* Carbondale: Southern Illinois University Press.

8. The Deep Semiotic Structure of Deservingness

Discourse and Identity in Welfare Policy

Sometime near the end of the last century, a prominent commentator in the field of public policy analysis stated in one of the leading mainstream journals in the field that "post-positivists have a very long way to go if they are to be relevant to the practical challenges of democratic governance" (Lynn 1999). With hindsight we can now say: au contraire! Not to be too argumentative, but this sequel to *The Argumentative Turn* stands as proof positive that this prediction was dead wrong. Instead, much has been gained by the postpositivist turn away from literal depictions of public policy to examining policy from a more constructivist perspective that emphasizes how figurative practices make some things seem to be true irrespective of whether they really are. Constructivism emphasizes how public policy is no different from any other realm of social experience, that it is never experienced in unmediated form, that we come to understand the alleged facts of public policy via how they are framed and articulated in discourse, and that the narration of public policy is inevitably done in a way that is not only mediated but also selective, partial, incomplete, highly contestable, and always politically biased. The power of this orientation for analyzing public policy has been demonstrated many times over in a growing number of important studies (for a review, see Dodge, Ospina, and Foldy 2005).

With time, the "argumentative turn" has moved in different directions, each offering different ways of contextualizing how social processes are constructed and contextualized. One turn of particular note has focused on discourse as its own source of political influence, giving rise to a growing number of insightful analyses about how the politics of public policy is often found by reading between the lines (Feldman et al. 2004). I say "reading between the lines" because discourse is, for me (along with others), the unsaid more than the said: it is that unsaid underlying structure of intelligibility that creates a referential context for deriving meaning from what is said (Felluga 2003). As Barry Laga clarifies: "by 'discourse,' I mean not only the way we use language, but also the assumptions, attitudes, values, beliefs, and hierarchies that are attached to the way language is used. [The] task is to show how a text functions within a discourse or show how a text attempts to negotiate among competing discourses" (2009). Just as Jacques Lacan could effectively suggest that the unconscious is structured like a language (see Dean 2006), discourse is in significant part like the unconscious, hidden in plain sight, available to be referenced even if not explicitly so.

In this rendering, discourse is different than narrative. Narratives are the surface textual representations of actions and events, while discourse is the underlying interpretive context for making sense of those surface narratives. Consciously or not, we inevitably rely on the underlying discourse for interpreting the implicit understandings that are only suggested by the explicit, surface narratives. Just as we rely on implicit understandings to interpret nonverbal cues, we rely on the structure of intelligibility associated with any discourse for connecting the dots in any narrative. Narratives are a portent with meaning in ways that only discourse can reveal. To focus on the explicit narratives at the expense of the implicit discourse is, metaphorically speaking, to miss the forest for the trees.[1]

One effective way of highlighting the role of discourse in constituting a context for what we say and do comes from semiotics, which strictly speaking is the study of signs (Pierce 1977). In recent years, a number of anthropologists, sociologists, and others in the social sciences, myself included (1995, 2000, 2006), have been drawn to using a semiotic approach to the study of social phenomenon, and I develop a version of this approach for my analysis in this chapter.

The semiotic approach to the study of culture leavens the social structural analysis of thinkers such as Émile Durkheim with the semiotic perspective of linguists such as Ferdinand Saussure. The semiotic approach to the study of social phenomena starts with the assumption that the culture of any society is at its base grounded in an interpretive grid comprising interrelated binary distinctions about what is good and bad, moral and immoral, natural and cultural, rational and emotional, male and female, and so on (Balkin 2002). The semiotic approach to cultural analysis enables us to go beyond a structural analysis of how society is organized in ways that structure social choices and actions to show that emerging from material conditions grows a structure of intelligibility, or what Jeffrey Alexander (2003) calls an "interpretive grid" that informs, mediates, and constitutes our social relations. Alexander calls this type of analysis "cultural sociology," highlighting how the interpretive grid of any "culture-structure" becomes the basis for both factual assessments and moral judgments (Alexander and Smith 1999).

At the heart of the structure of intelligibility are deeply sedimented binaries or dichotomies that serve as the basic "codes" for structuring the making of meaning in any particular social order, including distinctions between fact and fiction, reality and fantasy, nature and culture, reason and emotion, good and bad, moral and immoral, pure and impure, and so on (Balkin 2002). For J. M. Balkin, these binary codes operate as "cultural software" that provides a set of "nested oppositions," trading on each other in a form of intertextuality to create hierarchies that privilege one side of a particular binary at the expense of the other (2002:52, 234–35). These codes are not epiphenomenal but central in providing the basis for narratives we use to make sense of social relations writ large. For instance, Alexander has effectively highlighted the power of the underlying coded binaries that form the basis of a culture in writing about election campaigns in the United States:

> Difference is a semiotic truism, but it is also one of the major strategies of politics. As campaigns work the binaries, they try to simplify the meaning of every issue that comes up, bringing it into semiotic alignment, on one side or the other of the great divide. Everything must be made clean or dirty, and, whenever possible, the newly pure and polluted folded into the narrative arc of historical transformation. This spinning machine comes to an end on 4th November, when the act of voting allows a purging catharsis, a spitting out of the negative, and a transformation of the individual into the collective will. Until that day, politics is about creating difference, not overcoming it. The principal strategy for protecting the purity of your candidate's image is to categorize the other candidate in polluted ways. If we are to be coded as clean and democratic, he must be made dirty in the litany of tried and true, antidemocratic themes. If we are to be narrated as heroic, he must become a villain. (2009:81)

My version of a semiotic approach is informed by a variety of different theorists who do not necessarily always agree with each other in all respects. Yet, I draw on them eclectically to develop a semiotic approach to social performances associated with the enactments of public policy. This semiotic approach to policy analysis draws from Stuart Hall (1973), others associated with the Birmingham School in Cultural Studies, and scholars aligned with the Strong Program in Cultural Sociology to show how these coded binaries provide a critical basis for social performances that privilege some identities at the expense of others. The Strong Program allows us to theorize the relative autonomy of culture and how it is not entirely an artifact of the state or the market but an important source of meaning making that becomes its own site of contestation. It is a particularly important source of political power for conservative groups who can insist that various social changes need to be evaluated according to whether they violate basic social norms that are deeply entrenched in the social order as it has come to be reinforced via daily practices over time. As Roland Barthes (1972) once argued, "the left has no culture" in the sense that the right can use the embedded codes of the dominant culture as a cudgel to bash social change agents for seeking to unsettle established social norms. As a result, the conservatives are more often keen to invoke the established binaries that privilege some identities and practices over others as an adroit political move to undermine social change initiatives or even to reform public policy to make it continue to be consistent with established values.

Yet it is not just conservatives who end up reinforcing the dominant distinctions embedded in the culture. There are ways in which everyone participating in a social order is at risk of being implicated in reinscribing the embedded cultural distinctions. From the semiotic perspective on social relations, there is a performative dimension to the relationship between the underlying structure of intelligibility and how it is enacted by social actors through representational practices in everyday social life. For Hall, we need to pay attention to both how the enactment of social performances encode meaning and how their reception by audiences decodes it. Actors encode their representational practices, and audiences decode to make sense of what they are seeing and hearing (Hall 1973). Hall showed how powerful actors could promote a "moral panic" about things such as crime among the mass public that then could be interpreted variously. The power of these performances derives from how they activate scripts that social actors perform, though their performativity can be enacted with varying degrees of virtuosity, with some actors, especially those who are already advantageously positioned in social relations, having more or less compelling interpretations that move in new directions (Alexander 2006). Yet, depending on context, the performances can take on new meaning; there can be what Balkin calls "ideological drift" (2002). The power of the underlying codes is therefore never complete; instead, they are a site for contestation (Alexander and Smith 1999:458; Hall 1973). In this way, the underlying structure of intelligibility can give rise to competing narratives for making sense of social relations. Further, as I will demonstrate, these cultural contests can morph to become the basis for structuring social relations, as suggested by Pierre Bourdieu (1998), or even to become the basis for state action, as suggested by Michel Foucault (1991). My sort of semiotic structuralism enables people to see how culture is constitutive of social practices and social policies and how it is the basis of social change.

In what follows, I develop a semiotic analysis of social performance to show how the unsaid of an underlying discourse allows the said metaphors of policy narratives to indicate points of reference, especially privileged identities that are deeply established in the culture of the broader society. My example is welfare reform as it emerged from the Personal Responsibility and Work Opportunity Reconciliation Act of 1996. I show how the metaphors used in contemporary policy narratives about welfare frame their objects of concern in ways that point to implied understandings that were always available in the broader culture but were made ascendant starting with the culture wars coming out of the 1960s, when powerful, conservative business lobbies championed them as the basis for attacking the welfare state as not just expensive but immoral. A relentless campaign to promote a "moral panic" eventually resulted in today's popular assumptions that being on welfare is assumed to be a sign of not being the "good mother" who is practicing "personal responsibility," demonstrating that the "dependency" associated with taking welfare is analogous to other bad dependencies, for instance, a chemical dependency. These framing metaphors of welfare policy narratives are simultaneously moralizing and medicalizing the problem of welfare dependency as well as immediately suggesting that its treatment be undertaken in ways similar to the treatment of drug addictions. A semiotic analysis enables us to see the deeply embedded cultural bases for social change, for better or for worse. The transformation of social welfare policy for dispossessed single mothers begins with the discursive transformation of how we talk about the problem. In the current period, what begins as the semantic abolition of welfare departments, the renaming of agencies by government officials as "departments of self-sufficiency," has been followed by drastic cuts in access to needed cash aid. In other words, these issues are not "merely cultural" (Butler 1997).

A Semiotic Approach to Policy Discourse

It is my argument that this sort of eclectic semiotics of social performance (combining Hall with Bourdieu and Foucault) can add significantly to any analysis of social processes by highlighting how an underlying structure of intelligibility serves as the primary culture force for shaping how we interpret what we say and do. In this way, an underlying discourse serves as a cultural resource for making meaning from the narratives we create about ourselves. We get to see what emotional and political labor gets done when surface narratives tap into the implied identities associated with the underlying structure of intelligibility, that is, the discourse. Yet, this interpretive grid is in itself inert until it is enacted by social actors. This is another way of saying that discourse is about more than words; it is lived language, embodied in experience and enacted in practice. Discourse comes alive when it is embodied in practices, written on our bodies, enacted in our communities, and disseminated across the different domains of public policy. In this sense, discourse has, as Pierre Bourdieu (1998) once emphasized, the power to make itself real. Through reiteration, by being repeatedly enacted and performed, a discourse can make itself a self-fulfilling prophecy in which we talk the talk and walk the walk—where we do what we say and say what we do—to the point that the saying becomes an accurate depiction even if we had the possibility of being and doing differently. Ian Hacking calls it the "looping effect" (2000). Jennifer Dodge, Sonia Ospina, and Erica Foldy add: "Narrative as metaphor emphasizes the assumption that narratives are constitutive: People shape stories and, in turn, stories shape people. In this view, as notions of self, existence, and identity are named through language, they begin to feel real in their consequences. People take for granted that they are objective and preexisting realities. Over time, this process becomes automatic and usually unconscious" (2005:293).

For instance, if we think, breathe, and talk about an "underclass" constantly, after a certain point even the people who are said to inhabit that world against their will come to enact its nightmares. Once incorporated into the world of today's highly medicalized system of social service provision, they may become clients who let the therapy do their talking such that they become people preoccupied with overcoming their "deficits," surmounting their "barriers," and taking the "steps" (usually twelve, as required by any credible twelve-step program) to defeat their "demons" and join the mainstream, middle-class society of "self-sufficient" autonomous beings (who unfortunately often, but not at the same rates, confront similar psychological problems but with more economic resources at their disposal to counter them). (For more, see Schram 2006.)

Therefore, to study discourse is to recognize how the discourse "speaks us" as much as we speak it (Ball 1990:18). People embody discourse, enacting its articulations of who they are and how they relate one to the other; without discourse, they cannot know themselves and who it is they have become. This is true for social formations as much as individuals. Take class as a social formation. Whether it is the "middle class" or even the "underclass," these are discursive fictions of a highly politicized sort; they are often the underlying reference points of policy discourse, held in reserve, rarely explicitly examined, but often assumed to be real, to the point that people of various levels of economic well-being organize their lives in just such terms.

For Michel Foucault (1991), the self-fulfilling prophecy of discourse becomes what he called "governmentality," as in "governing mentalities" (Campbell 1999), in which the state proliferates categories of population and then gets people to populate those categories in self-regulating ways, all in the name of helping to stabilize the social order and further assist the state in fulfilling its governance responsibilities. That is what is so "under" about the underclass: this positional metaphor locates the denizens of the underclass *below* the class system, where they are unable to rise to the threshold of participation in the class system and where they fail to meet the requisites of appropriate class behavior. The "underclass" implies a group of people who need to be disciplined to learn how to become the self-regulating sort of people who are willing to take up their assigned positions in the social order and to ensure they execute them appropriately.

Yet it is important to recognize that the internalization of discourse is never complete and people embody the dominant narrations of who they are incompletely and strategically. Consistent with Hall's emphasis on coding and decoding, members of subordinated groups often have their own selective interpretations of what the powerful have championed and how they should seem themselves. Members of the underclass selectively interpret how they must practice discipline if they are to be included in the mainstream according to a self-conscious "practical rationality" (March and Olsen 2006). It is as if the underclass pierces the veil of ideology even as it continues to wear its masks (Žižek 1989).

Today, welfare policies as reformed seem less focused on addressing the structural causes of people's lack of economic resources and more intent on helping people overcome the exclusion associated with their engaging in pathological individual behaviors that earned them the designation as members of the "underclass." Yet these inclusionary policies often reinscribe their subordination by assuming that inclusion is satisfied by getting welfare-to-work participants to become willingly compliant low-wage workers in the emerging globalizing economy. The result is what Joel Handler calls the "paradox of inclusion" (2004). The goal of these welfare-to-work policies is to make members of the underclass into less unruly members of the lower class, but still lower than all the other people who are in the class system. Raised up from beneath the class system, the former members of the underclass now get to be, once appropriately disciplined, low-wage workers on the bottom of the socioeconomic order. The discourse of contemporary welfare policy enacts what Giorgio Agamben calls the "inclusive exclusion" (1998). As a result, even as we rework welfare policy to activate the underclass's participation in the mainstream society, we risk reinscribing deeply embedded, well-established binaries of self and other, normal and deviant, and so on, that privilege some identities and subjectivities over others. And it comes to be that the poor shall always be with us, if for no other reason than because of how discourse as that underlying structure of intelligibility informs our policy narratives.

Consistent with my eclecticism, a semiotic approach for Alexander does not supplant, but instead supplements, a structural analysis (Alexander 2003). Structuralism was predicated on the idea that fundamental binaries built right into the classifying way humans put real structural limits on the ways we act in interrelated ways—nature and culture, emotion and reason, man and woman, and so on. Poststructuralism argues that these are but artificial distinctions that deconstruct. It enables us to see how these distinctions practice their own intertexuality, that is, how each claims to refer to a real binary but in fact its ability to reference the real world is infinitely deferred. The distinctions refer instead to each other, one text to the next endlessly, never quite getting to anchor their particular distinctions in the material world. In fact, the historically privileged citizen-subject of Western, liberal political discourse—the rational, autonomous, self-sufficient male—emerges out of the intertextuality of nested oppositions that suggests that women are more emotional than men because they are more tied to humans' biological nature due to their child-bearing capacities. Therefore, poststructuralism enables us to see the cultural biases of structuralism. The relevance of poststructuralism for critiquing policy discourse is acute. For instance, it helps question the dichotomy of structure and agency that lies problematically at the base of the still-hegemonic, Western, liberal-capitalist political discourse that assumes at its foundation the independent, self-sufficient, autonomous citizen-subject—for example, a male breadwinner—who is therefore to be privileged over those subjectivities that imply dependency and an inability to act for oneself on one's own terms—for example, a female welfare recipient.

A semiotic approach to policy discourse builds on these insights. It enables us to demonstrate how beginning with the culture wars coming out of the 1960s, powerful actors could effectively champion new interpretations of deeply sedimented cultural biases to undermine established social policy. Questioning the implied subjectivities of all policy discourses is in fact political work that is critical. At the center of the imaginaries of most policy discourses is the implied subject of that policy: the policy identity assumed to be reflective of the citizen-subject who is the target of that policy, be he or she citizen, taxpayer, worker, voter, business owner, homeowner, welfare recipient, retiree, illegal immigrant, ex-con, terrorist, green consumer, hedge fund manager, and so on (see Cruikshank 1999). The implied subject position so defined by any one particular public policy is the quintessential example of how policy discourse operates by creating an unsaid, assumed reference point to the ostensible metaphors of the surface narrative of any policy gesture (see figure 1). Heuristically, there is arguably value in suggesting that there are levels of policy discourse, much like the idea that there are

The Deep Semiotic Structure of Deservingness 245

FIGURE 1. The Levels of Policy Discourse.

Surface Level

Narrative
often including a story of how a policy problem and its solution came to be

Framing Metaphors
always present in any policy narrative referencing an underlying discourse for making sense of the narrative and its story

Underlying Structure

Discourse
comprising critical distinctions for making sense of particular policy narratives

Subjectivities
key distinctions that reference why some identities are to be privileged in a policy narrative

---

levels of consciousness. On the surface, there are key framing metaphors embedded in any policy narrative that point to an underlying discourse that provides reference points for making meaning from the framing metaphors and the ostensible narratives with which they are associated.

As Deborah Stone (1988) has insightfully noted, policy narratives often tell politically convenient "just so" stories, often championed most effectively by the most powerful groups active in the public policy process, that suggest why it makes sense to see a policy and its problem of concern a particular way. The policy narrative and the story it provides inevitably include framing metaphors that suggest the saga told about a policy, its problem, and the people associated with dealing with it are analogous to other situations and characters. The context for interpreting these metaphors is that underlying structure of intelligibility, or what I am calling here the discourse, which itself relies on key binary distinctions for privileging certain practices and people. The policy narrative and its framing metaphors rely on that discourse for implying there is a certain type of identified citizen-subject who is assumed to be the focus of concern (either as a problem person or praiseworthy protagonist, as, for example, in the case of welfare policy in the United States today, where such a protagonist is either a demonized "welfare mother" or a "personally responsible mother," the latter of which means, ironically for welfare reform, a "working mother" who puts taking paid employment outside the home as her top priority). As Frank Fischer has written, "Employing literary and rhetorical devices for symbolic representation, policy stories are tools of political persuasion. As strategies for depicting problems and interests, discursive devices such as synecdoches (which represent the whole by one of its parts) or metaphors (which make implied comparisons) are pervasive throughout policy stories. Such linguistic constructions are designed and introduced to convince an audience of the necessity of a political or policy action; they help identify the responsible culprits and the virtuous saviors capable of leading us to high ground" (2009:206).

Therefore, one important dimension of semiotic policy analysis is that it begins to investigate how the underlying cultural interpretive grid in any society provides the basis for providing the implied subjectivities of any public policy. Related questions are: Who are these imagined personas that inhabit any particular policy discourse? How do they get created? How do they get to act? What kind of agency do they have? What is their power over us? And how can we engage them in ways that are democratic and that enable us to make our own gestures toward a more social just set of public arrangements? These are questions that a revitalized form of discourse analysis provokes.

The inquiry into the discursive construction of policy identities has the potential to make a distinctive, democratizing contribution to public policy analysis (Fischer 2009). More so than conventional approaches, semiotic policy analysis offers the opportunity to interrogate assumptions about identity embedded in the analysis and making of public policy, thereby enabling the questionable distinctions that privilege some identities at the expense of others to be rethought and resisted. Public policy analysis can benefit from the emphasis that postmodernism places on how discourse constructs identity.

In what follows, I offer an in-depth example of how a semiotic approach to interrogating policy discourse provides a window into how every policy has its "other"—its unsaid, implied citizen-subject that makes us assume that the policy is logically related to real people when in fact that other is an artifact of the policy discourse that personifies its political biases. Social welfare policy in the contemporary postindustrial United States is shown to participate in the construction and maintenance of identity in ways that affect not just the allocation of public benefits but also economic opportunities outside of the state. Yet this is a well-established black art. Mired in old, invidious distinctions, welfare policy discourse today helps to re-create the problems of yesterday. An examination of the implied citizen-subject of welfare policy in the post-reform period is my object of inquiry. I conclude with a discussion of the democratic consequences for learning to challenge the implied citizen-subject of contemporary welfare policy.

Dependency Discourse: The "Poor" as Other

History teaches us that there is a deep semiotic structure of deservingness undergirding contemporary welfare policy discourse in the United States. It is deeply embedded in the nation's roots, stretching back over two centuries (Somers and Block 2005). This discourse is anchored in the contrast between two central subjectivities: the deserving autonomous, self-sufficient individual and the undeserving dependent who fails to exhibit the independence assumed to be central in the making of the liberal citizen who can be counted on to act for himself or herself (see figure 2).

These two central subjectivities not only anchor how we approach thinking about the public realm generally but also serve to create a basis for questioning whether to extend aid to the needy. We can see this in the debates about welfare that have historically informed welfare policy discourse in the United States. From before Thomas Malthus wrote his infamous *Essays on the Principles of Population* in 1798 in England to after Charles Murray reiterated those arguments in *Losing Ground* in 1984 in the United States, social welfare policy discourse has been dominated by what Albert Hirschman has called the "perversity thesis" (as discussed in Somers and Block 2005). The perversity thesis in Malthus's hands combined classical liberal economic theory and Christian morality to suggest that, contrary to the apparent reality that offering financial aid to the "poor" was a kind and charitable act of assistance, such interventions actually undermined the natural order of things and corrupted individuals who took such succor so that they lost the ability to practice self-discipline and to exercise personal responsibility. The the-

FIGURE 2. The Levels of Welfare Reform Discourse.

Surface Level

The Welfare Dependency Narrative
including stories of how relying on welfare is an addiction, means you are a bad mother, makes you a bad role model, and so on

Dependency, Personal Responsibility, Self-Sufficiency as Key Welfare Policy Metaphors
these framing metaphors suggest that accepting welfare is to be understood by referencing an underlying discourse that connects welfare reliance to other denigrated practices

Underlying Structure

Welfare Reform Discourse
comprising critical distinctions for making sense of welfare reform narratives: active and passive, independent and dependent, work and care, and so on

Subjectivities
identities to be privileged in the welfare reform narrative: the self-sufficient, autonomous subject

---

ory held that helping poor people in this way actually had perverse effects because the poor are different from other people and lack the capacity of self-discipline when it comes to issues of work and family: the poor are lazy and promiscuous. If you give them financial assistance, they will just squander it, and if you persist in helping them, they will just take society down with them. The perversity thesis has proven resilient even in the face of secularization. For well over two centuries, at varying points in time and to varying degrees, much success has come to the perversity thesis and its related cousin, the futility thesis, which maintains that "the poor" will always be with us no matter what we do.

This success testifies to the power of discourse. Arguments like the perversity thesis can be persuasive independent of historical circumstances. The facts of "welfare dependency" at any time seem far less significant than the enduring power of the perversity thesis to appeal to ingrained moralisms of Western, liberal-capitalist societies about public aid corrupting the individual and undermining the self-discipline assumed to be central in the making of the autonomous, self-sufficient, liberal citizen-subject. Taking welfare is therefore often characterized as "welfare dependency" because it is associated with undermining the autonomy and independence associated with the model type of citizen-subject we are all in need of becoming to take on the subject position in the liberal public sphere. If we are all dependents, then who will be able to fulfill the role of the independent citizen free to act on his or her own accord in the public sphere, politically, socially, economically, and so on? The entire edifice of the liberal, democratic, capitalist order is built on the assumption that there are free consenting individuals who enter into economic, social, and political contracts and other arrangements. Any behaviors that suggest we are not free or independent, but instead beholden to others or dependent, undermine the plausibility of this assumed subjectivity and pose a risk to that order that must be resisted.

The facts of welfare dependency in this sense are always already there, ready to be materialized in quotidian practices of welfare administration that treat welfare recipients in self-fulfilling, denigrating ways. All it takes is a less-than-active imagination willing to interpret welfare participation unreflectively, as if it were without question a sign of personal deficiency. Sadly, the modern history of the Western world, especially in the United States and England, is replete with such instances of underutilized imagination placing whatever facts were offered about welfare use in terms of this argument about an unchanging underlying moral order. And the facts of welfare dependency are less than apparent.

In the run-up to welfare reform in the 1990s, no amount of piling up of facts about the myths of alleged welfare dependency crisis did any good whatsoever in undermining the ideological juggernaut the conservative, right-wing cultural warriors had developed to impugn the already sullied image of welfare recipients as malingerers and no-counts, that is, promiscuous women lazily living off of welfare. Racial bias figured prominently in the narratives that circulated among welfare reform supporters and highlighted how deeply embedded racialized distinctions of who is deserving permeated policy discourse (Gilens 1999; Neubeck and Cazenave 2001). The gender bias of the discourse was equally stunning, overlooking that the overwhelming majority of recipients of cash assistance to poor families are single mothers who are trying to handle both the breadwinning and caregiving responsibilities on their own (Reese 2005). Yet the mere recitation of factual evidence about contemporary welfare recipients was to prove woefully inadequate in the face of an argument that had endured at least since the eighteenth century and had convinced people to ignore empirical information in order to appreciate the underlying "natural order of things." And in the Western, liberal political imaginary, the underlying natural order of things was assumed to be one in which the privileged citizen-subject was an autonomous, self-sufficient, male head of a family. It was as if extending aid to black, single mothers jeopardized the perpetuation of the natural order of things and needed to be resisted.

Therefore, dependency discourse in the United States is arguably paradigmatic of discourse in general. It provides an exemplar of how discourse operates to make itself real. Like all discourse, it takes symptoms as signs of some preexisting, underlying condition that it retroactively imputes as always already having been there, often for reasons attributable to the characteristics or traits of some implied type of person associated with a particular identity, that is, a subjectivity. In this way, it can be said that all discourses, welfare policy or otherwise, have their "others." Discourse implies identities, both a privileged identity and an "othered," denigrated identity. In the case of welfare policy discourse, from Malthus on, dependency discourse with its perversity thesis imputes a preexisting set of pathological behaviors in a timeless way to the "poor" as an othered group comprising distinctive types of people that then in their otherness give rise to the poverty and welfare dependency that we see before us in the contemporary scene.

Contemporary Welfare Policy Discourse: Medicalizing Dependency

Today, the age-old perversity thesis is being reincarnated in highly technocratic ways for the new forms of governance. Contemporary welfare policy discourse understands reliance on public assistance in highly medicalized terms by borrowing metaphors from other service domains that end up imputing the causes of poverty and reliance to the individual and her or his personal deficiencies. Medicalization is arguably the main way that welfare policy discourse today creates a stage for enacting Foucault's governmentality.

The medicalization of what has come to be called "welfare dependency" is fast becoming a major administrative focus under the new welfare reform regime instituted in the 1990s. It is as if the aphasia of welfare discourse prevents us from confronting the trauma of poverty, and we use euphemistic substitutes like welfare dependency to paper over our complicity in perpetuating other people's destitution while simultaneously shifting the blame away from the structure of society to the individual behavior of those who are forced to live in poverty. With this old aphasic shift taking new form, welfare dependency becomes the center of our discursive terrain about how, in the contemporary parlance of our therapeutic culture, to "treat" recipients for their diseased condition of dependence on welfare. Welfare use beyond the shortest periods of time as a form of transitional aid, as, say, when a single mother relies on welfare while working through a divorce, is now considered an abuse. In other words, welfare use beyond a few months is now welfare abuse, signaling the need to undergo treatment to overcome one's dependency on welfare. The dependency metaphor operates more like a metonymy in which a contiguous reference point is emphasized rather than the original object of concern. The poverty that precedes welfare dependency is ignored, and instead we are asked to focus on the reliance on welfare. This semiotic shift is arguably most convenient for the rich and powerful in the United States, who increasingly need to deflect attention from the lack of upward mobility afforded to the lower classes in the ossifying and deeply unequal class structure that has emerged with the changing economy associated with the globalizing economy and the proliferation of low-wage jobs as the only recourse for subsistence for many. Dependency becomes a displacement for talking about the underlying structural poverty of that economy that our liberal, individualistic, agentistic political discourse cannot effectively address. So "welfare use," "welfare receipt," and the especially verboten "welfare taking" are all being replaced by "welfare dependency." As a result, reliance on welfare is articulated as a sign that a single mother suffers from "welfare dependency," which, like other dependencies, is something from which the client needs to be weaned with an appropriate therapeutic treatment. Under welfare reform, all applicants for assistance are screened, diagnosed, assessed, and referred for the appropriate treatment to accelerate the process by which they can overcome their vulnerability to being dependent on welfare.

Medicalization represents modernity's emphasis on science over religion. It is associated with the growing propensity to conceive myriad personal problems in medicalized terms. It envisions the poor as sick as opposed to bad. Yet that improved outlook comes with a price: welfare dependency is a product of an individual's behavior more so than the inequities in the social structure or political economy. In this way, medicalization becomes a way of suggesting that upward mobility is still possible. The poor are not fated to be poor; they can be cured of their ills and thereby then activated to advance economically. This convenient displacement story, away from the structural embeddedness of persistent poverty in the changing economy, serves the political interests of powerful groups invested in not having to attack those structural roots of contemporary poverty. By highlighting that the poor can be cured of their dependency on welfare, medicalizing implies mobility is still possible when in fact it is less than likely.

A manifestation of how medicalization implies mobility is the proliferation of "barriers" talk in welfare policy implementation. A major preoccupation in welfare reform as a new form of governance is assisting recipients to overcome "barriers" to self-sufficiency. "Barriers," contrary to the term's ostensible meaning, is most often construed under welfare reform as personal problems. Racial and sexual discrimination in the workplace or the lack of decent paying jobs is not usually featured in state welfare programs as a barrier to moving from welfare to work. Instead, barriers are most often discussed as personal problems the client must correct. As a result, more and more programming under welfare reform is concentrated on what are seen as the related conditions that give rise to welfare dependency, be they mental health issues, behavioral problems, or addictions. In the masculinized discourse of welfare reform, even children are now at risk of being referred to as barriers to work (Stone 2008). The goal is to get single mothers to be comfortable being the breadwinner for their families, even if it means cutting back on their commitments to their children (Dodson 2010). Yet the idea of instilling a commitment to taking paid employment is couched in the terms of liberal political discourse. Self-esteem classes as well as psychological counseling have become common features of welfare-to-work programs as ways of engendering the self-confidence needed for participants to become the autonomous, self-sufficient actors assumed by liberal political discourse.

Over time, these issues of self become their own self-fulfilling prophecy. As more and more of the welfare population exits under welfare-to-work programs that require recipients to make "rapid attachment" to paid employment in the labor force, the remaining population is increasingly made up of recipients who do indeed incur certain personal problems at high rates. For instance, it is estimated that "a growing share of [those individuals receiving] Temporary Assistance for Needy Families, which offers cash support to low-income single caregivers, is composed of individuals with mental illness, as new work requirements result in faster exits of those without mental health conditions" (Danziger, Frank, and Meara 2009). Rates for depression among the welfare reform population have been growing for some time. This ironically reinforces the medicalized character of welfare dependency as if it were a real phenomenon that was in fact always already there in the first place, as if most recipients were always suffering from the illness of welfare dependency and its related medicalized conditions. Just like any good discourse, "welfare dependency" then becomes its own self-fulfilling prophecy, making itself real, manufacturing the reality that it claims pre-existed it. Reliance on welfare becomes seen less as an economic problem and more as a mental health issue.

Borrowing the dependency metaphor from other medicalized discourses is, however, no historical accident.[2] People spoke the discourse even as they were being spoken by it. The contemporary discourse of welfare dependency grew out of an extensive campaign that corporate interests started in the mid-1970s to roll back the welfare state. Part of the campaign to discredit the welfare state was economic: it led to higher taxes, increased business regulation, heightened inflation, lower productivity, decreased work effort, and a growing federal deficit. Certain elements of the business coalition, especially leaders in the fast-food industry, argued that welfare retrenchment was needed to increase the efficiency of local economies and enable the United States to compete in a globalizing economy. A major economic goal was to push the poor off welfare and into low-wage work so that employers could simultaneously lighten their tax burden and prevent the development of a labor force that could rely on welfare state protections to bargain more aggressively for better wages. Yet the campaign was not strictly economic. Moral conservatives added a cultural dimension to the attack on the welfare state as part of a broader countermovement against changes in gender and race relations, consumption patterns, and sexual and familial norms that they saw as evidence of moral decline.

In addition, starting in the 1980s, private foundations with extensive funding from corporations and certain wealthy families with a morally conservative agenda supported the work of a number of critics whose writings reemphasized the age-old perversity thesis and its argument that helping the poor only mired them in a life of welfare dependency, passivity, and personal irresponsibility. Government officials who saw political rewards in attacking federal welfare programs joined the chorus and emphasized devolving responsibility for welfare to states and localities. Advocates for low-income families were forced to defend an unpopular program that they perceived as inadequate, but they failed to establish a positive alternative to "dependency" as the frame for understanding welfare use by the poor.

Further, as more working- and middle-class mothers were able to find paid employment as it became more acceptable for women to work, single mothers who remained on welfare increasingly were at risk of being those different, other people who did not adhere to middle-class work as well as family values (see Reese 2005). This perspective overlooked two facts: many mothers were forced into the paid labor force due to declines in the real value of their husbands' wages, and single mothers on welfare were often already working, if most often part-time, as they supplemented their wages with welfare while assuming responsibility for breadwinning as well as homemaking all on their own. All this was swept under the rug by a dependency discourse that redefined single mothers on welfare as pathologically dependent and in need of a paternalistic form of treatment to wean them from their irresponsible addiction to public aid. In contemporary welfare policy discourse, being a good mother had now largely come to mean being a mother who took paid employment in addition to fulfilling her caregiving and homemaking responsibilities.

This political campaign against welfare was strikingly successful in laying the groundwork for the eventual passage in the 1990s of welfare reform legislation that significantly retrenched public assistance to low-income families and individuals. Yet the campaign's success was not because it changed fundamental attitudes about welfare, which remained ambivalent. After the campaign ended, most Americans still did not in principle oppose government assistance for low-income families and in fact continued to believe that we have a collective obligation to help the poor. For instance, from the 1980s through 2009, 60 to 70 percent of Americans indicated they supported government assistance for the poor and believed government had a responsibility to guarantee every citizen food to eat and a place to sleep (PRC 2009). At the same time, most Americans also continued to believe that those in need should receive assistance only if they maintain a commitment to personal responsibility and a work ethic (see Schram and Soss 2001; Soss and Schram 2007). The campaign against welfare dependency was successful not because it changed this mix of attitudes. Instead, its success was in reframing the issue to focus on welfare dependency as a problem that needed immediate treatment. The problem of dependency came to be seen as a major source of society's economic as well as social and cultural ills. It increasingly was framed as creating a significant drain on the economy even as it encouraged out-of-wedlock births, single-parent families, and a decline in the work ethic. The dependency frame saw public assistance not as a hard-won protection *for* poor workers and their families; instead, it viewed welfare as a policy imposed *against* workers' values as well as their bank accounts.

This "us versus them" identity politics reframing of welfare was facilitated by the fact that welfare was at this time also increasingly depicted in the mass media using highly misleading racial terms and imagery. As a result, the public started to exaggerate grossly the extent to which blacks received public assistance and in turn became increasingly critical of welfare as a program for poor blacks, who were seen as these "other" people who were not like most white middle-class families and were not adhering to work and family values (see Neubeck and Cazenave 2001). Racial resentments and old stereotypes of black laziness became more influential in spawning growing hostility toward welfare (see Gilens 1999).

The reframing of the welfare issue as a problem of dependency concentrated in a black underclass involved the policy equivalent of a Gestalt switch by which the same facts came to be seen through a new lens, leading to a different interpretation. In an earlier era, liberals had framed "troubling" behaviors among the poor as products of poverty and used images of social disorganization, especially among poor blacks, as evidence for the necessity of extending aid. The conservative campaign against welfare dependency, however, reframed these same behaviors as products of "permissive" social programs that failed to limit program usage, require work, or demand functional behavior. "Long-term dependency" became a key phrase in welfare debates, usually treated as part of a broader syndrome of underclass pathologies that included drug use, violence, crime, teen pregnancy, single motherhood, and even poverty itself. Gradually, permissiveness and dependency displaced poverty and structural barriers to advancement as the central problems that drew attention from those designing welfare policy.

The discursive turn to dependency had important political consequences. First, welfare dependency and its effects on the poor set the agenda for poverty research in the 1980s and 1990s. To distinguish myths from realities, researchers expended great effort identifying the typical duration of participation spells and the individual-level correlates of long-term program usage. Structural questions received less attention as defenders responded to critics in a debate that focused on work effort, program usage, and poor people's behaviors. Second, as dependency came to be seen as a cause of intergenerational poverty, it became a kind of synecdoche, a single part used to represent the whole tangle of problems associated with the poor. To fight dependency was, in essence, to fight a kind of substance abuse that led to unrestrained sexuality, drug problems, violent crime, civic irresponsibility, and even poverty itself.

As a synecdoche for diverse social ills, dependency became the basis for a powerful crisis narrative in the 1980s and 1990s. Critics spoke of a "crisis of dependency," often in conjunction with fellow travelers such as the "teen pregnancy crisis" and the "underclass crisis." As Murray Edelman (1977) explains, such crisis language evokes perceptions of threat, conveys the need for immediate and extraordinary action, and suggests that "now is not the time" to air dissent or seek deliberation. Claims about the prevalence of long-term program usage were often overblown, and images of wholesale social disintegration depended on highly selective readings of poor people's attitudes and behaviors. But by applying the label of "crisis," critics turned ambiguous trends among the poor (many of which also existed in the rest of society) into a fearsome threat to the values of "middle America."

Just as the "drug crisis" seemed to require a tough, incarceration-minded "war on drugs," the crisis of dependency called for nothing short of an assault on permissiveness. In this environment, poverty advocates who tried to direct attention toward issues other than dependency were seen as fiddling while Rome burned. Long-term program usage was viewed as a major social problem requiring a bold solution; it called for extraordinary measures, not tepid liberal palliatives. The only suitable response was to attack dependency at its root by imposing a new regime of welfare rules designed to dissuade and limit program usage, enforce work, and curb unwanted behaviors. In 1996, that is exactly what welfare reform did.

This reframing of welfare dependency as a manifestation of the pathologies of the poor, and most especially black, underclass created the political climate that led to President Bill Clinton joining with a Republican Congress to "end welfare as we know it." The result was the Personal Responsibility and Work Opportunity Reconciliation Act of 1996 that abolished the sixty-one-year-old Aid to Families with Dependent Children (AFDC) program, which had come to be an entitlement that citizens had a right to receive once determined to be eligible. In its place, states would now receive block grants under the Temporary Assistance for Needy Families (TANF) program that could be used to provide cash assistance as AFDC did, but they had to meet quotas in moving recipients into paid employment. In addition, recipients face work requirements, time limits, caps on benefits, and the possibility of sanctions when not complying with contracts they sign promising to take steps to leave welfare for work. The purging of the welfare rolls that had started in the early 1990s with waivers allowing states to experiment with some of these new restrictions accelerated after 1996 until the economy slowed in 2001. As a result, the number of recipients receiving welfare fell from 13,242,000 in 1995 to 4,076,764 by September 2009—a decline of 69.2 percent (USHHS 2009). And while welfare reform has been widely heralded as a success for this reason alone, it resulted in most single mothers leaving TANF to become mired in poverty, earning on average no more than $7.50 an hour, often without benefits, and most often with increased out-of-pocket expenses associated with taking paid employment, most especially for child care (see Schram 2006). These hardships were more frequently visited on black single mothers, who were also more likely to be forced off welfare by sanctions and more likely to have to cycle back on if they had time-limited eligibility remaining.

Welfare was thus retrenched in no small part because of the way welfare dependency discourse had reframed this policy issue in gendered and racialized ways that portrayed welfare use as a pathology that had to be treated therapeutically. Borrowing metaphors from allied arenas of service provision laid the basis for a veritable medicalization of welfare dependency as a personal pathology that required individualized treatment as much as any other behavioral problem. With such a reframing, it became all the more difficult to see reliance on welfare as a product of structural problems in the economy or society. Public opinion was not so much changed as mobilized to support the retrenchment of welfare as the primary means by which we as a society could attack not just the scourge of welfare dependency but the cluster of pathological behaviors with which it was associated.

Now, with the medicalized discourse of welfare dependency firmly entrenched in public deliberations about welfare use, welfare reform increasingly has turned into the social policy equivalent of a twelve-step program. Rather than being a program to redistribute needed income to poor families with children, it has become a behavioral-modification regime centered on getting the parents of these children to become self-disciplined so that they in turn will become self-sufficient according to ascendant work and family values. Increasingly, this behavioral-modification regime is implemented via public-private partnerships in which state and local governments contract with private, often for-profit, providers to move single mothers with children off welfare and into jobs and marriages. The medicalized discourse of dependency logically calls forth new forms of governance that can practice the governmentality needed for regimenting low-income parents into the low-wage labor markets of the globalizing economy. The net result is that poverty is displaced as the persistent underlying problem that it is, and welfare policy comes to be focused ever more so on reducing welfare dependency as an end in itself.

The medicalized discourse of welfare dependency may have made relying on welfare the social policy equivalent of an addiction, thereby making welfare recipients out to be "sick" rather than "bad" (see Conrad 2007). Yet, this discursive shift did not exonerate the poor. The medicalization of welfare dependency simply reinforced the belief that most welfare recipients were passive dependents who were idle when they could have been working; and it further reinforced the idea that offering the poor aid only perversely encouraged the bad habit of idleness (see Soss and Schram 2007). In fact, in today's medicalized parlance, offering aid was characterized as "sick," as Newt Gingrich and others noted in the years just before welfare reform was adopted by the United States Congress (O'Brien 1995). From this perspective, it became that much easier to believe that if welfare recipients were treated for their condition, they could be taught how to do what is right and then they could take their place in the workforce and begin to work their way to self-sufficiency, if not quite out of poverty. Indeed, although the rolls have declined and the labor force participation rate and earnings of former adult welfare recipients are up, the underlying poverty that afflicts their families persists. The "welfare poor" have been replaced by the "working poor." And the metonymy of dependency as a product of individual choice continues to leave us in denial about the structural causes of poverty in our economic system.

Today's welfare system trades on a discourse dedicated to making itself real by becoming its own self-fulfilling prophecy. The governmentality associated with contemporary welfare policies has been aptly described as "a political project that endeavors to create a social reality that it suggests already exists" (Lemke 2001:203). In fact, poverty governance today assumes that welfare recipients are already market actors even before they start taking paid employment. As a result, the different dimensions of their lives, from mental health issues to child-rearing responsibilities, are termed "barriers" to work that must be overcome (Stone 2008). This reconstruction is but one element of a broader rewriting of identity that is well captured by the exhortations of a welfare "job club" instructor observed by Anna Korteweg: "No one in this room has been out of work, the way we're going to write your résumé. You're working in the house, you're a taxi driver, a budget planner, you volunteer at your children's school, you're a food preparer. You're self-employed, you're not receiving the income but you're working all the time. You have been successfully and diligently working daily" (2003:468). Welfare policy discourse repositions single mothers on welfare as protoworkers who are to prove their worth to society by taking paid employment under almost any conditions and regardless of how poor the pay. They are to be regimented into the bottom of a globalizing economy of declining wages. There they learn to be the compliant members of that subordinate caste. Their inclusive exclusion is executed when we come to see them as no longer the "welfare poor" but now the "working poor."

New Identities through Counterdiscourses

A semiotic approach to the study of public policy enables us to see how an underlying structure of intelligibility informs how we interpret the narratives we provide for understanding policy problems. It goes further to show how policy itself becomes a site for narrating privileged identities. As the foregoing analysis has shown, the favored subjectivity of contemporary welfare policy discourse in the United States continues to be the privileged subject of liberal political discourse: the autonomous, self-sufficient head of the traditional family (usually the white male husband and father). This subjectivity is matched by its denigrated other, the welfare dependent (still most often vividly portrayed in the popular imaginary as a black single mother). These subjectivities continue to anchor welfare policy discourse in the United States. Welfare policy remains mortgaged to a deep semiotic structure of deservingness that comes close to insisting that "if you don't work, you don't eat!"

Attention to discourse is not epiphenomenal but is instead central to democratic politics focused on making the state more responsive to people's economic concerns. Challenges can begin with questioning welfare policy's Malthusian assumptions—all of them—from how there is an underlying natural order to things that must not be tampered with, to how giving aid corrupts and undermines commitment to work and family values, to questioning the poor as different from everyone else. A good empirical base can be invoked by pointing to the experiences of other advanced industrial societies that have far more generous terms of social provision and do not see the deleterious effects predicted by the perversity thesis. Yet this kind of factual base is never dispositive. For instance, in this case, countries with stronger welfare states tend to have higher levels of unemployment. Nonetheless, there is a need for a counterdiscourse that does not rely on the implied subjectivities that anchor welfare policy discourse today. While no discourse will ensure absolute social justice and no discourse is beyond contestation, a less exclusionary discourse less tied to the image of the poor as qualitatively different people is a good place to begin.

Comparisons with other countries are especially pertinent in the quest for a counterdiscourse because they show the extent to which our forms of social provision are distinctively vindictive, given the high degree to which they are structured by the perversity thesis. In comparison to other advanced industrialized countries, social policies are to a far greater degree structured to "assume the worst" about low-income people who receive aid. And ironically this "assume-the-worst" mentality ends up a self-fulfilling prophecy. Programs are designed to emphasize suspicion, surveillance, and a reluctance to provide aid except under the most extreme circumstances in which people demonstrate that they are in desperate need for assistance. Cash, food, housing, and health assistance for low-income families all have operated under the assume-the-worst mentality. This leads to targeted, means-tested programs that are designed to guard covetously against providing aid to families with incomes above strict cut-off levels. As a result, recipients must of necessity restructure their identities, conform their behaviors, and fit themselves into the systems of assistance to make it seem that they are the most desperate of all and therefore should be provided with aid. Therefore, ironically, the conservatives who complain about how our welfare system creates dependency are in fact responsible for creating such a self-defeating mechanism that traps people in a system that forces them to prove their deservingness by keeping themselves poor so that they can tap much-needed aid. Only when we begin "assuming the best" in people will we start to break the cycle of dependency that conservatives are so concerned about. This then means moving to systems of assistance that rely less on suspicion and surveillance, less on targeting and means-testing. Instead, we need more universal programs. But we need to move to them in ways that will not jeopardize the assistance that targeted programs provide to low-income families.

This then is the beginning of a counterdiscourse that highlights how the discourse that assumes the worst of dependency is the self-defeating and self-fulfilling prophecy of a welfare system thoroughly grounded in the perversity thesis. It provides the initial outlines of an argument that not only points to the fallacious reasoning of the perversity thesis but offers a counterdiscourse that explains the same phenomenon in terms that create the basis for supporting more generous forms of social provision. Such a counterdiscourse does not so much try to convince with facts as provide an alternative basis for explaining facts. And it arguably ends up creating a potentially more enduring basis for achieving the progressive agenda. This is but an initial challenge to the dominance of the perversity thesis and the assume-the-worst mentality. Much more work is needed to develop a counterdiscourse that will be a compelling challenge that will resonate with the public and create the basis of support for more generous forms of social provision. Yet it is my argument here that this is where the critical energy of welfare rights activism needs to be focused if it is to be politically effective. Democratically effective welfare activism must challenge the reigning ideology of stinginess and its assumptions about people as identified in policy discourse.

Martha Fineman (2008) has gone to the heart of the matter when she says we need to rethink the privileged citizen-subject assumed by the discourse of deservingness that informs social policy today. Rather than an entitlement discourse that assumes the privileged deserving person is one consistent with the model of the autonomous, self-sufficient citizen-subject of the liberal political imaginary, we should shift to a need-based formulation that assumes the universal identity of the "vulnerable subject." Fineman astutely argues that our shared vulnerability, economically and otherwise, is a more universally shared basis for an assumed subjectivity of the citizen. Given the structural inequities that shape our political economy, the state should be organized around addressing our shared vulnerabilities rather than rewarding us for our less-than-shared opportunities to demonstrate our ability to be autonomous, self-sufficient political and economic actors who have earned their benefits. Our vulnerabilities that emerge as children, vulnerable older persons, and dependent caregivers should inform the basis for determining our eligibility for aid rather than the liberal political and economic subject that is falsely assumed to be autonomous and self-sufficient. Fineman writes that "the 'vulnerable subject' must replace the autonomous and independent subject asserted in the liberal tradition. Far more representative of actual lived experience and the human condition, the vulnerable subject should be at the center of our political and theoretical endeavors. The vision of the state that would emerge in such an engagement would be both more responsive to and responsible for the vulnerable subject, a reimagining that is essential if we are to attain a more equal society than currently exists in the United States" (2008:1–2). Once we center discourse on our shared vulnerability, we can begin to build a state around the idea that we care for each other and are prepared to compensate people for their disadvantage in how they are positioned institutionally in ways that deny them access to needed assets. "By recognizing that privilege and disadvantage migrate across identity categories, we are forced to focus not only on individuals, but also on institutions—the structures and arrangements that can almost invisibly produce or exacerbate existing inequality" (Fineman 2008:22). Once we do this, we can begin to see that the autonomy of the implied citizen-subject of the prevailing liberal political discourse is not a natural phenomenon but a product of the very social policies whose discourse assumes autonomy as a precondition.

Conclusion

As the foregoing demonstrates, discourse analysis, especially one that focuses on the semiotics of social performance, is the melding of intellectual and political work that can create critical resources for resisting oppressive social and economic policies in today's age of globalization and in the future. Discourse itself is not critical, but we can cast a critical eye on how it structures the narrative practices of public policy. When we do that, a discourse analysis becomes one of the more effective ways to highlight how the age-old attitude of assuming the worst about the poor becomes a politically convenient resource for underwriting collective inaction and outright denial about the structural roots of poverty and inequality in the contemporary globalizing society (Peck 2002). In the foregoing, I have tried to demonstrate that my own eclectic approach to studying welfare policy discourse in the United States can help challenge the willful ignorance about poverty that persists to this day. It might even prove useful in tracking the contemporary spread of dependency talk around the developed world. Discourse analysis can highlight how welfare policy today replaces concerns about economic subordination with a therapeutic orientation for treating the poor as deficient people in need of paternalistic policies that will regiment them into the emerging low-wage labor markets of the globalizing economy. Discourse analysis can shine a bright light on today's implied standard that taking available work no matter how poorly it pays is a precondition for full citizenship in an era of globalization.

Since discourse's power is never complete, the dominant readings of dependency discourse need to be challenged by pursuing alternative ones that highlight the dignity and earnest efforts of those who are being marginalized as allegedly passive dependents content to subsist on welfare payments. Encoded discourse can be decoded transgressively. Alternative readings can highlight how all citizens in the globalizing work-first regime are subsidized in various ways by the welfare state. Our shared vulnerabilities are hidden in plain sight. Studying semiotic sources of identity can enable us to see how we rely on an underlying structure of intelligibility in ways that risk reinscribing old prejudices even in new contexts. A semiotic analysis of performance can highlight how welfare policy discourse makes the relative distinction of who is dependent versus independent into a naturalized, reified difference that it does not deserve to be but which our contemporary market-centered society so desperately needs to make appear to be real. In this way, we can show that while discourse is not the only force propelling the push to regiment the poor into the bottom of the occupational structure in the face of the declining wages of a globalizing economy, it is a powerful resource that already-powerful actors can draw upon to make it seem inevitable that the poor shall always be with us.

The political impasse created by the Great Recession that unfolded in the first decade of the twenty-first century highlights the persistence of a deep semiotic structure of deservingness that undergirds social welfare policy in the Western world, after all these years, and still today. The mortgage meltdown that propelled Western economies into crisis was very much framed as a result of risky loans to an undeserving poor who could not responsibly save and pay off their mortgages. The resulting Eurozone financial crisis was in turn framed as largely the result of a profligate welfare state that rewarded undeserving citizens for their lack of work effort. The power of this discourse of deservingness remains real and needs to be challenged. Attention to identity in discourse in particular can therefore help strengthen challenges to the injustices of welfare policy today, locally and globally.

Notes

1. In criticizing reviews of Stanley Kubrick's film *Barry Lyndon*, Michael Klein distinguishes discourse and narrative: "There seems to be an expectation, virtually prescriptive, that the core of the film should reside in the narrative, in the sequence of events and point of view of the main characters. However Kubrick's modernist perspective is somewhat different.

While the events do shape the characters' lives, they are relatively neutral, incomplete signs. The characters are devoid of self-consciousness. The total configuration of visual and aural signs (including the music and the voice-over), that is the discourse, defines and determines our response to and comprehension of the events. . . . The discourse is ironic and analytic (places the characters and events in a larger perspective); it also engages our sympathy (defines value and meaning). A discourse is a configuration of [s]igns . . . that overdetermines the narrative" (1981:95, 107).

2. The remainder of this section draws heavily on Schram and Soss (2001).

References

Agamben, Giorgio. 1998. *Homo Sacer: Sovereign Power and Bare Life.* Stanford: Stanford University Press.
Alexander, Jeffrey. 2003. *The Meanings of Social Life: A Cultural Sociology.* New York: Oxford University Press.
——. 2006. "Cultural Pragmatics: Social Performance between Ritual and Strategy." In *Social Performance: Symbolic Action, Cultural Pragmatics and Ritual,* edited by Jeffrey C. Alexander, Bernhard Giesen, and Jason L. Mast, 29–90. Cambridge: Cambridge University Press.
——. 2009. "The Democratic Struggle for Power: The 2008 Presidential Campaign in the USA." *Journal of Power* 2:65–88.
Alexander, Jeffrey, and Philip Smith. 1999. "Cultural Structures, Social Action, and the Discourses of American Civil Society: A Reply to Battani, Hall, and Powers." *Theory and Society* 28:455–61.
Balkin, J. M. 2002. *Cultural Software: A Theory of Ideology.* New Haven: Yale University Press.
Ball, Stephen J. 1990. *Politics and Policymaking in Education: Explorations in Policy Sociology.* London: Routledge.
Barthes, Roland. 1972. *Mythologies.* Translated by Annette Lavers. New York: Farrar, Straus and Giroux.
Bourdieu, Pierre. 1998. *Practical Reason: On the Theory of Action.* Stanford: Stanford University Press.
Butler, Judith. 1997. "Merely Cultural." *Social Text* 52–53(Fall):33–44.
Campbell, Nancy. 1999. *Using Women: Gender, Drug Policy, and Social Justice.* New York: Routledge.
Conrad, Peter. 2007. *The Medicalization of Society: On the Transformation of Human Conditions into Treatable Disorders.* Baltimore: Johns Hopkins University Press.
Cruikshank, Barbara. 1999. *The Will to Empower: Democratic Citizens and Other Subjects.* Ithaca: Cornell University Press.

Danziger, Sheldon H., Richard Frank, and Ellen Meara. 2009. "Mental Illness, Work and Income Support Programs." *American Journal of Psychiatry* 166(4):398–404.

Dean, Jody. 2006. *Žižek's Politics.* New York: Routledge.

Dodge, Jennifer, Sonia Ospina, and Erica Foldy. 2005. "Integrating Rigor and Relevance in Public Administration Scholarship: The Contribution of Narrative Inquiry." *Public Administration Review* 65(3):286–300.

Dodson, Lisa. 2010. *The Moral Underground: How Ordinary Americans Subvert an Unfair Economy.* New York: New Press.

Edelman, Murray. 1977. *Political Language: Words that Succeed and Policies that Fail.* New York: Academic.

Feldman, Martha, Kaj Sköldberg, Ruth Nicole Brown, and Debra Horner. 2004. "Making Sense of Stories: A Rhetorical Approach to Narrative Analysis." *Journal of Public Administration Research and Theory* 14(2):147–70.

Felluga, Dino. 2003. "Verse's Perversity." *Victorian Poetry* 41(4):490–99.

Fineman, Martha Albertson. 2008. "The Vulnerable Subject: Anchoring Equality in the Human Condition." *Yale Journal of Law and Feminism* 20(1):1–23.

Fischer, Frank. 2009. *Democracy and Expertise: Reorienting Policy Inquiry.* New York: Oxford University Press.

Foucault, Michel. 1991. "Governmentality." In *The Foucault Effect: Studies in Governmentality,* edited by Graham Burchell, Colin Gordon, and Peter Miller, 87–104. Chicago: University of Chicago Press.

Gilens, Martin. 1999. *Why Americans Hate Welfare: Race, Media, and the Politics of Antipoverty Policy.* Chicago: University of Chicago Press.

Hacking, Ian. 2000. *The Social Construction of What?* Cambridge: Harvard University Press.

Hall, Stuart. 1973. "Encoding and Decoding in Television Discourse." Stenciled paper 7. Birmingham: Center for Contemporary Cultural Studies, University of Birmingham.

Handler, Joel. 2004. *Social Citizenship and Workfare in the United States and Western Europe: The Paradox of Inclusion.* New York: Cambridge University Press.

Klein, Michael. 1981. "Narrative and Discourse in Kubrick's Modern Tragedy." In *The English Novel and the Movies,* edited by Michael Klein and Gillian Parker, 95–107. New York: Frederick Ungar.

Korteweg, Anna. 2003. "Welfare Reform and the Subject of the Working Mother: Get a Job, a Better Job, Then a Career." *Theory and Society* 32(4):445–80.

Laga, Barry. 2009. "Reading with an Eye on Discourse: The New Historicism," on the author's page on the web site of Colorado Mesa University.

Lemke, Thomas. 2001. "The Birth of Bio-Politics: Michel Foucault's Lecture at the Collège de France on Neo-Liberal Governmentality." *Economy and Society* 30(2):190–207.

Lynn, Laurence E., Jr. 1999. "A Place at the Table: Policy Analysis, Its Postpositive Critics, and the Future of Practice." *Journal of Policy Analysis and Management* 18(3):411–24.

Malthus, Thomas. (1798) 1985. *Essays on the Principles of Population*. London: Penguin.

March, James G., and Johan P. Olsen. 2006. "The Logic of Appropriateness." In *The Oxford Handbook of Public Policy*, edited by Michael Moran, Martin Rein, and Robert Goodin, 689–708. Oxford: Oxford University Press.

Murray, Charles. 1984. *Losing Ground: American Social Policy, 1950–1980*. New York: Basic.

Neubeck, Kenneth, and Noel Cazenave. 2001. *Welfare Racism: Playing the Race Card against America's Poor*. New York: Routledge.

O'Brien, Sue. 1995. "Outraged Watchers Eye Newt." *Denver Post*, December 10.

Peck, Jamie. 2002. "Political Economies of Scale: Fast Policy, Interscalar Relations, and Neoliberal Workfare." *Economic Geography* 78(3):331–60.

Pierce, Charles S. 1977. *Semiotics and Significs*. Edited by Charles Hardwick. Bloomington: Indiana University Press.

PRC (Pew Research Center). 2009. "Independents Take Center Stage in Obama Era," on the Center's web site.

Reese, Ellen. 2005. *Backlash against Welfare Mothers: Past and Present*. Berkeley: University of California Press.

Schram, Sanford F. 1995. *Words of Welfare: The Poverty of Social Science and the Social Science of Poverty*. Minneapolis: University of Minnesota Press.

———. 2000. *After Welfare: The Culture of Postindustrial Social Policy*. New York: New York University Press.

———. 2006. *Welfare Discipline: Discourse, Governance, and Globalization*. Philadelphia: Temple University Press.

Schram, Sanford F., and Joe Soss. 2001. "Success Stories: Welfare Reform, Policy Discourse, and the Politics of Research." *Annals of the American Academy of Political and Social Science* 577 (September):49–65.

Somers, Margaret, and Fred Block. 2005. "From Poverty to Perversity: Ideas, Markets, and Institutions over 200 Years of Welfare Debate." *American Sociological Review* 70:260–87.

Soss, Joe, and Sanford F. Schram. 2007. "A Public Transformed? Welfare Reform as Policy Feedback." *American Political Science Review* 101(1):111–27.

Stone, Deborah. 1988. *Policy Paradox and Political Reason*. Boston: Scott Foresman.

———. 2008. *The Samaritan's Dilemma: Should Government Help Your Neighbor.* New York: Nation Books.
USHHS (US Department of Health and Human Services). 2009. TANF-Caseload Data 2009, on the web site of the USHHS.
Žižek, Slavoj. 1989. *The Sublime Object of Ideology.* New York: Verso.

PART V
Policy Argumentation in Critical Theory and Practice
COMMUNICATIVE LOGICS AND POLICY LEARNING

HUBERTUS BUCHSTEIN AND DIRK JÖRKE

9. The Argumentative Turn toward Deliberative Democracy

Habermas's Contribution and the Foucauldian Critique

The argumentative turn in policy analysis and planning is based on the insight that our language does not simply mirror the world but that instead language profoundly shapes our view of the world. Since "public policy is made of language," as Giandomenico Majone (1989:1) famously puts it, the ways policy analysts represent the social reality in their research are deeply embedded in controversies about the truth of their claims and about social power.

The debates in social philosophy and epistemology about the essential status of language in the sciences and its implications were inspired by philosophers like Ludwig Wittgenstein, Martin Heidegger, Hans-Georg Gadamer, J. L. Austin, and Jacques Lacan. But it was eventually the work of Jürgen Habermas and Michel Foucault that kept the debate moving in the direction later aptly coined "the argumentative turn in policy analysis" by Frank Fischer and John Forester (1993). In assessing policy analysis as argumentation, Fischer and Forester made use of the ambiguity of the term "argument," referring both to an analytical content and to a practical performance. In retrospect, it is in particular Habermas's early criticism of positivism in the social sciences and his later conceptual work on discourse theory, in which he developed this ambiguity of content and performance, which became the crucial step in bridging the gap between language philosophy and public policy analysis.[1] In addition, Foucault's theory of discourse and power inspired a new area of academic inquiry: the discourse analysis. Today, the work of Habermas as well as that of Foucault has become the point of reference for two altercating strands of research in public policy.

Habermas is still regarded as one of the most influential academic thinkers of our times in the fields of philosophy, sociology, linguistics, and political science.[2] In addition, his contributions as a public intellectual have triggered many political debates both in Europe and in the United States.[3] In the first part of this chapter, we reevaluate Habermas's influence on critical policy studies. First, we look back on his path from a critique of positivism to democratic theory and his theory of deliberative policy. We discuss whether Habermas has made an epistemic turn in his more recent writings on democratic theory and its implications for policy making. Then, we turn to current empirical studies about deliberative policy making. In the second part of the chapter, we reevaluate Foucauldian critiques of the Habermasian approach to democratic theory, beginning with a reconstruction of the internal links between Foucault's theory of discourse, knowledge, and power, and moving to an outline of their implications for a critical analysis of deliberative policy and politics. Finally, we reflect on the consequences of late Foucault's understanding of governmentality for critical policy studies today and argue that Foucault's ethos of critique is indeed in some respects not far away from the intentions of Habermas's discourse ethics.

Jürgen Habermas: From Postpositivism to Deliberative Democracy

In retrospect, the impact of Habermas's contribution to the argumentative turn in the study of public policy can be seen on three different levels. First, Habermas's work became a prominent point of reference for critical policy scholars as a result of his contributions to the field of *democratic theory*. His work was read as having a participatory impulse, which attracted academics interested in democratic reforms. Starting in the 1950s with a radically democratic reformulation of Franz L. Neumann's famous statement that democracy is the realization of human freedom through political participation, Habermas became politically engaged in his early days as a proponent of a socialist and participatory concept of democracy.[4] His outspoken support for the protest movements against German remilitarization in the 1950s, as well as his support for the protest movements of the late 1960s and his engagement with democratic university reform, created his public image as an advocate of participatory democracy. In the field of university politics, for example, Habermas put on the political agenda the "democratization of the university" through the institutionalization of open and nonhierarchical discussions and through politically decided topics of research (1970:6). In addition, he defended "student's participation in research processes" (1970:9). However, Habermas understood political participation in his writings (and his political activities) in a certain normative sense: as an activity of equal involvement in processes of discursive will-formation. At this point in his intellectual development, Habermas diagnosed a tension between democracy and capitalism. In his programmatic introduction to *Theory and Practice*, he spoke of the "incompatibility of the imperatives that rule the capitalistic economic system with a democratic process for forming the public will" and called for the "discursive formation of the will as an organizational principle for the social system as a whole" (1973:4, 27). Habermas hoped that the political forces pressing toward a democratization of society would "succeed in penetrating the total complex of production" (232). This understanding of the democratization of society and the essential role of "rational arguments" in political debates were confirmed again in the mid-1970s in the final chapters of Habermas's programmatic essay *Legitimation Crisis* (1975).

Second, Habermas has been read by social scientists as an author who reconceptualized the tradition of critical theory of the Frankfurt School of western Marxism. From his early book *The Structural Transformation of the Public Sphere* (originally published in 1961) to his *The Theory of Communicative Action* (originally published in 1981) and *The Future of Human Nature* (2003), Habermas intended to lay the ground for a "theory of society" that would be capable of formulating a critical perspective on the processes of reification and alienation in modern capitalist societies (see Iser 2009; Strecker 2012; White 1988). Since the 1980s, this work has contributed to *metatheoretical* debates among many policy scholars about basic questions of social philosophy, theories of society, and the policy process.

Third, this interest in Habermas's work has stimulated debate on the *methodological level* in the field of policy studies and discourse analyses. This started with his early critique of positivism and neopositivism in the 1960s and was complemented in the 1970s by his critique of Gadamer's hermeneutics.[5] It was, in particular, Habermas's claim, in his *Knowledge and Human Interest* (originally published in 1968), that Freudian psychoanalysis might serve as a paradigmatic case for an emancipating and participatory social science that laid the ground for the search for postpositivist methodologies among scholars of public policy (see Fischer 1980). Thus, Habermas's attack on positivism and his attempt to overcome the shortcomings of pure hermeneutic alternatives became a crucial steppingstone for the argumentative turn in the social sciences.

Revisions and New Turns in Habermas's Thought

Since the mid-twentieth century, starting with the publication in 1953 of his first articles on Heidegger's philosophy and his sociological studies of consumerism, Habermas has shown a tremendous capability and willingness to engage in debates with his critics. More than once he has reacted to substantial objections to his ideas by making radical theoretical changes and revisions. The best-known of these changes are those that led him away from his early, Adorno-like cultural critique, first to an epistemological foundation for critical theory, and subsequently to a theory of communicative rationality.[6] However, Habermas's later work has also constantly undergone revisions, mostly triggered by the need to bring in new topics and to respond to his critics. Due to the vast amount of literature by and on Habermas, it can be easy to overlook some of these lesser-known revisions, even though they may be of importance for an assessment of his contributions to critical policy studies, including policy discourse analyses. With respect to the significant role of Habermas's work in shaping the formative phase of the argumentative turn, we mention three of these changes.

First, revisions occur on the *methodological level*. Although Habermas is still a critic of positivism (as well as of rational choice) in the social sciences, he has distanced himself from his harsh and polemical attacks of the 1960s. As early as 1982, in the new German edition of his book on positivism, he acknowledged the relevance of mainstream empirical research in the social sciences. As a consequence, he developed the concept of "rational reconstruction" as a suitable methodology for empirical policy research (e.g., into the deliberative quality of public discussion) and discourse analyses.[7] Unfortunately, Habermas has not developed this methodological concept very far (see Habermas 2005; Koller 2009; Gaus 2009:106–10). And so, it comes as less of a surprise when one gets the impression, in some of his other writings, such as *Between Facts and Norms* (originally published in 1992), that he has returned to a traditional distinction between political philosophy (which deals with normative issues only) and empirical social sciences (which use all sorts of methodologies). Thus, scholars in critical policy studies are left without clear answers to questions about the methodological status and potential of Habermas's more recent work: what is left of his critique of positivism, which inspired the early postpositivist movement? It is doubtful whether postpositivist scholars today still may learn new lessons from Habermas's later take on methodology.

In addition, Habermas has made changes, clarifications, concessions, and revisions on the metatheoretical level. With respect to the field of discourse analyses, the main clarification has concerned the different types of discourse. With the publication in 1991 of *Erläuterungen zur Diskursethik*, Habermas began to differentiate between three types of discourse, moral, ethical, and pragmatic, each with its own communicative claims and internal logic (see Habermas 1993). The differences between Habermas's understanding of a discourse as a source for normative standards and Foucault's conceptualization of discourses as spaces of power relations, which had already worked out a couple of years earlier in his lecture *The Philosophical Discourse of Modernity* (originally published in 1985), finally became more clear-cut.

However, it is not fully clear to what extent these categorical and conceptual differentiations are relevant to the argumentative turn in general and to empirical research on public policy issues. Questions may be asked about the consequences of the distinction between weak and strong forms of communicative action to empirical discourse analyses. To what extent can the revised role of imperatives within Habermas's linguistic framework reinvigorate the empirical identification of arguing and bargaining in political deliberations? And how can the analysis of political debate make use of the distinction between the three types of discourse? It is obvious that the analytical differentiation between moral, ethical, and pragmatic types of discourse—each with its own communicative claims and internal logic—is supposed to have conceptual as well as normative consequences for empirical research on policy formation processes. But what exactly these analytical distinctions lead policy analysts to has not been worked out yet.

To some readers of Habermas such as Nancy Fraser, William Scheuerman, Hans Joas, or Rainer Schmalz-Bruns, however, the most disturbing revisions they find in Habermas's work are in the field of *democratic theory*. In the final chapters of *The Theory of Communicative Action*, in which Habermas integrates systems theory into his theory of society to such a degree that, in the end, system media such as "money" and "power" seem to dominate (or, in Habermas's word, "colonize") the realm of politics. Against this tendency of modern societies, Habermas has insisted on the relevance of participatory politics, in particular through social movements and an activist civil society. Even though these movements were interpreted by Habermas as a defensive social force against the colonization of the life-world by the system, active members of social movements were understood as crucial policy makers to fight pathologies of modernity. In his later writings, Habermas has distanced himself from any earlier aspirations to democratize society as a whole. According to Habermas, one has to take the arguments of modern systems theorists such as Niklas Luhmann more seriously than he did earlier: "All the modern economies are so complex that a complete shift to participatory decision-making processes, that is to say, a democratic restructuring at *every* level, would inevitably do damage to some of the sensitive requirements of contemporary organization" (Habermas 1987:324). As a consequence, he placed political participation within the sphere of the life-world, where it is expected to defend communicative rationality against the colonization of the life-world with the instrumental rationality of systems imperatives. This conceptualization served as a source of inspiration for radical politics and new social movements. In addition, it provided a starting point for a number of scholars of critical public policy who had been interested both in radical democracy and in a sociological analysis of public discourses. So in the 1990s, Habermas's work again was cited as a normative and methodological cornerstone for the movement toward a more democratic and civil society (Arato and Cohen 1992).

The development of Habermas's ideas about democracy culminated in the publication in 1992 of *Between Facts and Norms*. This book was the first by Habermas devoted exclusively to questions of democratic principles and democratic institutions. Shortly after its publication, the book made Habermas, and continues to make him, one of the—if not *the*—most widely read authors dealing with the concept of "deliberative democracy." In particular, in the second part of the book, Habermas delineates a "two-track" model of the public sphere. In a wider and mostly unorganized public sphere, the members of civil society discuss political issues and create communicative power. If this power is strong enough, it may undermine the institutionalized realm of the governmental system (consisting in legislative bodies and other formal political institutions such as constitutional courts). But it is not allowed to occupy the state. Rather, in the passage from the wider public sphere to the inner realm of the political system, a deliberative laundering of communicative power has to take place.

Habermas's procedural reformulation of deliberative democracy and his two-track model seemed to bridge the gap between an elaborated normative program and empirical research in democratic policy making (see Benhabib 1996; Bohman 1996). Even though some authors criticized *Between Facts and Norms* for what they perceived as a lack of consistency with its radical democratic normative starting point (see Buchstein 1994; Scheuerman 1999; Schmalz-Bruns 1995), the theory of deliberative democracy, in its Habermasian version, still seemed to offer at least a normative orientation for a certain strand of scholars in the public policy research community. According to their understanding, the theory of deliberative democracy has to be worked out in more detail into a concept in which practical public policy problems would be settled in a way that emphasizes simultaneously the egalitarian and rational promises of modern democracy (see Chambers 1996; D'Entréves Passerin 2006).

An Epistemic Turn in Habermas's Theory of Democracy?

Since the publication of *Between Facts and Norms*, Habermas has carefully distinguished between the mode of "routine politics," which is within the institutions of the political system, and the mode of "exceptional politics," in which citizens get more deeply involved in political participation. According to Habermas, this model is normatively sufficient as long as the political apparatus is under the critical supervision of a professional public sphere. Today, Habermas is distancing himself from most of his early writings on democracy. In the German edition of his selected works published in 2009, in the volume collecting his main articles on political philosophy, he included no article written earlier than 1992. He justified this editorial decision with the argument that it was not until he completed *Between Facts and Norms* that he fully understood the proper role of democracy in modern societies (see Habermas 2009a:21).

Habermas is in line with the basic argument stated by other proponents of the deliberative theory like John Dryzek or Joshua Cohen that one of its major strengths lies in its particular suitability for offering a conceptual framework for democracy beyond the nation-state. According to Dryzek, the discursive theory of democracy "is particularly conducive to international society, because unlike older models of democracy, it can downplay the problem of boundaries" (2000:129). During its shift in focus from civil society actors in the framework of the nation-state to international organizations and supranational bodies, the deliberative theory of democracy quietly underwent a revision of its legitimating point of departure, as a result of which it has joined the trend of the "rationalization of the theory of democracy." Although the deliberative theory of democracy at first had its place in the tradition of radically democratic approaches that attempted to make a contribution to reform policy by strengthening forums of participation, its source of legitimacy has successively shifted ever more toward engendering "reasonable results" as a normative point of reference. There is especially the danger of a slippery slope from deliberative politics, through epistemic communities, to the rule of experts. This trend can be observed especially in the context of so-called comitology research on the political system of the European Union. After research uncovered that the expert bodies with international membership within the multilevel European system not only negotiate interests with one another but also make numerous decisions after exchanging arguments, these bodies were presented as examples par excellence of successful political processes of deliberation (see Joerges and Neyer 1997; Joerges 2002). After a deliberative redescription of "democracy," it is only a small step to regard the decision-making processes of the European comitology, which both lack transparency and are highly exclusive, as "democratic." Habermas's deliberative theory of democracy at the very least gives support to this democratic rereading of a highly technocratic governmental apparatus (Scheuerman 2004), even though he himself charges that the political elites in the EU have acted like technocrats in the recent financial and political crisis in Europe (Habermas 2010, 2011).

In the context of the debates about transnational democracy, Habermas has recently introduced an additional distinction between "voluntaristic" and "epistemic" understandings of democratic politics. According to him, it is the postnational constellation that "calls for further adjustments within the conceptual apparatus of political theory" (2008: 319) if we want to enable the theory of democracy to catch up with the realities of a world organized at a supranational level. For the normative core of his understanding of democracy, this means undertaking a shift in emphasis requiring that "we also ascribe an epistemic function of democratic will-formation" (Habermas 2001:110). In Habermas's approach of "epistemic proceduralism" (2006:413), democratic processes obtain their legitimizing power "not only and not mainly from participation and will-articulation," but from the general accessibility of "a deliberative process whose structure grounds an expectation of rationally acceptable results" (110; for a critique, see Jörke 2009).

The benefit that Habermas expects from this shift toward the epistemic dimension, as the move is coined by Rainer Schmalz-Bruns (1995: 274), is its particular suitability in the deliberative theory of democracy for meeting the requirements of a conceptualization of democracy that transcends national boundaries. By doing so, Habermas can easily and critically counter an understanding of democracy that insists that in a democracy citizens first of all must have the same opportunities to bring their authentic preferences to bear through elections or referenda that are "voluntaristic" (Habermas 2001:110). Habermas thus assigns to the participatory element in the concept of democracy the status of a dependent variable of the rationality wished for in political processes. Reasonable deliberation and inclusive participation are not simply two sides of democratic policy making, which is how Habermas in some of his writings tends to reconcile the two different strands (Habermas 2009a:12), but there is a priority for the cognitive element. The logical consequence of this priority is that democratic participation is subordinated to the demands of rationality posed by modern politics. Thus, a deliberative theory of democracy interpreted in this vein has a problem concerning its democratic nature when it comes to its input dimension (see Buchstein and Jörke 2007).

The influence of the changing sociological view of the forces and developments that are constitutive of modern societies, which Habermas took from Niklas Luhmann's systems theory approach to democratic theory, can hardly be overestimated (see Schmalz-Bruns 2009: 449). However, one would have a hard time trying to identify Habermas's distinction between a "voluntaristic" strand and an "epistemic" strand in democratic thought as something like a fundamental turn in his work in the field of democratic theory. As Thomas Saretzki indicates, there had been quite a number of "concretistic (mis-)interpretations of his concepts (e.g., concerning the ideal speech situation)" (2009:428), since for some of his readers his concepts seem to suggest practices of direct democracy and direct political involvement by all citizens. Habermas himself undoubtedly invited some of these concretistic readings by the way he illustrated his concepts and the way he took sides in political controversies in the 1960s, 1970s, and early 1980s. But despite these statements, the lack of an answer for the question of proper institutionalization of democratic principles in his work before *Between Facts and Norms*, in which he finally worked his ideas through the institutional setting of modern Western democracies, invited readers to fill the gaps with their own radical democratic aspirations.

On the other hand, Habermas explicitly rejected the idea of any totalizing visions of modern society that run counter to the complexity and plurality of modern society in the name of democracy (Habermas 1982). To him, the associative vision of a radical democracy is utopian in the negative sense, for it is based on unrealistic assumptions about the possibility of reducing the complexity of modern societies. A democratic theory that has no sociological plausibility is a hopeless project for him. And for this reason, Habermas focused his understanding of "democratization" on the options within the context of institutionalized will-formation and decision making in political parties, parliamentary legislation, the judiciary, and the political administration. So, despite the new Habermasian language of "voluntaristic" versus "epistemic," there should be no misunderstanding that Habermas from early on— for example, in the final sections of *The Structural Transformation of the Public Sphere*—put an emphasis on reasonable will-formation and not just the articulation preferences in polls or political activities (Habermas 1989).

So, Habermas can indeed be seen as a radical democrat even today. Radical, however, in a very special sense. He is not radical in the traditional meaning of having a totalizing and participatory democratic vision of modern society. His theory is radical with respect to the normative foundation of his democratic thought. In his view, any proper account of democracy has to be radical in the sense of being deeply connected to the fundamental rationalities that characterize the normative infrastructure of modernity.

Deliberating Deliberative Democracy

Since *Between Facts and Norms,* Habermas has devoted a certain amount of his intellectual energy to coming to terms with the institutional setting of democracies, both on the national and on the supranational level. According to Habermas, it is the deliberative "structure" (2001: 110) of institutions that can produce rationality in democratic decision making. The idea of seeing a close connection between the process of deliberation, political rationality, and a certain type of institution is not new; already Hegel in 1821 characterized the institution of the criminal jury according to the "deliberation of the members of the courts" and its potential to come to a fair verdict due to the different perspectives and the local knowledge that jurors may bring into the process (Hegel 1952:§224).

By focusing on the institutional aspects of deliberative democracy, Habermas has created a prolific source of troubles for his democratic thought. Recent research on deliberative practices identifies different areas in which institutions of deliberative democracies have in their practice proven susceptible to falling behind the normative expectations placed on them. There are three difficulties that are the focus of the critical debate.

First is the *problem of strategic exploitation.* Even if sometimes deliberative practices only gradually develop a universally normative characteristic within small bodies, they do remain susceptible to strategically minded actors who merely simulate the mode of debate, while simultaneously attempting to obtain as many benefits as possible through rhetoric.[8] The strategic aspect intensifies if participants in deliberative processes are pressured by the expectations of their political clientele. Jon Elster concludes from this susceptibility that it is better to give up Habermas's requirement of public scrutiny in favor of the view that deliberative processes are at times better served if they are conducted behind closed doors (see Elster 1997).

Second is the *problem of motivation.* Not all deliberative contexts equally motivate their participants to encumber themselves with the cognitive and moral exertion required to carry on rational discourse. Problems of motivation can partly be solved by the skillful work of professional moderators (see Fishkin 2009:132–34); however, participants often weigh the costs and benefits of deliberative processes and question whether their committed involvement is worthwhile if the result of political deliberations does not lead to binding political decisions (Ryfe 2005).

Next is the *problem of polarization*. The success of the deliberative process depends not least on the overall composition of those taking part. Apparently, homogeneous social settings do not invite rational communication but instead trigger a repeating process of participants confirming each other's opinions (Mutz 2006:16). If we follow Cass Sunstein's thesis, taking the next step forward from social-psychological research, one can even formulate a "law of group polarization" (2003:81; see also Ryfe 2005:54–60; Schweitzer 2004:91–97). According to this law, discussions in homogeneous groups or in groups that display a clear hegemony of one point of view do not have the effect of opening up horizons, but merely result in everyone in the group (or the group forming the majority) taking a more extreme position after the debates than before. On the other hand, researchers have been able to observe that all the participants in heterogeneous groups are more prepared to enter into a conversation about the deliberations of the other participants in the debate (see Druckman 2004; Fishkin 2009:131–34).

Putting these three problems together, we see that the problem of Habermas's deliberative theory of democracy is obviously not just one of democracy but also one of deliberation. And the problems become even more pressing when we take a closer look at processes of deliberation from a Foucauldian point of view.

Foucault and Deliberative Politics

One of the focal points of the sociophilosophical discussion in the 1980s and 1990s was the controversy between Habermasians and Foucauldians. Starting with Habermas's critique in *The Philosophical Discourse of Modernity* of the contradictions and blind spots in Foucault's concept of power, this debate evoked reams of articles on the relationship between power, critique, and subjectivity (see Bernstein 1989; Habermas 1987; Honneth 1991; McCarthy 1990). Habermas and his followers argue that power in the work of Foucault is too undifferentiated and that, for conceptual reasons, Foucault cannot distinguish between those forms of power that are the product of democratic action and those forms of power that are typical for totalitarian societies. But this is not the only problem with Foucault's concept of power. According to Habermas, Foucault also commits a performative contradiction insofar as he uses his insights to critique the power relations in contemporary societies. For example, when he describes in *Discipline and Punish* (1977) how subjects are produced by modern institutions such as the school and the army, this is clearly intended as a critique of those institutions and their corresponding disciplines. But he is not able to spell out the normative ground of this critique. On the contrary, in Foucault's work all normative thoughts are the result of the interrelation between power and knowledge. They are generated and reproduced by discursive formations and therefore cannot serve as a solid ground for critique. In a famous article, Nancy Fraser summarizes this critique: "On the one hand, he adopts a concept of power that permits him no condemnation of any objectionable features of modernity. But at the same time, and on the other hand, his rhetoric betrays the conviction that modernity is utterly without redeeming features. Clearly what Foucault needs—and needs desperately—are normative criteria for distinguishing acceptable from unacceptable forms of power" (Fraser 1981:286; see also Bernstein 1989; Honneth 1991).

In reaction, Foucauldians have emphasized the difference between the form of critique in the tradition of critical theory and Foucault's method of genealogy. According to David Owen, it is a categorical mistake to interpret Foucault's writings as a form of ideology critique (Owen 1999, 2003). Instead, it is a form of critique that shows, not our ideological captivity and therefore the falsehood of our beliefs, but rather their aspectival captivity. The difference between these two modes of critique is that the latter is no longer searching for an Archimedean point as the normative ground. For Foucauldians, such a point simply does not exist. However, what can be shown is the contingency of those discursive structures, which are fundamental for the reproduction of society. Thus, genealogy "opens a space in which what are experienced as immobile, irreversible and stable limits to reflections are re-experienced as mobile, reversible and unstable bounds" (Owen 1999:36; see also Dean 1999:183). James Tully goes even a step further and argues that, in comparison with Foucault's writing, the work of Habermas "is a less effective critique of limits of the present" and that "Habermas' normative analysis is [in a negative sense] utopian whereas Foucault's is not" (Tully 1999:91).

We do not wish to resurrect this more philosophical debate. Our aim here is rather to use some basic insights of Foucault for a discussion of the epistemic turn in Habermas's theory, especially with regard to his model of deliberative democracy. What can central concepts of Foucault contribute to the understanding of the democratic promises of deliberative procedures? To answer this question, we begin with a brief reconstruction of the links between discourse, power, and knowledge in his work and then try to develop the implications of such an approach for a Foucauldian understanding of deliberative practices. In Foucault's view, they are instruments for the fabrication of subjects and social consent which coordinate perfectly with the power structures of the disciplinary society. However, in his later writings, Foucault slightly moved away from such a one-dimensional concept of power. Especially in his lectures about governmentality, we can find an analysis of policy practices that is able to cast new light on the interplay of power and freedom in modern societies. Later in the chapter, in a part of our discussion that is more empirical, we adopt the concept of governmentality for an analysis of deliberative policy making, where the interplay between techniques of domination and techniques of the self can be seen eminently and clearly.

Discourse, Power, and Knowledge

One of the central but also one of the most problematic concepts in Foucault's work is that of "discourse." It is central insofar as his oeuvre can be read as analyzing those discourses that are constitutive for the modern world. In Foucault's view, discourses or discursive formations produce the modern understanding of truth, rationality, subjectivity, and legitimacy. Discursive formations are also constitutive for practices that reproduce those understandings of truth, subjectivity, and the like, such as telling the truth or acting like a democratic citizen. Thus, many scholars argue that he never described the relationship between so-called discursive and nondiscursive practices in a convincing way. Nevertheless, it is this ambiguity of "discourse" that is so inspiring for social scientists when they analyze the structure of modernity or the contemporary world.

For Foucault, discourses are not "a mere intersection of things and words: an obscure web of things, and a manifest, visible, colored chain of words." They are rather "practices that systematically form the objects of which they speak" (Foucault 1972:48–49). In other words, discourses are historically located systems that construct the social world through the practices of subjects. But, according to Foucault, subjects should not be considered as autonomous and unconstrained actors; they are rather themselves the product of discourses. The subjects are not speaking; the discourse is speaking through the productions of speaking subjects. Thus, Foucault breaks with the idealistic notion of a transcendental ego or consciousness as something that is before society.

Foucault differs from the philosophical tradition in general and the philosophy of enlightenment in particular in another crucial way, namely, in his contextualization of truth and rationality. For example, in *The Order of Things* (1970), Foucault analyzes different regimes of rationality and the discursive practices that are constitutive for these regimes. In that book, he distinguishes between the classical order and the modern order of knowledge. For Foucault, one cannot conceptualize the succession of these two orders as a growth in rationality or say that one order is truer than the other. Rather, there are simply different forms of rationality that can only be described and analyzed but that should not be categorized in a narrative of progress.

In *The Archaeology of Knowledge* (1972), which reflects his theoretical assumptions, Foucault declares that social practices, located in "different bodies of learning, philosophical ideas, everyday opinions," as well as in mores, institutions, and commercial and policy activities, all refer "to a certain implicit knowledge" special to a certain regime of rationality (261). This implicit knowledge, which is produced and reproduced in daily practices, decides what is intelligible and what is not, what can be articulated according to the rules of rationality and what is considered as a senseless or even insane utterance. However, how does discourse create the order of things? How is implicit knowledge produced? Finally, and importantly, where does discourse come from? To answer these questions, Foucault in the early 1970s developed his genealogical method, a method that more complements than substitutes for the archaeological method of his earlier writings.

In his genealogical writings such as *Discipline and Punish* (1977) and the first volume of *The History of Sexuality* (1982a), Foucault crucially enlarges his earlier method with his concept of power. For Foucault, power is not something possessed by individuals or a class. Rather, power is exercised in myriads of actions and has no center. Power, therefore, does not flow from top (e.g., the state) to bottom (e.g., the individual) but is actualized at the microlevel of individual actions. And, most crucial, power for Foucault is primarily not repressive but productive (see Kelly 1994:374). Power is productive insofar as it constitutes the order of things, the regimes of rationality, and the subjects and their daily practices. Thus, in *Discipline and Punish*, Foucault gives a detailed description of the fabrication of the modern subject and modern society through disciplinary institutions such as the prison, the school, and the army. In these institutions, a "microphysics of power" is at work through daily routines aiming to produce bodies and minds that are needed in a capitalist society, for example, bodies that stand up early in the morning, care for their health, and enjoy, at least to the necessary degree, their work.

It is the punch line of Foucault's genealogy that power and knowledge are complementary. On the one hand, the use and concentration of power in disciplinary institutions needs knowledge about effective strategies for the fulfillment of the disciplinary goals. On the other hand, knowledge is itself produced in institutions that are constituted by power. For example, the university is structured by constitutive rules that lay down who has the right to speak in the name of science and who does not, what is a scientific utterance, and so on. According to Foucault, these and many other rules are not the precondition for a never-ending scientific progress but are instruments for the regulation of "the great proliferation of discourse" (Foucault 1971:21). Therefore, Foucault's aim is to scrutinize this politics of truth, that is, "the types of discourse which [a society] accepts and makes function as true; the mechanisms and instances which enable one to distinguish true and false statements, the means by which each is sanctioned; the techniques and procedures accorded value in the acquisition of truth; the status of those who are charged with saying what counts as true" (Foucault 1984:73).

In other words, telling the truth and trimming the discourse, for Foucault, are the obverse and reverse of the same coin. To be productive, the discourses have to be structured by procedures of control and scarcity. And here power comes into play, insofar as it draws the line between those statements that can claim to be scientific and those that cannot. Thus, the sciences are themselves constituted by a politics of truth that establishes the very precondition of scientific knowledge. At the same time, the human sciences in particular are powerful insofar as they constitute, legitimate, and foster those social technologies and disciplinary practices that establish the difference between the normal and the abnormal.

What are the implications of this theory of discourse, power, and politics of truth for Habermas's epistemic understanding of deliberative democracy? As seen in Habermas's theory of deliberative democracy, institutions and policy practices come to the fore to sort out all those interests that cannot be justified in a universal discourse. This model is epistemic insofar as, for Habermas, political issues and policy conflicts can be solved in a rational way. In other words, the use of reason through the give-and-take of arguments can and should guide political action. Therefore, political actions should be regulated by institutions so that their outcomes will be "rationally acceptable." For Habermas, "the democratic procedure no longer draws its legitimatizing force only, indeed not even predominantly, from political participation and the expression of political will, but rather from the general accessibility of a deliberative process whose structure grounds an expectation of rationally acceptable results" (2001:110). Habermas is eager to sort out all those political actions and policy demands that cannot be justified in a universal way. But why is this epistemic understanding of democracy problematic?

First, one can ask whether this is an adequate theory of policy and politics in modern societies. As some scholars following Foucault have argued (see, e.g., Butler 1990; Connolly 1991), policy and politics is about power and difference and not about reason. Against this, a Habermasian may argue that it is the role of power in politics that is the starting point of deliberative democracy insofar as it tries to check unjustified forms of power. But this misses the point of the criticism. The objection is not against undertaking to regulate the use of power, but against the assumption that this can be done in a rational and nonpolitical way. Every institutional framework is the product of past political struggles and therefore always a contingent and historical discursive order. This is also true for the liberal-democratic framework that is the reference point of Habermas's deliberative account.

From a Foucauldian point of view, the institutional design of Habermas's two-track model of politics is also problematic insofar as it leaves only a limited space for political action that does not correspond to the hegemonic understanding of politics and society. In consequence, Habermas's political theory, against all presumptions or claims to the idea of "radical democracy," becomes conservative. This, in particular, is the case with the center of the political system, where according to Habermas a system of sluices (*Schleusen*) should guarantee the moral and epistemic character of political decisions. Such sluices are the main institutions of representative democracy, such as the party system, elections, the decision-making process in the parliament, and the opportunity for a juridical review of the laws. However, these liberal institutions and their policy practices work like a filter, sorting out those political initiatives that are not formulated by the powerful players of liberal democracy, for example, political parties or constitutional courts. Therefore, the "rationally acceptable results" are mainly a mirror of the power structure or—in Foucault's terms—the discursive formation of the society. They reflect the accepted assumptions about the "common good" and the main goals of politics, for example, economic growth or the protection of the capitalist order. In other words, the institutional channels of liberal democracy are biased insofar as they privilege mostly those political demands that are already hegemonic in the society.

The Government of Modern Freedom

In a famous and often-quoted passage, Foucault speaks of the disciplines as the other side of modern liberal democracy: "although, in a formal way, the representative regime makes it possible, directly or indirectly, with or without relays, for the will of all to form the fundamental authority of sovereignty, the disciplines provide, at the base, a guarantee of the submission of forces and bodies. The real, corporal disciplines constituted the foundation of the formal, juridical liberties" (1977:222). However, in the years after the publication of *Discipline and Punish* and the first volume of *The History of Sexuality*, he slightly moved away from this gloomy image of modern societies.[9] Especially in his lectures in 1977–78 and 1978–79 (2007, 2008), he sketched a theory of governmentality in which power is no longer a disciplinary entity but rather works in and through individual freedom. According to this new theory, the individual is not simply a product of power. Foucault also no longer grasped modern society as only disciplinary. Now, it is the interplay between freedom as the technologies of the self and freedom as the technologies of power that at the same time generates the basic structures of modern societies and individual identities. Through the technologies of the self, one shapes his identity and habits, for example, the identity of a good democrat and the corresponding habits of voting, reading the newspapers, and being engaged in civil society or in political parties.

Foucault has developed his concept of the technologies of the self mainly in the examination of antique cultures. However, in his lectures on governmentality, he has also shown how modern identities are shaped by practices that originate in the pastoral techniques of leading a fold on the one hand and hearing confession on the other hand. In modern societies, these practices have loosened their connection to Christianity. They are mostly habitual structures that can be filled with other goals, for example, the already-mentioned goal to be a good democrat. Thus, for Foucault, power in the sense of shaping individual mentalities and habits and individual freedom—the technologies of the self—are two sides of the same coin. The crucial difference from his former, one-dimensional theory of power as disciplinary is that there is more space for individual choices and also more space for resistance in liberal regimes. But he still understands individual freedom and power not as opposites, but rather as the prerequisite of each other.

The medium that binds individual freedom and power is government. One "has to take into account the interaction between two types of techniques—techniques of domination and techniques of the self. . . . The contact point, where the individuals are driven by others is tied to the way they conduct themselves, is what we can call, I think, government. Governing people, in the broad meaning of the word, is not a way to force people to do what the governor wants; it is always a versatile equilibrium, with complementarity and conflicts between techniques which assure coercion and processes through which the self is constructed or modified by himself" (Foucault 1993:203–4).

According to Foucault, government is the sum of those institutions, practices, and belief systems through which people are directed. The subject of this government can be the children, your partner, your employees, the members of a party, or the whole society. Thus, the concept of governmentality is not tied to the state. Foucault also regards the state not as an unchangeable entity but as a shifting ensemble of institutions, practices, and knowledge. The liberal state is therefore a historical, contingent way to govern modern societies. The liberal state has developed from two separate traditions: the sovereign state of the seventeenth and eighteenth centuries and pastoral techniques: "Never, I think, in the history of human societies—even in the old Chinese society—has there been such a tricky combination in the same political structures of individualization techniques and of totalization procedures" (Foucault 1982b:782). The goal of the pastoral techniques is the government of the soul; the goal of the political techniques of the sovereign state is the welfare and the security of the whole society. Together they are constitutive of the modern, liberal state whose main focus is the government of freedom.

To govern the society, liberal regimes do not, or only in exceptional cases, coerce. They rather try to lead the behavior and thoughts of the individuals through incentive structures, through the creation of likelihoods and possibilities. For Foucault, modern power "is a total structure of actions brought to bear upon possible actions; it incites, it induces, it seduces, it makes easier or more difficult; in the extreme it constrains or forbids absolutely; it is nevertheless always a way of acting upon an acting subject or acting subjects by virtue of their acting or being capable of action. A set of actions upon other actions" (1982b: 789). Modern power, thus, is a soft power, and it is a form of power that is compatible with different ways of life, different religious belief systems, and different political convictions. Its goal is the welfare and the security of the society, which is to be achieved while maintaining and using the liberties of the individuals. However, Foucault did not develop a coherent and complete theory of governmentality. But the lectures from 1977 to 1979 and some connected interviews and essays have stimulated a whole branch of inquiry, so-called governmentality studies (see Barry, Osborne, and Rose 1996; Burchell, Gordin, and Miller 1991; Dean 1999). And this approach has thrown a new light on policy practices in general and deliberative procedures in particular.

The Government of Mentalities through Deliberative Practices

Habermas's discourse ethics has inspired many scholars to shift the focus from ordinary party politics and institutionalized legislative bodies to smaller deliberative arenas where citizens directly participate. There is a still growing literature on discursive policy arenas such as deliberative opinion polls, planning cells, and consensus conferences (e.g., Brown 2006; Dryzek 2002). Habermas himself considers these new forms of citizen participation at least as a complement to more ordinary forms of party politics. The hope is that these new models of citizen involvement can lead to an improvement of both democracy and policy decisions in two ways. One way is to foster the legitimacy of political decisions through the participation of ordinary citizens. Some authors also argue that the consideration of as many different views as possible will raise the rationality of the outcomes. The second goal refers to the educational effects on the involved people (Fishkin 2009). The experience of deliberative processes will contribute to a better understanding of democratic rules, norms, and policies in the citizenry. Proponents of deliberative democracy argue that the experience of real participation will increase the democratic skills and attitudes of the citizen. For example, they will learn to follow the arguments of the other parties or will get an insight in the complexities of policy making. The more citizens participate in deliberative settings, the more widespread these democratic virtues will be.

The increase of deliberative procedures in the field of policy making can be seen as a model case of the interplay between technologies of the self and technologies of power. The political beliefs of the participants are guided in these arenas by the give-and-take of arguments. In the following, we will illustrate this understanding of deliberative practices as governmental technologies with the help of two examples. The first is from Alexis de Tocqueville's *Democracy in America*; the second is taken from a recent policy study about bioethical regimes.

In his famous book about American democracy in the middle of the nineteenth century, Tocqueville not only outlines the main political institutions but also focuses especially on the "habits of the heart" of the citizens. The main thesis of the book is that these habits are even more significant for the reproduction of the democratic order than the institutional design of American politics. According to Tocqueville, these democratic virtues are on the one hand established by religious feelings of guilt and shame; they are necessary for behaving as a reasonable citizen in public. On the other hand, these feelings are strengthened and completed by the respect and honor created by deliberative institutions such as New England town meetings or citizen juries. These deliberative settings are schools for democracy, where "school" can be read in a Foucauldian sense as a governmental institution. Indeed, Tocqueville does not characterize the citizen jury as an egalitarian, participative setting; rather, he stresses the positive role of the judges in the forming of democratic habits: "the jury, and more especially the civil jury, serves to communicate the spirit of the judges to the minds of all the citizens" (1990:284). The judges with their knowledge and their habits govern the micropolitics of the deliberative setting and in this way function as a role model for democratic citizenship. Indeed, "the jurors look up to him with confidence and listen to him with respect, for in this instance, his intellect entirely governs theirs" (285–86).

Viewed through Foucault, these deliberative settings are governmental procedures to foster those habits of the heart that are the necessary foundation of liberal democracy. The participating citizen learns to argue correctly and to listen to the policy experts (the judges), who are the possessors of the better argument. In reading this passage from Tocqueville through the lens of Foucault, one gets an insight into those soft powers that work beneath the surface of the give-and-take of arguments. The forging of consent is thus scarcely free of power. Rather, it is the interplay between the political goals of the experts and the aim of the citizen to become a good democrat.

Much the same can be seen if we take a look at an empirical study about new bioethical regimes. In an inquiry into bioethical debates, Herrmann and Könninger (2007) explicitly refer to Foucault's concept of governmentality to explain the rise of deliberative procedures in this policy arena. The starting point of the inquiry is the development of human genetics and biomedical technologies such as in vitro fertilization (IVF). These scientific developments raise ethical questions about the degree to which artificial reproductive techniques should be allowed or even fostered by the state. These questions are highly controversial because they are deeply connected to our idea of humanity and to our religious feelings. Thus, many citizens face these new biotechnologies with unease and even resistance. Herrmann and Könninger delineate how in this policy field deliberative procedures such as consensus conferences and the inclusion of the public in ethics bodies such as the French Comité Consultatif National d'Ethique pour les Sciences de la Vie et de la Santé and the German Nationaler Ethikrat aim to govern the thoughts and the knowledge of the people. Like the jury in Tocqueville's *Democracy in America*, these bodies try to educate the citizen by initiating public dialogues. This new ethical regime is especially at pains to widen the appropriate knowledge and the habits of deliberative debate through the public. Thus, they are often eager to gain disseminators, who expand the ethical knowledge and deliberative habits through their social environment.

Central to the desired deliberative habits is the premise that "each (even the most troublesome) perspective is worth the deliberation, that everyone has to have an opinion on each and every issue, and that each and every opinion is equally valid and has to be taken into account" (Herrmann and Könninger 2007:218). The participants of public debate have to be modest, tolerant, and informed. The paradoxical effect of such regimes is, of course, the exclusion of "fundamentalist" positions and people; they simply lack the "appropriate knowledge" and the "appropriate ways of deliberation" (219). Against this background, it is no accident that the conclusions of the deliberative settings in the field of bioethics are mostly moderate and open to the new biotechnologies. However, according to the authors it is more the educational result than the direct impact on policy making that is remarkable. The new ethics regime "establishes a mentality, a guiding frame for self-government as regards individual bodily existence as well as the participation in public debates on bioethics" (210).

Through participation in those deliberative settings, one surely is not dominated by policy experts or governmental authorities. Participation is voluntary, and often it is seen as an honor to have a role in a deliberative arena. Members might even get the impression that they are taken seriously as citizens. One can argue with other citizens and policy experts about crucial issues. In other words, one is acknowledged as a self-governed person. On the other hand, the participant learns in these settings to deliberate like a good democrat. She learns to reflect on her beliefs, to discuss in a moderate way, and to be open to scientific progress. It is exactly this interplay between individual freedom and the shaping of mentalities and habits that can be seen using the concept of governmentality. In this way, deliberative settings are a particularly smart technique for governing modern societies.

Looking at other empirical research about deliberative procedures, the findings of Herrmann and Könninger are confirmed. For example,

John Parkinson in studies about the reform process of the British health care system has shown that the adoption of deliberative procedures in the context of new public management results in a dual gap between normative theory and political practice. One gap is that the scope of deliberation is limited from the beginning. At the outset, the policy experts define the realm of possible outcomes: "Thus people find themselves deliberating about topics that are constrained by larger forces over which they have no control" (Parkinson 2004:392). The other gap refers to "the collision between the deliberative concern for rationality and the public management construction of that concern" (391), which leads to a separation between knowledgeable experts and "ordinary" citizens. The experts try to regulate the opinions of the citizens through deliberative processes. In deliberative processes, the use of speech, as well as the way one presents the arguments, is crucial. And it is crucial who is speaking, that is, who has the authority to start, manage, and determine the process of deliberation. This gives room for the manipulation of these processes by administrative and policy elites. In other words, deliberative settings can be used for a managerial fabrication of consent and legitimacy. In accordance with Foucault's writings and lectures about governmentality, one can view deliberative democracy as a government technology that tries to guide the conduct of the participants.

But what is the lesson of these Foucauldian insights for democratic politics? Because deliberation is constitutive for democracy, one should not see in deliberative procedures only an insidious power game. Rather, it is necessary to use Foucault's concept of governmentality as a reminder of the fact that no human interaction is powerless, even if the participants are oriented toward communicative action.

Habermas and Foucault on the Use of the Better Argument in Deliberative Decision Making

To show what this could mean for the practice of deliberative democracy, we now view some later writings of Foucault and then argue for a recombination of Habermas's normative theory and Foucault's insights in the strategic character of deliberative policy making. In his later works, Foucault's attention not only shifts from the investigation of the power effects of discourses and the different dispositives to an inquiry into the technologies of the self. He also mentions in some interviews a closeness of his work to that of the Frankfurt School, even to the work of Habermas. And as Thomas McCarthy (1990) has shown, Foucault's differentiation between three comprehensive social techniques, namely, those of production, of signification, and of domination, resembles the program that Habermas developed in his inaugural lecture, "Knowledge and Human Interests." In addition, in Foucault's "What Is Enlightenment" lecture, delivered in 1984, he comes close to a neo-Kantian notion of critique, which may lead a hasty reader to wonder whether there is in the end any difference between him and Habermas.

However, Foucault did not make a turnaround; rather, he moved his focus of attention from discourse and power to the technologies of the self and governmentality. As a consequence, he slightly changed his evaluation of the interplay between power and freedom. Regarding the latter point, he now distinguishes between relations of domination and relations of power. Relations of domination on the one hand are a given when there is no leeway, no opportunity to act in a different way. Relations of power on the other hand leave space for resistance, that is, one can reject the wishes of others or their social expectations: "a power relationship can only be articulated on the basis of two elements which are each indispensable if it is really to be a power relationship: that 'the other' (the one over whom power is exercised) be thoroughly recognized and maintained to the very end as a person who acts; and that, faced with a relationship of power, a whole field of responses, reactions, results, and possible inventions may open up" (Foucault 1982b:789). Thus, for Foucault, power and freedom are no antipodes; rather, one is the precondition of the other. Using power is to enhance the probability, but not the necessity, of certain kinds of behavior of others. Person B is to a certain degree also able to refuse A's aim to direct his conduct and B can even try himself to influence the behavior of A. There is always a strategic game between actors, regardless of whether they are located in the political sphere, the academic realm, or the field of family relations.

What are the implications of this new concept of power and freedom for democratic practices and institutions? First of all, Foucault is still convinced that a powerless discourse is unrealizable. In one of his last interviews, he states with explicit reference to Habermas, "The thought that there could be a state of communication that would be such that the games of truth could circulate freely, without obstacles, without constraint and without coercive effects, seems to me to be Utopia" (Foucault 1988:18). It is utopian insofar as there never could be a give-and-take of arguments free from power relations. A Habermasian may reply that the noncoercive discourse is only a regulative ideal and that the challenge is to frame real deliberations in a way that the influence of power is restrained as much as possible. Nevertheless, there remains a crucial discrepancy between Habermas's and Foucault's social ontologies.

Habermas's central differentiation between communicative and strategic speech acts is according to Foucault not sustainable. There are only strategic acts: even if the speaker tries to give arguments, he still operates in the field of power insofar as he tries to influence the beliefs as well as the acts of others. Deliberative settings are a certain way to govern the conduct of the participants and the relations of power as strategically oriented speech acts such as rhetoric or the holding back of information, which are an essential part of this game: "Relationships of communication imply finalized activities (even if only the correct putting into operation of elements of meaning) and, by virtue of modifying the field of information between partners, produce effects of power. They can scarcely be dissociated from activities brought to their final term, be they those which permit the exercise of this power (such as training techniques, processes of domination, the means by which obedience is obtained) or those, which in order to develop their potential, call upon relations of power (the division of labor and the hierarchy of tasks)" (Foucault 1982b:787).

Again, we do not wish to resuscitate the Habermas-Foucault debate on a philosophical level. Nevertheless, regarding Foucault's axiom that all human interactions are strategic, one may ask whether this is not too one-sided. As has already been shown, Foucault in his last writings moved from a monolithic theory of discursive and disciplinary power to a more differentiated conception of freedom in and through power. And this led him not only to a separation between power and domination, but also to a normative understanding of politics that is not so far away from the program of Habermas's discourse ethics. Foucault formulates an ethos for strategic interaction that shares common ground with Habermas's discourse ethics: "I don't believe there can be a society without relations of power, if you understand them as means by which individuals try to conduct, to determine the behaviors of others. The problem is not of trying to dissolve them in the utopia of a perfectly transparent communication, but to give one's self the rules of law, the techniques of management, and also the ethics, the ethos, the practice of the self, which would allow these games of power to be played with a minimum of domination" (Foucault 1988:18).

Of course, on a rhetorical level Foucault still distances himself from Habermasian discourse ethics. But what are the institutional consequences of Foucault's claim to limit relations of domination in the field of public policy? Is it not to give the people a voice in those political fields where the social conditions of their life are decided? And is this not the aim of Habermas's theory of deliberative democracy? In other words, Habermas's ethical and political theory offers a normative foundation for those institutions and practices that Foucault postulates to minimize the relations of domination. This thesis gains strength if we look at the beginning of his last lectures at the Collège de France, in which he reconstructs the development of the Greek concept of *parrēsia* (Foucault 2010).

According to Foucault, parrēsia is not just the right but also the courage to tell the truth. It is to speak, whereof one is deeply convinced, even if this act evokes the anger of the powerful. Foucault shows in detail through an interpretation of Euripides' *Ion* that a democratic order is a precondition of the use of parrēsia. Only in a democratic order does one not have to fear being persecuted for telling the truth. At the same time, a democratic order depends on the praxis of parrēsia, insofar as the political decisions are to be taken by deliberative practices. It is, in other words, the give-and-take of arguments that should result in decisions. Thus, the right of telling the truth is a fundamental constituent of democracy and of deliberative politics. But the other side of Foucault's lectures is that parrēsia is also a concept that goes in dual ways beyond democracy. First, even if everybody has the right to tell the truth, not everybody is able to do that. As he shows, only the best citizens are able to tell the truth, and for this reason there is a small but crucial difference between parrēsia and *isegoria*, or democratic equality. A well-functioning democratic order requires advice from wise people. But, "only a few can tell the truth" (Foucault 2010:183). Second, there is always the danger of a false parrēsia, namely, the practice of demagoguery. Foucault argues in a reconstruction of the work of Thucydides, Socrates, and Plato that the antique democracy was haunted by a populist style of politics: "The bond between *parrēsia* and democracy is problematic, difficult, and dangerous. Democracy is in the process of being overrun by a bad *parrēsia*" (Foucault 2010:168). And to Foucault, it was this false parrēsia that fostered the decline of the Athenian democracy.

What are the normative and even institutional implications of Foucault's reconstruction of the antique concept of parrēsia for political debate and deliberation in modern democracies? Surely, there is a large gulf between the antique democracy of Athens and our modern democratic practices. And it is not very obvious whether or not Foucault regards the antique concept of parrēsia as an archetype for a contemporary deliberative politics. But maybe it is not too audacious to argue that Habermas in *Between Facts and Norms* provides a comprehensive theory of exactly those liberal-democratic institutions that are the precondition for the use of parrēsia in modern societies. According to Habermas, the institutions of the democratic constitutional state afford not only the opportunity of collective self-legislation through deliberative practices, but also some shelter against a populist takeover. Therefore, one can argue that the difference between Habermas and at least the later Foucault is not implacable. On the contrary, beyond rhetorical statements, which may be owed to academic rituals, Habermas's political theory seems to be a necessary complement of Foucault's conceptions of freedom as nondomination and parrēsia as the courage of telling the truth.

Notes

1. For the relevance of the work of Habermas in the early phase in the formation of the argumentative turn, see Bernstein 1978; Dryzek 1990:11–21; Fischer 1980:36–40, 91–95; and Healey 1993.

2. See, e.g., the contributions by a number of international scholars in Brunkhorst 2009.

3. For Habermas's role as a public intellectual, see Holub 1991.

4. This article has not yet been translated into English. At least one crucial paragraph is worthy of being quoted: "Democracy, as we can learn from Franz L. Neumann, is not a form of state like any other. It aims at far reaching social changes which enhance and finally fully realize freedom. Democracy aims at the self-determination of mankind. Only when this has become real, democracy is true" (Habermas 1958:12). As the source for Habermas's reference to Neumann, see Neumann 1957.

5. See Habermas 1980 and 1993a. For this debate on methodology, see Bernstein's classical study (1978).

6. These early changes and revisions are reconstructed by McCarthy 1978.

7. On Habermas's concept of rational reconstruction, see Pedersen 2008 and Gaus 2009.

8. On the role of rhetoric in democratic discourses, see Dryzek 2010.

9. The development of Foucault's thought in the late 1970s and early 1980s is shown by Lemke 1997.

Bibliography

Arato, A., and J. Cohen. 1992. *Civil Society*. Cambridge: MIT Press.
Barry, A., T. Osborne, and N. Rose, eds. 1996. *Foucault and Political Reason: Liberalism, Neoliberalism and Rationalities of Government*. Chicago: University of Chicago Press.
Benhabib, Seyla. 1996. "Towards a Deliberative Model of Democratic Legitimacy." In *Democracy and Difference*, edited by Seyla Benhabib, 67–94. Princeton: Princeton University Press.
Bernstein, Richard J. 1978. *The Restructuring of Social and Political Theory*. Philadelphia: University of Pennsylvania Press.
———. 1989. "Foucault: Critique as a Philosophical Ethos." In *Zwischenbetrachtungen im Prozeß der Aufklärung*, edited by Axel Honneth, Thomas McCarthy, Claus Offe, and Albrecht Wellmer, 395–425. Frankfurt am Main: Suhrkamp.
Bohman, James. 1996. *Public Deliberation*. Cambridge: MIT Press.
Brown, M. B. 2006. "Survey Article: Citizen Panels and the Concept of Representation." *Journal of Political Philosophy* 14(2):203–25.
Brunkhorst, Hauke, ed. 2009. *Habermas-Handbuch*. Stuttgart: Metzler.
Buchstein, Hubertus. 1994. "Von den Neuen Sozialen Bewegungen zum zivilgesellschaftlichen Akteur." *Forschungsjournal Neue Soziale Bewegungen* 1:104–8.
———. 2009. "Jürgen Habermas and Critical Policy Studies." *Critical Policy Studies* 3(3–4):421–25.
Buchstein, Hubertus, and Dirk Jörke. 2007. "Redescribing Democracy." *Redescriptions* 11:178–202.
Burchell, G., C. Gordin, and P. Miller, eds. 1991. *The Foucault Effect: Studies in Governmentality*. Chicago: University of Chicago Press.
Butler, Judith. 1990. *Gender Trouble*. London: Routledge.
Chambers, Simone. 1996. *Reasonable Democracy: Jürgen Habermas and the Politics of Discourse*. Ithaca: Cornell University Press.
Connolly, William. 1991. *Identity/Difference*. Ithaca: Cornell University Press.
Dean, Mitchell. 1999. "Normalising Democracy: Foucault and Habermas

on Democracy, Liberalism and Law." In *Foucault Contra Habermas: Recasting the Dialogue between Genealogy and Critical Theory*, edited by Samantha Ashenden and David Owen, 166–94. London: Sage.
———. 2009. *Governmentality*. 2nd ed. London: Sage.
D'Entréves Passerin, M., ed. 2006. *Democracy as Public Deliberation*. New Brunswick, N.J.: Transaction.
Druckman, James. 2004. "Political Preference Formation." *American Political Science Review* 98(4):671–86.
Dryzek, John. 1990. *Discursive Democracy: Politics, Policy, and Political Science*. Cambridge: Cambridge University Press.
———. 2000. *Deliberative Democracy and Beyond: Liberals, Critics, Contestations*. Oxford: Oxford University Press.
———. 2010. "Rhetoric in Democracy: A Systematic Appreciation." *Political Theory* 38(3):319–39.
Elster, John. 1997. "The Market and the Forum." In *Deliberative Democracy: Essays on Reason and Politics*, edited by James Bohman and William Regh, 3–34. Cambridge: MIT Press.
Fischer, Frank. 1980. *Politics, Values and Public Policy: The Problem of Methodology*. Boulder, Colo.: Westview.
Fischer, Frank, and John Forester, eds. 1993. *The Argumentative Turn in Policy Analysis and Planning*. Durham: Duke University Press.
Fishkin, James. 2009. *When the People Speak: Deliberative Democracy and Public Consultation*. Oxford: Oxford University Press.
Foucault, Michel. 1970. The Order of Things: An Archaeology of the Human Sciences. London: Tavistock.
———. 1971. "The Order of Discourse." *Social Science Information* 10(2):7–31.
———. 1972. *Archaeology of Knowledge*. New York: Pantheon.
———. 1977. *Discipline and Punish*. Harmondsworth: Penguin.
———. 1982a. *The History of Sexuality*. Vol. 1. Harmondsworth: Penguin.
———. 1982b. "The Subject and Power." *Critical Inquiry* 8(4):777–95.
———. 1984. *The Foucault Reader*. Edited by Paul Rabinow. Harmondsworth: Penguin.
———. 1988. "The Ethic of Care for the Self as a Practice of Freedom." In *The Final Foucault*, edited by James William Bernauer and David M. Rasmussen, 1–21. Cambridge: MIT Press.
———. 1993. "About the Beginning of the Hermeneutics of the Self: Two Lectures at Dartmouth." *Political Theory* 21(2):198–227.
———. 2007. *Security, Territory, Population: Lectures at the Collège de France 1977–1978*. Basingstoke: Palgrave Macmillan.
———. 2008. *The Birth of Biopolitics: Lectures at the Collège de France, 1978–1979*. Basingstoke: Palgrave Macmillan.
———. 2010. *The Government of Self and Others: Lectures at the Collège de France, 1982–1983*. Basingstoke: Palgrave Macmillan.

Fraser, Nancy. 1981. "Foucault on Modern Power: Empirical Insights and Normative Confusions." *Praxis International* 7(3):272–87.
Gaus, Daniel. 2009. *Der Sinn von Demokratie*. Frankfurt am Main: Campus.
Habermas, Jürgen. 1958. "Zum Begriff der politischen Beteiligung" (On the concept of political participation). In *Kultur und Kritik*, 9–60. Frankfurt am Main: Suhrkamp.
———. 1970. *Toward a Rational Society: Student Protest, Science, and Politics*. Boston: Beacon.
———. 1971. *Knowledge and Human Interests*. Boston: Beacon.
———. 1973. *Theory and Practice*. Boston: Beacon.
———. 1975. *Legitimation Crisis*. Boston: Beacon.
———. 1980. "The Hermeneutic Claim to Universality." In *Contemporary Hermeneutics*, edited by Josef Bleicher, 181–211. London: Routledge.
———. 1982. "A Reply to My Critics." In *Habermas: Critical Debates*, edited by J. B. Thompson and David Held, 219–83. Cambridge: MIT Press.
———. 1984. *The Theory of Communicative Action*. 2 vols. Cambridge, England: Polity.
———. 1986. *Autonomy and Solidarity: Interviews*. Edited by Peter Dews. Cambridge: Verso.
———. 1987. *The Philosophical Discourse of Modernity*. Cambridge: MIT Press.
———. 1989. *The Structural Transformation of the Public Sphere*. Cambridge: MIT Press.
———. 1993a. *On the Logic of the Social Sciences*. Cambridge: MIT Press.
———. 1993b. *Justification and Application: Remarks on Discourse Ethics*. Cambridge, England: Polity.
———. 1996. *Between Facts and Norms: Contributions to a Discourse Theory of Law and Democracy*. Cambridge: MIT Press.
———. 2001. *The Postnational Constellation*. Cambridge: MIT Press.
———. 2003. *The Future of Human Nature*. Cambridge: MIT Press.
———. 2005. "Concluding Comments on Empirical Approaches to Deliberative Politics." *Politica* 40(3):384–92.
———. 2006. "Political Communication in Media Society." *Communication Theory* 16(4):411–26.
———. 2008. "The Constitutionalization of International Law and the Legitimation Problems of a Constitution for World Society." *Constellations* 15(4):444–55.
———. 2009a. "Einleitung." In *Rationalitäts- und Sprachtheorie*, vol. 2 of *Philosophische Texte*, 14–46. Frankfurt am Main: Suhrkamp.
———. 2009b. "Einleitung." In *Politische Theorie*, vol. 4 of *Philosophische Texte*, 14–58. Frankfurt am Main: Suhrkamp.
———. 2010. "Wir brauchen Europa." *Die Zeit*, May 20.
———. 2011. *Die Verfassung Europas*. Frankfurt am Main: Suhrkamp.

Healey, Patsy. 1993. "Planning through Debate: The Communicative Turn in Planning Theory." In Fischer and Forester, *The Argumentative Turn in Policy Analysis and Planning*, 233–53.

Hegel, Friedrich Wilhelm Georg. 1952. *Philosophy of Right*. Oxford: Oxford University Press.

Herrmann, S. L., and S. Könninger. 2007. "'... But You Can Not Influence the Direction of Your Thinking': Guiding Self-Government in Bioethics Policy Discourse." *Advances in Medical Sociology* 9:205–23.

Holub, R. 1991. *Jürgen Habermas: Critic in the Public Sphere*. London: Routledge.

Honneth, Axel. 1991. *The Critique of Power*. Cambridge: MIT Press.

Iser, Mathias. 2009. *Empörung und Fortschritt*. Frankfurt am Main: Campus.

Joerges, Christian. 2002. "Deliberative Supranationalism—Two Defenses." *European Legal Journal* 8(2):133–51.

Joerges, Christian, and Jürgen Neyer. 1997. "From Intergovernmental Bargaining to Deliberative Political Processes: The Constitutionalization of Comitology." *European Law Journal* 3(3):273–99.

Jörke, Dirk. 2009. "The Epistemic Turn of Critical Theory: Implications for Deliberative Politics and Policy-Making." *Critical Policy Studies* 3(3–4):440–46.

Kelly, Michael. 1994. "Foucault, Habermas, and the Self-Referentiality of Critique." In *Critique and Power: Recasting the Foucault Habermas Debate*, edited by Michael Kelly, 365–400. Cambridge: MIT Press.

Koller, A. 2009. "Kontrafaktische Voraussetzungen." In *Habermas-Handbuch*, edited by Hauke Brunkhorst et al., 338–43. Stuttgart: Metzler.

Lemke, Thomas. 1997. *Eine Kritik der politischen Vernunft: Foucaults Analyse der modernen Gouvernementalität*. Berlin: Argument.

Majone, Giandomenico. 1989. *Evidence, Argument, and Persuasion in the Policy Process*. New Haven: Yale University Press.

McCarthy, Thomas. 1978. *The Critical Theory of Jürgen Habermas*. London: Hutchinson.

———. 1990. "The Critique of Impure Reason: Foucault and the Frankfurt School." *Political Theory* 18(3):437–69.

Mutz, Diana C. 2006. *Hearing the Other Side: Deliberative versus Participatory Democracy*. Cambridge: Cambridge University Press.

Neumann, Franz L. 1957. "The Concept of Political Freedom." In *The Democratic and the Authoritarian State*, edited by Herbert Marcuse, 160–200. New York: Free Press.

Niesen, Peter. 2006. "Deliberation ohne Demokratie? Zur Konstruktion von Legitimität jenseits des Nationalstaats." In *Transnationale Verrechtlichung*, edited by Regina Kreide and Andreas Niederberger, 240–59. Frankfurt am Main: Campus.

Owen, David. 1999. "Orientation and Enlightenment: An Essay on Critique and Genealogy." In *Foucault Contra Habermas: Recasting the Dialogue between Genealogy and Critical Theory*, edited by Samantha Ashenden and David Owen, 21–44. London: Sage.
———. 2003. "Kritik und Gefangenschaft: Genealogie und Kritische Theorie." In *Michel Foucault: Zwischenbilanz einer Rezeption*, edited by Axel Honneth and Martin Saar, 122–44. Frankfurt am Main: Suhrkamp.
Parkinson, J. 2004. "Why Deliberate? The Encounter between Deliberation and New Public Managers." *Public Administration* 82(4):377–95.
Pedersen, J. 2008. "Habermas' Method: Rational Reconstruction." *Philosophy of the Social Sciences* 38(4):457–85.
Ryfe, David M. 2005. "Does Deliberative Democracy Work?" *Annual Review of Political Science* 8:49–71, 122–44.
Saretzki, Thomas. 2009. "Habermas and Critical Policy Studies: Legitimation, Judgment, and Participation." *Critical Policy Studies* 3(3–4): 426–33.
Scheuerman, William E. 1999. "Between Radicalism and Resignation. Democratic Theory and Habermas's *Between Facts and Norms*." In *Habermas: A Critical Reader*, edited by Peter Dews, 153–77. Oxford: Blackwell.
———. 2004. "Critical Theory beyond Habermas." In *The Oxford Handbook of Political Theory*, edited by John Dryzek, Bonny Honig, and Anne Phillips, 228–38. Oxford: Oxford University Press.
Schmalz-Bruns, Rainer. 1995. *Reflexive Demokratie*. Baden-Baden: Nomos.
———. 2007. "An den Grenzen der Entstaatlichung: Bemerkungen zu Jürgen Habermas' Modell einer 'Weltinnenpolitik ohne Weltregierung.' " In *Anarchie der kommunikativen Freiheit: Jürgen Habermas und die Theorie der internationalen Politik*, edited by Peter Niesen and Benjamin Herborth, 269–93. Frankfurt am Main: Suhrkamp.
———. 2009. "Habermas' Theory of Democracy and Critical Policy Studies: An (Undistorted) Elective Affinity?" *Critical Policy Studies* 3(3–4):447–52.
Schweitzer, Eva. 2004. *Deliberative Polling*. Wiesbaden: Verlag für Sozialwissenschaften.
Strecker, David. 2012. *Logik der Macht*. Weilerwirst: Velbrück.
Sunstein, Cass. 2003. "The Law of Group Polarisation." In *Debating Deliberative Democracy*, edited by James S. Fishkin and Peter Lasslett, 80–101. Oxford: Oxford University Press.
Tocqueville, Alexis de. 1990. *Democracy in America*. Vol. 1. New York: Vintage.
Tully, James. 1999. "To Think and Act Differently: Foucault's Four Reciprocal Objection to Habermas' Theory." In *Foucault Contra Habermas: Recasting the Dialogue between Genealogy and Critical Theory*, edited by Samantha Ashenden and David Owen, 90–142. London: Sage.
Warren, Marc E. 2009. "Governance-Driven Democratization." *Critical Policy Studies* 3(1):3–13.

White, Stephen K. 1988. *The Recent Work of Jürgen Habermas: Reason, Justice and Modernity.* Cambridge: Cambridge University Press.

Young, Iris Marion. 2000. *Inclusion and Democracy.* Oxford: Oxford University Press.

———. 2001. "Activist Challenges to Deliberative Democracy." *Political Theory* 29(5):670–90.

10. Poststructuralist Policy Analysis
Discourse, Hegemony, and Critical Explanation

A number of contemporary innovators in the field of policy studies draw sustenance from the "discursive turn" in the human and social sciences, as well as from the ideas of poststructuralism that often accompany this trend. This turn to discourse focuses our attention on the need for understanding, interpretation, and critical evaluation in social and political analysis, rather than the search for lawlike or causal explanations. A range of discourse analysts and interpretivists thus privilege the political construction of meanings and identities in and through the policy process, and they question the sharp separation between questions of fact and questions of value. In pursuing these ideals, they have developed notions such as narratives, story lines, framing, discourse coalitions, interpretation, rhetoric, and argumentation to critically explain the initiation, formation, implementation, and evaluation of public policies in various contexts and settings.

Yet the injection of poststructuralist ideas and techniques into the field of policy studies has been diverse and complex, causing discursive policy analysis to assume various shapes and sizes. It includes those who wish to break radically from positivist perspectives (Fischer 2003), as well as those who seek mainly to supplement positivist viewpoints by treating discourses as particular systems of belief or conceptual frameworks for apprehending the world (Dryzek 1997:8; Weale 1992). In this chapter, we demonstrate how one particular type of discursive policy analysis, poststructuralist policy analysis, when articulated with elements of critical discourse analysis and rhetorical political analysis, can contribute important tools and concepts to the conduct of critical policy studies. Our approach goes beyond a minimal and cognitive conception of discourse, in which the concept of discourse is reduced to simply another variable that can be subjected to empirical testing, and which often gives rise to what we might term "discourse-lite" forms of explanation and interpretation (Torfing 2005:25). Rather, we employ a "thicker" conception of discourse theory in which discourse does not just consist in an abstract cognitive system of beliefs and words, but is a constitutive dimension of social relations that does not merely describe or make known a preexisting or underlying reality, but instead helps to bring that reality into being (Gottweis 2003:251).

In expounding our approach, we begin by setting out the ontological assumptions of poststructuralist discourse theory, showing how its categories and logics can help us to analyze the politics of policy change as a hegemonic struggle, while also foregrounding the affective dimension of policy making. Using the category of discourse, we thus develop a poststructuralist reading of the Gramscian concepts of hegemony and power, and we employ the Lacanian logic of fantasy to focus our attention on the enjoyment subjects procure from their identifications with certain policy practices, signifiers, and figures. We then turn to questions of methodology and the techniques of discursive policy analysis. Those who employ a "thicker," more constitutive conception of discourse have often faced charges of failing to critically reflect upon questions of method and research strategy and of not properly attending to the normative implications of policy making (Townshend 2003). In response to such claims, we outline the steps of what we term the logics of critical explanation, focusing our attention on problematization; social, political, and fantasmatic logics; and articulation, judgment, and critique (Glynos and Howarth 2007). We start by discussing how poststructuralist policy analysis helps us to reconceptualize mainstream approaches to public policy.

Poststructuralist Policy Analysis: Questions of Ontology

The idea of poststructuralist policy analysis includes various approaches that share a series of family resemblances (for further discussion, see Howarth 2012). Alongside other types of interpretive policy analysis, its proponents focus on the role of meanings in shaping human actions and social institutions in the policy-making process. Yet they are equally concerned with the ways in which meanings are created and contested by rival political forces in particular policy settings, and how these settings are related to wider social systems and power relations. The approach thus assumes that even the most sedimented practices, objects, and categories of policy making are ambiguous and radically contingent entities, whose meaning can be articulated in various ways by differently positioned social actors (cf. Fox and Miller 2007; Miller 2002). Poststructuralist policy analysts also explore the way in which subjects are formed and act in the policy-making process, as well as the wider structures of social relations within which subjects operate.

In this perspective, natural, physical, and cultural phenomena acquire their meaning in specific discourses; in our jargon, they are "discursively constructed." Objects and things in this approach certainly "exist" independently of any particular discourse, but their meaning and significance—and how they are engaged by social actors—depend on their position within particular symbolic frameworks. Poststructuralist policy analysis thus rejects essentialist accounts of policy making which assume that objects, human subjects, or social formations have underlying and fixed essences, which are evident, for example, in the economic determinism and class reductionism in explanations of social and political change in Marxism. By contrast, it assumes that "social, political, or natural phenomena and, inseparately from them, their meanings, are constantly moving, changing and shifting in various directions" (Gottweis 2003:249).

Against this background, we conceptualize policy programs such as new public management, social inclusion, or sustainable development, as well as institutions such as administrative systems or governance networks, as more or less sedimented systems of discourse. As Ernesto Laclau and Chantal Mouffe insist, "a discursive structure is not a merely 'cognitive' or 'contemplative' entity; it is an articulatory practice which constitutes and organizes social relations" (Laclau and Mouffe 1985:96). Discourses in our perspective are thus partially fixed systems of rules, norms, resources, practices, and subjectivities, which are constituted politically by the construction of social antagonisms and the creation of political frontiers. They are thus finite and contingent constructions, whose production involves the exercise of power, as well as certain forms of exclusion. This means that every discursive structure is uneven and hierarchical (Howarth 2009:313). Bearing this in mind, we shall say a little more about our conception of discourse before turning to its broad implications for policy analysis.

Our understanding of discourse rests on three moves. First, as we have already suggested, we extend the scope of discourse theory beyond the analysis of "texts and talk in contexts" to social actions and political practices, so that all objects and social practices are objects and practices of discourse in that their meaning depends upon their articulation within socially constructed systems of rules and differences (Howarth and Stavrakakis 2000:3; Laclau and Mouffe 1985). For example, the discourse of new public management in the United Kingdom is not exhausted by the "talk" or language of new public management as it is expressed in policy guidance, ministerial speeches, or managerial textbooks. It includes a diverse array of actions and practices such as the technologies of performance measurement, the coaching practices of transformational leadership, the conventions and tasks of project management, and the competition of quasi markets across the public sector. In other words, language, actions, and objects are intertwined in what we call "discourse."

Second, by grounding our understanding of discourse in the work of Saussure (1983) and structural linguistics more generally, we understand discourses as relational and differential configurations of elements that comprise agents (or subjects), words, and actions. These elements are individuated and rendered intelligible within the context of a particular practice in which each element acquires its meaning only in relation to the others (Howarth 2009:311–12). For example, the meaning of the word "governance" depends on its difference from related terms such as "government," "governmentality," "hierarchy," "market," and so on. Because the identity of each element depends on its relation to others, and because an articulatory practice is a dynamic process that links contingent elements together in a new way, the identity of each element is modified in each particular construction. For example, the discourse of new public management establishes systems of relations between different objects and practices—markets, contracting out, constructing evidence bases or league tables, and so forth—while providing a range of subject positions with which social agents can identify, including the "consumer," the "performance manager," or the "service provider." To borrow from the work of Rein and Schön (1993:153), discourse thereby installs a particular kind of coherence by bringing "things named" into a "composite whole." But in so doing, the identities of elements are modified. This is evident, for example, in the transformation of the understandings of "markets" and "choice" when they were articulated into the discourse of new public management.

Finally, drawing on poststructuralists like Jacques Derrida, Michel Foucault, and Jacques Lacan, we stress the radical contingency and structural undecidability of discursive structures (Howarth 2009:312). This arises because we assume that all systems of meaning are in a fundamental sense incomplete. By saying that discourses are incomplete, we do not mean that they are simply missing something, as when we say that we have not ticked all the boxes on a bureaucratic form. Incompletion in our view highlights an absence or negativity that structurally prevents the completion of a discourse, thereby indicating its limits. Discourses are thus incomplete systems of meaningful practice, because they are predicated on the exclusion of certain elements. At the same time, however, these excluded elements are required for the very identity of the discourse (Griggs and Howarth 2012). With the discourse of new public management, its identity thus rests upon its construction of antagonisms with "old public administration" and thus involves the institution of political frontiers or boundaries between insiders and outsiders, which exclude particular practices and possibilities. This means that any identity or order is marked by what Henry Staten and Ernesto Laclau call a "constitutive outside" (Laclau 2005:69–71; Staten 1984). This absence or negativity prevents the full constitution of a discursive structure, so that every structure is thus dislocated. Yet this "out-of-joint-ness" is only evident in particular dislocations or events that show their incompletion, while the construction of social antagonisms signifies the limits of any discourse or social order, that is, its contestation by competing political forces. Discourses are thus contingent and historical constructions, which are always vulnerable to those political forces excluded in their production, as well as the dislocatory effects of events beyond their control (Howarth 2000:109).

What does this mean for the study of public policy? First, it suggests that one of the primary tasks of policy analysis is to critically explain why and how one particular policy has been formulated, accepted, and implemented, rather than others. It thus privileges the general concern with policy change or policy reversal, on the one hand, and policy inertia and policy sedimentation, on the other. This focus gives rise to a particular set of questions for the policy analyst. What are the conditions for particular policy discourses to become dominant or hegemonic? How do we account for the reproduction and transformation of such hegemonic policy orders and practices? How do we explain the "grip" of certain policy discourses? And how are such dominant orders contested?

Second, in our view, poststructuralist policy analysis must situate the practices of policy making in relation to wider social and political contexts. Policy analyses and evaluations thus have to be conducted in relation to broader societal tendencies and changes (see, e.g., Fischer 1995, 2000). Yet, because policy making emerges and operates in different social contexts, its analysis must be located at the intersection of processes operating at *multiple* spatial scales, be they the microprocesses of an organization or the more macroprocesses of national government (Bridge and McManus 2000:13) It is also shaped by the overall balances of political forces in society and the changing configurations of hegemony therein. In addition, these political practices are intimately related to other socioeconomic processes, such as the contradictions and dynamics of the local, national, and global political economy, as well as other social practices and cultural representations.

Third, and in equal fashion, meaningful policy analysis in our view must have a critical and normative commitment. Policy analysts should seek to deconstruct "taken for granted" regimes of policy practices and objects, while exposing their particular exclusionary logics and proposing alternative counterlogics. This means that our particular understanding of policy making privileges the role of power and political processes, characterizing policies as the contingent outcomes of political struggles between competing discourses. Politics here is understood as the contestation and institution of social relations and practices, and it discloses the contingent character of any practice or institution by showing the role of power and exclusion in its formation. Every discursive structure, as we argue, will be uneven, heterogeneous, and hierarchical. Yet what are the implications of this primacy of politics for our understanding of policy making? Why do particular policies become sedimented? How are they overthrown? By radicalizing the insights of the Marxist theorist Antonio Gramsci, and by drawing on the work of Laclau and Mouffe, we argue that policy discourses are stabilized and challenged by multiple hegemonic operations, whose general structure consists in the logics of equivalence and difference. This means that the concept of hegemony is central to the perspective we put forward here.

Policy change or policy inertia will be the outcome of hegemonic struggles (Howarth 2009). We need, therefore, to say a few words about the concept of hegemony by focusing on its emergence.

Neo-Gramscian Approaches to the State: Political Economy, Hegemony, and Public Policy

The concept of hegemony is complex and contested. Various conceptions, elaborated in rival theoretical frameworks, compete to fix and de-contest its meaning. To tease out some of this variation, we begin by returning to Antonio Gramsci. As a committed Marxist revolutionary, Gramsci's mature political theory explored the obstacles to and prospects for socialist revolution (led of course by the political representatives of the organized working classes) in the new conditions of "organized capitalism," which were emerging in Western Europe and elsewhere in the first part of the twentieth century (Lash and Urry 1987). The growth of the state, the expansion and complexification of civil society, and the appearance of new forms of economic production (exemplified, for example, in the emergence of Fordism) prompted Gramsci to rethink questions of power, domination, ideology, and political strategy, especially in the distinctive conditions of his native Italy in the 1920s and 1930s. But though the reflections collected together in his *Prison Notebooks* are concerned with the pressing specificity of Italian politics, Gramsci also advances a more general political theory, constructed around the category of hegemony, to transcend the economic determinism and class reductionism associated with classical Marxism (Femia 1981; Gramsci 1971).

In seeking to deconstruct and transcend the essentialism of classical Marxism, especially as it was developed in the Second International, Gramsci embarked on a fundamental reworking of the Marxist concept of society, which was expressed in the famous base-superstructure model of social relations. For example, in his justly famous Preface to *A Contribution to the Critique of Political Economy*, Karl Marx summarizes his materialist conception of history as follows:

> In the social production of their life, men enter into definite relations that are indispensable and independent of their will, relations of production which correspond to a definite stage of development of their material productive forces. The sum total of these relations of produc-

tion constitutes the economic structure of society, the real foundation, on which rises a legal and political superstructure and to which correspond definite forms of social consciousness. The mode of production of material life conditions the social, political and intellectual life process in general. It is not the consciousness of men that determines their being, but, on the contrary, their social being that determines their consciousness. (1997:425)

One immediate implication of Marx's picture of social life is the importance he places on the "economic structure of society" in shaping and conditioning the ideas and beliefs of social agents, as well as the legal and political systems that govern their conduct. This economic structure is in turn rooted in a particular mode of material production, whether feudalism, capitalism, or socialism, which consists in the relations and forces of production and their dialectical interaction. The role of the superstructures in ensuring the reproduction of social relations in this perspective depends on the coercive power of the state and the propagation of false and distorted forms of consciousness (see Howarth 2012).

Within this schema, as Noberto Bobbio (1988) puts it, Gramsci engineers a twofold inversion of the Marxist base-superstructure model of society. Whereas Marx privileges the role of economic production, focusing his attention on the contradictory relationship between the forces and relations of production, Gramsci emphasizes the ideological superstructures ("state plus civil society") over the economic structure. In addition, within the realm of the "complex superstructures," Gramsci (1971:182) asserts the priority of civil society (the moment of consent and consensus) over political society (the moment of force or coercion). But though Bobbio correctly pinpoints the principal elements of Gramsci's contribution to Marxist political theory, his insinuation of a simple reversal of the classical oppositions crucially misses Gramsci's endeavors to deconstruct and reconnect the dualisms he introduces (Gramsci 1971:169–70; see also Texier 1979). For instance, although Gramsci problematizes the relationship between state and civil society in Marxist theory, he also introduces the idea of the "integral state" to account for both the hegemonic and dictatorial aspects of political rule. The integral state thus leads to a general redefinition of the state in Marxist theory. Rather than just an instrument of class rule, it is identified by Gramsci with "the entire complex of practical and theoretical activities with which the ruling class not only justifies and maintains its dominance, but manages to win the active consent of those over whom it rules" (1971:244). Similarly, his concept of a "historical bloc" articulates both structural and superstructural elements of society—the "decisive economic nucleus," political society, and civil society—as a "unity of opposites and distincts" (137). Historical blocs are thus configurations of related elements, although they are ultimately organized around a fundamental social class and a dominant mode of production.

In short, by challenging the economism of classical Marxism, in which dominant productive structures are sustained by the coercive power of the state and the propagation of various forms of false consciousness (or ideology), Gramsci argues that the maintenance of class rule should be explained via a reworked conception of hegemony. Hegemony is not identified with the political leadership of a certain class in a strategic alliance struggling for state power, as Lenin had argued, but involves the construction and dissemination of "intellectual and moral leadership" throughout society (Gramsci 1971:57). It comprises a complex set of practices designed to win the active and passive consent of key social actors in a particular historical bloc, while securing the compliance of others. Hegemony is not to be identified with a narrow notion of domination and government, because the "general notion of State" includes "elements which need to be referred back to the notion of civil society (in the sense that one might say that State = political society + civil society, in other words hegemony protected by the armour of coercion)" (263).

Finally, as Gramsci argues, different forms of hegemony are put together by organic intellectuals, whose political and ideological task is to elaborate and inculcate the new "common sense" that is to form the basis of a particular historical bloc. This idea of "common sense" corresponds to Gramsci's reworked conception of ideology, which for him is not a purely negative notion that connotes illusory forms of representation. Instead, ideology is understood as a positive material force that is vital in advancing the interests and objectives of various hegemonic projects. Importantly, Gramsci distinguishes between ideologies that are "historically organic" and can thus form the connective tissue of a new common sense, and those that are "arbitrary, rationalistic or 'willed'" and are thus unlikely to form the basis of a successful hegemonic project (1971:376–77). In this way, organic ideologies provide the means to create collective wills and hegemonic projects that have the capacity to transform societies in various ways.

There are at least three major strands of neo-Gramscian theory that are evident in contemporary debates in political theory, public policy, and political economy. Under the leadership of Andrew Cox and Stephen Gill, one group of theorists has employed Gramsci's original concepts to develop an alternative approach to international political economy (e.g., Cox 1981, 1983, 1987; Gill 2008; Gill and Law 1988). For example, Robert Cox draws upon Gramsci to focus on the construction of hegemony and historical blocs at the global level. For him, regimes comprise three basic elements—ideas, material capabilities, and institutions—which are concretely articulated into different historical configurations at both the national and international levels. More precisely, at the international level, Cox's object of study centers on the dialectical interaction between social forces (situated principally below the national state level), national state actors, and an overall "world order" or regime—say, Pax Britannica in the nineteenth century or Pax Americana in the twentieth—that has achieved hegemony (cf. Glynos and Howarth 2007:126). According to Cox, a hegemonic world regime only obtains if there is a coherent fit between material economic power, a dominant collective image of the world order, and a particular set of global institutions that can regulate and administer a specific order (Cox 1981, 1987). Once established, a hegemonic regime facilitates a certain range of policies at the national level—those that are compatible with the dominant values and images—while placing significant constraints on the development and pursuit of others. Cox also stresses the emergence and consolidation of institutional linkages and regimes of a transnational character, which can take the form of international policy networks (Cox 1981, 1996, 1999).

Engaging with the work of Marx, Gramsci, Louis Althusser, Nicos Poulantzas, and Ernesto Laclau and Chantal Mouffe, Bob Jessop is the most prominent exponent of a second strand of neo-Gramscian theory in the domain of hegemony and state theory. He elaborates a "strategic-relational approach" toward the capitalist state that builds on Marx's theory of capital as a "social relation" (rather than a thing) and the later Poulantzas's relational (rather than regional) conception of the modern capitalist system (Poulantzas 1978). Jessop accepts the neo-Marxist premise that the modern capitalist state crystallizes a tension between two contradictory logics and features. On the one hand, the modern capitalist state brings about an institutional and functional separation of the state from the "economy" and "civil society," in which state managers and officials achieve a degree of "operational autonomy" from other members of the polity. Yet, at the same time, its emergence also results in the actual intertwining of different functional subsystems, as well as the modern state's claim to stand for the public and national interest: it is thus "open," in principle, to competing social forces that express their demands in terms of these principles. At the same time, the birth of the modern state ushers forth the selective integration of officials and politicians into the wider society (Jessop 1990, 2007).

In accounting for this structural tension, Jessop foregrounds the relational character of the state. More precisely, drawing on the later Poulantzas, he argues that "state power is a form-determined material condensation of the balance of (class) forces in struggle," in which the role of the state is to crystallize and mediate the competing demands and interests that are voiced and articulated in society by representing them in its different institutional sites and by producing various interventions that are designed to respond to them (Jessop 2002a:6, 37, 40, 70, 95). State interventions are thus embodied in particular policies, decisions, actions, pronouncements, ideological forms, and so forth. Yet, in keeping with liberal democratic ideology, the state, although in principle open to all interests and identities, still exhibits a "strategic selectivity," so that its accessibility and responsiveness to various demands reflects the dominant forces that have inscribed their interests and ambitions into the "institutional materiality" of the state (Jessop 1982, 1990). (In this regard, the state may be understood as having different degrees of "relative autonomy" from conflicting interests and groups in society, thus enabling it to facilitate the reproduction of capitalist relations, while remaining accessible to different, perhaps noncapitalist, representations [cf. Miliband 1969; Poulantzas 1969, 1973, 1978].)

With respect to the practices of policy making in modern capitalist societies, Jessop explores the ways in which various state forms and regimes exert a differential impact on the processes of policy formulation and implementation. For example, forms of representation associated with pluralism consist in a series of "institutionalized channels of access to the state apparatuses for political forces representing interests and/or causes rooted in civil society (as opposed to function in the division of labor) and recognised as legitimate by relevant branches of the state," whereas corporatism involves forms of interest mediation that are grounded in functionally differentiated groups such as "business" and "labour" (Jessop 1982:230). Other systems of representation include clientelism, parliamentarism, raison d'état, and so on (229–30). Any concrete political system will tend to exhibit various syntheses and combinations of these basic representational systems.

More concretely, Jessop has integrated selected concepts and logics in French regulation theory and then employed his framework to analyze the emergence, consolidation, and policy impact of hegemonic projects, such as Thatcherism and New Labour in the British context (Jessop 2002b, 2004a; Jessop et al. 1988). For example, against the backdrop of the contradictions and crises of the Keynesian welfare state in the 1960s and 1970s, Jessop charts the way Thatcherism combined a neoliberal accumulation strategy, which promoted a market-driven transition from the flawed Keynesian model, with a stronger yet smaller and more centralized state, which could enforce its policy commitments while imposing its will on those recalcitrant elements that sought to defend the old order or that dared to propose alternatives. In policy terms, the new economic strategy involved a commitment to privatization, deregulation, and the introduction of commercial criteria into existing state practices and activities; the deregulation and liberalization of the City in an effort to establish London as the center of international finance and to secure an export role for Britain through its specialization in financial services; the sponsoring of a market-generated industrial recovery—the so-called supply-side revolution—which concentrated on the encouragement of inward investment, the promotion of small business, the expansion of new technology, and the development of labor policies that emphasized greater flexibility; reduced direct taxes to expand the scope of the operation of market forces through enhanced investor and consumer choice; and the attempt to position the economy of the United Kingdom into "a dynamic multinational space" (Jessop et al. 1988:171). Beneath the commitment to its macroeconomic austerity strategy—the commitment to monetarism and various drives to curb public expenditures—these five connected sets of policies constituted the microeconomic supply-side dimension of neoliberalism.

In his more recent writings, along with Ngai-Ling Sum, Jessop has supplemented his strategic relational approach by elaborating a method of "cultural political economy" to explore, for example, the shift from Fordist to post-Fordist social formations (Jessop 2004b, 2009; Jessop and Sum 2006). While accepting the material constraints of social structures—or "structural selectivities"—this "cultural turn" recognizes the role of meaning making in sustaining the conditions for capital accumulation, and it draws attention to particular forms of argumentation, narratives, and economic imaginaries in the production and reproduction of social relations. The turn to culture, meaning, and the semiotic dimension of social relations has also led Jessop to engage more fully with contemporary forms of discourse analysis, especially critical discourse analysis, which has been developed by Norman Fairclough, Ruth Wodak, and Lilie Chouliaraki (Chouliaraki and Fairclough 1999; Fairclough 2001; Fairclough and Wodak 1997).

A Poststructuralist Conception of Hegemony

Jessop's turn to culture brings us neatly to a third group of neo-Gramscians who have developed Gramsci's theory of hegemony and ideology in a more poststructuralist direction. Laclau, Mouffe, and other proponents of the Essex school of discourse analysis have combined Gramsci's pathbreaking reflections on hegemony with more recent developments in critical theory (such as structural Marxism, genealogy, and psychoanalysis) to engage in a wider deconstruction of the Marxist tradition (Howarth and Stavrakakis 2000; Laclau and Mouffe 1985). Against Jessop's commitment to critical realism, they reject a sharp distinction between the material/real and the discursive/symbolic, in which the former simply reflect or represent the latter in particular ways. They choose instead to embrace a constitutive conception of discourse that goes beyond the narrow confines of linguistic representation to include material objects and practices. The result of these developments is the elaboration of a discourse theory approach to the state, public policy, and our conceptions of political intervention that is grounded in a poststructuralist conception of hegemony.

Working within this perspective, we delineate two aspects of hegemony that are vital in developing a viable approach to critical policy analysis.[1] On the one hand, hegemony is a type of rule or governance that captures how a regime, practice, or policy *holds sway* over a set of subjects with a particular entwining of consent, compliance, and coercion. On the other hand, hegemony is a practice of politics that involves the linking together of disparate demands to forge projects or "discourse coalitions," which can *contest* a particular form of rule, practice, or policy (Howarth 2009:317). In practice, of course, these aspects are intimately related. Hegemony as a form of rule presupposes various practices of transformism, negotiation, compromise, and bargaining, while the struggle to develop counterhegemonic movements presupposes certain forms of rule, which the movements challenge and seek to transform. Yet, on analytical, if not ontological, grounds, it is possible to separate these two aspects. We shall explore each dimension in turn, drawing upon the case of the politics of aviation policy in the United Kingdom to develop our arguments. The hegemonic regime of aviation expansion, which emerged during the Second World War, was sustained during the postwar consensus and then gathered momentum during the 1980s and 1990s when successive governments pursued an agenda of liberalization, reregulation, and privatization. Yet, more recently, it has increasingly been associated with collective environmental costs and climate change, as well as noise pollution and disruption for those living in the surrounding airport communities, prompting the emergence of counterhegemonic discourse coalitions (Griggs and Howarth 2012).

Hegemony as a form of rule speaks in general to the way subjects accept and conform to a particular regime, practice, or policy, even though they may have previously resisted or opposed it. As such, it enables us to characterize different forms of concrete governance, shedding light on how different policy regimes are stabilized and reproduced through diverse practices of transformism, negotiation, compromise, and bargaining (Howarth 2009:318–20). Indeed, two opposed ideal types of hegemony as a form of rule can be specified, each of which comprises different blends of force and consent. What we might term a situation of "organic hegemony" represents a type of rule in which subjects actively consent to a particular practice or regime, so that the role of force or domination recedes into the background. At the opposite pole of the continuum, we find a situation of "inorganic hegemony," which designates a practice or regime where subjects at best comply with, or even actively resist, such forms so that relations of force, coercion, and compulsion are necessary to secure an order.

If we turn to the governance of aviation in the United Kingdom, we can note that the opposition to the postwar regime of airport expansion was repeatedly met with different forms of consultation in which local communities had little or no say over final decisions, such as short-term concessions that imposed limits on noise or runway use at airports, and a set of procedural mechanisms, notably official hearings and public inquiries, that framed decisions not according to the environmental impact but as narrow technocratic planning decisions. However, the inorganic character of this hegemonic regime of expansion was repeatedly manifested when such mechanisms failed to gain consent or compliance for expansion plans, and local campaigners turned to direct action and protest to challenge proposals for expansion. Thus, at the Manchester airport in the late 1990s, local residents rejected the outcome of the public inquiry and joined forces with direct action environmentalists to combat the second runway (Griggs and Howarth 2002). More recently, John Stewart, the leader of HACAN ClearSkies, one of the local resident groups against expansion at London Heathrow airport, demonstrated the inability of government to generate consent and compliance, proclaiming after further announcements of expansion in 2006 that "there will be the mother of all battles if the Government tries to expand Heathrow," declaring that "the Government doesn't seem to realise the forces lining up against it. . . . We've stopped speaking to the Department for Transport. We've started speaking to Earth First!"[2]

However, it is important to stress that in whatever ways we employ these terms to characterize different forms of concrete governance, the rhetorical dimension of a hegemonic relation retains a similar form: a particular set of demands and values comes to function as universal demands and values, thus representing a concrete "totality" or order that exceeds them (Laclau 2005:72). In this model, each demand is split between a universal and a particular dimension. Let us say in the case of airport expansion in the United Kingdom that this universal dimension is the demand for growth. Airlines might demand an expansion of the aviation industry (the universal dimension), but lobby for such expansion in different locations such as London Heathrow, Manchester, or Birmingham (the particular dimension). The hegemonic relation rests upon one of the demands—in this instance, the desire for growth—coming to play a universal function, thus representing and giving sense to the entire chain of demands. Expressed in rhetorical terms, this relation is best captured by the figure of synecdoche, in which a part represents the whole. The relation between part and whole thus furnishes an important means for conceptualizing the hegemonic relation, though a thorough empirical analysis will also require an account of the identifications and attachments through which subjects are gripped by such regimes and practices. In turn, this involves a passage through the categories of fantasy and ideology, as well as the operation of hegemony as a political practice, which as we shall see involves the interplay between metonymy and metaphor.

Hegemony is thus a form or type of rule. But it is also a kind of political practice that involves the making and breaking of political coalitions. The second aspect of hegemony thus highlights the linking together of different demands and identities to challenge and even replace a given practice or social order. Here, hegemony is a type of political relation or practice that involves the drawing of equivalences between disparate elements via the construction of political frontiers that divide social fields into opposed camps (Howarth 2009:318). In this way, the identities that compose such equivalential chains are modified by the practice. For example, local campaigns to oppose particular airport expansions can be linked together into a broader coalition against airport expansion generally, which in turn may also be linked to wider adjacent social demands for environmental protection and corporate regulation by finding points of equivalence among these struggles. Indeed, local residents campaigning against New Labour proposals for a third runway at London Heathrow drew equivalences between their demands against expansion at the airport and the demands of direct action environmentalists for action on climate change and the reduction of carbon emissions. In this case, the very identities of local struggles were modified to reflect their more universal character, while the content of the new demand was given by a more general opposition to a government's overall national policy of airport expansion and to its environmental consequences (Griggs and Howarth 2004, 2008, 2012).

This second aspect of hegemony foregrounds in rhetorical terms the metonymical dimension of political practices. As a rhetorical strategy, metonymy refers to the substitution of an attribute or aspect of the object or concept that is meant (let us say "the House" as a substitute for Members of Parliament). Here, we use it to symbolize the way in which a particular group or movement located in a particular sphere begins to take responsibility for tasks and activities in adjacent or contiguous spheres of social relations, thus seeking to hegemonize such demands. Yet this focus does not preclude the metaphorical dimension. On the contrary, the role of metaphor is essential because if a group is to successfully hegemonize the demands and identity of others, it must create analogical relations—forms of resemblance—between such demands, while articulating empty signifiers that can partially fix or condense such demands into a more universal (if ultimately precarious) unity. Here again, one particular difference will begin to assume a more universal function, with empty signifiers acting as a means of representation, which enables the articulation of internal differences, while simultaneously showing the limits of a group's identity and its dependence on opposition to other groups (see Howarth 1997, 2000; Laclau 1996).

If we revisit our example of airport expansion, we can see that those subjects who sought to garner support for expansion endeavored to link together more and more demands, not only for growth at particular airports, but also for jobs across manufacturing and high-technology sectors, cheap leisure flights and increased mobility, the protection of the tourist industry, and so on. As more and more demands were added to the chain of equivalences, the universal signifier—"expand the aviation industry in the United Kingdom"—was emptied of content, thus becoming a "tendentially empty signifier" to use Laclau's (1996:47) terms. In the case of the public consultation surrounding the future of airport expansion in the United Kingdom in 2003, it was the name of the progrowth coalition Freedom to Fly that came to signify the universal need for growth, thus functioning as an empty signifier that unified the coalition around something that was perceived to be lacking, or at least that was under threat from those protesting against expansion (Howarth and Griggs 2006).

The Affective Dimension of Policy Practices

Hegemony is thus a form of rule and a quintessential type of political practice. However, we have yet to say something about why and how particular policies "stick." How and why are subjects gripped by particular devices or signifiers? Or, conversely, how and why are subjects not held fast by a discourse? We address these questions by turning to the affective dimension of policy change and by considering the related notion of lack and the unconscious and affective investments of subjects in certain rhetorical devices, signifiers, and images. It is here that the Lacanian logic of fantasy, which has been developed by theorists such as Slavoj Žižek, can focus our attention on the enjoyment subjects procure from their identifications with certain signifiers and figures (Glynos 2001; Lacan 2006; Žižek 1989, 1997).

It is important to stress that fantasy is not an ideological illusion or a form of false consciousness that comes between a subject and social reality. On the contrary, in the Lacanian approach, fantasies partly organize our perceptions of reality and structure our understanding of social relations by covering over their radical contingency. Social relations thus appear to subjects as natural and sedimented (Glynos and Howarth 2007:117–20). Indeed, one of the indicators of the "success" of a fantasy is its invisibility: the fact that it supports social reality without our being conscious of it. On the other hand, the visibility of fantasmatic figures and devices—their disclosure and appearance as fantasies—means that they cease to function properly in this regard. Of course, there are different ways to come to terms with social fantasies and their grip, ranging from repression to traversal.

The logic of fantasy thus operates to bring a form of ideological closure to the radical contingency of social relations and to naturalize the different relations of domination within which a subject is enmeshed. It does this through a fantasmatic narrative or discourse that promises a fullness-to-come once a named or implied obstacle is overcome—the beatific dimension of fantasy—or that foretells of disaster if the obstacle proves insurmountable, which might be termed the horrific dimension of fantasy, though in any particular instance the two work hand in hand (Stavrakakis 1999:108–9, 2007). The beatific side, as Žižek (1998:192) puts it, has "a stabilizing dimension" on policy regimes, while the horrific aspect possesses "a destabilizing dimension," where the other is presented as a threatening or irritating force that must be rooted out or destroyed. On the whole, fantasmatic logics capture the various ways subjects organize their enjoyment by binding themselves to particular objects and representations "to resolve some fundamental antagonism" (Žižek 1997:11).

In fact, we can see such fantasmatic appeals in operation in the postwar development of aviation policy in the United Kingdom. Throughout the postwar institution of the regime of aviation expansion, the threat of foreign competition, in particular from the United States, operated as something akin to a horrific fantasy for British policy makers and manufacturers. If actualized, this fantasy carried the threat of destroying aviation in the United Kingdom and its drive to secure global markets in the postwar period. At the same time, politicians and policy makers repeatedly articulated fantasmatic appeals to aviation: the growth of civil and military aircraft manufacturing, the development of more sophisticated and safer technologies, the very experience of flying and the "jet set," and the promise of mass tourism were intimately connected with a discourse of modernization and progress, which was an essential ingredient in countering Britain's inexorable economic decline. More recently, in the run-up to the public consultation over the future of aviation in 2003, the Labour government and supporters of expansion sought (but ultimately failed) to rhetorically redefine the question of airport expansion in terms of "sustainable aviation," articulating a beatific fantasy in which aviation expansion and environmental sustainability could be linked in a harmonious and mutually reinforcing fashion.

The role of subjective desire and attachment therefore adds further elements to the conceptual grammar of poststructuralist policy analysis by providing the means to explore how identities are stabilized and given direction, as well as the moments when such identifications begin to lose their adhesion or fail to resonate at all. Yet this ontological focus must still be articulated in particular empirical contexts; in other words, the basic categories and logics of the approach have to inform our concrete analysis of particular practices, thus modifying or adding to our existing interpretations of policy change or stability. In short, they must be employed at the ontical level of investigation (Mulhall 1996:4). This raises methodological questions about the operationalization of psychoanalytical categories and logics. How do we study discourses? How do we describe, explain, criticize, and evaluate? Here, we turn to the logics of critical explanation.

Conducting Critical Policy Analysis: Logics of Critical Explanation

What we shall term discourse analysis involves the more ontical investigation of specific discourses in particular times and places, though such analysis is always informed by the ontological presuppositions of discourse theory. More precisely, it captures the process of analyzing a whole range of meaningful practices and regimes as discursive forms by focusing on how such objects can be translated into discursive sequences and then empirically investigated. The discussion of discourse analysis also ought to touch upon the epistemological status of the outcomes of such research (Howarth 2005). We take discourse analysis to be a problem-driven approach to policy analysis, rather than a method, technique, or theory-driven perspective. It thus involves the construction of particular problems in particular policy contexts. Equally, it does not search for general laws or causal theories, though a wider set of inferences might be constructed as a result of particular analyses. Yet it does pose some general questions. How can we characterize a discourse or discursive practice? Where did it come from and how was it formed? How and why is it sustained? How can we evaluate and criticize discursive formations? This last question suggests that discourse theory is a species of critical theory (Howarth 2009:324).

Building on Glynos and Howarth's *Logics of Critical Explanation in Social and Political Theory* (2007), our answers to these questions can be summarized in a five-step approach to critical policy analysis. First, following Foucault, we begin by problematizing a particular phenomenon. This problematization is related both to the field of academic questions and to the social and political issues that confront us in a specific historical conjuncture. Second, the form of explanation is retroductive rather than exclusively inductive or deductive. Derived from the American pragmatist Charles Sanders Peirce, our explanatory task thus begins with an anomalous phenomenon—an explanandum—which would be rendered intelligible were a putative explanans (explanation) to hold. Third, the content of any putative explanation—any explanans—is couched in terms of logics rather than laws, causal mechanisms, or contextual self-interpretations. Fourth, any putative explanans will comprise a plurality of logics—social, political, and fantasmatic—which must be linked together in relation to a particular set of circumstances to render a problematic phenomenon intelligible. It is here that we stress the concept of articulation as a practice of linking together elements in a logic that modifies each particular element in an explanation that consists in a "synthesis of many determinations" (Marx 1973). Finally, our approach posits an internal connection between explanation, critique, and policy evaluation. With respect to the formulation, analysis, and explanation of policy problems, as well as our critical interventions into particular situations, evaluation and critique are internal components of the explanatory endeavor. We shall now explore these steps in more detail.

Problematization

An essential, and often difficult, starting point in critical policy analysis is to problematize a pressing problem in the present.[3] In the field of policy studies, this task is immensely complex and complicated. For one thing, it is unusual for a single "problem" to emerge for description and analysis. Instead, there is a range of ongoing problematizations of different facets of the policy under consideration by various groups and subjectivities. For example, the task of problematizing aviation policy in the United Kingdom raises a range of ongoing problematizations of different facets of the aviation industry by various groups and subjectivities. The "problem" of aviation is different for the U.K. government, the airport operators, the airlines, the environmental protesters, the local communities affected or threatened by airport expansions, the passengers, and so on. These subjectivities and constituencies are themselves complex and differentiated entities. Moreover, the "problem" exhibits various dimensions: the political economy of aviation; questions about planning, public policy, and administration; the role of protest and direct action in shaping policy and attitudes; the environmental impact of aviation; and so on. Each dimension contains a further range of issues and questions. For example, the political economy of aviation in the United Kingdom concerns questions about the net contribution of aviation to the British economy, the changing ownership patterns of the airports, the relationship between the airlines and the airport operators, the external costs of aviation for the environment and the wider community, and so on.

Our first analytical task is thus to problematize the various problematizations of the issue under consideration, so that we can construct a viable object of research (Howarth 2009:324–25). But this task immediately raises questions about the notion of problematization and its connection to a network of related concepts and logics to which we have already alluded: demands, grievances, dislocations, antagonisms, contradictions, and so forth. Our conception of problematization stems mainly from the work of Michel Foucault, who in turn draws upon Martin Heidegger (see Rayner 2004). It concerns "a movement of critical analysis in which one tries to see how the different solutions to a problem have been constructed; but also how these different solutions result from a specific form of problematization" (Foucault 1997:118–19). For example, the "problem" of aviation in the United Kingdom, like other fields of transport policy, was framed in the postwar period in terms of "predict and provide" policies or as ensuring the provision of sufficient airport infrastructure, runways, and terminals to meet rising passenger demand and to protect the interests of the national carrier, British Airways. That this particular problematization of airport policy came to frame deliberations surrounding airports involved a privileging of specific technologies of government and modes of argumentation. It enshrined the art of forecasting as one of the primary technologies of government, while privileging particularistic arguments about the development needs of individual airports, as well as the advantages and disadvantages of one site location over another. Indeed, airport policy itself was often played out "in the future," as rival stakeholders articulated competing projections of rising demands on airports in the next ten or twenty years, with recourse to the horrific fantasy of a "capacity overload" a regular trope of government.

In this approach, an object of study is always constructed, which means that a range of disparate empirical phenomena has to be constituted as a problem and that the problem has to be located at the appropriate level of abstraction and complexity. The problem then has to be resolved—or better, perhaps, "dissolved"—by a careful genealogical disentangling that exposes the various historical threads and trajectories that constitute the problems and identities we confront in the present, which only emerge via the various struggles and political clashes between forces in critical conjunctures over time (Foucault 1984). Indeed, this genealogical accounting of a problem and its ensuing identity lays bare excluded possibilities that can, in turn, form the basis for alternative problematizations and projects.

In our perspective, we connect the construction of problems to the expression of grievances and the articulation of demands. What is more, demands and grievances are the products of various problematizations, or the different ways "being offers itself to be . . . thought," to use

Foucault's rather abstract, Heideggerian formulation (Foucault 1985: 11). For example, the problem of aviation for environmentalists and many local residents in the United Kingdom (and elsewhere) is the damaging impact of airport expansion and global air travel on the environment and local communities, coupled with a weakly regulated aviation industry that is conceded a privileged role in state policy making. Over the last ten or fifteen years, these developments have given rise to demands for better management of aviation expansion, more control on the numbers and types of flights, and so forth (Griggs and Howarth 2004, 2008; Howarth and Griggs 2006). Alternatively, for those favoring more expansion—airlines, big business, airport operators, sections of the tourist industry, the city, and so on—the strategic advantage enjoyed by the British aviation industry is increasingly under threat from "capacity overload," poor infrastructure, and foreign competition, be it from Frankfurt, Amsterdam, or new airports in China. They have charged the government with "dithering" and "piecemeal development," articulating demands for the government to take the lead and put in place a long-term strategic plan for aviation expansion (Caves and Gosling 1997:320). In short, demands are thus the product of the various ways troubling issues confront subjects and engage their attention. Yet such "thinking" is also rooted in the various practices from which the issues themselves arise, be they local resident experiences of noise pollution, environmental degradation, or the repeated failure of participation in public inquiries to prevent expansion. More precisely, demands thus arise out of the failures and dislocations of social practices and regimes, which only "appear" when normal ways of "going on" are interrupted.

However, although grievances and demands are rooted in these disrupted practices, they can, as already suggested, be linked together to form wider identities and political projects, which can challenge existing relations in the name of something new. These identities and projects may constitute the raw materials for the construction of other problems in different social contexts or at different institutional levels of a particular social system. At the same time, demands and claims can be disarticulated and rearranged by the operation of other political logics. Importantly for us, the role of government, and more broadly the state, in contemporary societies has become a privileged site for constructing and dealing with the problems that arise from a variety of competing social demands and claims. However, in seeking to tackle these problems, those in government first need to "know" the character of the problems before endeavoring to address them in various ways. For instance, this mediation process may involve the attempt by governments to deal with a combined set of social demands by addressing each of them in a punctual and singular fashion, thus processing them on the government's own terms and thereby weakening a wider challenge to its authority. Or it may involve redescribing a set of demands in new terms, so that the demand seems more manageable. Equally, it may involve the marginalization of certain demands by rendering them equivalent to unpopular or extremist grievances and desires, thus weakening their import. To examine these issues, we propose three basic types of logic—social, political, and fantasmatic—with which to critically explain the problem under investigation (see Glynos and Howarth 2007).

Retroduction

This brings us to the second step of our approach, which focuses on the form of a putative explanation of a problematized phenomenon in policy studies, while offering us logics as a way to think about the units that make up the content of that explanation. Although Aristotle has been credited with its original identification, retroduction has been insightfully developed and applied in the philosophy of science by Charles Sanders Peirce and Norwood Hanson. In contrast to induction and deduction, retroduction implies that the single most important criterion for admitting a hypothesis, however tentatively, is that it accounts for the phenomenon or problem at stake. More specifically, retroductive reasoning takes a threefold form. To begin with, a surprising, anomalous, or wondrous phenomenon is observed (P). For example, we might observe the government's continued sponsorship of aviation expansion despite the growing recognition of aviation's contribution to climate change and the government's own commitment to the reduction of carbon emissions. We then proceed "backward" to furnish an account of how and why this is so. So, we conjecture that this phenomenon (P, or the continued expansion of aviation) "would be explicable as a matter of course" if a hypothesis (H, or the continued "grip" of aviation expansion and the success of political parties in managing dissent) were true, and so there is good reason to think that H is true (Hanson 1961:86). In other words, the hypothesis is not inferred until its content is already present in the explanation of P. This contrasts with inductive accounts that "expect H to emerge from repetitions of P" and with hypothetico-deductive accounts that "make P emerge from some unaccounted-for creation of H as a 'higher-level hypothesis'" (86).

Logics

We couch the content of any putative explanans in terms of logics rather than laws, causal mechanisms, or contextualized self-interpretations. What are logics and how might they help us to describe and explain the dynamics of policy discourses? Logics, in our view, are not causal laws or causal mechanisms, which are independent of an actor's meaning. And although their discernment must take the actors' own meanings into account, they do not simply reflect an actor's self-interpretations. Instead, the logic of a discourse captures the rules that govern a meaningful practice, as well as the conditions that make the operation of such rules possible. Yet, because of the contingency and undecidability of these rules, in certain circumstances such conditions also render them vulnerable to change. Logics thus provide answers to questions about the nature and function of various social practices, as well as their overall purposes, meanings, and effects. What makes a practice tick? What are its purpose, meaning, and effect for the analyst? What is the "essence" of a practice (in Wittgenstein's sense of the term)?

In fleshing out our answers to these questions, we can single out three types of logic: what we shall term social, political, and fantasmatic logics. When harnessed together to develop a critical explanation of a problematized phenomenon, these logics are not reducible to the empirical phenomena they purport to characterize and critically explain, nor can they be accorded a fully transcendental role and function, which can furnish explanations from a position completely outside social phenomena. Social logics enable one to characterize social practices in different contexts. They are thus multiple and contextual. This is because there are as many logics as there are various situations that an investigator explores. These logics can capture economic, social, cultural, and political processes: a particular logic of competition or commodification, for example, or a specific logic of bureaucratization in a particular social context (Howarth 2009:325).

Political logics enable analysts to explain and potentially criticize the emergence and formation of a social practice or regime. Of particular importance in this regard are the logics of equivalence and difference. The logic of equivalence entails the construction and privileging of antagonistic relations; it grasps the way political frontiers are constructed via the linking together of social demands and identities. The logic of difference draws on other discourses in an attempt to break down these chains of equivalence. The age-old practice of "divide and rule," for instance, in which an occupying power seeks to separate ethnic or national groups into particular communities or indirect systems of rule, is invariably designed to prevent the articulation of demands and identities into a generalized challenge to the dominant regime. In other words, it captures the way demands are negated, disarticulated, mediated, and negotiated by various institutions. Logics of equivalence and difference thus emphasize the dynamic process by which political frontiers are constructed, stabilized, strengthened, or weakened.

For example, if we return to the case of aviation policy in the United Kingdom and the proposal of the Labour government under Gordon Brown to expand London Heathrow, it is possible to discern an array of political logics that attempted to ward off the growing grievances and demands which accompanied plans for a third runway and a sixth terminal at the London airport (Griggs and Howarth 2012). Indeed, the Brown government endeavored to impose clear boundaries on the process of consultation over the third runway through what we term the logic of managed consultation. These strategies coexisted with a wider logic of deferred responsibility or individualization which captures the way the government in the United Kingdom endeavored to incorporate multiple stakeholders into the shared ownership or management of a desired policy outcome. Equally, logics of incentivization capture the various ways the Brown government adopted a hands-off approach to the environmental regulation of the air transport industry by developing and supporting the development of an emissions trading scheme. Finally, in what we term the logic of brokerage, government rearticulated its attempts to position itself as an "honest broker" seeking to accommodate and balance various interests and demands in order to produce a partial and acceptable equilibrium. But one important consequence of the logic of brokerage was that it reproduced the fantasy of sustainable aviation that reconciled in some way competing demands for growth and environmental protection.

Fantasmatic logics provide the means to explain and potentially criticize the way subjects are gripped by discourses. They enable us to detect the particular narratives that provide ideological closure for the subject. As we have said, fantasy is intimately connected to the category of ideology. Drawing upon the work of Laclau and Mouffe, we understand ideology to be the logic of concealing the contingency of social relations and naturalizing the relations of domination in discourses or meaningful practices that thus appear to subjects as natural and "given." In this context, the production of certain fantasmatic narratives is intertwined with the logic of ideology, for such narratives structure the way different social subjects are attached to certain signifiers and focus our attention on the different types of "enjoyment" subjects procure in identifying with discourses and believing the things they do. In this regard, the logic of fantasy, which is predicated on the Lacanian category of enjoyment (*jouissance*), points to the way in which subjects are rendered complicit in concealing or covering over the radical contingency of social relations. As such, the grip of the fantasmatic appeals of aviation in postwar Britain masked over considerations such as the poor profit returns of carriers, noise complaints, and political opposition to new infrastructure. Britain was considered a world leader in aviation, and any government would be misguided if it failed to pursue and secure such advantages.

To analyze these logics at the ontical level, we can deploy a range of different techniques and tools as long as these approaches are articulated in a way that meets the ontological commitments of discourse theory. So, for example, we can turn to the rhetoric political analysis (RPA) of Alan Finlayson, which elaborates a more constitutive conception of rhetoric (Finlayson 2007). Starting with a distinctive agonistic conception of politics, which is understood as "the 'arena' within which we see expressed the irreducible and contested plurality of public life, the ineradicable contestation of differing world-views," RPA focuses on the role of argumentative practices and persuasion in the inevitable disputes over political decisions and courses of action that are the very stuff of democratic politics (Finlayson 2007:552). An important strength of Finlayson's proposal is that he provides a series of analytical strategies for investigating different kinds of argumentative practice in different contexts of political life. For example, he draws attention to various "rhetorical situations" that provide the rules within which arguments take place; the form and content of arguments, that is, the type of argument and the substantive subject under dispute; the various problematizations and framings of issues; the various genres of rhetoric, especially deliberative political rhetoric; the role of narratives and commonplaces in the structuring of arguments; and finally, the three basic forms of appeal in rhetorical strategies, that is, logos, ethos, and pathos (Gottweis 2006).

Equally, we can draw upon the tools of critical discourse analysis (CDA), which have been developed by theorists such as Norman Fairclough and Ruth Wodak (1997). They draw, among other things, on Foucault's various conceptions of discourse to elaborate another variant of discursive policy analysis, which they use to study various policy responses to globalization and the politics of New Labour in Britain. According to Norman Fairclough (2001), CDA aims to address social and political issues and problems by conducting a close study of texts, linguistic interactions, and other forms of semiotic material to detect changes taking place around key policy issues such as governance, education, media, and democracy, while also looking for unrealized possibilities for transforming the way social life is currently organized. CDA emphasizes the role and impact of ideology in policy making. Ideology is not defined by comprehensive and coherent worldviews, but by a discursive naturalization of contingently constructed meanings and identities. New public management can thus be seen as an ideology insofar as it presents a totalizing story about how public administration and policy can be subject to new ideas associated with "managerialism." Particular groups and elites may have an interest in reproducing and propagating particular ideologies that might help them to maintain, or even enhance, their political power.

With our distinction between the ontological and the ontical, we do indeed focus both on the constitutive character of rhetoric (and language more generally) in our understanding of social relations and on the instrumental use of particular figures (such as metaphors that are condensed in particular signifiers, phrases, and images) in constructing coalitions and hegemonic projects; we can also focus on particular tropes and the role of arguments in practices of decision making and persuasion; and our focus can seek to understand and critique arguments in relation to broader discourses and ideologies. For example, metaphor helps us to develop a grammar of concepts for understanding practices and regimes, as well as the particular devices that can hold divergent demands and interests together in precarious fixations (see Schön 1993).

However, we draw particular attention to the technique of rhetorical redescription and the figure of catachresis and the process of naming. Quentin Skinner reactivates Quintilian's technique of rhetorical redescription, which involves the restating of facts "but not all in the same way; you must assign different causes, a different state of mind and a different motive for what was done" (cited in Skinner 2002:183). Of particular interest for discourse theorists is the substitution of a rival (yet neighboring) evaluative term "that serves to picture an action no less plausibly, but serves at the same time to place it in a contrasting light" (Skinner 2002:183). In the case of air transport policy in the United Kingdom, the collocation "sustainable aviation," which was made to serve during the consultation for the air transport white paper in 2003 (DfT 2003) as the universal demand of the progrowth coalition, was the product of a metaphorical redescription, which was then universalized by organic intellectuals intent on developing the case for expansion. Efforts were made not just to redescribe aviation as "sustainable aviation," but to redefine the very terms of argumentation themselves away from concerns about the environment, the control of demand, and issues about equality and social justice to questions about our freedom to fly, the threat to jobs and economic competitiveness, and our opportunities for pleasure, if expansion was threatened (Howarth and Griggs 2006).

Following poststructuralist theorists such as Derrida, Foucault, and Laclau, we also attribute the figure of catachresis a more fundamental role in our understanding of rhetoric and in our analysis of political logics. Catachresis "is a transfer of terms from one place to another employed when no proper word exists" (Parker 1990:60). For example, to speak of "the leg of a table" or "the foot of a mountain" is to apply a term to a thing that the term does not literally refer to, either because our language lacks such a term or because we encounter or invent new objects in need of a name. The process of naming has itself a constitutive function. Indeed, drawing upon Žižek's (1989:95) account of the retroactive effect of naming, Laclau (2005:100) argues that in certain specific circumstances—for example, the failure of an institutional order to contain demands or the emergence of antagonisms and demands that cannot be represented within such an order—"the name becomes the ground of the thing," partly constituting the meaning of the objects to which it applies. Thus, with our example of air transport in the United Kingdom, the act of naming the progrowth coalition Freedom to Fly (the catachrestic moment par excellence) brought into being a new object (the coalition demanding sustainable growth) and provided the ideological means of representing a perceived threat or lack (being prevented from flying) that could be overcome by a particular policy (a progrowth expansion strategy) (Howarth and Griggs 2006).

Of course, the integration of such tools and techniques depends upon their articulation by the policy analyst or researcher in each problematization. The overriding condition is that they fit the ontological presuppositions of poststructuralist discourse theory and do not leave our approach with a debilitating eclecticism. In fact, this raises further questions about the practice of articulation, as well as that of judgment and critique in policy analysis, to which we now turn.

Articulation, Judgment, and Critique

Any putative explanans of a policy problem will inevitably comprise a plurality of logics—social, political, and fantasmatic—which will have to be linked together in relation to a particular set of circumstances to render a problematic phenomenon intelligible. It is here that we stress the concept of articulation as a practice of linking together elements in a logic that modifies each particular element in the "synthesis of many determinations" (Marx 1973). Moreover, to think about this practice of articulation, we stress the role of judgment as a kind of situated ability in which a subject—a researching subject in a particular case—acquires and enacts the capacity to connect a concept to an object or to "apply" a logic to a series of social processes within a contingent and contestable theoretical framework (Glynos and Howarth 2007:184–85).

Indeed, a question that often arises with respect to this approach concerns the identification of relevant rhetorical figures or theoretical concepts. How do we know what counts in reality as an empty signifier, or as a relevant metaphor, or as a metonym? Against subsumptive logics, which are invariably built upon a spurious logic of scientific "operationalization" that sets out the necessary and sufficient conditions for "applying" a concept to an object, we favor an approach based on intuition, theoretical expertise, and the method of articulation. This means that, having immersed oneself in a given discursive field consisting in texts, documents, interviews, and social practices, the researcher draws on her or his theoretical and practical expertise to make particular judgments about whether something counts as an "x" (is "x" a metaphor, logic of equivalence, empty signifier, or whatever?) and then to decide upon its overall import for the problem investigated. The theoretical expertise is acquired by learning and using the specific language-games that form the grammar of the researcher's theoretical approach. And if indeed a practice or signifier does count as an instance of an "x," an integral part of this logic of judgment consists in deciding what the precise relevance and importance of the "x" is in constructing a narrative that explains a phenomenon or dissolves a particular paradox. These elements—"intuitions," "theoretical expertise," "practical wisdom," "judgments," and so forth—form part of what we call the method of articulation. This method consists in a practice of explanation that links specific theoretical and empirical elements together (explanans) to account for a singular, problematized phenomenon (explanandum). In this picture, the ultimate "proof" consists in the production of narratives explaining problematized phenomena, which in turn depends partly on the relevant community of critical scholars (Howarth and Griggs 2006:31).

Critical Explanation and Normative Evaluation

Finally, we posit an internal connection between explanation, critique, and normative evaluation. With respect to the formulation, analysis, and explanation of policy change, as well as our intervention into particular instances of change or stasis, evaluation and critique are internal to the logic of investigation. As discourse theorists, we are thus firmly opposed to positivist and purely descriptivist approaches to political theory and social science. But we also eschew an overhasty and overreaching normativism that too quickly prescribes an a priori set of norms and principles with which to evaluate and then reorder existing institutions, policies, and practices. More concretely, the practice of critique is predicated on the centrality of political and fantasmatic logics, for their discernment enables us to highlight the contingency and undecidability of particular social relations and structures. The political is evident in those conjunctures where social relations are formed and challenged by the exercise of power and where exclusions and foreclosures occur. They thus indicate the moments of the potential reactivation of political institution and thus the possibility of resistance against various forms of domination. The ideological is evident in those fantasmatic narratives that function to conceal contingency and naturalize relations of domination.

Recognizing the centrality of political and fantasmatic logics to the practice of critique, we elude the risks of limiting policy evaluation to the surfacing of the different contextualized self-interpretations of those engaged in the formulation and implementation of a particular program or policy. These risks, we suggest, are particularly pertinent to those who might frame evaluation as a form of practical hermeneutic inquiry, thereby privileging "practical wisdom" and characterizing the art of evaluation as "dialogical encounters" in which evaluators become "partners in an ethically informed, reasoned conversation about essentially contested concepts like welfare, health care, education, justice, work life and so forth" (Schwandt 1997:79). Such approaches recognize the constitutive role of the process of evaluation itself. They accept that the evaluator does not stand "outside" the object of study as a spectator. However, against the backdrop of our emphasis on the role of articulation in critical policy studies, such approaches may well run the risk of offering no explicit critical engagement since, in the words of Geertz, "their contextualized self-interpretations 'hover' too close to the practices they seek to elucidate" (cited in Glynos and Howarth 2007:64). Most importantly, however, they may well underplay the political dimension of the constitution of meanings since the political is potentially mobilized out of or removed from any such hermeneutical approach through the insistence on the possibilities of reaching deliberative consensus (see, e.g., Schwandt's optimism that "different interpretations can be adjudicated by appealing to transcendental conditions of ideal speech communities"; 1997:80).

However, we have not addressed the implications of our approach for understanding democratic policy making. It is thus with a brief discussion of our understanding of democratic policy making that we move toward the conclusion of this chapter. The primacy of political practices and processes, which underpins our poststructuralist account of policy making, challenges the temptation to reify rational consensus as the desired outcome of policy formulation, implementation, and evaluation. It does so by rendering obsolete the belief in the potential eradication of antagonism through negotiation and dialogue. The policy process will inevitably draw boundaries between different social groups and their demands, while the formation of policy regimes understood as "sites" for political contestation will be predicated upon patterns of exclusion, as conflicting groups seek to universalize their narrow sectional interests and values (Howarth 2006). The challenge for critical policy studies is thus to evaluate the extent of inclusion and exclusion within policy processes and the forms of antagonism that structure patterns of inclusion and exclusion. First, some policy actors will forge equivalential chains and popular demands that are more inclusive of "relevant and affected actors" in the policy subsystem (Sørensen 2005: 354). Second, antagonisms, as Mouffe argues, do not necessarily have to take the form of the division between "us" and "them" or of distinctions between "friends" and "enemies" where the existence of the "other" threatens the identity of the "we" (2005:20–21). Although not eliminating antagonism, we can envisage agonistic "we-they" relations in which adversaries recognize the legitimacy of their opponents, so that "while in conflict, they see themselves as belonging to the same political association, as sharing a common symbolic space within which the conflict takes place" (Mouffe 2005:20). As such, the art of democratic policy making, to paraphrase Mouffe, rests on our capacity to transform antagonism into agonism.

Conclusions

This chapter has outlined a poststructuralist approach to critical policy studies that emphasizes the centrality of politics and power in the forging, sustenance, and grip of various policy frames and discourses in particular social and historical contexts. In substantive theoretical terms, this involves the articulation of the concept of hegemony to account for the emergence and formation of policy discourses, and it draws on Lacanian psychoanalysis and the category of fantasy to account for the stabilization and grip of policies. In developing how such concepts and categories may be employed to analyze particular fields of policy making, we outline a five-step method for investigating problematized policy issues. Critical policy studies, we suggest, should thus offer retroductive explanations couched in terms of social, political, and fantasmatic logics that are articulated together in a particular set of circumstances to render a problematic phenomenon intelligible. The practice of critique itself is predicated on the centrality of political and fantasmatic logics to policy inquiry. It is their discernment that enables us to highlight the contingency and undecidability of particular social relations and structures and to move beyond "negative critique" to the generation of positive alternatives for social and political organization.

Notes

We would like to thank the editors and the two anonymous readers for their helpful comments on this chapter. The chapter builds on ideas developed by members of the Essex School of Discourse Analysis, as well as previous theoretical research about the relationship between discourse, power, and critical policy analysis. It also draws upon ongoing empirical research undertaken by the authors, some of which is presented in a forthcoming book titled *Resignifying "Sustainable Aviation" in the United Kingdom* to be published by Manchester University Press.

1. This section builds upon Howarth 2000, 2009.
2. *The Observer*, January 1, 2006.
3. In this regard, we are assisted by the fact that the strategy of problematization has been adopted by a number of poststructuralists and critical theorists in the fields of social and political analysis (e.g., Campbell 1998; Fischer 2003; Rose 1999).

Bibliography

Bobbio, N. 1988. "Gramsci and the Concept of Civil Society." In *Civil Society and the State: New European Perspectives*, edited by J. Keane, 73–100. London: Verso.

Bridge, G., and P. McManus. 2000. "Sticks and Stones: Environmental Narratives and Discursive Regulation in the Forestry and Mining Sectors." *Antipode* 31(4):10–47.

Campbell, D. 1998. *National Deconstruction*. Minneapolis: University of Minnesota Press.

Caves, R. E., and G. D. Gosling. 1997. *Strategic Airport Planning*. Oxford: Pergamon.

Chouliaraki, L., and N. Fairclough. 1999. *Discourse in Late Modernity*. Edinburgh: Edinburgh University Press.

Cox, R. 1981. "Social Forces, States, and World Orders." *Millennium* 10(2): 126–55.
———. 1983. "Gramsci, Hegemony and International Relations: An Essay in Method." *Millennium* 12(2):162–75.
———. 1987. *Production, Power and World Order*. New York: Columbia University Press.
———. 1996. "A Perspective on Globalization." In *Globalization: Critical Reflections*, edited by J. H. Mittelman, 21–30. Boulder, Colo.: Lynne Rienner.
———. 1999. "Civil Society at the Turn of the Millennium: Prospects for an Alternative World Order." *Review of International Studies* 25(1):3–28.
DfT (Department for Transport). 2003. *The Future of Air Transport Cm 6046*. London: DfT.
Dryzek, J. 1997. *The Politics of the Earth: Environmental Discourses*. Oxford: Oxford University Press.
Fairclough, N. 2001. "Critical Discourse Analysis as a Method in Social Science Research." In *Methods of Critical Discourse Analysis*, edited by R. Wodak and M. Meyer, 121–38. London: Sage.
Fairclough, N., and R. Wodak. 1997. "Critical Discourse Analysis." In *Discourse as Social Interaction*, edited by T. van Dijk, 258–84. London: Sage.
Femia, J. 1981. *Gramsci's Political Thought: Hegemony, Consciousness and the Revolutionary Process*. Oxford: Clarendon.
Finlayson, A. 2007. "From Beliefs to Arguments: Interpretive Methodology and Rhetorical Political Analysis." *British Journal of Politics and International Relations* 9(4):545–63.
Fischer, F. 1995. *Evaluating Public Policy*. Florence, Ky.: Wadsworth.
———. 2000. *Citizens, Experts and the Environment*. Durham: Duke University Press.
———. 2003. *Reframing Public Policy: Discursive Politics and Deliberative Practices*. Oxford: Oxford University Press.
Foucault, M. 1984. "Nietzsche, Genealogy, History." In *The Foucault Reader*, edited by P. Rabinow, 76–100. Harmondsworth: Penguin.
———. 1985. *The Use of Pleasure*. New York: Pantheon.
———. 1997. *Ethics*. New York: New Press.
Fox, C. J., and H. T. Miller. 2007. *Postmodern Public Administration*. Rev. ed. Armonk, N.Y.: M. E. Sharpe.
Gill, S. 2008. *Power and Resistance and the New World Order*. 2nd ed. London: Palgrave.
Gill, S., and D. Law. 1988. *The Global Political Economy: Perspectives, Problems, and Policies*. London: Harvester.
Glynos, J. 2001. "The Grip of Ideology." *Journal of Political Ideologies* 6(2): 191–214.

Glynos, J., and D. Howarth. 2007. *Logics of Critical Explanation in Social and Political Theory*. London: Routledge.

Gottweis, H. 2003. "Theoretical Strategies of Poststructuralist Policy Analysis: Towards an Analytics of Government." In *Deliberative Policy Analysis: Understanding Governance in the Network Society*, edited by M. Hajer and H. Wagenaar, 247–65. Cambridge: Cambridge University Press.

———. 2006. "Rhetoric in Policy Making: Between Logos, Ethos, and Pathos." In *Handbook of Public Policy*, edited by F. Fischer, G. J. Miller, and M. S. Sidney, 237–50. London: Taylor and Francis.

Gramsci, A. 1971. *Selections from Prison Notebooks*. London: Lawrence and Wishart.

Griggs, S., and D. Howarth. 2002. "An Alliance of Interest and Identity? Explaining the Campaign against Manchester Airport's Second Runway." *Mobilization* 7(1):43–58.

———. 2004. "A Transformative Political Campaign? The New Rhetoric of Protest against Airport Expansion in the UK." *Journal of Political Ideologies* 9(2):167–87.

———. 2008. "Populism, Localism and Environmental Politics: The Logic and Rhetoric of the Stop Stansted Expansion Campaign." *Planning Theory* 7(2):123–44.

———. 2012. "Phronesis, Logics, and Critical Policy Analysis: Heathrow's 'Third Runway' and the Politics of Sustainable Aviation in the UK." In *Real Social Science: Applied Phronesis*, edited by B. Flyvbjerg, T. Landman, and S. Schram. Cambridge: Cambridge University Press.

Hanson, N. R. 1961. *Patterns of Discovery*. Cambridge: Cambridge University Press.

Howarth, D. 1997. "Complexities of Identity/Difference." *Journal of Political Ideologies* 2(1):51–78.

———. 2000. *Discourse*. Buckingham: Open University Press.

———. 2005. "Applying Discourse Theory." In *Discourse Theory in European Politics*, edited by D. Howarth and J. Torfing, 316–43. London: Palgrave.

———. 2006. "Space, Subjectivity and the Political." *Alternatives* 31(2):105–34.

———. 2009. "Discourse, Power, and Policy: Articulating a Hegemony Approach to Critical Policy Studies." *Critical Policy Studies* 3(3–4):309–35.

———. 2012. *Poststructuralism and After*. London: Palgrave.

Howarth, D., and S. Griggs. 2006. "Metaphor, Catachresis and Equivalence: The Rhetoric of Freedom to Fly in the Struggle over Aviation Policy in the UK." *Policy and Society* 25(2):23–46.

Howarth, D., and Y. Stavrakakis. 2000. "Introducing Discourse Theory and Political Analysis." In *Discourse Theory and Political Analysis*, edited by D. Howarth, A. J. Norval, and Y. Stavrakakis, 1–23. Manchester: Manchester University Press.

Jessop, B. 1982. *The Capitalist State: Marxist Theories and Methods.* Oxford: Martin Robertson.
———. 1990. *State Theory.* Cambridge, England: Polity.
———. 2002a. *The Future of the Capitalist State.* Cambridge, England: Polity.
———. 2002b. "Revisiting Thatcherism and its Political Economy: Hegemonic Projects, Accumulation Strategies and the Question of Internationalization." In *Critical Political Studies,* edited by A. Bakkan and E. MacDonald, 41–56. Montreal: McGill University Press.
———. 2004a. "Comments on 'New Labour's Double Shuffle.'" *Soundings* 24:25–30.
———. 2004b. "Critical Semiotic Analysis and Cultural Political Economy." *Critical Discourse Studies* 1(2):159–74.
———. 2007. *State Power: A Strategic-Relational Approach.* Cambridge, England: Polity.
———. 2009. "Cultural Political Economy and Critical Policy Studies." *Critical Policy Studies* 3(3–4):336–56.
Jessop, B., K. Bonnett, S. Bromley, and S. Ling. 1988. *Thatcherism: A Tale of Two Nations.* Cambridge, England: Polity.
Jessop, B., and N.-L. Sum. 2006. *Beyond the Regulation Approach: Putting Capitalist Economies in their Place.* Cheltenham: Edward Elgar.
Lacan, J. 2006. *Écrits.* New York: W. W. Norton.
Laclau, E. 1996. *Emancipation(s).* London: Verso.
———. 2005. *On Populist Reason.* London: Verso.
Laclau, E., and C. Mouffe. 1985. *Hegemony and Socialist Strategy: Towards a Radical Democratic Politics.* London: Verso.
Lash, S., and J. Urry. 1987. *The End of Organized Capitalism.* Cambridge, England: Polity.
Marx, K. 1973. *Grundrisse.* London: Allen Lane.
———. 1997. "Preface to a Contribution to the Critique of Political Economy." In *Karl Marx: Selected Writings,* edited by D. McLellan, 424–27. Oxford: Oxford University Press.
Miliband, R. 1969. *The State in Capitalist Society.* London: Weidenfeld and Nicolson.
Miller, H. T. 2002. *Postmodern Public Policy.* Albany: SUNY Press.
Mouffe, C. 2005. *On the Political.* London: Routledge.
Mulhall, S. 1996. *Heidegger and Being and Time.* London: Routledge.
Parker, P. 1990. "Metaphor and Catachresis." In *The Ends of Rhetoric: History, Theory, Practice,* edited by J. Bender and D. E. Wellbery, 60–76. Stanford: Stanford University Press.
Poulantzas, N. 1969. "The Problem of the Capitalist State." *New Left Review* 58:67–78.
———. 1973. *Political Power and Social Class.* London: Verso.
———. 1978. *State, Power, Socialism.* London: New Left.

Rayner, T. 2004. "On Questioning Being: Foucault's Heideggerian Turn." *International Journal of Philosophical Studies* 12(4):419–38.

Rein, M., and D. A. Schön. 1993. "Reframing Policy Discourse." In *The Argumentative Turn in Policy Analysis and Planning*, edited by F. Fischer and J. Forester, 145–66. Durham: Duke University Press.

Rose, N. 1999. *Powers of Freedom*. Cambridge: Cambridge University Press.

Saussure, F. de. 1983. *Course in General Linguistics*. London: Duckworth.

Schön, D. A. 1993. "Generative Metaphor: A Perspective on Problem-Setting in Social Policy." In *Metaphor and Thought*, 2nd ed., edited by A. Ortony, 137–63. Cambridge: Cambridge University Press.

Schwandt, T. 1997. "Evaluation as Practical Hermeneutics." *Evaluation* 3(1):69–83.

Skinner, Q. 2002. *Visions of Politics*. Vol. 1. Cambridge: Cambridge University Press.

Sørensen, E. 2005. "The Democratic Problems and Potentials of Network Governance." *European Political Science* 4:348–57.

Staten, H. 1984. *Wittgenstein and Derrida*. Lincoln: University of Nebraska Press.

Stavrakakis, Y. 1999. *Lacan and the Political*. London: Routledge.

———. 2007. *The Lacanian Left*. Edinburgh: Edinburgh University Press.

Texier, J. 1979. "Gramsci, Theoretician of the Superstructures." In *Gramsci and Marxist Theory*, edited by C. Mouffe, 48–79. London: Routledge.

Torfing, J. 2005. "Discourse Theory: Achievements, Arguments, and Challenges." In *Discourse Theory in European Politics*, edited by D. Howarth and J. Torfing, 1–32. Basingstoke: Palgrave Macmillan.

Townshend, J. 2003. "Discourse Theory and Political Analysis: A New Paradigm from the Essex School." *British Journal of Political Science* 5(1):129–42.

Weale, A. 1992. *The New Politics of Pollution*. Manchester: Manchester University Press.

Žižek, S. 1989. *The Sublime Object of Ideology*. London: Verso.

———. 1997. *Plague of Fantasies*. London: Verso.

———. 1998. "The Seven Veils of Fantasy." In *Key Concepts of Lacanian Psychoanalysis*, edited by D. Nobus, 190–218. London: Rebus.

FRANK FISCHER AND ALAN MANDELL

11. Transformative Learning in Planning and Policy Deliberation

Probing Social Meaning and Tacit Assumptions

This chapter examines the concept of social learning and its import for policy learning, a topic that has taken on particular importance in recent times in planning and policy analysis.[1] Much of the current work in these disciplines has focused on the technical dimensions of learning in policy inquiry, neglecting a deeper attention to the policy paradigms of which they are a part. Since a critical perspective on policy and planning requires a reflexive examination of the basic assumptions informing a progressive action-orientation, the chapter seeks to first draw out the implications of policy paradigms and the basic beliefs and values that they embody, and then explores the ways that these underlying assumptions can be part of the work of the planner and policy analyst. Toward this end, the discussion then turns to the theory of transformative learning as it has emerged in progressive adult educational theory. This work assists us in better understanding the process of attitudinal and cognitive change and suggests ways that such change can be facilitated. Two brief examples of facilitation are offered. The chapter closes with a discussion of the implications of such learning for professional education and practice.

Social Learning in Policy and Planning

Social learning is today a central concept in the social sciences. This reflects the recognition that learning is basic to social and political life. Given this reality, the concept of learning has emerged in nearly every corner of the social and managerial sciences—indeed, in some cases, this emphasis on "learning" has become something of an ideology. Countless texts on business and public administration, for example, speak of the "learning organization" as the model for effective administration, especially in difficult times characterized by rapid social change. Concepts of adult life-long learning and personal flexibility have become a basic part of the standard normative framework for employees—professional and otherwise—in uncertain times requiring high degrees of flexibility.[2]

The concept of learning, understood as a change in thinking, perception, and attitude, has taken on an important role in policy analysis and planning, given the ever-growing number of problems in need of solution—poverty, environmental deterioration, educational failure, crime, drugs, and more. In policy studies, learning is generally dated to the work of Hugh Heclo (1972). Attention to learning would, in his view, lead to better explanations of policy outcomes than the theories based solely on social and economic variables.

More specifically, Heclo has theoretically and empirically concentrated on the role of policy learning in the political decision process. For Heclo, "politics finds its sources not only in power but also in uncertainty—men collectively wondering what to do" (1974:305–6). Policy making is thus conceptualized as "a form of collective puzzlement on society's behalf," entailing not only knowing and deciding but also learning. In his theory, such learning is mainly a task that falls to the civil servants who gather, code, and store policy experiences.

Where Heclo has mainly sought to identify and examine learning in the political system, Paul Sabatier has researched the ways in which interest groups sometimes learn from each other in policy deliberation. The central feature of his influential "advocacy coalition framework" turns on the ways in which members of different policy coalitions, organized around competing policy beliefs, can learn from technical policy research and debates in policy communities (Sabatier 1988). This orientation stresses the role of policy ideas and analysis in the policy process.

Both Heclo and Sabatier emphasize the need for empirical and analytical explanation of the role of learning in policy change. Their work, however, focuses on the more technical aspects of debate and assumes that changes in more fundamental beliefs are atypical. Thus, they tend to examine instrumental learning based on technical information. For some, however, such a perspective is rather narrow and technocratic at its core (Fischer 2003; Freeman 2006).

Peter Hall, by contrast, has identified the more fundamental importance of "paradigmatic change." He defines "social learning as a deliberate attempt to adjust the goals or techniques of policy in response to past experience and new information," with learning occurring "when policy changes as the result of such a process" (1993:278). While he recognizes the technical dimensions of policy deliberation, Hall goes beyond setting technical levels of policy instruments (e.g., degrees of permissible pollution) and changing of policy instruments (e.g., carbon trading or carbon taxes). That is, he extends learning to include changes in the "policy paradigm," defined as the "framework of ideas and standards that specifies not only the goals of policy and the kinds of instruments used to attain them, but also the very nature of the problems they are meant to be addressing" (279). Hall's work acknowledges that change in policy paradigms does not happen regularly, but that when it does, such changes—the result of new learning—are of crucial importance.

The policy paradigm is an "interpretive framework" for understanding policy goals and the instruments to achieve them, but even more importantly, it offers a framework for understanding the nature of the issues to be dealt with. As Richard Freeman puts it, a paradigm makes "sense of the world by identifying particular phenomena as problematic and suggests courses of action to deal with them" (2006:375). Policies are formulated within frameworks of beliefs and ideas—and the norms and standards drawn from them—that are intelligible to those engaged in the process. In this sense, discussion and deliberation of policy take place within a political discourse. As Freeman observes, the discursive framework, "like a Gestalt, is embedded in the very terminology through which policy makers communicate about their work, and it is influential precisely because so much of it is taken for granted and unamenable to scrutiny as a whole" (2006:279).

While writers such as Heclo and Sabatier have sought an empirical explanation of learning in the institutional structures of policy processes, planners have tended to focus more normatively on the role of agency, including the facilitation of learning. This is the result of the action-oriented nature of planning. Rather than focusing on development of empirical theory as such, the applied assignment of planners and policy analysts is to develop courses of action based on relevant knowledge. From this perspective, learning is a practical rather than a theoretical endeavor.

John Friedmann has conceptualized planning itself as social learning, explaining that the "principle focus of the social learning approach is on action—that is, on purposeful activity undertaken by an actor, individual or collective—within the actor's environment" (1987:183). It mainly "manifests itself as a change in practical activity" and thus "it is rarely systematized or articulated in the formal language of scientific discourse" (185). Rather, social learning involves a more informal, discursive process facilitated by "change agents who encourage, guide, and assist an actor in the process of changing social reality." Such agents serve as facilitators "who bring certain kinds of formal knowledge to the ongoing social practice of their 'client group.'" They do this by developing "a transactive relationship with their clients conducive to *mutual learning*" (185). Such learning is typically carried out in small groups, whether in the planning office or in civil society.

Drawing on John Dewey, Friedmann (1987) emphasizes a consensus theory of knowledge. Important here are the ways we learn through dialogical action to probe and test our assumptions, particularly as they relate to proposals for action. In this understanding, knowledge is ultimately validated when it helps to settle or dispose of a problem in a particular context. But this validation does not rest on a narrow empirical understanding of either the problem or the test. Rather, it is the result of a dialectical interaction between theoretical perspectives and everyday practices that probe the underlying assumptions that structure perceptions of social problems. Here, Friedmann recognizes the need to get at the deeper, often tacit, assumptions that underlie and often plague decision making. Similar to Hall's emphasis on the underlying policy paradigm, Friedmann's is a call for planners to assist citizens and clients in identifying and assessing the deeper interpretive frameworks that more fundamentally shape their immediate problems.

An important step forward, which Friedmann encourages us to take, is reflected in the work of Donald Schön, who has focused on the need for learning in the face of the growing uncertainty confronting contemporary societies, largely the result of increasing complexity. For Schön, the loss of the "stable state" for decision makers, institutions, and the larger society requires planners and policy analysts to "learn about learning" (1973:28). It becomes essential to learn about conditions of complexity, uncertainty, and instability as they pertain to planning and social change. Toward this end, Schön calls for a rethinking of government and its institutions as "a learning system."

Fundamentally, Schön was concerned with what he called the "crisis of the professions," a topic that engaged him throughout his long and productive career. He sought to move planners, managers, and policy analysts beyond the limiting confines of technical rationality and the principles of rational decision making that have long governed these professions. He attributed the failure of expertise in planning and policy analysis to an outdated adherence to the technical model of rationality and to the superior-subordinate relationship between experts and clients that it demands. He thus focused on the need for open and authentic interactions between experts and clients in planning and policy science. To avoid distorted communications between practitioners and their clients, Schön emphasized the need for more open interactions as the key to the reconstruction of expert practices. As an alternative to the technical approach to problem solving, he advanced the nontechnical, interpretive practice of "problem setting" based on a "conversation with the situation."

Engaging Schön's approach, John Forester (1999) draws out its transformative dimensions and their implications. Arguing for a move beyond the standard understanding of dialogue to the processes of transformative learning, Forester explores the ways that "learning occurs not just through arguments, not just through the reframing of ideas, not just through the critique of expert knowledge, but through transformations of relationships and responsibilities, of networks and competence, of collective memory and memberships." He asserts that "many analyses of dialogue and democratic argument do not go nearly far enough to do justice to the learning that dialogical and argumentative processes can really promote." The standard approach to deliberation and empowerment tends to reduce these processes to a matter of "being heard" (115).

Within such an approach, learning is thus reduced to knowing information, and deliberation is treated as merely speaking. In the process, the transformation of passive citizens into active participants tends to get lost. As Forester puts it, "much more is at stake in dialogic and argumentative processes than claims about what is or is not true (as crucial and essential as factual analyses . . . are)" (1999:115–16). Also involved are questions "of political membership and identify, memory and hope, confidence and competence, appreciation and respect, acknowledgement and the ability to act together. The transformations at stake are those not only of knowledge or class structure, but of people more or less able to act practically together to better their lives, people we might call citizens" (115–16).

While writers like Schön and Forester make clear the need to include basic policy beliefs—as paradigms—and their assumptions in practical deliberation, the epistemology of this process has received far less attention. An approach is needed that recognizes the technical component of planning and policy analysis, but that also seeks to critique and reconstruct the technocratic approaches that have often wittingly or unwittingly emerged. Fischer and Mandell (2009) have also sought to connect the methods relevant to such policy learning to a postempiricist conception of planning and policy analysis. Taken in this way, the goal of the postempiricist planner and policy analyst is to confront the fact that many contemporary problems are too complex, uncertain, and messy to lend themselves to the methods of rational empirical analysis. Understanding thus depends on the interpretation of a multiplicity of uncertain events through dialogic deliberation. It requires new learning.

From this perspective, policies and plans must be understood as social constructions. They are discursively created sociopolitical agreements that set out courses of action that rest on understandings based on normative and empirical beliefs. While policies and plans have a substantive content, they cannot simply be empirically researched; more fundamentally, they have to be interpreted. Hence, an understanding of policies and plans, as well as their outcomes, cannot be separated from the ideas, theories, and criteria by which the policy is analyzed and described (Majone 1989:147). Policy making, in this view, is regularly a discursive struggle over the assumptions that shape problem definitions, the boundaries of the categories used to explicate them, the evaluative criteria for their assessments, and the social and political meanings of the ideals that guide particular actions (Stone 1989). Thus, policies and plans can always be seen as doing two things at once: they attempt to effectively solve a problem and, at the same time, they seek to do it in ways that reproduce the norms and values of particular societal arrangements and the politics supporting them (Fischer 1995). The task of the analyst must include helping the client learn about and understand the multiple understandings of what otherwise appears to be a single concept. A new kind of learning emerges, one that must involve uncovering the hidden assumptions embedded in a policy concept that can illuminate and even at times resolve the conflicts at hand.

Fischer and Mandell (2009) have extended this constructivist perspective and its emphasis on social and political assumptions by turning to the work on "transformative learning" in progressive educational theory. As a deeper form of learning—a form of Schön's "reflection in action"—it takes on special importance today as the issues facing contemporary societies have gradually (and sometimes not so gradually) moved from incremental problems to matters of crisis that raise profound questions about the very nature of the societies of which they are a part. Urgent matters such as climate change, the collapse of the international financial system, international terrorism, and pandemic medical emergencies all indicate that more than new policy regulations are required. They suggest that the very assumptions that inform our thinking and behaving about these issues are at the root of the problem. Such a reality demands a different, deeper transformational perspective.

The goal of this perspective is thus to develop a more discursive relationship between planners and policy analysts and those they seek to advise—decision makers, clients, citizens, and so on: to develop more critical action-oriented arguments in and for policy and planning processes. That is, there needs to be an ongoing, participatory, communicative interaction between them.

But can we be more specific about the nature of the learning practices that this involves and how they relate to policy analysis and planning? The sections that follow seek to extend this perspective by drawing out the components of transformative learning, first by pulling together and illustrating the various—and often disparate—methodological elements involved and then by attempting to integrate them in a more systematic perspective. We therefore turn now to the theory and practice of transformative learning.

Transformative Learning as Problematization: Social Meaning and Reflexivity

The theory and practice of transformative learning focuses on the examination of social meaning through narration and dialogue. Largely developed for the education of adults, it involves "becoming critically aware of one's own tacit assumptions and expectations and those of others and assessing their relevance for making an interpretation of the ongoing social narratives, both one's own and those of others" (Mezirow and Associates 2000:4). Such learning is based on a constructivist understanding of action-oriented knowledge and social meaning. The approach is generally founded on Paulo Freire's (1973) critique of the "banking" model of schooling. In this model, teachers fill students' minds with the content of their expert narratives about which learners are supposed to be either ignorant or misinformed. Students are passive; they take notes and regurgitate what are deemed the important points on examinations. Although the critique of the banking model is typically focused on the problematic realities of the schooling experience, the assumptions of the banking model extend further into other realms of human interaction, including the policy sciences. Indeed, it is the pedagogical orientation that shapes much of the thinking about learning in planning and policy analysis, framing an architecture of subjects and objects that is reflected in understandings of public sector information-gathering and advice-giving. This is particularly evident in the construction of data banks (emphasizing information storage and retrieval), now greatly facilitated by new computer technologies and the Internet.

Even more important, a "banking" orientation reflects the practices governing relations between professionals and citizens. Professionals are trained to explain to clients and citizens who are expected to listen. They explain problems and options to a largely passive audience of citizens and decision makers who seek their advice. Discussion often occurs, but it is largely framed by the expert advice.

On the other hand, in transformative learning, teachers and students collaborate reflexively to create knowledge about the social world that, in turn, can be used to help develop courses of action based on their own goals and interests. The teacher (professional) and his or her student (client) cooperatively seek to uncover and validate knowledge in the sociocultural realm in which it is created. A claim is accepted or rejected as a result of deliberation based on relevant discourses; participants negotiate the meanings attached to information, objects, stories, events, and symbols.

Particularly useful is the conception of the process developed by Danny Wildemeersch and Walter Leirman (1988). They emphasize the importance of movement toward reflectivity through educational interventions geared to the learner's particular ability and experience. Although transformative theory is not formally a "stage theory," they identify three dialogic phases in the development of transformation. The first is a "narrative dialogue," which involves telling a story or describing an action. The story affirms or reaffirms a subjective and objective reality—that is, the otherwise self-evident character of the social life-world—making actions seem true and normal. Seemingly settled issues may turn out to be unsettled, thus leading to intellectual and emotional apprehensiveness. In such a context, new ideas can be seen as threats rather than opportunities.

The second phase involves a threatening situation in the individual's or group's life-world. In transformational theory, this is understood as the "dilemma" and becomes the object of exploration. The deliberative task is to make apparent and identify the problematic narrative contradictions related to the anxiety-producing dilemma, or what Wildemeersch and Leirman call the "manifest situational contradictions." In this phase, a transactional conversation takes place, involving an analytical dialogue about the evidence and arguments pertaining to alternative viewpoints.

The third phase involves a critical discourse that explores the relationship between the person's or group's own problematic situation—that is, dilemma—and similar themes related to other places and possibilities. Learners perceive these problems and conflicts in the context of the larger social framework of which they are a part, and they develop their reflective capacities to identify and interpret different perspectives from alternative points of view. Engaging in such a process holds out the possibility of the learner gaining insights into the "ruptured situation" that can lead to a new perspective and a narrative to convey it (Loder 1981). This involves a "revised narrative-dialogic process" through which disordered beliefs come to make sense. The result is a new story that helps us better understand the problematic situation: how it came to be, and what to do about it.

Although this description of the transformative learning process seems to be quite removed from standard approaches to professional practices, there is an important linkage that provides a convenient opening for further theorizing and experimentation in this direction. This is found in the close resemblance between Freire's concept of "problematization" and Schön's (1983) concept of "problem setting." For Freire (1970:67), problematization is a fundamental challenge to the hierarchy of the teacher (or professional) and the student (or client). As coproducers of knowledge, teachers and students, clients and professionals become "jointly responsible for a process in which all grow" (Freire 1970:67). Similarly, Schön is concerned with the same issue as it manifests itself in planning and policy science. Designed to avoid the one-dimensional, hierarchical, and thus generally distorted communications between practitioners and their clients (resulting from an adherence to the technical model of rationality and the superior-subordinate relationship between experts and clients), Schön advances his concept of "problem setting."

Problem setting, for Schön, is nontechnical and contrasts sharply with "problem solving." Where the latter emphasizes technical knowledge and skills, problem setting is fundamentally normative and qualitative. In technical analysis, values and goals are taken as given; in problem setting, analysis focuses on their identification and discovery. At times, problem setting also involves the consensual shaping of new value orientations.

Problem setting for both Freire and Schön concerns two interrelated learning tasks: first, the determination of the problem situations to be addressed; and second, the normative forms that shape our understanding of policy issues, including the criteria for their evaluation. Analytically preceding technical problem solving, problem setting requires professionals to initiate what Schön (1983) calls "a conversation with the situation." Focusing on naming situations and defining the problems that arise in them, this "reflection in action" necessitates a broader epistemological orientation. The quantitative modes of reason that have shaped policy and planning must, in short, make room for qualitative, interpretive modes of reason.

Applied to the deliberative process in public policy and planning, this approach begins with the recognition that policies and plans are social constructions built around particular social meanings. Although this is not the usual way of looking at policies and plans, Dvora Yanow opened the issue with her book *How Does a Policy Mean?* (1996). Policy making and implementation, she shows, is as much about the creation of meanings as it is about substantive policy content. Public policies and plans seek to solve objective economic and social problems, but they are constructed in the realm of public discourse (Edelman 1988; Yanow 1996). They thus reinforce particular belief systems and the ideologies that promote them. From this perspective, a policy is a mix of empirical and normative components—combining opinion, evidence, norms, and so on—pulled together through an argument.

Next, we take up a more detailed examination of the ontological and epistemological elements that come into play in this process of transformational learning. We begin with the most basic element, social meaning.

Learning Social Meaning: Multiple Realities and Tacit Assumptions

Grounded in a constructivist ontology, the methodology of transformative learning recognizes human experience to be enveloped in a nonmaterial social, cultural, and personal realm of thought and meaning. Transformative learning theorists begin from the understanding that people are born into a world of preexisting social meanings. Through socialization, the dominant meanings come to all of us more or less as a given, as a fixed reality that we treat as such. Many of the ideas and social understandings upon which peoples' worlds are constructed are difficult to recognize, because they are typically buried in everyday practices. We thus tend to neglect the many other realities that exist in society, for example, those of people with different experiences, social backgrounds, and beliefs. Some of these multiple realities differ only in details. But others can differ fundamentally (Fischer 2003). Through transformative learning, the social worlds of individuals and groups are understood to be enlarged as a result of new experiences and thoughts. Facilitated by competing meanings, social worlds are continuously evolving through communication, reflection, and the practices to which they give rise. Changing over time through the interactions of people's cognitive schemes with their social environment, social worlds are thus interpretive linkages of social perceptions, recollections, and expectations, all of which are grounded in subjective experience and understanding of the social and physical realms and in the ideological givens of a particular society.

Social action is thus based on meaning shaped by motives, intentions, goals, and values. Constructed through language, its analysis has more in common with history and literature than with physical science. Rather than seeking proofs through formal logic and empirical experimentation, the investigation of social action requires the use of metaphoric processes that pull together and connect different experience. The meaning of a social experience is assessed in transformational learning by examining its relationship to the larger patterns of which it is a part, be it a situation, a social system, or an ideology.

Mezirow's (2004) approach to transformative learning is based on a distinction between meaning "schemes" and meaning "perspectives." The former constitute the more concrete sets of understandings that emerge from meaning perspectives. They are oriented to specific beliefs, attitudes, and emotional reactions and can more easily be thought about and corrected. Transposed into policy learning, meaning schemes constitute the level at which policy is normally debated and deliberated —for example, what measures would meaningfully respond to the problems of air and water pollution? How might new regulations be introduced to deal with them?

Learning at the level of a meaning perspective, by contrast, assesses the more abstract beliefs, norms, and values within which the discussion of regulations takes place. They are examined according to their larger implications for society. That is, the very assumptions grounding the ideas or understandings that are normally taken for granted are identified and called into question. In this case, the discussion moves from specific environmental regulations to a deeper examination of the political, economic, and cultural system that is creating the pollution and probes the system's relationship to both nature and the condition of human kind. Such a discussion involves a search for dysfunctional, systemic patterns (e.g., an overemphasis on consumption) and contradictions in the system that create the problem or hinder its amelioration (e.g., the capitalist drive to grow and accumulate).

Meaning perspectives, as such, are broadly conceived frameworks that provide basic orientations to objects, events, and ideas in the social world. Much like political ideologies and policy paradigms, they provide understandings of how the world works and how it should work. Uncovering meaning perspectives requires a deeper form of self-reflection than the kind of thought engaged in everyday life. Transforming a meaning perspective involves becoming critically aware of how and why assumptions have come to shape and constrain the way we perceive, narrate, and feel about our world and thus entails learning that can change the structures of habitual expectation to make possible a more inclusive, discriminating, and integrative story upon which action can be based. Often this requires critical reflection on the "distorted" premises sustaining one's narrative understandings and expectations. And, given the embeddedness of meaning perspectives in the very core of self-definition, such reflection often encounters resistance, including deeply felt emotional resistance.

These two levels of meaning can be conceptualized in terms of first- and second-order learning (Bateson 2000; Fischer 1995). They can also roughly be understood in terms of Argyris and Schön's (1996) concept of "double-loop" learning focused on underlying assumptions in learning organizations, which can also be applied to policy analysis. "Single-loop" learning involves a reflective process in which individuals, groups, or organizations modify their actions according to the differences between expected and obtained outcomes (e.g., the expected effectiveness and outcomes of air pollution regulations). In double-loop learning, by contrast, these same learners question the assumptions that led to the actions in the first place (e.g., the nature of the underlying production process). If they are able to view and modify those taken-for-granted assumptions, then double-loop learning—as a form of learning about single-loop learning—has taken place.[3]

Finally, it is essential to recognize that meaning is often embedded in less visible—often hidden—policy assumptions. Based on past experiences—social traditions and conventions—tacit knowledge, as a repertoire of understandings and beliefs that support any pursuit of knowledge, is the very fulcrum from which otherwise objective knowledge acquires both its possibility and significance. As Michael Polanyi (1966) demonstrated, cognitive knowing begins implicitly in the tacit realm before becoming explicit. Fischer and Mandell (2009), moreover, have shown the ways these tacit assumptions are often part of an implicit social theory that informs political and policy deliberations.

While the discussion of tacit knowledge might sound rather removed from the concrete practices of policy makers and planners, the topic has been taken up by a number of scholars in fields as diverse as medicine, law, management, and education. These researchers have sought to understand the ways in which important aspects of professional knowledge and skills are not captured or taught in either textbooks or in the classroom. Tacit knowledge, as they understand it, refers to nonverbal, unarticulated dimensions of professional knowledge that are mainly acquired through direct practical experience in real-world environments. It is uncovered by identifying action-oriented assumptions, social biases, and ways of looking at things.

Revising Narrative-Dialogics: Social Meaning in Narrative Storytelling

In transformative learning, social meaning is understood to be embedded in and carried by social narratives and their story lines. Such learning involves an evaluation of the assumptions relevant to the assessment of narratives. The first step, as outlined by Wildemeersch and Leirman (1988), is the identification and discussion of a narrative or narratives that tell a story or describe an action, typically based on the subjective and objective reality of an otherwise self-evident dimension of the social life-world. The task, which they refer to as the development of a "narrative-dialogic," is to organize and facilitate a process that unsettles settled issues. In such a process, new ideas are typically encountered with intellectual and emotional apprehensiveness; they are treated more as threats than as opportunities. The narrative-dialogic process strives for a revised story that can make sense of the disordered beliefs that emerge with the unsettled issue. When successful, the new story offers a better explanation of the problematic situation—how it can be rethought, how it came to be, and what to do about it.

This dialogic turn to narratives rests on an essential cognitive reality: Narratives and stories are basic to social understanding; through stories we make meaning in our lives. They do this by imposing a coherent interpretation on the whirl of events and actions around us. At the cultural level, narratives serve to give cohesion to shared beliefs and to transmit basic values. At the individual level, people tell narratives about their own lives that enable them to understand both who they are and where they are headed. The narrative form—or storytelling—is thus the domain of the individual's pattern of making sense of his or her experience and the domain of the spoken exchange in everyday interactions, including learning. In particular, the narrative form furnishes communication with the particular details that constitute the stuff of which meaning is made.[4] Through the dialogic act of storytelling, individuals describe and assess their social positions in their communities, grasp the goals and values of their groups, internalize social conventions, and understand who they are vis-à-vis one another.

Policy makers as learners turn to narratives to make sense of their own situation and to develop strategies for change, incremental or transformational. Public policy easily translates into the narrative form: the problem situation to be solved is laid out as the beginning of the policy story, the middle or event introduces the policy interventions, and the end shows the consequential outcomes. Deborah Stone (1989) makes it clear that the reliance on policy narratives is evident even in the most casual examination of policy discussions, whether in everyday or official form. She shows the ways in which policy controversies often turn on the story lines—typically about crisis or decline in the state of things— rather than on the facts typically presented by the policy analysis. What frequently seems to be a conflict over facts, as Stone explains, is, in actuality, a disagreement about the basic story.

Deliberation: Reflexivity and Dialectics

After the narrative phase, the transformative learning turns to a deliberative confrontation with the problem or threatening situation. This is understood as the "dilemma" and becomes the object of exploration. The task in both learning theory and policy analysis is to make apparent the contradictions related to this anxiety-producing dilemma. During this phase, a "transactional" conversation takes place, involving an analytic deliberation about the evidence and arguments pertaining to alternative viewpoints.

The emphasis on deliberation resonates with the extensive discussion of deliberative politics and deliberative democracy in contemporary political theory (for example, see the Dryzek and Hendriks chapter in this book). Even though deliberation seldom solves the policy problems at issue, engagement in the process itself typically facilitates various kinds of learning. Some participants, in fact, describe the experience as self-development, even as potentially personal self-transformation, that leads to new social engagements. Through the experience of deliberation, these actors could be said to have engaged in processes of transformative learning.

But realizing this potential is more the exception than the rule. Basically, most deliberative practices are rather narrowly problem-oriented; they are geared to conflicts that revolve around established interests. As such, these strategies fail to take into account the fact that the problems to which they are addressed often have much deeper roots. So designed, deliberation cannot untangle the problems it sets out to "solve." Typically, only topics deemed politically acceptable are available for discussion. Discussions about restructuring basic social and political power relationship or redistributing resources are seldom options.

Deliberation in transformative learning approaches this process of enlightenment through a dialectical logic. In contrast to analytical logic, which is based on consensus, dialectical logic uses methods of conflict to surface underlying assumptions, including tacit assumptions. It seeks to represent the discursive confrontation of subjective interpretations; its goal of a dialectical clash among interpretations is a constructive synthesis that leads to new understandings (Lincoln and Guba 1985:41). Such dialectically generated consensus does not rest on a reality independent of those who shape and share it. As long as there remains the possibility of further confrontation with other points of view, the construction of a consensus is never finished or complete. The continuing discursive confrontation with other constructs is the essential epistemological principle of transformative learning. There can be progress in the production of consensus, but such knowledge can never be proven in the standard scientific sense of the concept.

An essential part of the "transactional conversation" is an analytic deliberation about the evidence and arguments pertaining to alternative narratives and the points of view they represent. The job of the planner or analyst—now understood as facilitators of new learning—is not just to tell a story. It is to discursively translate a narrative into an argument, or to tease out the argument implicitly embedded in the story. This is important to recognize, since different people construct different arguments out of the same narrative, even though the author or storyteller may have had something in particular in mind.

Facilitating Transformative Learning:
Contending with Reason and Emotion

The facilitation of transformative learning has roots in the emancipatory orientation of critical theory. Grounded in the ideal of deliberative empowerment, transformative learning sets out an alternative approach that assists both citizens and decision makers in understanding proposed courses of action according to their implications for democratic politics and social justice. Such work has often presented itself as an effort to further develop both Dewey's (1927) idea of the social sciences taking on the task of citizen enlightenment through the facilitation of public deliberation and, in more practical terms, Lasswell's (1951) concept of a "policy science of democracy."

Insofar as the goal is public enlightenment, the question of learning is once again front and center; that is, the underlying issue is that of social and political learning. Working at the intersection between narrative dialogue and formal disciplinary discourses, transformative learning assists clients and citizens in engaging in deliberation about evidence and arguments. It does this by posing questions, bringing relevant information to bear on them, or, in some cases, by helping citizens conduct their own local investigations. In the process, it takes into account the deeper experiential and emotional components that underlie the issues. As such, the task of transformative planners or policy analysts has to be reconfigured; they become facilitators of learning. Such facilitation can take place in two ways. It can involve a written text that lays out and discursively explores the various second-order relationships—social meanings and ideological elements—that underlie particular courses of action, with the objective of making the arguments and the assumptions on which they are based both accessible and clear. Or, second, it can involve direct personal interactions with citizens that assist them in thinking through a problem and the issues it raises. These could include opportunities for deliberations such as citizen juries or consensus conferences.

The goal of facilitation is "challenging learners with alternative ways of interpreting their experience" and presenting them with "ideas and behaviors that cause them to examine critically their values, ways of acting and the assumptions by which they live" (Brookfield 1986:3). Rather than distorting the totality of human experience by reducing it to dimensions amenable to treatment—that is, to difficulties to be solved—these processes of problematization help people develop an alternative narrative about their own social reality that can facilitate a critical understanding that can empower them to change their own relationship to the social and natural worlds in which they live (Freire 1973).

The concept of facilitator is not new to the policy and planning literature. Indeed, in recent decades facilitation has become something of formal service offered by consultants. Facilitation of this sort typically focuses on the first-order issues posed by the problem at hand. But there are also others, such as Fischer (2003:221), Healey (2006), Innes and Booher (2003), Forester (1999), and Allain (2010), who call for a more critical approach to deliberative facilitation. Forester (1999) conceptualizes the task as assisting planners to critically reflect on practices in ways that make them more aware of the hidden forms of communicative power involved in planning practices. As Sophie Allain (2010) put it, "beyond helping citizens or clients to analyze the logic of their situation through their discourses, the analyst strives to link this specific situation to the larger social structures, which shape it." The task of such policy analysts and planners "is not only to give an account of the arguments given by the participants, in order to understand the local situation, but also to conduct a critical assessment of the warrants, in order to identify the ideological and values assumptions involved in justifying the backing of the warrants."

Lyn Carson and Janette Hartz-Karp argue that the facilitator must "provide open dialogue, access to information, respect, space to understand and reframe issues and movement towards consensus" (2005: 122). Facilitation further needs to maintain a focus on the issues while remaining comfortable enough for those involved that they feel free not only to speak but to change their views as a result of discursive interactions. Emotional expression is also welcomed, but it should contribute to facilitating constructive argumentation.

Fischer (2000) has illustrated this process through a case study of the People's Planning Campaign in Kerala, India. Pursuing a devolutionary program of village-level participatory planning as a strategy to both change the existing power structure and improve governmental effectiveness, the government of Kerala established district planning councils empowered to establish the state's Five-Year Plan (Isaac and Heller 2003). Each village formulated a development plan that spelled out local needs, specific projects to be advanced, financing requirements, procedures for deciding beneficiaries, and a system for monitoring the outcomes. Basic to the process of empowerment was the task of deliberative facilitation, carried out by the Science for the People movement (referred to as "KSSP"), a unique sociocultural movement influenced by Freire's pedagogical approach.

The process included working with people who had never participated—people who typically began with the belief that they did not have the capacities to be a part of a deliberative process; the main contribution of the approach was to make clear a basic message: these deliberations were for the people on their own terms. Toward this end, the approach began by drawing out the relevant community histories and local knowledge. That is, by "problematizing" the social marginality of the community members, particularly peasant farmers, these narratives were then used to assist them in examining their own beliefs and identities in ways that helped them reflect on established understandings of the existing relationships of the social structure (Fischer 2000). In the process of learning and discussing the ways in which the social order is structured and communicated, community members were assisted in exploring the cultural politics that define and solidify their own "subject positions" in the dominant discourses of those who exercise social and political power. Through the construction of alternative understandings, the participants fashioned networks of solidarity, built confidence in their own knowledge and capabilities, and, in the process, developed a sense of own their abilities to address their own interests and needs.

After the campaign's decentralized participatory structures were developed, the project confronted a more specific question: what body of information would be the basis upon which the discussions in the decentralized deliberations would took place? Much of the information needed to assess the physical and social characteristics of the local areas was unavailable. To deal with this, KSSP combined the methods of critical pedagogy with techniques of rural resource mapping to develop a way of gathering the information needed for the deliberations. The bridge across these two activities—pedagogy and resource mapping—was the community members' "local knowledge" of their local districts, social as well as physical. Such knowledge became a vehicle for both the data collection and the cultural valorization of the political context that enlivened and gave substance to the deliberations of the popular assemblies.

One of the major challenges of the practice of such facilitation concerns the question of how to deal with passion and emotional expression. More than just the rational exchange of ideas, the facilitation of a transformational interaction involves a highly complex dialogue "in which the personalities of the individuals involved, the contextual setting for the educational transaction, and the prevailing political climate affect the nature and form of learning" (Brookfield 1986:3). The dialogue is likened to a "transactional drama" in which the philosophies, personalities, and priorities "of the chief players interact continuously to influence the nature, direction, and form of subsequent learning" (Brookfield 1986). Sometimes this dialogue can take the form of a story or a drama, using video equipment, drawings, mapping procedures, and forms of role playing.

Delving into the deeper emotional realm plays a special role in transformational learning. Many of our social meanings and tacit understandings are anchored to specific emotions and are not readily available for rational deliberation. Often, as David Howarth and Steven Griggs argue in chapter 10 of this book, particular political and social views are emotionally grounded in ways that stabilize difficult situations and make them manageable. Drawing on Lacan's "logic of fantasy," they point to the ways that ideological assumptions and basic worldviews are emotionally forged to protect individuals from the uncertainties of particular social conflicts and, in effect, to naturalize particular relations of domination in which a subject is enmeshed. Although this deeper psychological dimension poses difficult problems for social deliberation and learning, it needs to be recognized and dealt with.

The role of emotions is beginning to get more attention in planning and policy deliberation. Emotion and the kinds of impassioned rhetoric associated with it have long been portrayed as the enemy of rationality. But more recent investigation in both philosophy and neuroscience show the intricate ways that reason and emotion are bound together, even depend on one another. Martha Nussbaum (2001) persuasively argues that emotions are themselves suffused with a form of tacit intelligence. Emotions are, in this view, composites of feelings and beliefs. Such a perspective is supported by contemporary research in neuroscience, which shows that emotions often actually trigger rather than hinder reason (Marcus 2002).

Social transformations in politics, as with successful therapy, require political and psychological breakthroughs capable of opening new pathways to individual growth and social engagement. They involve processes of public learning aimed at shifting social values and the institutional practices that embody them. Although there is no guarantee of success, such processes appear to be the only way forward in cases where deep-seated, emotionally based social conflicts have long stymied conventional techniques of conflict negotiation.[5] Particularly important to such processes is the role of empathy—the capacity to experience and understand things the way someone else does—as a basic aspect of social life. When people empathize with one another, the process tends to connect their sense of identity and can also facilitate social trust.

We can gain important insights into how to deal with such emotional conflict from several planning experiences reported by Leonie Sandercock. As she explains, when the conflicting parties "involved in a dispute have been at odds for generations, or come from disparate cultural traditions, or where there is a history of marginalization, something more than the usual methods of negotiation and mediation are needed" (2003:159). In cases in which face-to-face exchanges are unworkable owing to histories of conflict, discursive design processes are needed that offer the parties opportunities to uncover problems and issues that are difficult to approach—if they are at all approachable—through rational-deliberative processes (159). When emotional intensity hinders a more formal deliberation, participants need a forum that allows them to tell the stories—that is, to make public the narratives—that convey their feelings.

Drawing on a number of practical experiences, Sandercock (2003) presents an approach that begins with the introduction of an expressive state before moving on to deliberation and negotiations. Such a process relies on a series of preparatory meetings in which a planning team meets separately with the conflicting groups. Focused on the hopes and fears of those involved, such meetings would typically take place in emotionally secure settings, such as the living spaces of the various parties. The activity in this initial phase is primarily focused on storytelling. Just as the residents tell their stories to each other, here they present them to the planners, whose goal is to listen rather than to intervene.

After these preparatory discussions, a "speak-out" is organized in which each of the groups is encouraged to participate (Sandercock 2003:159). The goal here is to get community groups to express their feelings before the discussion turns to specific plans or programs. Specifically, the objective is to encourage people to say what they feel in the presence of the other groups—to speak the unspeakable—no matter how unpleasant or how painful it might be for the others to hear (Forester 2000). This "speaking out" can also serve to generate empathy among those carrying destructive anger, fear of betrayal, grievances over previous losses, and the like. It is not that through their simple articulation conflicts will be altogether eliminated, but rather that the speak-out can be used to reduce the levels of tension enough to make possible a workable level of discussion. Organizing this airing of underlying concerns and feelings can create a basis for building a new trust capable of encouraging the participants to engage in the kinds of discussion that can make new agreements possible and move the community forward.

To be sure, this kind of work requires practitioners to be knowledgeable and fluent in various modes of communication, from storytelling and listening to interpreting visual and body language. We thus turn to the concluding discussion of this chapter, in which we focus on methods and their implications for a new kind of professional education.

Methods and Educational Implications

It should be clear that various kinds of learning—and unlearning—are taking place at every turn and that there is nothing simple about transformational learning. Given its multidimensionality—both cognitive and emotive—there can be no one single way to approach this work. Most importantly, the approach has to be imaginatively conceived, based on the particular circumstances of the situation to be dealt with, attentive to the experiences and educational levels of the participants, aware of cultural assumptions, however implicit they may be, and sensitive to power dynamics that have shaped the situation. The approach relies on modes of reasoning that focus on social meaning, that are pursued through discourse and dialectical argumentation, and that are understood as the specialized use of dialogue in search of common understandings and evaluations of interpretations or beliefs. It also involves assessing the reasons (both normative and factual) advanced for supporting evidence and arguments and examining alternative meanings perspectives. When such discourse is encouraged, and thus becomes the stuff of deliberation, it can tap individual and collective experiences in ways that lead to deeper understandings and more informed judgments.

Transformative learning thus poses many sophisticated challenges for professional education. One concerns the educational curriculum itself. Once we recognize that this professional work is grounded in a kind of teaching that is more a creative art than a science, we venture into relatively unknown pedagogical territory. Scientific methodology texts can be organized as if they were straightforward, though not simple, cookbooks. However, not only are there no formulas for the art form upon which transformative learning depends, but also little is known about the creative impulse itself and about the kinds of experiences in which it might be called upon and strengthened. How do we develop practitioners who can intuitively sense openings and opportunities to gain insights into complex human affairs? How do we make evident to professionals that their expertise is only tentative, that grappling with questions and a wide range of meanings and interpretations is at the very heart of their work? How do we encourage policy analysts to recognize and take seriously the fact that their clients also bring their own valuable knowledge to the table? If there are answers to these kinds of questions, they no doubt include greater exposure to the creative arts, to history, literature, and to an array of cultural studies—all areas typically neglected in professional education.

An inherently creative exercise, problem posing in transformative learning can be neither explained nor taught from the technical, positivist perspective that has informed much of professional practice in planning and policy science. There is no particular textbook methodology for engaging in this kind of transformative learning. Indeed, different practitioners discuss it in different terms, based in significant part on their own experiences.

When it comes to interactive facilitation, it is generally agreed that an authentic, democratic discursive process depends on particular conditions for its realization. To participate fully and freely, people have to find themselves in situations in which they are free of coercive pressures, have accurate information, are able to assess arguments and examine evidence, can be empathetically open to others' points of view, are able to carefully attend to how others think and feel, and have equal chances to participate in the deliberative process (see, e.g., Mezirow 2009; Mezirow and Associates 2000:13). Such conditions of "ideal speech" can never be fully realized, but the criteria can be used to judge some discursive spaces as better than others and to assess whether or not enough of the conditions are met to even enter into such a process.

If new forms of cooperative learning are to work, they have to be conducted by people with high levels of personal awareness, with a willingness to accept the tentativeness of their own conclusions, with an interest in acknowledging and evaluating their own tacit assumptions, with a tolerance for ambiguities, with a desire to listen to ideas and feelings often very different from what they best know, and, overall, with a genuine reflective spirit. This requires confronting the social, emotional, and intellectual distances that separate the professional from the client's experiential life-world. Greater emphasis has to be placed on interpersonal skills and on what William Torbert (1991) has defined as "transformational leadership."

This new role of the educator-as-facilitator, as mentor, has to be learned (Herman and Mandell 2004). The situation is made even more difficult by the fact that discussions touching upon social and political problems and policy often move toward ideological critique. This raises often subtle ethical questions and can easily close off discussions that need to take place. Although clearly political, a commitment to dialogue is not to be confused with a commitment to a doctrine or ideology. The transformative practitioner, the professional committed to guiding a deliberative process, needs to be committed to democratic values. The facilitation of transformative learning must follow ethical guidelines that themselves need to be articulated and agreed upon. Ruling out manipulation, educators must encourage learners to choose freely from among a wide range of viewpoints.

Professional practitioners need to have sufficient self-knowledge and sensitivity to others to be able to help learners deal with personal and interpersonal conflicts in "meaning perspectives" that often create barriers to the negotiation of difficult issues and life transitions. And educators need to be able to distinguish between these participants and those whose personal problems require professional psychotherapeutic attention. Learning to acknowledge and work within the limits of one's understanding is a key element of the development of transformative professionals.

Conclusion

The notion of learning has become ubiquitous in the social sciences. And surely some of the focus on learning has gained a distinctive ideological tint, as institutions of all kinds, searching for flexibility and grappling with problems that betray easy technical fixes, look for ways to think about what needs to be known and what problems need to be solved. Still, attention to learning also opens up a rich and critical orientation to planning and policy analysis. It pushes us to acknowledge the limits of a technocratic orientation and demands that we ask questions about the ways in which our decisions and the policy and planning processes upon which we depend are themselves embedded in assumptions that often go unacknowledged.

Taking seriously the insights of transformational learning theory thus not only offers a new perspective on the role of the expert and calls into question the very notion of expert knowledge; it also asks about the ways in which all participants in any policy arena can be understood to be co-learners seeking the kind of knowledge and insight needed to respond to any question. In this way, the call to learning makes us aware of the limits of what we know and of the factors that often make changing what we take for granted extremely difficult. By reimagining policy analysts as facilitators of learning and the public as citizens actively engaged in making sense of their world, a focus on learning can be seen as integral to more participatory and democratic politics.

Notes

1. As noted in the introduction to this book, policy analysis has become one of the methods of planning as well as political science and policy studies generally. Although there used to be a discussion about the differences between policy analysis and planning, many scholars and practitioners in planning have dropped the distinction and define themselves as policy analysts. Policy analysis, in this regard, is today primary understood to be an interdisciplinary enterprise.

2. This is also the case in the European Union as well as in the United States. See the Lifelong Learning page on the web site of the European Union.

3. Argyris and Schön apply their model to learning in business organizations that are embedded in a capitalist economy. Double-loop learning, as they present it, thus tends to neglect underlying ideological premises and thus can be seen as unnecessarily truncated (Brookfield 2005:11). Still, the very notion of "double-loop learning" alerts us to and opens up this deeper level of taken-for-granted assumptions and structures.

4. A good narrative, as Kaplan explains, "grasps together a variety of disparate information and thoughts by weaving them into a plot. Stringing together the beginning and middle of a story with a conclusion, a narrative pulls together a variety of components—metaphors, categories, markings, and other sense-making elements—to come to a conclusion that flows naturally out of these factors." It assists us "to make sense of complex

situations occurring with an environment of conflicting values" (1993:172). In the process, the story typically forges the unknown with the known patterns. More than a chronicle of events, which simply lists things according to their place on a time line (Kaplan 1993), a good narrative not only conveys a meaning to the listener but offers the listener or reader a way of seeing and thinking about events that points to implications requiring further attention or consideration.

5. One of the most important examples of such a process was that carried out by the South African Truth and Reconciliation Commission (described on the web site of the Commission).

References

Allain, S. 2010. "Framing the Policy Analyst as a Mediator to Cope with the Problem of Collective Action." Paper presented at the International Conference on Interpretive Policy Analysis, Grenoble, June 23–25.
Argyris, C., and D. A. Schön. 1996. *Organizational Learning II: Theory, Method and Practice.* Reading, Mass.: Addison-Wesley.
Bateson, G. 2000. *Steps to an Ecology of the Mind: Collected Essays in Anthropology, Psychiatry, Evolution and Epistemology.* Chicago: University of Chicago Press.
Brookfield, S. D. 1986. *Understanding and Facilitating Adult Learning.* San Francisco: Jossey-Bass.
———. 2005. *The Power of Critical Theory: Liberating Adult Learning and Teaching.* San Francisco: Jossey-Bass.
Carson, L., and J. Hartz-Karp. 2005. "Adapting and Combining Deliberative Designs: Juries, Polls, and Forums." In *The Deliberative Democracy Handbook,* edited by J. Gastl and P. Levine, 120–38. San Francisco: Jossey-Bass.
Dewey, J. 1927. *The Public and Its Problems.* New York: Swallow.
Edelman, M. 1988. *Constructing the Public Spectacle.* Chicago: University of Chicago Press.
———. 1995. *Evaluating Public Policy.* Belmont, Calif.: Wadsworth.
———. 2000. *Citizens, Experts and the Environment: The Politics of Local Knowledge.* Durham: Duke University Press.
———. 2003. *Reframing Public Policy: Discursive Politics and Deliberative Practices.* Oxford: Oxford University Press.
Fischer, F., and A. Mandell. 2009. "Transformative Learning through Deliberation: Social Assumptions and the Tacit Dimension." In *Democracy and Expertise: Reorienting Policy Inquiry,* ed. F. Fischer, 214–44. Oxford: Oxford University Press.
Forester, J. 1999. *The Deliberative Practitioner: Encouraging Participatory Planning Processes.* Cambridge: Cambridge University Press.

———. 2000. "Multicultural Planning in Deed: Lessons from the Mediation Practice of Shirley Solomon and Larry Sherman." In *Urban Planning in a Multicultural Society*, edited by M. Burayidi. Westport, Conn.: Praeger.

Freeman, R. 2006. "Learning in Public Policy." In *The Oxford Handbook of Public Policy*, edited by M. Moran, M. Rein, and R. E. Goodin, 367–88. Oxford: Oxford University Press.

Freire, P. 1970. *Pedagogy of the Oppressed*. New York: Seabury.

———. 1973. *Education for Critical Consciousness*. New York: Seabury.

Friedmann, J. 1987. *Planning in the Public Domain: From Knowledge to Action*. Princeton: Princeton University Press.

Hall, P. A. 1993. "Policy Paradigms, Social Learning and the State: The Case of Economic Policymaking in Britain." *Comparative Politics* 25:275–96.

Healey, P. 2006. *Collaborative Planning*. London: Palgrave Macmillan.

Heclo, H. 1972. "Review Article: Policy Analysis." *British Journal of Political Science* 2:83–108.

———. 1974. *Modern Social Politics in Britain and Sweden: From Relief to Income Maintenance*. New Haven: Yale University Press.

Herman, L., and A. Mandell. 2004. *From Teaching to Mentoring: Principle and Practice, Dialogue and Life in Adult Education*. London: Routledge.

Innes, J. J., and D. E. Booher. 2003. "Collaborative Policymaking: Governance through Dialogue." In *Deliberative Policy Analysis*, edited by M. A. Hajer and H. Wagenaar, 33–59. Cambridge: Cambridge University Press.

Isaac, T. H., and P. Heller. 2003. "Democracy and Development: Decentralized Planning in Kerala." In *Deepening Democracy*, edited by A. Fung and E. O. Wright, 77–102. New York: Verso.

Kaplan, T. J. 1993. "Reading Policy Narratives: Beginnings, Middles, and Ends." In *The Argumentative Turn in Policy Analysis and Planning*, edited by F. Fischer and J. Forester, 167–85. Durham: Duke University Press.

Kitchenham, A. 2008. "The Evolution of Jack Mezirow's Transformative Learning Theory." *Journal of Transformative Education* 6(2):104–23.

Lasswell, H. 1951. "The Policy Orientation." In *The Policy Sciences*, edited by H. Lasswell and D. Lerner. Stanford: Stanford University Press.

Lincoln, Y. S., and E. G. Guba. 1985. *Naturalistic Inquiry*. Newbury Park, Calif.: Sage.

Loder, J. I. 1981. *The Transforming Moment: Understanding Convictional Experiences*. San Francisco: Harper and Row.

Majone, G. 1989. *Evidence, Argument, and Persuasion in the Policy Process*. New Haven: Yale University Press.

Marcus, G. E. 2002. *The Sentimental Citizen: Emotion in Democratic Politics*. University Park: Pennsylvania State University Press.

Mezirow, J. 2009. "Transformative Learning Theory." In *Transformative Learning Theory in Practice: Community, Workplace, and Higher Educa-*

tion, edited by J. Mezirow, E. Taylor, and Associates, 18–32. San Francisco: Jossey-Bass.

Mezirow, J., and Associates. 2000. *Learning as Transformation: Critical Perspectives on a Theory in Progress.* San Francisco: Jossey-Bass.

Nussbaum, M. 2001. *Upheavals of Thought: The Intelligence of Emotions.* Cambridge: Cambridge University Press.

———. 2004. *Hiding from Humanity: Disgust, Shame, and the Law.* Princeton: Princeton University Press.

Polanyi, M. 1966. *The Tacit Dimension.* Garden City, N.Y.: Doubleday.

Sabatier, P. A. 1988. "An Advocacy Coalition Framework of Policy Change and the Role of Policy-Oriented Learning Therein." *Policy Sciences* 21: 129–68.

Sandercock, L. 2003. "Dreaming the Sustainable City: Organizing Hope, Negotiating Fear, Mediating Memory." In *Story and Sustainability: Planning, Practice, and Possibility for American Cities*, edited by B. Eckstein and J. A. Throgmorton, 143–64. Cambridge: MIT Press.

Schön, D. A. 1973. *Beyond the Stable State: Public and Private Learning in a Changing Society.* Harmondsworth: Penguin.

———. 1983. *The Reflective Practitioner: How Professionals Think in Action.* New York: Basic.

Stone, D. 1989. "Causal Stories and the Formation of Policy Agendas." *Political Science Quarterly* 104:281–300.

Torbert, W. 1991. *The Power of Balance: Transforming Self, Society, and Scientific Inquiry.* Newbury Park, Calif.: Sage.

Wildemeersch, D., and W. Leirman. 1988. "The Facilitation of the Life-World Transformation." *Adult Education Quarterly* 39:19–30.

Yanow, D. 1996. *How Does a Policy Mean?* Washington: Georgetown University Press.

Contributors

GIOVANNI ATTILI is a researcher and teacher of urban and regional systems at University of Rome, La Sapienza, where he received his Ph.D. He received the "G. Ferraro" award for the best urban planning Ph.D. thesis in Italy in 2005. His research interests are focused in particular on the use of "images" and multimedia as catalysts of social interactions in urban-planning processes, storytelling in planning theory and practice, and the challenges of coexistence in ethno-diverse landscapes.

HUBERTUS BUCHSTEIN is Professor for Political Theory and the History of Political Ideas at Greifswald University, Germany, and Fellow at the Wissenschaftskolleg Berlin in 2012–13. Currently, he is the president of the German Political Science Association as well as a member of the editorial board of *Constellations*. His research interests are focused on theories of democracy, in particular on political procedures; the history of political science as a discipline; and critical theory. His recent publications include *Demokratie und Lotterie* (Campus Verlag, 2009), "Randomizing Europe—The Lottery as a Decision-Making Procedure for Policy Creation in the EU" (*Critical Policy Studies* 3:29–59), and *Demokratiepolitik* (Nomos, 2011).

STEPHEN COLEMAN is Professor of Political Communication at the Institute of Communications Studies, University of Leeds. His two most recently published books are *The Internet and Democratic Citizenship: Theory, Practice, and Policy* (with Jay G. Blumler, Cambridge University Press, 2009) and *The Media and the Public: "Them" and "Us" in Media Discourse* (with Karen Ross, Wiley-Blackwell, 2010). His next book, exploring the affective and aesthetic dimensions of democratic engagement, will be published by Cambridge University Press.

JOHN S. DRYZEK is Australian Research Council Federation Fellow and Professor of Political Science in the Centre for Deliberative Democracy and Global Governance, Australian National University. His recent books include *Theories of the Democratic State* (with Patrick Dunleavy, Palgrave Macmillan, 2009), *Foundations and Frontiers of Deliberative Governance* (Oxford University Press, 2010), and *The Oxford Handbook of Climate Change and Society* (coedited with Richard B. Norgaard and David Schlosberg, Oxford University Press, 2011).

FRANK FISCHER is Professor of Politics and Global Affairs at Rutgers University, and he teaches about public policy and planning at the university's E. J. Bloustein School of Planning and Public Policy. He is a senior faculty fellow at the University of Kassel in Germany, where he teaches about global public policy, foreign policy in the United States, and comparative and global environmental politics. In addition, he is a co-organizer of the APSA Conference Group on Critical Policy Studies and a member of the Advisory Committee of the European Consortium of Political Research's Standing Committee on Theoretical Perspectives in Policy Analysis. He is also a coeditor of the journal *Critical Policy Studies*.

HERBERT GOTTWEIS is a professor in the Department of Political Science at the University of Vienna. He is also a visiting professor at the United Nations University, Tokyo, and at Kyung Hee University, South Korea. Among his book publications are *The Global Politics of Human Embryonic Stem Cell Science: Regenerative Medicine in Transition* (with Brian Salter and Catherine Waldby, Palgrave, 2009), *Biobanks: Governance in Comparative Perspective* (coedited with Alan Petersen, Routledge, 2008), and *Governing Molecules: The Discursive Politics of Genetic Engineering in Europe and the United States* (MIT Press, 1998).

STEVEN GRIGGS is Reader in Local Governance in the Department of Politics and Public Policy at De Montfort University. He has research interests in political discourse theory and local government and environmental policy making, particularly aviation policy and protests against airport expansion. Steven is a coauthor with David Howarth of *The Politics of "Sustainable Aviation"* (Manchester University Press, forthcoming). Currently he is engaged in a two-year research program into the strategic policy responses of local government's response to public spending cuts in the United Kingdom. He is also a coeditor of *Critical Policy Studies*.

MARY HAWKESWORTH is Professor of Women's and Gender Studies and Political Science at Rutgers University. Her teaching and research interests include feminist theory, women and politics, contemporary political philosophy, philosophy of science, and social policy. Her major works include *Political Worlds of Women: Activism, Advocacy, and Governance in the Twenty-First Century* (Westview, 2012), *War and Terror: Feminist Perspectives* (coedited with Karen Alexander, University of Chicago Press, 2008), *Globalization and Feminist Activism* (Rowman and Littlefield, 2006), *Feminist Inquiry: From Political Conviction to Methodological Innovation* (Rutgers University Press, 2006), *Women, Democracy and Globalization in North America* (Palgrave, 2006), *The Encyclopedia of Government and Politics* (2nd revised ed., Routledge, 2003), and *Gender, Globalization and Democratization* (as coeditor, Rowman and Littlefield, 2001). She currently serves as the editor of *Signs: Journal of Women in Culture and Society*.

PATSY HEALEY is Professor Emeritus in the School of Architecture, Planning and Landscape at Newcastle University (United Kingdom). She is a specialist in planning theory and the practice of strategic planning and urban regeneration policies, and has worked on planning and development practices in various parts of the world. She is the author of several widely read books in the planning field, including *Collaborative Planning: Shaping Places in Fragmented Societies* (1997, 2nd ed., Palgrave, 2006), *Urban Complexity and Spatial Strategies* (Routledge, 2007), and *Making Better Places* (Palgrave, 2010).

CAROLYN M. HENDRIKS is a Senior Lecturer at the Crawford School of Economics and Government at the Australian National University. Her work examines the democratic practices of contemporary governance, particularly with respect to public deliberation, inclusion, and political representation. She has taught and published widely on the application and politics of inclusive and deliberative forms of citizen engagement. Her book *The Politics of Public Deliberation* (Palgrave, 2011) explores the interface between citizen engagement and interest advocacy.

DAVID HOWARTH is a Reader in Political Theory in the Department of Government at the University of Essex and Co-Director of the Centre for Theoretical Studies. His publications include *Discourse* (Open University Press, 2000) and *Logics of Critical Explanation in Social and Political Theory* (with Jason Glynos, Routledge, 2007). He is currently completing a book titled *Poststructuralism and After: Structure, Agency and Power* and (with Steven Griggs) a volume titled *Reframing Sustainable Aviation: Rhetoric, Power and Public Policy* (Manchester University Press, forthcoming).

DIRK JÖRKE, Heisenberg Fellow of the German Research Foundation and Assistant Professor of Political Science at the University of Greifswald (Germany), specializes in political theory with particular emphases on the democratic theory, American pragmatism, and the history of political ideas. His recent work includes *Kritik demokratischer Praxis: Eine ideengeschichtliche Studie* (Nomos, 2011), *Politische Anthropologie: Geschichte–Gegenwart–Möglichkeiten* (coedited with Bernd Ladwig, Nomos, 2009), "The Epistemic Turn of Critical Theory: Implications for Deliberative Politics and Policy-Making" (*Critical Policy Studies* 3:440–446), and *Demokratie als Erfahrung: John Dewey und die politische Philosophie der Gegenwart* (Verlag für Sozialwissenschaften, 2003).

ALAN MANDELL is College Professor of Adult Learning and Mentoring at SUNY Empire State College. He has served as administrator, mentor in the social sciences, and director of the college's Mentoring Institute. With Elana Michelson, he is the author of *Portfolio Development and the Assessment of Prior Learning* (Stylus, 2004). With Lee Herman, he has written many essays and book chapters on adult learning and mentoring, including *From Teaching to Mentoring: Principle and Practice, Dialogue and Life in Adult Education* (Routledge, 2004). One of Mandell and Herman's recent essays, "Mentoring: When Learners Make the Learning," is included in *Transformative Learning in Practice*, edited by Jack Mezirow and Edward Taylor (Jossey-Bass, 2009). His ongoing work with Frank Fischer includes the essay "Michael Polanyi's Republic of Science: The Tacit Dimension" (*Science as Culture*, 18[1], 2009).

LEONIE SANDERCOCK is a professor in the School of Community and Regional Planning at the University of British Columbia, and is the recipient of the Dale Prize for Excellence in Urban and Regional Planning, the Paul Davidoff Award for best book in planning, the Harmony Gold Screenwriting Award, and the BMW Award for Intercultural Learning. Her research interests focus on planning in multicultural cities, indigenous planning, and the importance of storytelling and multimedia in planning. She is the author of a dozen books, including *Towards Cosmopolis: Planning for Multicultural Cities* (John Wiley, 1998), *Cosmopolis II: Mongrel Cities of the 21st Century* (Continuum, 2003), and *Multimedia Explorations in Urban Policy and Planning* (coedited with Giovanni Attili, Springer, 2010). She has also directed two documentaries (with Giovanni Attili): one is about the immigrant experience in Vancouver and the other deals with conflicts between First Nations and settlers in Burns Lake, British Columbia.

VIVIEN A. SCHMIDT is Jean Monnet Chair of European Integration, Professor of International Relations and Political Science, Founding Director of the Center for the Study of Europe, and Director of the Center for International Relations at Boston University. Her recent publications include *Debating Political Identity and Legitimacy in the European Union* (coedited with S. Lucarelli and F. Cerutti, Routledge, 2011), *Democracy in Europe* (Oxford University Press, 2006), *The Futures of European Capitalism* (Oxford University Press, 2002), "Discursive Institutionalism: The Explanatory Power of Ideas and Discourse" (*Annual Review of Political Science*, 2008), and "Putting the Political Back into Political Economy by Bringing the State Back in Yet Again" (*World Politics*, 2009).

SANFORD F. SCHRAM teaches about social theory and social policy at the Graduate School of Social Work and Social Research, Bryn Mawr College, and is an affiliate to the National Poverty Center at the University of Michigan–Ann Arbor. He is the author of ten books, including *Words of Welfare: The Poverty of Social Science and the Social Science of Poverty* (University of Minnesota Press, 1995), which won the Michael Harrington Award from the American Political Science Association, and, most recently, *Disciplining the Poor: Neoliberal Paternalism and the Persistent Power of Race* (University of Chicago Press, 2011), coauthored with his longtime collaborators Joe Soss and Rich Fording.

Index

action: based on social meaning, 353; Foucault on power exercised through the individual, 286; policy analysis and action, 16; policy narratives used in social construction of policy, 221; Schön's "reflection in action," 348; social learning and, 345–46; speech act theory and action, 217; values, purposes, ideas, and goals motivating, 16. *See also* collective action

action research. *See* community-based action research

actor network, 150–55, 161–64; policy, 37, 40–45, 91–105, 150–74

advocacy coalitions, 101

agency: based on sentient agents' background and foreground abilities, 92–95; creative, 60; social interactions and role of, 60

agency-structure debate, 95

agendas: deliberation and agendas, 174n.5; deliberative forum, 40–41; policy entrepreneurs setting the agenda, 106

Alexander, Jeffrey, 24

Althusser, Louis, 314

AmericaSpeaks Foundation, 42

Amossy, Ruth, 22, 217

argumentative communication: causal influence on political change by, 17; Debategraph system to track online, 165–66; deliberative decision making and using better, 294–98; interests, institutions, and cultural context of, 16–17; policy analysis assessed as, 271; procedural rules for shared meaning of, 105–7. *See also* collective argumentation; communicative practices

argumentative policy discourse: argumentative situation, 10; communicative practices of, 14–15; constructing argumentation from, 11–12; deliberation versus argumentation in, 9–10; developing terminology for, 9; influences on development of, 7–9. *See also* discourse; rhetoric/rhetorical argument

argumentative policy inquiry: as challenging beliefs in value-free policy analysis, 2; examining the Internet as a policy deliberation space, 20–21; linking postpositivist epistemology with social and political theory, 1, 8. *See also* deliberation

argumentative turn: 271; characteristics of, 149–50

Argyris, C., 355

Aristotle, 22, 215, 216, 218

Attili, Giovanni, 21, 180

Austin, J. L., 8, 217, 271

Baiocchi, G., 47

Bakhtin, Mikhail Mikhailovich, 157

banking model of schooling, 349–50

beliefs: argumentative policy inquiry challenging, 2; meaning perspective narrative-dialogic process, 351. *See also* social meaning; values

Beneviste, E., 218
Bevir, Mark, 90
Bhashkar, Roy, 96
Bobbio, Noberto, 312
Booher, D. E., 359
Bourdieu, Pierre, 8, 90, 92, 93, 94, 241
BP oil disaster (2010), 5–6
British Columbia Citizens' Assembly, 47
Brundtland Commission, 137
Buchstein, Hubertus, 23, 271
Bush, George W., 222–23, 225, 229, 232
Bush administration: failed Iraq War policies of the, 5; stem cell policy of the, 222–25, 229

Canadian immigration policy, 180–81
capitalism: concerns over new varieties of, 4; Gramsci on "organized capitalism," 311; hegemonic discourses about, 16; Marxist perspective on, 314–15; new order of global and liberal, 3–4
Castells, M., 150, 152
Chambers, S., 35
change: political, 17, 90, 91–100, 105, 307; social, 240–41
Churchman, C. W., 181
citizens: collaborative governance planning inclusion of, 58–77; collaborative neighborhood change management role of, 64–67; collaborative planning driven by demands of, 62–63; deliberation "habits of the heart" of, 291–93; deliberation requiring representative sample of, 174n.5; as deliberative forum participants, 37, 40–45; facilitating transformative learning in, 358–64; Foucault's concept of governmentality and, 292–93; Internet's potential for construction of civic habits by, 170; lack of trust in representative government by, 169; online policy-making participation by, 167–69, 170; preparatory "speak-outs" held for, 363–64; regime exclusion of those lacking "appropriate" knowledge, 293, 294; Tocqueville on democratic political institutions and role of, 291–92; transformation through social learning, 347. *See also* deliberative forum participants; social movements
civil society: Gramsci's concept of, 313; interests rooted in, 316; separation of the state from, 315
Clinton administration, 222, 226, 229
cognitive dissonance theory, 93
Cohen, Joshua, 277
Coleman, Stephen, 20, 21, 149, 168, 174n.5
collaborative governance planning: citizen demands and, 62–63; ethical orientation of, 67, 76; managing neighborhood change through communicative, 64–67; promoting major projects through communicative, 68–70; reflecting on issues of communicative, 58–63; spatial development strategies for communicative, 70–75; three questions related to communicative approach to, 58, 75–77. *See also* policy planning
collective action: collaborative networking augmenting, 166; how the Internet solves problem of coordinating, 152–53. *See also* action; social movements
collective argumentation: Debategraph system to track online

deliberation and, 165–66; Internet impact on practices of, 150–74; online multivocal narratives to develop, 154–57; policy networking to develop and share, 161–64; procedurally governed form of, 9–10. *See also* argumentative communication

Collingwood Neighbourhood House (CNH) research study, 188–90, 201–3

communicative planning theory: collaborative dimensions of planning emphasized in, 59–63; description of, 59; managing neighborhood change application of, 64–67; promoting major projects application of, 68–70; spatial strategy making using, 70–75

communicative practices: argumentative policy application of, 14–15; collaborative planning through, 58–77; critical interpretive analysis emphasis on, 18; deliberation supported by, 11, 31–33, 34–37; description and uses of, 13; examining collaborative planning process use of, 19; how discursive institutionalism shapes discourse, 16, 19–20, 85–108; nondeliberative, 36; political action through institutional, 17; political discourse "pictorial turn" representation as, 13–14; reciprocity, 33–34; relationship between ideas and material interests in, 14–15; ruled out for deliberation, 34–35; social theory emphasis on, 13; Westminster-style adversarial debate, 31. *See also* argumentative communication; discourse; Internet

community-based action research: Collingwood Neighbourhood House (CNH), 188–200; dual inquiry, 180

consensus building, 35–36

consensus conferences (Denmark), 48

constructivism: narrative analysis perspective of, 186–87; public policy perspective in, 236; transformative social learning perspective in, 253, 348–49; understanding of action-oriented knowledge in, 349–50

constructivist-materialist debate, 95–96

Cox, Robert, 314

"crisis of the professions," 346–47

critical discourse analysis (CDA), 332

critical policy analysis, 324–25, 334–35; description and five-step process of, 323–25; explanation made in terms of logics, 324, 329–34; problematization, 324, 325–28; retroduction, 324, 328–29

critical realists, 96

critical theory: examining Foucauldian poststructuralism impact on, 23; Frankfurt-style, 1, 8, 23, 273, 274, 295; Habermasian reconceptualization of, 1, 23, 273, 274

cultural sociology, 238, 239

culture: discursive institutionalism on interplay of institutions, interests, and, 16–17; how speech is shaped by discourse and, 241; power to reinforce hegemony, 150–51; semiotic approach to the study of, 237–41. *See also* values

Dean, M., 170

Debategraph system, 165–66

decision making: Habermas and deliberative institutional aspects

378 Index

decision making (*cont.*)
of, 281–82; Habermas and Foucault on better argument used in, 294–98; problem of motivation in deliberative, 282–83; problem of strategic exploitation in deliberative, 281. *See also* problem solving
deliberation: argumentation constructed from discourse, 11; citizen "habits of the heart" for, 291–93; Debategraph system to track online, 165–66; definition of, 162–63; and the deliberative system, 48–50; emergence and focus of, 18–19; governmental technologies practice of, 290–94; Habermas focus on policy planning and, 9, 213, 281–82; the Internet as a new space for policy, 20–21, 149–74; meaning in context of public policy, 33–37; network actors and online, 161–64; public scrutiny of, 281; rhetoric in political text and, 225–30; seven ideal conditions for, 174n.5; social learning as central to, 344–49; "speak-outs" held prior to, 363–64; transformative learning and process of, 351, 357–58; transformative learning in planning and policy, 24, 343–68. *See also* argumentative policy inquiry; policy analysis; political discourse
deliberative democracy: content of deliberation, 34; Habermas on institutional aspects of, 281–82; Habermas's two-track model and, 276–77, 278, 288; Internet and new modes of accountability for, 152; movement to institutionalize forums of, 31–32; rhetoric role in, 34; tension between *parrēsia* and *isegoria* in, 297–98; viewed as government technology, 294;

Westminster-style political systems of, 31. *See also* democracy; democratic theory
deliberative forum design: authority and legitimacy issues of, 46–48; participants and roles considered in, 42–46; structure and rules consideration of, 39–42
deliberative forum participants: how structure and rules impact, 40–42; inclusion of, 37; "law of group polarization" and, 42–43; methods for recruiting and selecting, 43–45. *See also* stakeholders
deliberative forums: advisory versus decision-making power of, 47; communicative practices supporting, 11, 31–33, 34–37; debate over collective decisions through, 36–37; Discourse Quality Index measuring, 39–40; emphasizing inclusive forms of, 37; informality of everyday political discussion form of, 32, 36–37; institutionalized to foster deliberation, 31–33; institutionalizing, 31–33; Internet facilitation of online, 20–21, 150–74; preparatory "speak-outs," 363–64; rationality of, 34; shaping and facilitating, 37–48; spatial development strategies through, 72; types of communication not to use in, 34–35. *See also* citizens; discursive policy arenas
deliberative policy analysis, 32
deliberative systems: how forums function within, 33; in international negotiations, 32–33; meta-deliberation on, 50; promoting deliberation in the, 48–50
democracy: *isegoria* value of, 297; *parrēsia* requirement for, 297–98; "policy science of," 359; self-

determination aim of, 298n.4; system, 288; Tocqueville's examination of U.S., 291–92, 293. *See also* deliberative democracy

Democracy in America (Tocqueville), 291, 293

Democratic Party: Missouri senate campaign (2006) stem cell video supporting, 211–12, 218, 220, 221–22; policy analysts used by the, 101–2; "public interest" discourse of the, 15

democratic theory: Dryzek's discursive, 278; epistemic understanding of politics, 277–80; exploitation, motivation, and polarization problems of, 281–82; Habermas's deliberative, 272–73, 276–82; Habermas's two-track model of, 276–77, 278, 288; Luhmann's systems theory approach to, 279; participatory politics of, 272, 276; rationalization of the, 278. *See also* deliberative democracy

Denmark's consensus conferences, 48

Derrida, Jacques, 8, 309, 333

development policies: failure to achieve objectives by, 114–15; feminist critiques of, 123–25, 128–29; feminist framing of, 116, 120, 129–42; global North seen as telos of development, 125, 139–40; modernization theory as practice of, 120–23, 130, 139; moving toward discursive politics, 138–40; sustainable, 140–41; traditionally as "quality of life" strategy, 120; "underdevelopment" problem of, 121–23; undertaking a discursive analysis of, 115–16; "the Woman Question" in, 124–25. *See also* global poverty

Dewey, John, 212–13, 346, 358

digital ethnography: CNH research approach using, 190–98; reflections on use for policy inquiry and planning praxis, 201–3

digital storytelling: description and policy process role of, 155. *See also* film; narratives/stories

discourse: Bourdieu and institutional practices, 8; comparing Habermas's and Foucault's conceptualization of, 275, 296–98; comparing narratives and, 237, 264n.1–65n.1; constructing argumentation from, 11–12; development of argumentative, 7–18; Discourse Quality Index measuring, 39–40; discursive institutionalism on content of ideas and, 87–91; Foucauldian poststructuralism, 8, 23; Frankfurt-style critical theory, 8; Gramscian hegemonic, 16, 24, 94, 312–14; Habermas on three types of, 275; Hajer's definition of, 11; Howarth's definition of, 11; how discursive institutionalism shapes policy, 16, 19–20, 85–108; how ways of thinking are structured by, 16; international negotiations, 32–33, 105–7; narration used with, 12–13; narrativizing, 221; neo-Gramscian hegemonic, 8, 314–17; "planning through debate," 60; procedural rules for sharing meaning of, 105–7; Reaganism, 15; self-fulfilling prophecy of, 241, 242; semiotic approach to understanding public policy and, 237–64; social welfare reform, 22, 240–64; sociocultural macro level of, 11; surface and underlying structure levels of, 244–45*fig*, 248*fig*; Thatcherism, 15, 103, 316; the unsaid underlying

discourse (*cont.*)
structure and meaning of, 236–37. *See also* argumentative policy discourse; communicative practices; political discourse; speech

discourse coalitions: characteristics of members, 101; description of, 100–101; epistemic communities and advocacy coalitions subsets of, 101; information generated by, 101–2

Discourse Quality Index, 39–40

discourse surface level: narrative and framing metaphors as, 244, 245*fig*; welfare reform narrative and metaphors, 248*fig*

discourse theory, 271, 308, 324

discourse underlying structure level: discourse and subjectivities as, 245*fig*; welfare reform discourse and subjectivities as, 248*fig*

discursive communities: coordinative and communicative discourse within, 100–105; discourse coalition approach to conceive, 100–102; information generated by, 101–2

discursive institutionalism: content of ideas and discourse in, 87–91; context of ideas and discourse in, 105–7; coordinative and communicative discourses of, 100–105; definition of, 85–86; elite-led, 103–4; "epistemic communities" of, 101–2; institutions understood in context of, 86–87; on interplay of culture, interests, and institutions, 16–17; policy changes and movements spurred by, 104–5; policy discourse shaped by, 16, 19–20; sentient agents spreading ideas through practices of, 91–100, 105. *See also* institutions

discursive institutionalism theory, 16, 19–20

discursive interactions: coordinative and communicative, 100–105; of discourse coalitions, 101–2; formal institutions and procedures for, 105–7

discursive policy arenas: examples of, 291; Habermas on citizen participation in, 272–73, 276, 290–91; partially fixed systems of rules for, 307; Tocqueville on citizen role, 291–92. *See also* deliberative forums

Dodge, Jennifer, 241

double-loop learning, 355

Dryzek, John S., 18, 31, 35, 42, 277, 278

Easton, D., 37

Edelman, Murray, 256

elites. *See* political elites

emotions: Bush's stem cell speech use of, 222–25, 229, 232; facilitation and handling of, 361–62; logos used with, 218–19, 231; Michael J. Fox video in context of, 219, 229, 231, 232; rhetorical view of, 218–19; transformation learning role of, 362–64. *See also* ethos

empathy, 362–63

epistemic communities, 101

epistemology: essential status of language debates in, 271; Foucault's theory of discourse, 287–88; Habermasian epistemic understandings of democracy, 277–80; linking social/political theory to postpositivist, 1, 8; philosophic contributions to, 8–9; shift from traditional approach of, 181; "story turn" in planning, 181–82; ways of knowing through, 181

Essex School of Discourse Analysis, 338
ethical discourse, 275
ethnography: digital, 21, 180–84, 190–98, 201–3; as narrative analysis approach, 184–88
ethnomethodology, 8
ethos: distinguishing between two meanings of, 217; New Rhetoric understanding of, 217; "prior ethos" notion of, 224. *See also* emotions
Euripides, 297
Executive Order 13505, 230
expert knowledge, 367
explanandum: critical policy analysis and, 324; retroduction, 328–29

facilitation: as consulting service, 359; of deliberation, 48–50; designing deliberative forum, 41; educator-as-facilitator role of, 366; the goal of, 359; handling passion and emotional expression during, 361–62; People's Planning Campaign (Kerala, India) example of, 360–61; skills required for effective, 364; of transformative learning, 358–64
Fairclough, Norman, 160, 317, 332
fantasmatic logic, 329, 331, 336
feminist political economy: critiques of development from the, 123–25, 128–29. *See also* women
film: CHN research approach using, 190–98. *See also* digital storytelling
Finlayson, Alan, 331
Fischer, Frank, 1, 24, 59, 101, 166, 171, 246, 271, 343, 348, 355, 359, 360
Fishkin, F., 163
Forester, John, 1, 59, 63, 271, 347, 348, 359, 360
Fortenbaugh, William W., 218

Foucault, Michel: *The Archaeology of Knowledge*, 285; argumentative policy influenced by, 8, 23, 24, 271; on better argument used in decision making, 294–98; comparing Habermasian social ontology with that of, 296–98; concept of power critiqued by Habermas, 282–84; on "control society," 157; *Discipline and Punish* by, 283, 285, 286, 288; on discourse as spaces of knowledge and power relations, 275, 284–88; *The History of Sexuality* by, 285, 288; on ideational domination of the powerful, 94; method of genealogy used by, 283, 286; *The Order of Things* by, 285; poststructuralism of, 8, 23, 24, 309; problematization conception of, 326–27; scholarly influence of, 16, 92; on the self-fulfilling prophecy of discourse, 242; technologies of the government and self-study by, 290–94, 295; on truth of politics, 284, 286–87; "What Is Enlightenment" lecture by, 295. *See also* political theory
Fox, Michael J.: emotional context of message by, 219, 229, 231, 232
framing. *See* policy frames
Frankfurt-style critical theory, 1, 8, 23, 273, 274, 295
Fraser, Nancy, 275, 283
freedom: Foucault's changed evaluation of power interplay with, 295; Foucault's theory of governmentality on power and, 288–90
Freire, Paulo, 24, 351, 360
French, S., 165
French regulation theory, 316
Friedmann, John, 181, 345, 346
Fukushima nuclear disaster, 4
Fung, A., 44

Gadamer, Hans-Georg, 271
Geertz, Clifford, 336
Gender and Development (GAD), 116, 132–33, 139
Giddens, Anthony, 92
global poverty: failure of "trickle-down development," 133; per capita GNP measure of, 121–22; problem of, 114–15. *See also* development policies
Glynos, J., 324
Goldman, Michael, 138
Gore, Al, 203
Gottweis, Herbert, 21, 22, 171, 211
governance: characteristics of network, 153–54; citizens' lack of trust in representative, 169; collaborative and communicative planning for, 58–77; contextual differences in meanings of, 308; deliberative practices as governmental technologies, 290–94; Foucault on modern freedom and theory of governmentality, 288–90; growing interest in participatory approaches to, 61–62; hegemony conception as type of, 317–20; increasing dependence on technologies of connection by, 172–73
government technologies: deliberative democracy viewed as, 294; Foucault on deliberation practice of, 290–94, 295
Gramsci, Antonio: discourse of, 16, 24, 94, 312–14; hegemonic political theory on socialist revolution by, 311; policy making and, 310; *Prison Notebooks* by, 311; twofold inversion of Marxist model of society, 312–13
Gramscian hegemonic discourse: on capitalism and neoliberalism, 16; "common sense" approach of, 313–14; examining poststructuralist reading of, 24; on role of intellectuals in breaking hegemonic discourse, 94; twofold inversion of Marxist model of society in, 312–13. *See also* neo-Gramscian hegemonic discourse
Granovetter, M., 150
Griggs, Steven, 23, 362
Gutmann, A., 34

Habermas, Jürgen: academic influence of, 92, 271; argumentative turn contributions by, 1, 23, 24, 271, 272–82, 290–91; *Between Facts and Norms* by, 274, 276, 277, 280, 281, 298; communicative action view of, 94; democratic theory contributions of, 272–73, 275–82; *Erläuterungen zur Diskursethik* by, 275; *The Future of Human Nature* by, 273; on "ideal speech situation," 157, 166, 280, 365; *Knowledge and Human Interest* by, 273; "Knowledge and Human Interests" by, 295; *Legitimation Crisis* by, 273; participation in social movements supported by, 272–73, 276, 291–92; *The Philosophical Discourse of Modernity* lecture of, 275, 282; on policy making through deliberate argument, 233; positivism and neopositivism critique by, 273–74, 275; on public reasons/interests, 34; rational reconstruction methodology developed by, 274; *The Structural Transformation of the Public Sphere* by, 273, 280; *Theory and Practice* by, 273; theory of communication by, 39; *The Theory of Communicative Action* by, 273, 275

habitus, 154
"habitus" notion, 93
Hacking, Ian, 241
Hajer, Maarten, 11, 32, 119, 168
Hall, Peter, 24; social learning 344–45, 346
Hanson, Norwood, 328
Hartz-Karp, Janette, 37, 360
Hawkesworth, Mary, 20, 114
Healey, Patsy: collaborative planning 19, 58, 359
Heclo, Hugh, 344, 345
Heidegger, Martin, 271, 326, 327
Hendriks, Carolyn M.: deliberation, 18, 31
Howarth, David, 11, 23, 324, 362
Hurricane Katrina (2005), 5

"ideal speech situation," 157, 166, 280, 365
ideas: discursive institutionalism on content of discourse and, 87–91; discursive institutionalism on power provided by, 106–7; how actions are motivated by, 16; importance in ordinary course of public affairs, 16; new institutionalists' (or neoinstitutionalists') emphasis on, 17; relationship between material interests and, 14–15; sentient agents' discursive institutionalism practices to spread, 91–100, 105
identities, 260–63, 309; discourse and, 245*fig*; Foucault on power of shaping individual, 289; how discourse modifies, 308–9; named through language, 241; postmodernism on how discourse constructs, 246–47. *See also* self (Self)
ideology: fantasmatic narratives and logic of, 331; meaning of social experience as part of, 353; understandings provided by, 354
Innes, J., 60, 359
institutions: in context of discursive institutionalism, 86–87; Foucault on modern institutions and disciplinary discourses, 286; Habermas on the deliberative "structure" of, 281–82; interests as influenced by structures, norms, and rules of, 17; political action through communicative practices of, 17; Tocqueville on democratic political, 291–92. *See also* discursive institutionalism
interests: actions motivated by, 16; discursive institutionalism on interplay of institutions, culture, and, 16–17; e-communication strategies to utilize, 152; influenced by institutional structures, norms, and rules, 17; online deliberation impact on revealing, 165–66; rooted in civil society, 316
International Association for Public Participation (IAP), 38
Internet: argumentative turn dependence on communication networks of, 170–73; barriers to online democratic policy making, 167–69, 170; collaborative working practices facilitated by, 62; coordinating deliberation with argumentative turn, 149–50; Debategraph system to track online deliberation on the, 165–66; developing new civic practices for policy deliberation using the, 169–70; emergence as new space for deliberation, 20–21, 150–51; how policy networking is facilitated by, 158; increasing dependence of governance on networks

Internet (*cont.*)
  of the, 172–73; literature on how policy-making process is influenced by, 149; multivocal narratives spread through the, 154–57; online deliberation through the, 161–64; policy networking through the, 158–61; potential as site for construction of civic habits, 170. *See also* communicative practices
interpretive policy analysis, 18
Iraq War: failure of Bush policies during, 5; survey of British Internet users protesting against, 168; tragic consequences of the, 5
Issue Crawler, 160

Jessop, Bob, 314, 315–17
Joas, Hans, 275
Jörke, Dirk, 23, 271

Kerala's People's Planning Campaign (India), 360–61
Keynesian economic theory, 316
knowledge: based on experiences in world versus pictures of the world, 95–100; classical order versus modern order of, 285; collaborative process of transformative learning for, 350; constructivist understanding of action-oriented, 349–50; "crisis of knowing" and limitations of expert, 181; differences in kinds of, 91; expert, 367; Foucault's conception of discourse as spaces of power and, 275, 284–88; management of discursivity approach to ordering social, 171; mutual learning through experiential and expert, 181; regime exclusion of people lacking "appropriate," 293, 294; tacit, 355, 362. *See also* rationality
Kuhn, Thomas, 99

Lacan, Jacques, 237, 271, 309, 310, 331, 333
Laclau, Ernesto, 90, 307, 314
language: argumentative turn based on how reality is shaped by, 271; crisis narrative, 256–57; how self, existence, and identity are named through, 241; of new public management in the United Kingdom, 308. *See also* semiotics; speech
Lasswell, Harold, 119, 359
law of group polarization, 42–43, 282
Laws, David, 119
learning: banking model of schooling and, 349–50; social, 24, 344–49; transformative, 24, 348–64
learning organizations, 355
legitimacy: communicative policy, 102–3; deliberation forum, 46–48; Foucault's view of discourse as producing, 284; of narratives, 154–55
Lehmbruch, Gerhard, 100
logics: articulation, judgment, and critique of, 334–35; critical policy analysis explanation through, 324, 329–34; fantasmatic, 329, 331, 336; ideology, 331; Lacanian logic of fantasy, 24, 322–23, 331, 362; political, 329–30, 333–34, 336; regime of U.K. aviation expansion driven by, 322–23; social, 329. *See also* rationality
logos (reason): Aristotelian tradition of, 216, 217, 218–19; emotions used with, 218–19, 231
Luhmann, Niklas, 276, 279
Lundby, K., 155

Mackenzie, Donald, 99
Maingueneau, Dominique, 22, 217, 218, 224

Majone, Giandomenico: policy and arguments, 7, 215, 216, 271
Mandell, Alan: transformative learning, 24, 343, 348, 355
Mansbridge, J., 34, 36, 37, 43
Marxism: on economic structure of society, 312; Gramsci's twofold inversion of model of society by, 312–13; materialism conception of history in, 311–12; perspective of capitalism in, 314–15; on political change, 307
McCarthy, Thomas, 295
meaning perspectives: beliefs, norms, and values assessed through, 354; first- and second-order learning levels of, 355; transforming, 354–55
meaning schemes: first- and second-order learning levels of, 355; sets of understandings emerging from perspectives, 354
metaphors, developing of grammar for understanding arguments through, 332–33
metonymical dimension of politics, 320–21
Meyer, Michael, 214
Mezirow, J.: transformative learning, 354
modernization theory: and critique of Foucault's concept of power, 283; development policy practices using, 120–23, 130, 139; on integrating women into labor force, 124–25, 130; strategies to solve underdevelopment problem using, 121–23
Mouffe, Chantal, 90, 307, 310, 314, 331, 337
multiculturalism: embedded in Canadian society, 189; Ministry of Citizenship and Immigration Canada's implementation of policies supporting, 189–90

narration: discourse used with, 12–13; generated by deliberative forums, 46; how arguments can be constructed by, 13; the Internet and ability to spread, 154–57; social meaning through dialogue and, 349–50
narrative analysis: constructive perspective of, 186–87; critical reflections on, 201–3; ethnographic approach of, 184–88; interpretation focus of, 187; polyphonic, 180; reflexivity levels in, 187–88; as sense-making and discursive practice, 184–85
narrative-dialogic: description of, 356; examining social meaning embedded in, 349–50, 356; revising social meaning through storytelling process of, 356–57
narratives/stories: comparing discourse and, 237, 264n.1–65n.1; crisis language of, 256–57; ethnographic approach as in-depth exploration of, 184–88; examining discourse underlying metaphors of policy, 22; functioning as metaphor, 241; the Internet and multivocal, 154–57; legitimacy of, 154–55; scenography concept embedded in, 219–21; social meaning created and shaped by, 154, 237; as surface level of discourse, 244, 245*fig*, 248*fig*; three dialogic phases of transformational, 350–51. *See also* digital storytelling; policy dialogues; policy frames
narrativizing discourse, 221
nation-state: Foucault on modern freedom and theory of govern-

nation-state (*cont.*)
mentality by, 288–90; "governing mentalities" practice of, 242; *parrēsia* (courage to tell truth) in democratic, 297–98; transformation into "the network state," 150
neo-Gramscian hegemonic discourse, 8, 314–17. *See also* Gramscian hegemonic discourse
neoliberalism discourse, 16
neopositivism, 273–74
new institutionalists (or neoinstitutionalists), 17
"New Rhetoric" tradition: ethos in context of, 217; examining the, 22; origins and development of the, 215–16; rhetoric within perspective of, 217
normative theory, 37, 38, 294
Nussbaum, Martha, 362

Obama, Barack H., 230
online deliberation: advantages and opportunities provided by, 161–62; Debategraph system tool for, 165–66; Fishkin's deliberative polls as form of, 163–64; impact on transparency and revelation of interests, 165–66; issue of limited citizen-based, 164; three categories of, 163
Ostrom, E., 170

parrēsia: defined as courage to tell truth, 297; difference from *isegoria* (democratic equality), 297–98
Peirce, Charles Sanders, 324, 328
People's Planning Campaign (Kerala, India), 360–61
Perelman, Chaïm, 22, 215, 217
persuasion: Aristotle on achievement of, 215; examining logos, pathos, and ethos in politics of, 22; as performative and interactive process, 217; policy-making role of, 231; politics of, 213; rhetoric associated with the art of, 213–14. *See also* political discourse; rhetoric/rhetorical argument
phenomenology theory, 8
"pictorial turn," 13–14
Plato, 214, 215, 297
plebiscitary rhetoric, 35
Polanyi, Michael, 355
policy actors: deliberative forum participants as, 37, 40–45; discourse coalitions of, 101–2; discursive institutionalism role of, 91–100, 105; discursive interactions of, 100–105; impact of communication technologies on networking of, 150–74; policy process role of, 100
policy analysis: argumentative approach to, 1–2, 6–7; assessed as being a form of argumentation, 271; critical, 323–37; of development policy, 114–42; Habermas's methodological debate in field of, 273, 274–75; Habermas's rational reconstruction approach to, 274; how contemporary political and economic situations impact, 3–4; interpretive, 18; need for new models of explanation, 5–6; poststructuralist, 305–38; primary explanation task of, 309–10; problem-driven approach to, 324; rational model of policy modeling and, 2, 4–5; rhetoric political analysis (RPA), 331–32; semiotic approach to, 237–64. *See also* deliberation
policy consultation: discursive mismatch characterizing most, 167–68; Internet as a new space for

deliberation and, 20–21, 149–74; network actors' role in, 150–55, 161–64
policy dialogues: digital ethnography used for, 21, 180–84, 190–98, 201–3; digital storytelling used for, 155–57; film used for, 21, 180–84, 190–98; scenography tool for creating, 219–25, 229. *See also* narratives/stories
policy frames: description of, 116–17; examining the role of, 20; feminist approaches to development policy, 116, 120, 129–43; interpretive approach to, 117–19; methodological approach to, 117; multimedia role in creating communicative discourse, 103–4; poststructuralist approach to, 119–20; reproductive and "welfare" development, 125–28; welfare reform, 22, 240–64. *See also* narratives/stories
policy networking: comparing hierarchical bureaucracy to, 158; how the Internet has facilitated, 158; increasing dependence of governance on, 172–73; linkages between virtual networks contributing to, 160–61; Netmums' practice of, 158–59; wikis used for, 159–60
policy paradigms: challenging the dominant planning, 59; communicative and collaborative planning, 58–77; examining the policy implications of learning in, 24; extending learning to include changes in the, 345; as interpretive framework to understand policy goals, 345. *See also* public policy
policy planning: communicative and collaborative, 58–77; developing discursive relationships during, 349; Habermasian thought on deliberation role in, 9, 213, 281–82; how citizen demands drive, 62–63; inclusion of citizens in collaborative governance and, 58–77; "planning through debate" discourse approach to, 60; reflections on using digital ethnography as praxis for, 201–3; social learning as central to, 343–49; "story turn" in, 181–82. *See also* collaborative governance planning; public policy; urban policy and planning
"policy science of democracy," 359
political change: argumentative communication influence on, 17; Marxism on, 307; through communicative practices of institutions, 17; "web of beliefs" that become new traditions and, 90. *See also* social movements
political discourse: discursive institutionalism theory on, 16, 19–20; feminist development policies for moving toward discursive, 138–40; "pictorial turn" representation of, 13–15; Reaganism, 15; relationship between ideas and material interests in, 14–15; Thatcherism, 15, 103. *See also* deliberation; discourse; persuasion
political elites: barriers to citizen participation in online policy making by, 167–69, 170; discursive institutionalism led by, 103–4; French and U.K. reform agendas concentrated among, 106
political logics: catachresis role in, 333–34; as central to practice of critique, 336; description and use of, 329–30
political theory: communicative planning theory, 59–77; critical

political theory (*cont.*)
  theory, 1, 23, 273, 274; discursive institutionalism, 16, 19–20; Foucauldian poststructuralism impact on critical theory, 23; Frankfurt-style critical theory, 8; Gramsci's socialist revolution, 311; linking postpositivist epistemology with, 1, 8; Marxism, 307, 311–15; "pictorial turn" representation of discourse in, 13–14. *See also* Foucault, Michel; social theory
positivism, 273–74, 275
postmodernism: on how discourse constructs identity, 246–47; public policy and, 8
postpositivist epistemology, 1, 8
poststructuralism: conception of hegemony in, 317–21; critical theory influenced by Foucauldian, 8, 23; examining contribution to policy studies by, 23–24; Foucauldian, 8, 23, 24, 309; public policy and, 8; welfare reform in context of, 244. *See also* social theory
poststructuralist policy analysis: on affective dimension of policy change, 321–23; conception of hegemony in, 317–21; examining emergency of hegemony in context of, 311–17; examining the social relations dimension of, 305–6; logics of critical explanation through, 323–37; ontological assumptions of, 306–11; primary explanation task of, 309–10; situating policy making in social and political contexts, 310
Poulantzas, Nicos, 314, 315
power: discursive discourse involving exercise of, 307; discursive institutionalism on ideas and, 106–7; feminist framing of development policy to address issues of, 116; Foucault's changed evaluation of freedom interplay with, 295; Foucault's conception of discourse as spaces of knowledge and, 275, 284–88; Foucault's theory of governmentality on individual freedom and, 288–90; Gender and Development (GAD) framework on, 116, 132–33, 139; Habermas's critique of Foucault's concept of, 282–84; how networked politics impact established patterns of, 151; network governance changing access to, 153–54; new communication technology as decentered politics, 150; politics as arising from both uncertainty and, 344; position *qua* position source of, 107
pragmatic discourse, 275
pre-Aristotelian philosophy, 214–15
problematization: constructing research through, 325–26; critical policy analysis step of, 324; task and process of, 324–28; transformative learning as, 349–53; transformative learning process resemblance to, 351
problem-driven policy analysis, 324
problems: critical policy analysis step of problematization of, 324, 325–28; grievances and demands connected to construction of, 326–28; narrative form of the, 357; policy analysis as driven by, 324; retroduction to create hypothesis of, 324, 328–29; United Kingdom's aviation, 326, 327. *See also* decision making
problem setting, 347, 351, 352
problem solving: problem-setting step for, 347, 351, 352; retroduction

to create hypothesis for, 324, 328–29; social learning role in, 348. *See also* decision making
public policy: argumentative discourse on, 7–8; communicative and collaborative planning for, 58–77; constructivism perspective on, 236; deliberation in context of, 33–37; how the Internet changes the process of, 20–21, 149–74; John Dewey's definition of, 212–13; semiotic approach to discourse and, 237–64; translated into narrative form, 356–57. *See also* policy paradigms; policy planning
public policy change, critical explanation and normative evaluation of, 335–37

radical relativism, 93, 96, 98
rationality: Aristotelian tradition of, 216, 217, 218–19; "crisis of the professions" and moving past, 347; of deliberative forums, 34; emotions used with logos or, 218–19, 231; Foucault's analysis on different regimes of, 285; Foucault's view of discourse as producing, 284; world economy collapse (2008) due to failures of, 4–5. *See also* knowledge; logics
rational model of policy modeling: argumentative policy inquiry as challenging, 2; description of, 2; world economy collapse (2008) representing failure of, 4–5
Rawls, John, 34, 233
Reagan, Ronald, 15, 223
reciprocity, communication with, 33–34
Rein, M., 308
reproductive development initiatives, 125–28

retroduction: creating hypothesis through process of, 328–29; critical policy analysis step of, 324
rhetorical redescription technique, 333
rhetoric/rhetorical argument: Aristotle's definition of, 215; catachresis role in understanding, 333–34; deliberative democracy role of, 34; deliberative distinguished from plebiscitary, 35; description of, 10, 213–14; examining role in policy studies by, 21–22; George Bush's speech on stem cell research, 222–25, 229; historic development of, 214–16; metonymical dimension of political, 320–21; Michael J. Fox's video on stem cell research, 211–12, 218, 219–20, 224, 228, 229, 231, 232; "New Rhetoric" tradition of, 22, 215–16; pejorative connotation of, 214; Platonian tradition of, 215; policy texts and deliberation role of, 225–30; pre-Aristotelian philosophy connection to, 214–15; redescription technique of, 333; rethinking ethos and pathos notions of, 216–25; scenography concept of, 219–21; stem research policy text and deliberation using, 225–30. *See also* argumentative policy discourse; persuasion
Rhodes, R. A. W.: governance, 90
Risse, T.: international relations and communicative interaction, 32
Rose, N.: governmentality, 170
Rosenberg, S. W.: deliberation, 38
rules: as deliberative forum design consideration, 39–42; discourses as partially fixed systems of, 307; hegemony as type of governance and, 317–20; how interests are

rules (cont.)
  influenced by institutional, 17;
  shared argumentative meaning through procedural, 105–7

Sabatier, Paul A.: advocacy coalitions and policy learning, 344, 345
Sandercock, Leonie: planning and film, 21, 180, 196–97, 363
Saretzki, Thomas, 279–80
Saussure, F. de, 308
scenography: Bush's stem cell speech creating a, 222–25, 229; embedded in discourse structures, 220–21; Michael J. Fox's video use of, 219–20
Schmalz-Bruns, Rainer, 275
Schmidt, Vivien A., 16; discursive institutionalism, 19, 85
Schön, Donald A., 308, 346–47, 348, 349, 351–52, 355
Schram, Sanford F., 22, 236
Science for the People movement (KSSP), 360
Scott, James, 121
Searle, John, 92, 93, 96
self (Self): Foucault's concept of technologies of the, 289, 295; Michael J. Fox's video presentation of, 218, 224; named through language, 241; welfare reform discourse becoming self-fulfilling prophecy of, 253. See also identities
semiotics: on creating new identities through counter discourses, 260–63; description of, 237; study of culture using, 237–41; on surface and underlying structure levels of discourse, 244–45fig, 248fig; understanding policy discourse through, 241–47; on welfare reform dependency discourse on "poor" as other, 247–50; on welfare reform discourse medicalizing dependency, 250–60. See also language
Shapiro, I., 39
Simon, H. A., 38
Skinner, Quentin, 333
social learning: action as principal focus of, 345–46; as central to social and political life, 344–49; as change in thinking and perception, 344; constructivist perspective on transformative, 348–49; different practices leading to, 347; examining planning and deliberation transformative, 24; Peter Hall and policy learning, 344–45
social meaning: catachresis role in naming, 333–34; context of public policy deliberation, 33–37; created and shaped by narratives, 154, 237; definition and patterns of, 171–72; Mezirow's distinction between "schemes" and "perspectives" of, 354–55; narrative-dialogics used to understand and change, 349–50, 356–58; policymaking content created through, 352; procedural rules for shared argumentative communication, 105–7; social action based on, 353; transformative learning theory and, 349–50, 353–58; the unsaid in discourse underlying structure and, 236–37. See also beliefs
social movements: bottom-up communicative discourse of, 104; Habermas on exploitation, motivation, and polarization problems of, 281–82; policy change through communicative discourse of, 104–5. See also citizens; collective action; political change

social theory: Bourdieu-influenced emphasis on institutional practices, 8; communicative practices emphasized in, 13; ethnomethodology, 8; Frankfurt-style critical theory, 1, 8, 23, 273, 274; linking postpositivist epistemology with, 1, 8; neo-Gramscian hegemonic discourse on, 8, 314–17; phenomenology, 8; postmodernism, 8, 246–47; poststructuralism, 8, 23–24, 244, 309, 317–24; structuralism, 243–44; symbolic interaction, 8. *See also* political theory; poststructuralism

Socrates, 297

Sophists, 214–15

speech: Bakhtin on "eventness" of, 157; Foucauldian "control society," 157; Habermas's "ideal speech situation," 157, 166, 280, 365; *parrēsia* (courage to tell truth), 297–98; speech act theory interpreting action as form of, 217. *See also* discourse; language

speech act theory, 217

stakeholders: collaborative governance planning by, 58–77; collaborative neighborhood change management role of, 64–67; collaborative planning driven by demands of citizen, 62–63; ethics of commitment to respect, 67; problem of motivation in deliberative practices of, 281–82; problem of polarization during deliberation by, 282; problem of strategic exploitation in deliberative practices of, 281; promoting new arenas for discursive encounters between, 61. *See also* deliberative forum participants

stem cell policy: Bush administration's, 222–25, 229; Clinton administration's, 222, 226, 229; Dickey Amendment, 226, 230; Executive Order 13505, 230; long political battle over, 221, 225–26; National Institutes of Health role in developing, 222, 225, 226–27, 229, 230, 231; persuasion to help develop, 231; rhetoric in texts and deliberation over human embryonic, 225–30; transforming phenomena during process of, 230–31

Stone, Deborah, 245, 357

stories. *See* digital storytelling; narratives / stories

structuralism: behavioral assumptions of, 243–44; cultural biases of, 244

Sum, Nagi-Ling, 316

Sunstein, Cass, 42, 282

symbolic interaction theory, 8

systems theory, 279

tacit knowledge, 355, 362

Thatcher, Margaret: neoliberalism, 103

Throgmorton, James A., 216

Thucydides, 297

Tilly, C., 154

Tocqueville, Alexis de: democracy in America, 291–92, 293

Torbert, William: transformative leadership, 366

Toulmin, Stephen: the uses of argumentation, 105, 215

transformational leadership, 366

urban policy and planning: collaborative planning for major projects, 68–70; collaborative planning for neighborhood, 64–67; examining role of multimedia in, 21, 180–203; polyphonic narrative urban policy and planning (*cont.*) analysis as antidote to biases of research on, 180; reflections on digital ethnography use in, 201–3; resistance to London Heathrow airport expansion, 319; spatial development strategies for, 70–75; "story turn" in, 181–82; three questions related to collaborative, 58, 75–77. *See also* policy planning

values: actions motivated by, 16; communicative networks' potential for discussing public, 171; meaning perspective assessed through, 354. *See also* beliefs; culture

Wagenaar, H.: interpretive policy analysis, 32
Warren, M. E.: deliberative democracy, 47, 149
Weber, Max: role of ideas, 14–15
Weick, K., 17
welfare reform. *See* discourse: social welfare reform
welfarist development initiatives, 125–28
Wendt, Alexander, 95
White, Hayden, 221
wikis: Debategraph mapping form of, 165–66; description and functions of, 173–75n.3; policy networking through, 159–60
Wildemeersch, Danny: transformative learning, 350, 351, 356
Wittgenstein, Ludwig, 8, 93, 97, 98, 271, 306
Wodak, Ruth, 317, 332
women: Gender and Development (GAD) development focus on, 116, 132–33, 139; invisibility in global labor force of, 124; modern approach for integrating into labor force, 124–25, 130; reproductive and "welfare" development policies' focus on, 125–28; "reproductive tax" of unwaged labor of, 131–32; World Bank's "women's empowerment" policy on, 134–37. *See also* feminist political economy
Women's Role in Economic Development (Boserup), 128–29
World Bank: "women's empowerment" policy of, 134–37
world economy collapse (2008), 4–5

Yanow, Dvora: social meaning and social construction, 18, 120, 352

FRANK FISCHER is Professor of Politics and Global Affairs at Rutgers University and a senior faculty fellow at the University of Kassel in Germany.

HERBERT GOTTWEIS is Professor of Political Science at the University of Vienna and a research associate at the BIOS Center, London School of Economics.

Library of Congress Cataloging-in-Publication Data
The argumentative turn revisited : public policy as communicative practice / edited by Frank Fischer and Herbert Gottweis.
p. cm.
Continues: The Argumentative turn in policy analysis and planning.
Includes bibliographical references and index.
ISBN 978-0-8223-5245-7 (cloth)
ISBN 978-0-8223-5263-1 (pbk.)
1. Policy sciences. 2. Debates and debating. 3. Persuasion (Rhetoric). I. Fischer, Frank, 1942– II. Gottweis, Herbert, 1958– III. Argumentative turn in policy analysis and planning.
H97.A653 2012
320.6—dc23   2011053294

www.ingramcontent.com/pod-product-compliance
Lightning Source LLC
Chambersburg PA
CBHW061342300426
44116CB00011B/1950